THE ESSENTIAL
FEMINIST
READER

THE ESSENTIAL FEMINIST READER

Edited and with an Introduction by

Estelle B. Freedman

THE MODERN LIBRARY

NEW YORK

FOR JOHN

Contents

INTRODUCTION

Feminism is a recent term, coined in the nineteenth century, but its intellectual history goes back over half a millennium. Simply defined, feminism is the belief that women have the same human capacities as men. While this claim may no longer seem controversial, the "woman question" has provoked spirited debate in Western culture since at least the fifteenth century. At that time, deeply held beliefs about women's physical, moral, and intellectual inferiority justified patriarchal laws requiring female obedience to fathers and husbands. In response, critics began to argue passionately that the common humanity of women and men far overshadows the biological distinctions of sex. This central insight has evolved over the centuries into a variety of feminist ideas that continue to inspire political movements throughout the world.

Even when men held formal power, however, women across cultures found myriad ways to transcend or resist patriarchal rule. Elite women could enjoy wealth and political authority through their connections to powerful male relatives. Some women reigned as queens. More commonly, women's contributions to household production gave them leverage within their families. Buddhist and Catholic religious convents in Asia, Europe, and the Americas provided an alternative to marriage and opportunities for women to claim spiritual authority. When denied formal education, women still created poetry, music, and art. And in villages from Africa to North America, women's social networks attempted to regulate male authority, as when they publicly shamed abusive husbands.

Two features distinguish feminism from women's individual efforts to claim spiritual, familial, or political authority. First, feminism explicitly rejects the legitimacy of patriarchal rule. Second, feminism initiates social movements to alter laws and customs. A series of historical transformations over the past six hundred years—including democratic politics and industrial growth—made feminist critiques both possible and necessary. Intellectually, a new worldview associated with "modernity" questioned inherited dogma and favored individual reason. From this foundation a political theory based on individual rights encouraged the rejection of rule by elites in favor of representative government. Simultaneously, the shift from agriculture to manufacturing, from rural to urban life, and from family economies to market systems based on wage labor reinforced the critique of social hierarchy.

In the fifteenth century, humanist ideas about the capacity for reason inspired European women to question their relegation to second-class status. Exceptional women who had access to learning, like Christine de Pizan, used their knowledge to try to refute the negative depictions of their sex as evil, ignorant, or frivolous. With the expansion of learning in Europe during the Renaissance and the Enlightenment, both women and men questioned restrictions on female education. By the late eighteenth century, democratic theories inspired revolutions that overthrew monarchical rule in the United States and France. The ideal of individual rights also encouraged social movements to abolish slavery in the Americas, to emancipate serfs and Jews in Europe, and to extend suffrage to adult males. In this climate, feminists questioned the patriarchal privileges retained by men. Along with these political ideas, the transition from a family to a market economy, which gradually drew women into wage labor, further fueled feminism by creating a double bind for women, as mothers and as wage workers. Feminism responded to the contradictions in women's lives wrought by capitalist economic growth, as well as to the limitations of democratic political ideals.

Feminist critiques of patriarchy took various forms, depending on whether they originated in liberal, socialist, or other traditions. In the early 1800s, Elizabeth Cady Stanton in the United States and John Stuart Mill in England extended liberal political ideals when they championed education, property rights, and full citizenship for women. By 1900 an international women's movement advocated these goals in urban areas of Latin America, the Middle East, and Asia, where Francisca Diniz, Qasim Amin, and Kishida Toshiko publicly argued for a wider sphere for women beyond the family. At the same time, socialists from Friedrich Engels in Germany to Alexandra Kollontai in Russia rejected "bourgeois feminist" campaigns for legal rights in favor of organizing women within trade unions and establishing revolutionary socialist states. Throughout the world, grassroots women's movements formed when workers and peasants organized, as Domitila Barrios de la Chungara of Brazil illustrated in the late twentieth century.

Movements for racial and social justice also inspired critiques of patriarchy, along with insights into the connections between hierarchies based on gender and race. In America, activists from Sojourner Truth and Anna Julia Cooper in the nineteenth century to W.E.B. Du Bois and Pauli Murray in the twentieth century sought full participation of African American women in U.S. society. Within the antiapartheid movement, the Federation of South African Women insisted that national liberation include women's emancipation. The revival of feminism after the 1960s, known as the Second Wave, witnessed the flourishing of identity politics among women of color and lesbians. Those living with multiple identities, Gloria Anzaldúa and others explained, illuminate the inseparability of efforts to achieve racial, sexual, and gender justice.

Over the past six hundred years, wherever the principles of individual rights or social justice gained legitimacy, critical thinkers have incorporated women into these new worldviews. From the woman question in early-modern Europe to the feminist debates of the past century, a variety of philosophical and literary texts document this rich literary tradition. The following sixty-four selections represent a small sampling from this heritage, necessarily omitting some major works but introducing others that should be better known. Along with influential treatises, speeches, and reports, they include selected works of fiction, drama, and poetry chosen for their articulation of feminist political ideas. The majority of these works originated in Europe and the Americas, but writers from every region, both female and male, have contributed to this history.

Reading these documents over time and across countries reveals both persistence and change in feminist thought. The earliest writers refuted arguments about the natural inferiority of women and justified female education. Later texts, responding to the effects of democratic and industrial revolutions, reiterated these concerns but incorporated as well new arguments for political rights and economic opportunities. In recent decades feminists have addressed the inseparability of race and gender in determining women's identities, and they have increasingly named health, reproduction, and sexuality as political, and not merely personal, matters.

Feminist writers could not ignore the fact that religious and scientific institutions took for granted the notion that women were inferior to men. In Western culture, the representation of women as frivolous, evil, or dissipated rested in part on the myth of Eve bringing sin into the world, but images of female decadence and ignorance could be found in Chinese and Indian civilizations as well. These beliefs in women's incapacity for virtue and learning helped justify male control over daughters and wives, whether through law or through customs such as female seclusion. In response to negative stereotypes, writers from Christine de Pizan in fifteenth-century France to Qiu Jin in twentieth-century China compiled litanies of mythical and historical heroines who exhibited learning, valor, virtue, and piety. Other writers, including Li Ju-chen and Rokeya Sakhawat Hossain, used satire and fantasy to question male dominance. Over the centuries, and building on earlier feminist texts, Mary Wollstonecraft, Ding Ling, Simone de Beauvoir, Betty Friedan, and others insisted that women's common humanity with men overrode the biological fact of sexual difference. They argued that only social custom, and particularly economic dependence on men, produced the negative qualities associated with women and the superiority assumed by men.

Across cultures and centuries, education recurs in feminist thought as the key to creating virtuous and capable women who reject mere ornamental roles. If "the mind has no sex," as François Poullain de la Barre wrote in 1673, women had the capacity for reason and, with education, they could contribute to social progress. For Mary Wollstonecraft, Flora Tristan, and Anna Julia Cooper, creating better mothers initially justified female education. Writers from Harriet Taylor Mill to Virginia Woolf suggested that men would also benefit from the perspectives of educated women. Far more radical was the suggestion that education would prepare women to become full citizens, a prospect that even Wollstonecraft considered daring. Only gradually did feminists justify education for women's own development, as did Elizabeth Cady Stanton in the 1890s. By the 1960s, Betty Friedan reiterated Stanton's claims, reframing them in the psychological terms of self-actualization, or achieving one's full potential. In the interim, expressions of women's rising consciousness echoed internationally in prose, song, and poetry, such as Yosano Akiko's observation in 1911 that "All the sleeping women / Are now awake and moving."

Building on access to education, calls to extend the political "rights of man" to women gathered force in the nineteenth century. Where representative governments replaced monarchical rule, working-class men and slaves struggled to achieve citizenship. For women within antislavery movements, such as Sarah and Angelina Grimké, the plight of slaves, along with constraints on women's political efforts, triggered feminist consciousness. Feminism as a form of emancipation from slavery remained a central metaphor in the women's rights movements that formed in Europe and the Americas. Another recurrent rationale for women's rights, first articulated by the French utopian socialist Charles Fourier, declared that the progress of a civilization could be measured by the level of its women. His statement echoed in Kishida's speeches in Japan in the 1880s, de Beauvoir's classic *The Second Sex* in the 1940s, and the charter of the Federation of South African Women in the 1950s. Over the course of a century, middle-class women's campaigns persuaded most democratic governments to extend property rights and suffrage to women. These once radical demands, for which women like Susan B. Anthony and Emmeline Pankhurst risked imprisonment, are now considered basic human rights.

Measuring civilizations by the status of women provided ammunition for Western feminist politics, but it encouraged ethnocentric attitudes toward the rest of the world. In the nineteenth century Europeans imagined that they led the march of civilization across the globe, justifying colonial rule because they brought enlightenment to otherwise savage peoples. Feminist writers such as Harriet Taylor Mill reflected these views, while some colonial subjects exposed to European education also accepted this hierarchy of civilizations. Thus the Egyptian male feminist Qasim Amin urged the rejection of local customs, such as female veiling, because they signified cultural inferiority to European styles, even as he insisted that Islamic law granted women's rights.

Increasingly, however, feminists questioned the narrative of European progress. In Africa, Funmilayo Ransome-Kuti pointed out that European colonial rule had undermined, rather than elevated, women's authority in Nigeria. At international feminist conferences, activists such as Shareefeh Hamid Ali rejected the ethnocentric and patronizing assumptions expressed by many white Western women. In the postcolonial world, women from developing regions continued to define liberation on their own terms. Some Islamic feminists championed modest dress as an improvement on the sexualized fashions of the West. As the American poet Adrienne Rich realized, given the legacy of colonial domination by Western nations, feminists had to question Virginia Woolf's dictum that "As a woman I have no country" and recognize their own cultural biases. By the end of the twentieth century, women from the developing regions increasingly assumed leadership in articulating feminist goals, as they did at the United Nations Fourth World Conference on Women held in Beijing in 1995.

Along with the quest for self-representation and full citizenship, feminists have targeted economic dependence on men as a source of women's secondary status. In the nineteenth century, middle-class women's inability to manage property or control wages left them in a childlike position, a theme explored by Henrik Ibsen in his 1879 play *The Doll's House.* Most feminist economic critiques, however, concentrated on working-class women. Liberals John Stuart Mill and Susan B. Anthony, socialist Flora Tristan, and radical anarchist Emma Goldman all condemned limited opportunities for self-support, low wages, and the consequent plight of those working-class women who were forced into prostitution. Drawing on Engels's account of history, Alexandra Kollontai insisted that the socialist state would emancipate female workers. Other socialist women, such as the Chinese writer Ding Ling and the Bolivian activist Domitila Barrios de la Chungara, recognized as well the importance of changing the attitudes of revolutionary men.

Despite progress in the areas of education, employment, and suffrage, feminists struggled to resolve the conflicts faced by wage-earning women who raise children. In the early twentieth century both W.E.B. Du Bois and the Swedish feminist Alva Myrdal insisted that women should not have to choose between wage labor and maternity. Most working women, however, have not had the luxury of making such a choice. In the 1970s socialist feminists such as the Italian theorist Mariarosa Dalla Costa proposed paying wages for housework. To ease the dual burdens of female labor, the United Nations has encouraged male responsibility for parenting, but only recently have men such as Jonah Gokova of Zimbabwe advocated shared parenting as a means of undermining patriarchy.

Feminist writers have also identified the female body as a source of both oppression and empowerment. "One is not born, but becomes a woman," de Beauvoir famously wrote. Because cultures have elaborated on biological differences to reinforce gender hierarchy, feminists have looked skeptically on theories of natural femininity. Early texts deplored women's ornamental function and the focus on female beauty at the expense of female intellect. In the nineteenth century, as the authority of medical science expanded, women like Charlotte Perkins Gilman expressed discontent with their treatment from this male-dominated elite. Margaret Sanger's birth control crusade soon placed reproduction at the center of feminist politics by rejecting involuntary motherhood. By the late twentieth century, women's acknowledgment of their illegal abortions in Europe and of female genital cutting in Africa brought once private health concerns into public view. In the United States, revelations of continuing sexual harassment inspired younger women, such as Rebecca Walker, to declare a Third Wave of feminism.

Despite the association of women's rights with free love—stimulated in part by the personal lives of writers such as Wollstonecraft and de Beauvoir—most feminists wanted to improve, rather than reject, the institution of marriage. Until the late twentieth century, control over reproduction took precedence over sexual liberation. Emma Goldman voiced a rare alternative when she insisted that women's emancipation must include love and passion. After the 1960s, however, explorations of female passion proliferated as feminists attempted to redefine sexual empowerment. Hélène Cixous portrayed the emancipatory energies of writing as an expression of the female body, while lesbian feminists in Europe and the United States conceptualized female sexual pleasure without dependence on men. Outside the West, the assertion of lesbian rights remained controversial, as evidenced by debates over their inclusion in the platform at the U.N. Conference on Women in 1995.

At the beginning of the twenty-first century, feminist ideas have evolved from pleas for educational opportunity to claims that women's rights, broadly defined, are human rights, a creed adopted by the United Nations and most of its member nations. No one political theory or strategy delineates feminism. Arguments that women's unique capacities as mothers justify their inclusion in civic life endure, but they have been supplemented by the universalistic tenets embodied in equal rights laws. Gender-specific policies—such as "affirmative action" to redress historic inequalities in the workplace, or *parité* to increase the representation of women in public office—seek equality by acknowledging the different treatment of men and women.

In response to persistent challenges to its goals, feminism continues to evolve. Young women still confront stereotypes about evil and ignorant girls and they remain vulnerable to sexual violence. Third Wave feminists face the dilemma of affirming female sexual agency in cultures that market the hypersexuality of young women. In those parts of the world now plagued by political and economic instability, women struggle simultaneously for daily survival, democracy, and personal sovereignty. For millions, the goal of literacy remains elusive. By attempting to empower these women, feminism contributes to the broader project of redressing global inequalities. On every continent, contemporary feminist theorists, artists, and activists carry on the tradition documented in this collection, seeking full human rights for all women.

THE ESSENTIAL
FEMINIST
READER

1.

CHRISTINE DE PIZAN
(1365–c. 1430)

The Book of the City of Ladies

(FRANCE, 1405)

For centuries, European writers grappled with the querelles des femmes, *or the "woman question," in response to the work of Christine de Pizan. At a time when both the Catholic Church and medieval states reinforced patriarchal authority in the family, de Pizan questioned the biblical and natural justifications for men's rule over women. Whether cursed by the sin of Eve or presumed to be intellectually as well as physically weaker then men, women generally did not merit education. During the Renaissance, however, women who wished to extend humanist ideas about the importance of education to their own sex defended female intellectual capacity. Born in Venice and raised in Paris, Christine de Pizan read widely in the subjects of philosophy and science (her father was a scholar). When she became a young widow, she put her education to good use, supporting her family as a writer. In* Epistre au dieu d'Amours (Poems of Cupid, God of Love *1399), she defended Eve. In* The Book of the City of Ladies, *the character Christine converses with three Ladies—Reason, Rectitude, and Justice—who refute contemporary theories of female inferiority. The Ladies also catalogue the learned women of the Bible and of classical myth, as well as the women who illustrate female intellectual capability in history. Over the next six hundred years, feminists continued to place female education at the foundation of their quest to achieve women's full humanity.*

One day as I was sitting alone in my study surrounded by books on all kinds of subjects, devoting myself to literary studies, my usual habit, my mind dwelt at length on the weighty opinions of various authors whom I had studied for a long time. I looked up from my book, having decided to leave such subtle questions in peace and to relax by reading some light poetry. With this in mind, I searched for some small book. By chance a strange volume came into my hands, not one of my own, but one which had been given to me along with some others. When I held it open and saw from its title page that it was by Mathéolus, I smiled, for though I had never seen it before, I had often heard that like other books it discussed respect for women. I thought I would browse through it to amuse myself. I had not been reading for very long when my good mother called me to refresh myself with some supper, for it was evening. Intending to look at it the next day, I put it down. The next morning, again seated in my study as was my habit, I remembered wanting to examine this book by Mathéolus. I started to read it and went on for a little while. Because the subject seemed to me not very pleasant for people who do not enjoy lies, and of no use in developing virtue or manners, given its lack of integrity in diction and theme, and after browsing here and there and reading the end, I put it down in order to turn my attention to more elevated and useful study. But just the sight of this book, even though it was of no authority, made me wonder how it happened that so many different men—and learned men among them—have been and are so inclined to express both in speaking and in their treatises and writings so many wicked insults about women and their behavior. Not only one or two and not even just this Mathéolus (for this book had a bad name anyway and was intended as a satire) but, more generally, judging from the treatises of all philosophers and poets and from all the orators—it would take too long to mention their names— it seems that they all speak from one and the same mouth. They all concur in one conclusion: that the behavior of women is inclined to and full of every vice. Thinking deeply about these matters, I began to examine my character and conduct as a natural woman and, similarly, I considered other women whose company I frequently kept, princesses, great ladies, women of the middle and lower classes, who had graciously told me of their most private and intimate thoughts, hoping that I could judge impartially and in good conscience whether the testimony of so many notable men could be true. To the best of my knowledge, no matter how long I confronted or dissected the problem, I could not see or realize how their claims could be true when compared to the natural behavior and character of women. Yet I still argued vehemently against women, saying that it would be impossible that so many famous men—such solemn scholars, possessed of such deep and great understanding, so clear-sighted in all things, as it seemed—could have spoken falsely on so many occasions that I could hardly find a book on morals where, even before I had read it in its entirety, I did not find several chapters or certain sections attacking women, no matter who the author was. This reason alone, in short, made me conclude that, although my intellect did not perceive my own great faults and, likewise, those of other women because of its simpleness and ignorance, it was however truly fitting that such was the case. And so I relied more on the judgment of others than on what I myself felt and knew. I was so transfixed in this line of thinking for such a long time that it seemed as if I were in a stupor. Like a gushing fountain, a series of authorities, whom I recalled one after another, came to mind, along with their opinions on this topic. And I finally decided that God formed a vile creature when He made woman, and I wondered how such a worthy artisan could have deigned to make such an abominable work which, from what they say, is the vessel as well as the refuge and abode of every evil and vice. As I was thinking this, a great unhappiness and sadness welled up in my heart, for I detested myself and the entire feminine sex, as though we were monstrosities in nature. And in my lament I spoke these words:

"Oh, God, how can this be? For unless I stray from my faith, I must never doubt that Your infinite wisdom and most perfect goodness ever created anything which was not good. Did You yourself not create woman in a very special way and since that time did You not give her all those inclinations which it pleased You for her to have? And how could it be that You could go wrong in anything? Yet look at all these accusations which have been judged, decided, and concluded against women. I do not know how to understand this repugnance. If it is so, fair Lord God, that in fact so many abominations abound in the female sex, for You Yourself say that the testimony of two or three witnesses lends credence, why shall I not doubt that this is true? Alas, God, why did You not let me be born in the world as a man, so that all my inclinations would be to serve You better, and so that I would not stray in anything and would be as perfect as a man is said to be? But since Your kindness has not been extended to me, then forgive my negligence in Your service, most fair Lord God, and may it not displease You, for the servant who receives fewer gifts from his lord is less obliged in his service." I spoke these words to God in my lament and a great deal more for a very long time in sad reflection, and in my folly I considered myself most unfortunate because God had made me inhabit a female body in this world. . . .

After hearing these things, I replied to the lady [Reason] who spoke infallibly: "My lady, truly has God revealed great wonders in the strength of these women whom you describe. But please enlighten me again, whether it has ever pleased this God, who has bestowed so many favors on women, to honor the feminine sex with the privilege of the virtue of high understanding and great learning, and whether women ever have a clever enough mind for this. I wish very much to know this because men maintain that the mind of women can learn only a little."

She answered, "My daughter, since I told you before, you know quite well that the opposite of their opinion is true, and to show you this even more clearly, I will give you proof through examples. I tell you again—and don't fear a contradiction—if it were customary to send daughters to school like sons, and if they were then taught the natural sciences, they would learn as thoroughly and understand the subtleties of all the arts and sciences as well as sons. And by chance there happen to be such women, for, as I touched on before, just as women have more delicate bodies than men, weaker and less able to perform many tasks, so do they have minds that are freer and sharper whenever they apply themselves."

"My lady, what are you saying? With all due respect, could you dwell longer on this point, please. Certainly men would never admit this answer is true, unless it is explained more plainly, for they believe that one normally sees that men know more than women do."

She answered, "Do you know why women know less?"

"Not unless you tell me, my lady."

"Without the slightest doubt, it is because they are not involved in many different things, but stay at home, where it is enough for them to run the household, and there is nothing which so instructs a reasonable creature as the exercise and experience of many different things."

"My lady, since they have minds skilled in conceptualizing and learning, just like men, why don't women learn more?"

She replied, "Because, my daughter, the public does not require them to get involved in the affairs which men are commissioned to execute, just as I told you before. It is enough for women to perform the usual duties to which they are ordained. As for judging from experience, since one sees that women usually know less than men, that therefore their capacity for understanding is less, look at men who farm the flatlands or who live in the mountains. You will find that in many countries they seem completely savage because they are so simple-minded. All the same, there is no doubt that Nature provided them with the qualities of body and mind found in the wisest and most learned men. All of this stems from a failure to learn, though, just as I told you, among men and women, some possess better minds than others. Let me tell you about women who have possessed great learning and profound understanding and treat the question of the similarity of women's minds to men's." ...

"My lady, I see the endless benefits which have accrued to the world through women and nevertheless these men claim that there is no evil which has not come into the world because of them."

"Fair friend," she answered, "you can see from what I have already said to you that the contrary of what they say is true. For there is no man who could sum up the enormous benefits which have come about through women and which come about every day, and I proved this for you with the examples of the noble ladies who gave the sciences and arts to the world. But, if what I have said about the earthly benefits accruing thanks to women is not enough for you, I will tell you about the spiritual ones. Oh, how could any man be so heartless to forget that the door of Paradise was opened to him by a woman? As I told you before, it was opened by the Virgin Mary, and is there anything greater one could ask for than that God was made man? And who can forget the great benefits which mothers bring to their sons and which wives bring to their husbands? I implore them at the very least not to forget the advantages which touch upon spiritual good. Let us consider the Law of the Jews. If you recall the story of Moses, to whom God gave the written Law of the Jews, you will find that this holy prophet, through whom so much good has come about, was saved from death by a woman, just as I will tell you....

"My lady [Rectitude], you have given me a remarkable account of the marvelous constancy, strength, endurance, and virtue of women. What more could one say about the strongest men who have lived? Men, especially writing in books, vociferously and unanimously claim that women in particular are fickle and inconstant, changeable and flighty, weak-hearted, compliant like children, and lacking all stamina. Are the men who accuse women of so much changeableness and inconstancy themselves so unwavering that change for them lies outside the realm of custom or common occurrence? Of course, if they themselves are not that firm, then it is truly despicable for them to accuse others of their own vice or to demand a virtue which they do not themselves know how to practice."

She replied, "Fair sweet friend, have you not heard the saying that the fool can clearly see the mote in his neighbor's eye but pays no attention to the beam hanging out of his own eye? Let me point out to you the contradiction in what these men say concerning the variability and inconstancy of women: since they all generally accuse women of being delicate and frail by nature, you would assume that they think that they are constant, or, at the very least, that women are less constant than they are. Yet they demand more constancy from women than they themselves can muster, for these men who claim to be so strong and of such noble condition are unable to prevent themselves from falling into many, even graver faults and sins, not all of them out of ignorance, but rather out of pure malice, knowing well that they are in the wrong. All the same, they excuse themselves for this by claiming it is human nature to sin. When a few women lapse (and when these men themselves, through their own strivings and their own power, are the cause), then as far as these men are concerned, it is completely a matter of fragility and inconstancy. It seems to me right, nevertheless, to conclude—since they claim women are so fragile—that these men should be somewhat more tolerant of women's weaknesses and not hold something to be a crime for women which they consider only a peccadillo for themselves. For the law does not maintain, nor can any such written opinion be found that permits them and not women to sin, that their vice is more excusable. In fact these men allow themselves liberties which they are unwilling to tolerate in women and thus they—and they are many—perpetrate many insults and outrages in word and deed. Nor do they deign to repute women strong and constant for having endured such men's harsh outrages. In this way men try in every question to have the right on their side—they want to have it both ways! You yourself have quite adequately discussed this problem in your *Epistre au Dieu d'Amour*....

In brief, all women—whether noble, bourgeois, or lower-class—be well-informed in all things and cautious in defending your honor and chastity against your enemies! My ladies, see how these men accuse you of so many vices in everything. Make liars of them all by showing forth your virtue, and prove their attacks false by acting well, so that you can say with the Psalmist, "the vices of the evil will fall on their heads." Repel the deceptive flatterers who, using different charms, seek with various tricks to steal that which you must consummately guard, that is, your honor and the beauty of your praise. Oh my ladies, flee, flee the foolish love they urge on you! Flee it, for God's sake, flee! For no good can come to you from it. Rather, rest assured that however deceptive their lures, their end is always to your detriment. And do not believe the contrary, for it cannot be otherwise. Remember, dear ladies, how these men call you frail, unserious, and easily influenced but yet try hard, using all kinds of strange and deceptive tricks, to catch you, just as one lays traps for wild animals. Flee, flee, my ladies, and avoid their company—under these smiles are hidden deadly and painful poisons. And so may it please you, my most respected ladies, to cultivate virtue, to flee vice, to increase and multiply our City, and to rejoice and act well. And may I, your servant, commend myself to you, praying to God who by His grace has granted me to live in this world and to persevere in His holy service. May He in the end have mercy on my great sins and grant to me the joy which lasts forever, which I may, by His grace, afford to you. Amen.

2.

FRANÇOIS POULLAIN DE LA BARRE
(1647–1723)

On the Equality of the Two Sexes
(FRANCE, 1673)

Both men and women contributed to the debates over the "woman question" in early modern Europe. Most learned men depicted women as the physically and mentally inferior sex, ordained by God and limited by nature to wifely duties, and sometimes caricatured as monsters if they sought knowledge. The French writer François Poullain de la Barre broke with this tradition when he rejected the principle that a person's sex determined the capacity for learning. Strongly influenced by the rationalist theories of scientific philosopher René Descartes, de la Barre questioned Catholic doctrines and sought logical explanations for women's status. Like Christine de Pizan, he argued that social custom, not inherent capacity, stunted women's intellectual growth. Since the mind "has no sex," women as well as men have a right to knowledge and to pursue scientific and literary studies. During the 1670s, while he was studying for the priesthood, de la Barre wrote three treatises on the equality of the sexes and the education of women. He later became disenchanted with Catholic intolerance and moved to Geneva, where he converted to Calvinism, married, and had two children. Though unpopular in his lifetime, his ideas were revived in the twentieth century through the dictum of feminist theorist Simone de Beauvoir that biology is not destiny.

It is easy to see that the difference between the two sexes is limited to the body, since that is the only part used in the reproduction of humankind. Since the mind merely gives its consent, and does so in exactly the same way in everyone, we can conclude that it has no sex.

Considered independently, the mind is found to be equal and of the same nature in all men, and capable of all kinds of thought. It is as much exercised by small concepts as by large; as much thought is required to conceive of a mite as an elephant. Anyone who understands the nature of the light and heat of a spark understands also the nature of the sun. When one becomes used to contemplating the things of the mind, one understands them as clearly as material things that are known through the senses. I find no greater difference between the mind of a vulgar, ignorant man and that of a refined, enlightened man than between the mind of the same man at ten years old and at forty years old. Since there seems not to be any greater difference between the minds of the two sexes, we can say that the difference does not lie there. It is rather the constitution of the body, but particularly education, religious observance, and the effects of our environment which are the natural and perceptible causes of all the many differences between people.

A woman's mind is joined to her body, like a man's, by God himself, and according to the same laws. Feelings, passions, and the will maintain this union, and since the mind functions no differently in one sex than in the other, it is capable of the same things in both.

This is all the more obvious if we consider the head, which is the sole organ of knowledge and the place where the mind exercises its functions. A most minute anatomical study reveals no difference here between men and women; a woman's brain is exactly the same as ours. Sense perceptions are received and assembled there in the same way and are in no way differently stored for the imagination and the memory. Like us, women hear with their ears, see with their eyes, and taste with their tongues. There is nothing peculiar to one sex in the disposition of these organs, except that women's are usually more sensitive, which is an advantage. External objects affect them in the same way: light through the eyes and sound through the ears. Who, then, will prevent them from undertaking a study of themselves and examining the nature of the mind, from asking how many different kinds of thoughts there are and how these are stimulated by certain physical movements, from going on to examine the natural ideas they have of God and, starting with spiritual things, from putting some order into their thoughts and conceiving the science we call metaphysics?

Since they also have eyes and hands, could they not perform a dissection of the human body themselves, or watch other people do so? In this way they could observe the symmetry and the structure of its parts, they could note their differences and relationship, their configurations, movements, and functions, and the changes to which they are susceptible. Such observation would enable them to find ways of keeping these parts in a healthy state and of bringing them back to health should they ever be altered. All they would need for this would be to learn the nature of the external bodies that interact with their own bodies, to discover their properties and everything that enables them to have a good or bad effect upon them. These things are learned by the use of one's senses and by the various experiences one derives from them, and as women are perfectly capable of both, they can learn physics and medicine as well as we can....

In the case of women, however, we have not been content to refuse them access to the sciences and the civil service after a long prescription against them, but we have gone even further and imagined that their exclusion is based upon some natural feebleness. Nothing is more fanciful than this idea, for whether we look at the sciences themselves or at the faculties we use to apprehend them, we see that the two sexes have equal aptitude. There is one way and one way only to introduce into the mind the truth which is its nourishment, just as there is only one way to introduce foods into various kinds of stomachs for the sustenance of the body. As to the different aspects of the mind that make it more or less apt for the study of the sciences, we have to agree, if we look honestly at the facts, that the advantages are all on the side of women.

We cannot dispute that those men who are most coarse and heavy are usually stupid, and that, on the contrary, the more delicately built are always the cleverest. Experience is too widespread and uniform for me to have to appeal to reason to argue further. Therefore, since the fair sex is of a more delicate disposition than ourselves, women would be sure to be at least our equals if only they applied themselves to studying.

I foresee that this idea will not be appreciated by many who will think that I am going too far. There is nothing I can do about that. We have taken it into our heads to think that the honor of our sex depends on our being first in everything, whereas it is my belief that justice demands that we give both sexes their due.

Indeed, all of us, men or women, have an equal right to truth since the minds of both are equally able to apprehend it, and since we both react in the same way to objects that make an impression upon our bodies. The right to the same knowledge which is given to us all by nature stems from the fact that we all have the same need of it. There is no one who does not seek his own happiness—the goal of all our actions. No one can achieve happiness without clear and distinct knowledge. It is this, as JESUS CHRIST Himself and St. Paul give us to hope, that will constitute our happiness in the next life....

We should not therefore set too much store by those common expressions deriving from the state of the two sexes today. If we want to make fun of a man for having too little courage, resolution, and firmness, we call him effeminate, as if we mean to say that he is as weak and feeble as a woman. On the other hand, if we mean to praise a woman who has extraordinary courage, strength, or intelligence, we say that she is manly. These expressions which are so flattering to them contribute in no small way to the high opinion we have of men, all because we do not acknowledge that they are a mere approximation of the truth, and that their so-called truth depends indiscriminately upon nature or custom, so that they are completely contingent and arbitrary. Virtue, gentleness, and honesty are so intimately associated with women that if their sex had not been held in such low esteem we would have praised a man who possesses these qualities to an extraordinary degree by saying "he is a woman" if men had been willing to accept that kind of language into their speech.

Be all this as it may, men should not have to depend upon physical strength for distinction, otherwise animals would have the advantage over them, as would the physically strongest among us. Experience shows us, however, that brute force makes men unfit for anything but manual labor, whereas those who have less physical strength usually have greater intelligence. The most competent philosophers and the greatest princes have traditionally been quite delicate, and perhaps the greatest captains would not have relished combat with the most humble private. One has only to visit the courts of law to see whether the greatest judges necessarily rival the strength of the most insignificant ushers.

It makes no sense, then, to lay so much emphasis on the constitution of the body to justify the difference between the sexes when differences in mind are much more important.

3.

SOR JUANA INÉS DE LA CRUZ
(1651–95)

"The Reply to Sor Philotea"
(MEXICO, 1691)

*The Mexican nun Sor Juana Inés de la Cruz defended female intellec-
tual pursuits by citing the examples of wise women in the Bible and rein-
terpreting early Christian texts, such as the writings of Saint Paul.
Drawing on her Catholic foundation, she argued that the equality of
women's souls entitled them to education in order to prepare themselves
spiritually. The illegitimate daughter of a Spanish father and a Mexican
Creole mother, as a child Sor Juana learned to read from her grandfather.
She served at the royal court in Mexico City, where she earned a reputation as an intellectual prodigy. At age eighteen she chose to enter a con-
vent in order to pursue her studies. Over the next two decades she wrote
secular plays, love poems, and eventually theological treatises. When her
bishop, writing under the pseudonym Sor Philotea, complained of these
works, Sor Juana wrote in response that what God had inspired should
not be thwarted by the Church. For centuries feminists employed similar
arguments, drawing on biblical models of heroic women and suggesting
that women made particularly suitable teachers. Within a few years after publishing her response, however, Sor Juana acceded to the pressures
of the Church and withdrew from writing.*

Even if these studies were to be viewed, my Lady, as to one's credit (as I see they are indeed celebrated in men), none would be due me, since I pursue them involuntarily. If they are seen as reprehensible, for the same reason I do not think I should be blamed. Still, though, I am so unsure of myself, that neither in this nor in anything do I trust my own judgment. Hence I leave the decision up to your supreme talent, and will abide by whatever it decrees, with no antagonism and no reluctance, for this has been nothing more than a simple account of my inclination to letters.

I must admit, likewise, that although, as I have said, a truth such as this requires no exemplification; nevertheless the many precedents I have read about in both divine and humane letters have greatly assisted me. For I see a Debbora [Judges 4 and 5] setting up laws in both military and political spheres, and governing a nation that could boast so many learned men. I see a most wise Queen of Sheba [3 (1) Kings 10; 2 Paralipomenon (Chronicles) 9], so learned that she dared to challenge with enigmas the wisdom of the wisest of the wise, without suffering on that account any reproof. Rather, thanks to that, she becomes judge of the unbelieving. I see so many and such outstanding women, like Abigail [1 Kings (1 Sam.) 25], endowed with the gift of prophecy; others, like Esther, with that of persuasiveness; others, like Rahab [Josue 2], with piety; others, like Anna, mother of Samuel [1 Kings (1 Sam.) 1 and 2], with perseverance; and an infinite number of others, all possessing other gifts and virtues. . . .

The venerable Dr. Arce (in virtue and cultivation a worthy professor of Scripture) in his *Studioso Bibliorum*, raises this question: *An liceat foeminis sacrorum Bibliorum studio incumbere? eaque interpretari?* [Is it legitimate for women to apply themselves to study of the Holy Bible and to interpret it?] He brings in many opinions of saints in support of the opposing view, especially that of the Apostle: *Mulieres in Ecclesiis taceant, non enim permittitur eis loqui* etc. ["Let women keep silence in the churches, for it is not permitted them to speak" (1 Cor. 14:34)].

He then brings in other opinions and especially that of the same Apostle addressing Titus: *Anus similiter in habitu sancto, bene docentes* ["The aged women, in like manner, in holy attire...teaching well" (Tit. 2:3)], with interpretations of the Church Fathers. He finally decides, in his judicious way, that to lecture publicly in the classroom and to preach in the pulpit are not legitimate activities for women, but that studying, writing, and teaching privately are not only allowable but most edifying and useful. Of course this does not apply to all women—only to those whom God has endowed with particular virtue and discernment and who have become highly accomplished and erudite, and possess the talents and other qualities needed for such holy pursuits. So true is this that the interpretation of Holy Scripture should be forbidden not only to women, considered so very inept, but to men, who merely by virtue of being men consider themselves sages, unless they are very learned and virtuous, with receptive and properly trained minds. Failure to do so, in my view, has given rise precisely to all those sectarians and been the root cause of all the heresies. For there are many who study in order to become ignorant, especially those of an arrogant, restless, and overbearing turn of mind, who are partial to new interpretations of the Law (where precisely they are to be rejected). Hence, until they have uttered something heretical merely in order to say what no one else has, they will not rest. Of these the Holy Spirit says: *In malevolam animam no introibit sapientia* ["For wisdom will not enter into a malicious soul" (Wisdom 1:4)]. Learning does more harm to such than remaining ignorant would....

Oh, how much harm would be avoided in our country if older women were as learned as Laeta and knew how to teach in the way Saint Paul and my Father Saint Jerome direct! Instead of which, if fathers wish to educate their daughters beyond what is customary, for want of trained older women and on account of the extreme negligence which has become women's sad lot, since well-educated older women are unavailable, they are obliged to bring in men teachers to give instruction in reading, writing, and arithmetic, playing musical instruments, and other skills. No little harm is done by this, as we witness every day in the pitiful examples of ill-assorted unions; from the ease of contact and the close company kept over a period of time, there easily comes about something not thought possible. As a result of this, many fathers prefer leaving their daughters in a barbaric, uncultivated state to exposing them to an evident danger such as familiarity with men breeds. All of which would be eliminated if there were older women of learning, as Saint Paul desires, and instruction were passed down from one group to another, as is the case with needlework and other traditional activities.

For what drawback could there be to having an old woman, well-versed in letters and pious in conversation and way of life, in charge of the education of maidens? And what harm in preventing the latter from going to waste either for lack of instruction or from having it imparted to them through the dangerous medium of male masters? For even if there were no greater risk than the impropriety of having a strange man sit beside a bashful woman (who blushes even when her father looks directly at her) and treat her with offhand familiarity and with the informality of the classroom, her discomfiture at being in men's company and conversing with them suffices to forbid it. . . .

If all those interpreters and expositors of Saint Paul think otherwise, I should like them to explain to me how they understand the passage *Mulieres in Ecclesia taceant.* Because they must understand it either as referring concretely to pulpits and clerics' chairs, or immaterially to the whole multitude of the faithful, which is the Church. If they take it in the first sense (which, in my view, is the true one, since we see that women are not in fact allowed to lecture or preach publicly in the Church), why do they reprimand those who study in private? If they understand it in the second sense and take the Apostle's prohibition so sweepingly as not even in secret to allow women to write or study, how is it that we see the Church allowing a Gertrude, a Teresa, a Bridget, the nun of Agreda, and many more to study? And if it is answered that these women were saints, I agree, but this does not invalidate my argument: first, because Saint Paul's affirmation is absolute and refers to all women, not excluding saints—for in his day, in the fervor of the early Church, Martha and Mary, Marcella, Mary mother of Jacob, Salomé, and many other women were saints, and he does not except them. And nowadays we see the Church allowing women, both saints and not, to write, for the nun of Agreda and Maria de la Antigua are not canonized, yet their writings circulate, nor were Saint Teresa and the others when they wrote. Thus Saint Paul's prohibition referred only to speaking in public from pulpits; if the Apostle had prohibited writing, the Church would not allow it. So today I am not so bold as to teach—it would be the height of presumption in my case. Writing requires greater talent than I possess and a great deal of thought. So Saint Cyprian says: *Gravi consideratione indigent, quae scribimus* [The things we write need to be very carefully considered]. My whole wish has been to study so as to be less ignorant, for, as Saint Augustine has it, some things are learned with a view to action, others only for the sake of knowing: *Discimus quaedam, ut sciamus; quaedam, ut faciamus.* So what is there so criminal, considering that I refrain even from what is legitimate for women, which is to teach through writing, knowing that I do not have the background for it, and following the advice of Quintilian: *Noscat quisque, et non tantum ex alieniis praeceptis, sed ex natura sua capiat consilium* [Let everyone learn, and not so much through the precepts of others as by consulting his own nature]?...

4.

MARY ASTELL
(1666–1731)

A Serious Proposal to the Ladies
(ENGLAND, 1694)

Protestant countries lacked the religious convents that offered Catholic women an alternative to marriage and possibilities for literacy. In England, Mary Astell, a self-educated woman of modest means and a devoted Anglican, proposed the establishment of a seminary where Protestant women could enjoy a learned life. Like other early proponents of women's education, Astell framed her arguments in religious terms and assured readers that women would not try to usurp male authority. Yet she insisted that women were as rational as men, capable of rigorous scientific as well as religious thought. She also emphasized the importance of female community and of female self-esteem. A Serious Proposal *had wide circulation in England and influenced writers such as Daniel Defoe. In a later work,* Reflections upon Marriage *(1700), Astell accepted the authority of men in the family but insisted that women should have options besides marriage. She herself remained single and enjoyed the support of a circle of aristocratic female friends who shared her views. Although Astell never established a women's seminary, she and her friends helped create a charitable boarding school, where she lived until her death.*

Now as to the Proposal it is to erect a *Monastery*, or if you will (to avoid giving offence to the scrupulous and injudicious, by names which tho' innocent in themselves, have been abus'd by superstitious Practices,) we will call it a *Religious Retirement*, and such as shall have a double aspect, being not only a Retreat from the World for those who desire that advantage, but likewise, an institution and previous discipline, to fit us to do the greatest good in it; such an institution as this (if I do not mightily deceive my self,) would be the most probable method to amend the present and improve the future Age....

You are therefore Ladies, invited into a place, where you shall suffer no other confinement, but to be kept out of the road Of Sin: You shall not be depriv'd of your Grandeur, but only exchange the vain Pomps and Pageantry of the world, empty Titles and Forms of State, for the true and solid Greatness of being able to despise *them.* You will only quit the Chat of insignificant people for an ingenious Conversation; the froth of flashy Wit for real Wisdom; idle tales for instructive discourses. The deceitful Flatteries of those who under pretence of loving and admiring you, really served their *own* base ends, for the seasonable Reproofs and wholsom Counsels of your hearty wellwishers and affectionate Friends, which will procure you those perfections your feigned lovers pretended you had, and kept you from obtaining....

[Y]our Retreat shall be so manag'd as not to exclude the good Works of an *Active*, from the pleasure and serenity of a *contemplative* Life, but by a due mixture of both retain all the advantages and avoid the inconveniences that attend either. It shall not so cut you off from the world as to hinder you from bettering and improving it, but rather qualify you to do it the greatest Good, and be a Seminary to stock the Kingdom with pious and prudent Ladies; whose good Example it is to be hop'd, will so influence the rest of their Sex, that Women may no longer pass for those little useless and impertinent Animals, which the ill conduct of too many has caus'd them to be mistaken for.

We have hitherto consider'd our Retirement only in relation to Religion, which is indeed its *main*, I may say its *only* design; nor can this be thought too contracting a word, since Religion is the adequate business of our lives, and largely consider'd, takes in all we have to do.... But because, as we have all along observ'd, Religion never appears in its true Beauty, but when it is accompanied with Wisdom and Discretion; and that without a good Understanding, we can scarce be *truly*, but never *eminently* Good; being liable to a thousand seductions and mistakes; for even the men themselves, if they have not a competent degree of Knowledge, they are carried about with every wind of Doctrine. Therefore, one great end of this institution, shall be to expel that cloud of Ignorance, which Custom has involv'd us in, to furnish our minds with a stock of solid and useful Knowledge, that the Souls of Women may no longer be the only unadorn'd and neglected things....

For since GOD has given Women as well as Men intelligent Souls, why should they be forbidden to improve them? Since he has not denied us the faculty of Thinking, why shou'd we not (at least in gratitude to him) employ our Thoughts on himself their noblest Object, and not unworthily bestow them on Trifles and Gaities and secular Affairs? Being the Soul was created for the contemplation of Truth as well as for the fruition of Good, is it not as cruel and unjust to preclude Women from the knowledge of the one, as well as from the enjoyment of the other?...

We pretend not that Women shou'd teach in the Church, or usurp Authority where it is not allow'd them; permit us only to understand our *own* duty, and not be forc'd to take it upon trust from others; to be at least so far learned, as to be able to form in our minds a true Idea of Christianity....

But since such Seminaries are thought proper for the Men, since they enjoy the fruits of those Noble Ladies' Bounty who were the foundresses of several of their Colleges, why shou'd we not think that such ways of Education wou'd be as advantageous to the Ladies? or why shou'd we despair of finding some among them who will be as kind to their own Sex as their Ancestors have been to the other?...

The Men therefore may still enjoy their Prerogatives for us, we mean not to intrench on any of their Lawful Privileges, our only

Contention shall be that they may not out-do us in promoting his Glory who is Lord both of them and us; And by all that appears the generality will not oppose us in this matter, we shall not provoke them by striving to be better Christians. They may busy their Heads with Affairs of State, and spend their Time and Strength in recommending themselves to an uncertain Master, or a more giddy Multitude, our only endeavour shall be to be absolute Monarchs in our own Bosoms. They shall still if they please dispute about Religion, let 'em only give us leave to Understand and Practise it....

5.

MARY WOLLSTONECRAFT
(1759–97)

A Vindication of the Rights of Woman
(ENGLAND, 1792)

In the eighteenth century, Enlightenment political theory replaced the divine right of kings with the individual rights of man, but these principles did not apply to women. The British writer Mary Wollstonecraft, a former governess who had written in support of the French Revolution, extended the Enlightenment critique by rejecting both aristocratic hierarchies and conventional ideas about the family, including the rights of husbands over their wives. Women's unique biological functions, she acknowledged, created a measure of dependence on men, but she blamed the socialization of elite and particularly middle-class women as frivolous creatures, concerned only with beauty and idle pleasures, for creating artificial weaknesses in female character. A virtuous citizenry—necessary for the success of self-government—required virtuous mothers, which in turn required educated women. In contrast to earlier rationales for women's education, which rested heavily upon service to God, Wollstonecraft stressed the common humanity of women and men. Although she highlighted women's roles as mothers, she also recognized the importance of self-support, and she dared to imagine a time when women would have political rights. Her personal reputation—in 1794 she bore a child out of wedlock, and she later had an open affair with the radical editor William Godwin before they married—led conservatives to condemn both Wollstonecraft and her ideas as immoral. For more than a century after her death, however, her work inspired feminist movements internationally.

After considering the historic page, and viewing the living world with anxious solicitude, the most melancholy emotions of sorrowful indignation have depressed my spirits, and I have sighed when obliged to confess that either nature has made a great difference between man and man, or that the civilization which has hitherto taken place in the world has been very partial. I have turned over various books written on the subject of education, and patiently observed the conduct of parents and the management of schools; but what has been the result?—a profound conviction that the neglected education of my fellow-creatures is the grand source of the misery I deplore; and that women, in particular, are rendered weak and wretched by a variety of concurring causes, originating from one hasty conclusion. The conduct and manners of women, in fact, evidently prove that their minds are not in a healthy state; for, like the flowers which are planted in too rich a soil, strength and usefulness are sacrificed to beauty; and the flaunting leaves, after having pleased a fastidious eye, fade, disregarded, on the stalk, long before the season when they ought to have arrived at maturity. One cause of this barren blooming I attribute to a false system of education, gathered from the books written on this subject by men who, considering females rather as women than human creatures, have been more anxious to make them alluring mistresses than affectionate wives and rational mothers; and the understanding of the sex has been so bubbled by this specious homage, that the civilized women of the present century, with a few exceptions, are only anxious to inspire love, when they ought to cherish a nobler ambition, and, by their abilities and virtues, exact respect.

In a treatise, therefore, on female rights and manners, the works which have been particularly written for their improvement must not be overlooked; especially when it is asserted, in direct terms, that the minds of women are enfeebled by false refinement; that the books of instruction, written by men of genius, have had the same tendency as more frivolous productions; and that, in the true style of Mahometanism, they are treated as a kind of subordinate beings, and not as a part of the human species, when improvable reason is allowed to be the dignified distinction which raises men above the brute creation, and puts a natural sceptre in a feeble hand.

Yet, because I am a woman, I would not lead my readers to suppose that I mean violently to agitate the contested question respecting the quality or inferiority of the sex; but as the subject lies in my way, and I cannot pass it over without subjecting the main tendency of my reasoning to misconstruction, I shall stop a moment to deliver, in a few words, my opinion. In the government of the physical world it is observable that the female in point of strength is, in general, inferior to the male. This is the law of Nature; and it does not appear to be suspended or abrogated in favor of woman. A degree of physical superiority cannot, therefore, be denied—and it is a noble prerogative! But not content with this natural pre-eminence, men endeavor to sink us still lower, merely to render us alluring objects for a moment; and women, intoxicated by the adoration which men, under the influence of their senses, pay them, do not seek to obtain a durable interest in their hearts, or to become the friends of the fellow-creatures who find amusement in their society.

I am aware of an obvious inference—from every quarter have I heard exclamations against masculine women; but where are they to be found? If by this appellation men mean to inveigh against their ardor in hunting, shooting, and gaming, I shall most cordially join in the cry; but if it be against the imitation of manly virtues, or, more properly speaking, the attainment of those talents and virtues the exercise of which ennobles the human character, and which raise females in the scale of animal being, when they are comprehensively termed mankind, all those who view them with a philosophic eye must, I should think, wish with me that they may every day grow more and more masculine.

This discussion naturally divides the subject. I shall first consider women in the grand light of human creatures, who, in common with men, are placed on this earth to unfold their faculties; and afterwards I shall more particularly point out their peculiar designation.

I wish also to steer clear of an error which many respectable writers have fallen into; for the instruction which has hitherto been addressed to women has rather been applicable to *ladies*, ... but, addressing my sex in a firmer tone, I pay particular attention to those in the middle class, because they appear to be in the most natural state. Perhaps the seeds of false refinement, immorality, and vanity have ever been shed by the great. Weak, artificial beings, raised above the common wants and affections of their race, in a premature, unnatural manner, undermine the very foundation of virtue, and spread corruption through the whole mass of society! As a class of mankind they have the strongest claim to pity; the education of the rich tends to render them vain and helpless, and the unfolding mind is not strengthened by the practice of those duties which dignify the human character. They only live to amuse themselves, and by the same law which in Nature invariably produces certain effects, they soon only afford barren amusement.

But as I purpose taking a separate view of the different ranks of society, and of the moral character of women in each, this hint is for the present sufficient; and I have only alluded to the subject because it appears to me to be the very essence of an introduction, to give a cursory account of the contents of the work it introduces.

My own sex, I hope, will excuse me if I treat them like rational creatures, instead of flattering their *fascinating* graces, and viewing them as if they were in a state of perpetual childhood, unable to stand alone. I earnestly wish to point out in what true dignity and human happiness consist; I wish to persuade women to endeavor to acquire strength, both of mind and body, and to convince them that the soft phrases, "susceptibility of heart," "delicacy of sentiment," and "refinement of taste" are almost synonymous with epithets of weakness, and that those beings who are only the objects of pity and that kind of love which has been termed its sister, will soon become objects of contempt.

Dismissing, then, those pretty feminine phrases which the men condescendingly use to soften our slavish dependence, and despising that weak elegancy of mind, exquisite sensibility, and sweet docility of manners supposed to be the sexual characteristics of the weaker vessel, I wish to show that elegance is inferior to virtue, that the first object of laudable ambition is to obtain a character as a human being, regardless of the distinction of sex; and that secondary views should be brought to this simple touchstone....

The education of women has, of late, been more attended to than formerly; yet they are still reckoned a frivolous sex, and ridiculed or pitied by the writers who endeavor by satire or instruction to improve them. It is acknowledged that they spend many of the first years of their lives in acquiring a smattering of accomplishments; meanwhile strength of body and mind are sacrificed to libertine notions of beauty, to the desire of establishing themselves—the only way women can rise in the world—by marriage. And this desire making mere animals of them, when they marry they act as such children may be expected to act—they dress, they paint, and nickname God's creatures. Surely these weak beings are only fit for a seraglio! Can they be expected to govern a family with judgment, or take care of the poor babes whom they bring into the world?

If, then, it can be fairly deduced, from the present conduct of the sex, from the prevalent fondness for pleasure which takes place of ambition and those nobler passions that open and enlarge the soul, that the instruction which women have hitherto received has only tended, with the constitution of civil society, to render them insignificant objects of desire—mere propagators of fools!—if it can be proved that in aiming to accomplish them without cultivating their understandings, they are taken out of their sphere of duties, and made ridiculous and useless when the short-lived bloom of beauty is over,* I presume that *rational* men will excuse me for endeavoring to persuade them to become more masculine and respectable.

Indeed, the word "masculine" is only a bugbear; there is little reason to fear that women will acquire too much courage or fortitude; for their apparent inferiority with respect to bodily strength must render them, in some degree, dependent on men in the various relations of life; but why should it be increased by prejudices that give a sex to virtue, and confound simple truths with sensual reveries?

Women are, in fact, so much degraded by mistaken notions of female excellence, that I do not mean to add a paradox when I assert that this artificial weakness produces a propensity to tyrannize, and gives birth to cunning, the natural opponent of strength, which leads them to play off those contemptible infantine airs that undermine esteem even while they excite desire. Let men become more chaste and modest, and if women do not grow wiser in the same ratio it will be clear that they have weaker understandings. It seems scarcely

---

*A lively writer—I cannot recollect his name—asks what business women turned of forty have to do in the world?

necessary to say that I now speak of the sex in general. Many individuals have more sense than their male relatives; and, as nothing preponderates where there is a constant struggle for an equilibrium without it has naturally more gravity, some women govern their husbands without degrading themselves, because intellect will always govern....

Of the pernicious effects which arise from the unnatural distinctions established in society....

It is vain to expect virtue from women till they are in some degree independent of men; nay, it is vain to expect that strength of natural affection which would make them good wives and mothers. While they are absolutely dependent on their husbands they will be cunning, mean, and selfish; and the men who can be gratified by the fawning fondness of spaniel-like affection have not much delicacy, for love is not to be bought; in any sense of the word: its silken wings are instantly shriveled up when anything beside a return in kind is sought. Yet while wealth enervates men, and women live, as it were, by their personal charms, how can we expect them to discharge those ennobling duties which equally require exertion and self-denial?...

I mean, therefore, to infer that the society is not properly organized which does not compel men and women to discharge their respective duties, by making it the only way to acquire that countenance from their fellow-creatures which every human being wishes some way to attain. The respect, consequently, which is paid to wealth and mere personal charms, is a true north-east blast that blights the tender blossoms of affection and virtue. Nature has wisely attached affections to duties to sweeten toil, and to give that vigor to the exertions of reason which only the heart can give. But the affection which is put on merely because it is the appropriated insignia of a certain character, when its duties are not fulfilled, is one of the empty compliments which vice and folly are obliged to pay to virtue and the real nature of things.

To illustrate my opinion, I need only observe that when a woman is admired for her beauty, and suffers herself to be so far intoxicated by the admiration she receives as to neglect to discharge the indispensable duty of a mother, she sins against herself by neglecting to cultivate an affection that would equally tend to make her useful and happy. True happiness—I mean all the contentment and virtuous satisfaction that can be snatched in this imperfect state—must arise from well-regulated affections; and an affection includes a duty. Men are not aware of the misery they cause and the vicious weakness they cherish by only inciting women to render themselves pleasing; they do not consider that they thus make natural and artificial duties clash by sacrificing the comfort and respectability of a woman's life, to voluptuous notions of beauty, when in Nature they all harmonize....

A truly benevolent legislator always endeavors to make it the interest of each individual to be virtuous; and thus, private virtue becoming the cement of public happiness, an orderly whole is consolidated by the tendency of all the parts toward a common centre. But the private or public virtue of woman is very problematical; for Rousseau, and a numerous list of male writers, insist that she should all her life be subjected to a severe restraint, that of propriety. Why subject her to propriety—blind propriety, if she be capable of acting from a nobler spring, if she be an heir of immortality? Is sugar always to be produced by vital blood? Is one-half of the human species, like the poor African slaves, to be subject to prejudices that brutalize them, when principles would be a surer guard, only to sweeten the cup of man? Is not this indirectly to deny woman reason? For a gift is mockery, if it be unfit for use.

Women are, in common with men, rendered weak and luxurious by the relaxing pleasures which wealth procures; but, added to this, they are made slaves to their persons, and must render them alluring that man may lend them his reason to guide their tottering steps aright. Or, should they be ambitious, they must govern their tyrants by sinister tricks; for without rights there cannot be any incumbent duties. The laws respecting woman, which I mean to discuss in a future part, make an absurd unit of a man and his wife; and then, by the easy transition of only considering him as responsible, she is reduced to a mere cypher.

The being who discharges the duties of its station is independent; and, speaking of women at large, their first duty is to themselves as rational creatures, and the next in point of importance, as citizens, is that which includes so many, of a mother. The rank in life which dispenses with their fulfilling this duty necessarily degrades them by making them mere dolls. Or, should they turn to something more important than merely fitting drapery upon a smooth block, their minds are only occupied by some soft, platonic attachment, or the actual management of an intrigue may keep their thoughts in motion; for, when they neglect domestic duties, they have it not in their own power to take the field and march and counter-march, like soldiers, or wrangle in the senate, to keep their faculties from rusting.

I know that, as a proof of the inferiority of the sex, Rousseau has exultingly exclaimed, "How can they leave the nursery for the camp?" And the camp has by some moralists been termed the school of the most heroic virtues; though, I think, it would puzzle a keen casuist to prove the reasonableness of the greater number of wars that have dubbed heroes. I do not mean to consider this question critically; because, having frequently viewed these freaks of ambition as the first natural mode of civilization, when the ground must be torn up, and the woods cleared by fire and sword, I do not choose to call them pests; but surely the present system of war has little connection with virtue of any denomination, being rather the school of *finesse* and effeminacy than of fortitude!

Yet, if defensive war—the only justifiable war in the present advanced state of society, where virtue can show its face and ripen amid the rigors which purify the air on the mountain's top—were alone to be adopted as just and glorious, the true heroism of antiquity might again animate female bosoms. But, fair and softly, gentle reader, male or female, do not alarm thyself; for though I have compared the character of a modern soldier with that of a civilized woman, I am not going to advise them to turn their distaff into a musket, though I sincerely wish to see the bayonet converted into a pruning-hook....

[T]hough I consider that women in the common walks of life are called to fulfill the duties of wives and mothers by religion and reason, I cannot help lamenting that women of a superior cast have not a road open by which they can pursue more extensive plans of usefulness and independence. I may excite laughter by dropping a hint which I mean to pursue some future time; for I really think that women ought to have representatives, instead of being arbitrarily governed without having any direct share allowed them in the deliberations of government....

In the superior ranks of life every duty is done by deputies, as if duties could ever be waived....Women, in particular, all want to be ladies—which is simply to have nothing to do, but listlessly to go they scarcely care where, for they cannot tell what.

But what have women to do in society (I may be asked) but to loiter with easy grace? Surely you would not condemn them all to "suckle fools and chronicle small beer?" No! Women might certainly study the art of healing, and be physicians as well as nurses. And midwifery, decency seems to allot to them; though, I am afraid, the word "midwife" in our dictionaries will soon give place to *"accoucheur,"* and one proof of the former delicacy of the sex be effaced from the language.

They might also study politics, and settle their benevolence on the broadest basis; for the reading of history will scarcely be more useful than the perusal of romances, if read as mere biography—if the character of the times, the political improvements, arts, etc., be not observed—in short, if it be not considered as the history of man, and not of particular men who filled a niche in the temple of fame, and dropped into the black rolling stream of time, that silently sweeps all before it into the shapeless void called eternity—for shape, can it be called, "that shape hath none"?

Business of various kinds they might likewise pursue, if they were educated in a more orderly manner, which might save many from common and legal prostitution. Women would not then marry for a support, as men accept of places under government, and neglect the implied duties; nor would an attempt to earn their own subsistence—a most laudable one!—sink them almost to the level of those poor abandoned creatures who live by prostitution. For, are not milliners and mantua-makers reckoned the next class? The few employments open to women, so far from being liberal, are menial; and when a superior education enables them to take charge of the education of children as governesses, they are not treated like the tutors of sons—though even clerical tutors are not always treated in a manner calculated to render them respectable in the eyes of their pupils, to say nothing of the private comfort of the individual. But as women educated like gentlewomen are never designed for the humiliating situations which necessity sometimes forces them to fill, these situations are considered in the light of a degradation; and they know little of the human heart who need to be told that nothing so painfully sharpens sensibility as such a fall in life.

Some of these women might be restrained from marrying by a proper spirit or delicacy, and others may not have had it in their power to escape in this pitiful way from servitude. Is not that government, then, very defective, and very unmindful of the happiness of one-half of its members, that does not provide for honest, independent women, by encouraging them to fill respectable stations? But in order to render their private virtue a public benefit, they must have a civil existence in the State, married or single; else we shall continually see some worthy woman, whose sensibility has been rendered painfully acute by undeserved contempt, droop like "the lily broken down by a plow-share."

It is a melancholy truth—yet such is the blessed effect of civilization—the most respectable women are the most oppressed; and, unless they have understandings far superior to the common run of understandings, taking in both sexes, they must, from being treated like contemptible beings, become contemptible. How many women thus waste life away, the prey of discontent, who might have practiced as physicians, regulated a farm, managed a shop, and stood erect, supported by their own industry, instead of hanging their heads surcharged with the dew of sensibility, that consumes the beauty to which it at first gave lustre—nay, I doubt whether pity and love are so near akin as poets feign, for I have seldom seen much compassion excited by the helplessness of females, unless they were fair; then, perhaps, pity was the soft handmaid of love, or the harbinger of lust!

How much more respectable is the woman who earns her own bread by fulfilling any duty, than the most accomplished beauty! Beauty! did I say? So sensible am I of the beauty of moral loveliness, or the harmonious propriety that attunes the passions of a well-regulated mind, that I blush at making the comparison; yet I sigh to think how few women aim at attaining this respectability by withdrawing from the giddy whirl of pleasure, or the indolent calm that stupefies the good sort of women it sucks in....

Those writers are particularly useful, in my opinion, who make man feel for man, independent of the station he fills, or the drapery of fictitious sentiments. I, then, would fain convince reasonable men of the importance of some of my remarks; and prevail on them to weigh dispassionately the whole tenor of my observations. I appeal to their understandings; and, as a fellow-creature, claim, in the name of my sex, some interest in their hearts. I entreat them to assist to emancipate their companion, to make her a *help meet* for them.

Would men but generously snap our chains, and be content with rational fellowship instead of slavish obedience, they would find us more observant daughters, more affectionate sisters, more faithful wives, more reasonable mothers—in a word, better citizens. We should then love them with true affection, because we should learn to respect ourselves; and the peace of mind of a worthy man would not be interrupted by the idle vanity of his wife, nor the babes sent to nestle in a strange bosom, having never found a home in their mother's....

Some instances of the folly which the ignorance of women generates, with concluding reflections on the moral improvement that a revolution in female manners might naturally be expected to produce....

Ignorance and the mistaken cunning that Nature sharpens in weak heads as a principle of self-preservation, render women very fond of dress, and produce all the vanity which such a fondness may naturally be expected to generate, to the exclusion of emulation and magnanimity.

I agree with Rousseau that the physical part of the art of pleasing consists in ornaments, and for that very reason I should guard girls against the contagious fondness for dress so common to weak women, that they may not rest in the physical part. Yet, weak are the women who imagine that they can long please without the aid of the mind, or, in other words, without the moral art of pleasing....

Is it then surprising that when the sole ambition of woman centres in beauty, and interest gives vanity additional force, perpetual rivalships should ensue? They are all running in the same race, and would rise above the virtue of mortals if they did not view each other with a suspicious and even envious eye.

An immoderate fondness for dress, for pleasure, and for sway, are the passions of savages; the passions that occupy those uncivilized beings who have not yet extended the dominion of the mind, or even learned to think with the energy necessary to concatenate that abstract train of thought which produces principles. And that women, from their education and the present state of civilized life, are in the same condition, cannot, I think, be controverted. To laugh at them, then, or satirize the follies of a being who is never to be allowed to act freely from the light of her own reason, is as absurd as cruel; for that they who are taught blindly to obey authority will endeavor cunningly to elude it, is most natural and certain....

But, fulfilling the duties of a mother, a woman with a sound constitution may still keep her person scrupulously neat, and assist to maintain her family, if necessary; or, by reading and conversations with both sexes indiscriminately, improve her mind. For Nature has so wisely ordered things, that did women suckle their children they would preserve their own health, and there would be such an interval between the birth of each child that we should seldom see a houseful of babes. And did they pursue a plan of conduct, and not waste their time in following the fashionable vagaries of dress, the management of their household and children need not shut them out from literature, or prevent their attaching themselves to a science with that steady eye which strengthens the mind, or practicing one of the fine arts that cultivate the taste....

But we shall not see women affectionate till more equality be established in society, till ranks are confounded and women freed; neither shall we see that dignified domestic happiness, the simple grandeur of which cannot be relished by ignorant or vitiated minds; nor will the important task of education ever be properly begun till the person of a woman is no longer preferred to her mind. For it would be as wise to expect corn from tares, or figs from thistles, as that a foolish, ignorant woman should be a good mother....

The affection of husbands and wives cannot be pure when they have so few sentiments in common, and when so little confidence is established at home, as must be the case when their pursuits are so different. That intimacy from which tenderness should flow, will not, can not, subsist between the vicious....

Asserting the rights which women, in common with men, ought to contend for, I have not attempted to extenuate their faults, but to prove them to be the natural consequence of their education and station in society. If so, it is reasonable to suppose that they will change their character and correct their vices and follies when they are allowed to be free in a physical, moral and civil sense.

Let women share the rights, and she will emulate the virtues, of man; for she must grow more perfect when emancipated, or justify the authority that chains such a weak being to her duty. If the latter, it will be expedient to open a fresh trade with Russia for whips: a present which a father should always make to his son-in-law on his wedding-day, that a husband may keep his whole family in order by the same means; and, without any violation of justice, reign, wielding his scep-tre, sole master of his house, because he is the only being in it who has reason:—the Divine, indefeasible, earthly sovereignty breathed into man by the Master of the Universe. Allowing this position, women have not any inherent rights to claim; and by the same rule their du-ties vanish, for rights and duties are inseparable.

Be just then, O ye men of understanding! and mark not more se-verely what women do amiss than the vicious tricks of the horse or the ass for whom ye provide provender—and allow her the privileges of ignorance to whom ye deny the rights of reason, or ye will be worse than Egyptian task-masters, expecting virtue where Nature has not given understanding!

6.

LI JU-CHEN
(1763–1830)

Flowers in the Mirror

(CHINA, C. 1800)

The scholar Li Ju-chen or Li Ruzhen, who studied language, the arts, and the sciences, incorporated a critique of women's oppression into his satirical novel about Chinese social customs. Li lived during the Qing dynasty, when the painful practice of foot binding, which initially denoted a woman's high social status, had become widespread. Confucian ideals required women's obedience to their husbands, while husbands enjoyed the privilege of acquiring concubines. Earlier male writers had questioned these practices through satire, but in the late eighteenth century the commentaries escalated, from condemnation of widow suicide to contemplations of women's rights to education. Li's novel can be read as a feminist critique of the objectification of women, the practice of foot binding, and the use of physical coercion to subdue female resistance and produce submissive creatures who are concerned primarily with beauty. Set in the eighth century, when an empress had ruled in China, the fictional characters include intellectually superior women as well as female villains who misuse power. In the following chapter, the cosmetics merchant Lin travels to the Kingdom of Women, where men wear women's clothing and submit to female authority. By portraying men's experience of foot binding and concubinage, Li attempted to expose the absurdity and inhumanity of these practices. The novel gained popularity in the late nineteenth and early twentieth centuries, when both male and female Chinese reformers rejected foot binding and championed female education.

When Tang Ao heard that they had arrived at the Country of Women, he thought that the country was populated entirely by women, and was afraid to go ashore. But Old Tuo said, "Not at all! There are men as well as women, only they call men women, and women men. The men wear the skirts and take care of the home, while the women wear hats and trousers and manage affairs outside. If it were a country populated solely by women, I doubt that even Brother Lin here would dare to venture ashore, although he knows he always makes a good profit from sales here!"

"If the men dress like women, do they use cosmetics and bind their feet?" asked Tang Ao.

"Of course they do!" cried Lin, and took from his pocket a list of the merchandise he was going to sell, which consisted of huge quantities of rouge, face powder, combs and other women's notions. "Lucky I wasn't born in this country," he said. "Catch me mincing around on bound feet!"

When Tang Ao asked why he had not put down the price of the merchandise, Lin said, "The people here, no matter rich or poor, from the 'King' down to the simplest peasant, are all mad about cosmetics. I'll charge them what I can. I shall have no difficulty selling the whole consignment to rich families in two or three days."

Beaming at the prospect of making a good profit, Lin went on shore with his list.

Tang Ao and Old Tuo decided to go and see the city. The people walking on the streets were small of stature, and rather slim, and although dressed in men's clothes, were beardless and spoke with women's voices, and walked with willowy steps.

"Look at them!" said Old Tuo. "They are perfectly normal-looking women. Isn't it a shame for them to dress like men?"

"Wait a minute," said Tang Ao. "Maybe when they see us, they think, 'Look at them, isn't it a shame that they dress like women'?"

"You're right. 'Whatever one is accustomed to always seems natural,' as the ancients say. But I wonder what the men are like?"

Old Tuo discreetly called Tang Ao's attention to a middle-aged woman, who was sitting in front of her doorstep, sewing on a shoe. Her hair was braided and coiled smoothly on top of her head, and decorated with pearls and jade. She was wearing long golden loops of earrings with precious stones in them, and wore a long mauve gown with an onion-green shirt underneath, from which peeped the toes of tiny feet shod in red silk shoes. With long, tapering fingers, the woman was doing embroidery. She had beautiful eyes and was carefully powdered and rouged, but when she lifted her head, they saw that her lip was covered by a thick moustache.

Tang Ao and Old Tuo could not help laughing out loud.

The "woman" looked up and said, "What are you laughing at, lassies?"

The voice sounded as deep and hoarse as a cracked gong. Tang Ao was so startled that he took to his heels and ran.

But the "woman" shouted after them, "You must be women, since you have whiskers on your faces. Why are you wearing men's clothes and pretending to be men? Aren't you ashamed of yourselves! I know, you dress like this because you want to mingle with the men, you cheap hussies! Take a look at yourselves in the mirror. Have you forgotten that you are women? It's lucky for you you only met up with me! If it had been somebody else who had caught you casting those sneaky glances, you would have been beaten almost to death!"

"This is the first time I have ever had such an experience," muttered Tang Ao. "But I suspect Brother Lin will receive better treatment at their hands."

"Why?" said Old Tuo.

"Well, he is very fair, and since he lost his beard at the Country of Flaming People, he may be mistaken by these people for a real woman. But come to think of it, isn't it worrying?"

As they walked further on, they saw some "women" on the streets as well as "men." Some were carrying babies in their arms, and others leading children by the hand. All the "women" walked on dainty bound feet, and in crowded places, acted shy, as if they were embarrassed to be seen. Some of the younger ones were beardless, and upon careful study, Tang Ao discovered that some of the ageing or middle-aged "women" shaved their lips and chins in order to appear younger.

The two returned to the junk before Merchant Lin. But when the latter did not come back at supper time, and it was past the second drum, Mistress Lu began to be worried. Tang Ao and Old Tuo went on shore with lanterns to look for him, but discovered that the city gates were shut for the night.

The next day, they went to look again, but found not a trace of Lin. On the third day, some sailors went with them, but still they could not find him.

When a few days had passed, it seemed as if Merchant Lin had vanished, like a rock sinking to the bottom of the sea. Mistress Lu and Pleasant wailed with grief. Tang Ao and Old Tuo went to make inquiries every day.

They could not know that Merchant Lin had been told by one of his customers that the "King's uncle" wanted to buy some of his goods. Following instructions, he went to the "Royal Uncle's" Residence in the Palace, and handed his list of merchandise to the gatekeeper. Soon, the gatekeeper came back and said that it was just what the "King" was looking for for his "concubines" and "maids," and asked Lin to be shown into the inner apartments.

The attendant led Merchant Lin through guarded doors and winding paths until he was at the door of the inner apartments, where a guard told him, "Please wait here, madam. I shall go in and inquire what the royal wishes are." She took Lin's list, and after a short time, returned and said, "But madam hasn't put any prices on her list. How much do you charge for a picul of rouge? How much is a picul of perfumed powder? And hair lotion? And hair ribbons?"

Lin told her the prices, and the guard went in and came out again and asked, "How much is a box of jade ornaments, madam? And your velvet flowers? How much is a box of your fragrant beads? And what about the combs?"

Merchant Lin told her and the guard again went to report, and came back and said, "The King has been choosing imperial concubines and wants to buy some of your goods for them. He invites you to go inside, since you come from the Kingdom on Earth and we are friendly allies. However, madam must behave with courtesy and respect when she is in the presence of His Majesty."

Merchant Lin followed the guard inside, and was soon in the presence of the "King." After making a deep bow, he saw that she was a woman of some thirty years old, with a beautiful face, fair skin and cherry-red lips. Around her there stood many palace "maids."

The "King" spoke to Lin in a light voice, holding the list of articles in her slender hands, and looking at him with interest as he answered her questions.

"I wonder what she is staring at me like this for," Merchant Lin thought to himself. "Hasn't she ever seen a man from the Kingdom on Earth before?"

After a while, he heard her say that she was keeping the list of goods, and ordered palace "maids" to prepare a feast and wine for the "woman" from the Kingdom on Earth.

In a little time, Merchant Lin was ushered to a room upstairs, where victuals of many kinds awaited him. As he ate, however, he heard a great deal of noise downstairs. Several palace "maids" ran upstairs soon, and calling him "Your Highness," kowtowed to him and congratulated him. Before he knew what was happening, Merchant Lin was being stripped completely bare by the maids and led to a perfumed bath. Against the powerful arms of these maids, he could scarcely struggle. Soon he found himself being anointed, perfumed, powdered and rouged, and dressed in a skirt. His big feet were bound up in strips of cloth and socks, and his hair was combed into an elaborate braid over his head and decorated with pins. These male "maids" thrust bracelets on his arms and rings on his fingers, and put a phoenix headdress on his head. They tied a jade green sash around his waist and put an embroidered cape around his shoulders.

Then they led him to a bed, and asked him to sit down.

Merchant Lin thought that he must be drunk, or dreaming, and began to tremble. He asked the maids what was happening, and was told that he had been chosen by the "King" to be the Imperial Consort, and that a propitious day would be chosen for him to enter the "King's" chambers.

Before he could utter a word, another group of maids, all tall and strong and wearing beards, came in. One was holding a threaded needle. "We are ordered to pierce your ears," he said, as the other four "maids" grabbed Lin by the arms and legs. The white-bearded one seized Lin's right ear, and after rubbing the lobe a little, drove the needle through it.

"Ooh!" Merchant Lin screamed.

The maid seized the other ear, and likewise drove the needle through it. As Lin screamed with pain, powdered lead was smeared on his earlobes and a pair of "eight-precious" earrings was hung from the holes.

Having finished what they came to do, the maids retreated, and a black-bearded fellow came in with a bolt of white silk. Kneeling down before him, the fellow said, "I am ordered to bind Your Highness's feet."

Two other maids seized Lin's feet as the black-bearded one sat down on a low stool, and began to rip the silk into ribbons. Seizing Lin's right foot, he set it upon his knee, and sprinkled white alum powder between the toes and the grooves of the foot. He squeezed the toes tightly together, bent them down so that the whole foot was shaped like an arch, and took a length of white silk and bound it tightly around it twice. One of the others sewed the ribbon together in small stitches. Again the silk went around the foot, and again, it was sewn up.

Merchant Lin felt as though his feet were burning, and wave after wave of pain rose to his heart. When he could stand it no longer, he let out his voice and began to cry. The "maids" had hastily made a pair of soft-soled red shoes, and these they put on both his feet.

"Please, kind brothers, go and tell Her Majesty that I'm a married man," Lin begged. "How can I become her Consort? As for my feet, please liberate them. They have enjoyed the kind of freedom which scholars who are not interested in official careers enjoy! How can you bind them? Please tell your 'King' to let me go. I shall be grateful, and my wife will be very grateful."

But the maids said, "The King said that you are to enter his chambers as soon as your feet are bound. It is no time for talk of this kind."

When it was dark, a table was laid for him with mountains of meat and oceans of wine. But Merchant Lin only nibbled, and told the "maids" they could have the rest.

Still sitting on the bed, and with his feet aching terribly, he decided to lie down in his clothes for a rest.

At once a middle-aged "maid" came up to him and said, "Please, will you wash before you retire?"

No sooner was this said than a succession of maids came in with candles, basins of water and spittoon, dressing table, boxes of ointment, face powder, towels, silk handkerchiefs, and surrounded him. Lin had to submit to the motions of washing in front of them all. But after he had washed his face, a maid wanted to put some cream on it again.

Merchant Lin stoutly refused.

"But night time is the best time to treat the skin," the white-bearded maid said, "This powder has a lot of musk in it. It will make your skin fragrant, although I dare say it is fair enough already. If you use it regularly your skin will not only seem like white jade, but will give off a natural fragrance of its own. And the more fragrant it is, the fairer it will become, and the more lovely to behold, and the more lovable you will be. You'll see how good it is after you have used it regularly."

But Lin refused firmly, and the maids said, "If you are so stubborn, we will have to report this, and let Matron deal with you tomorrow."

Then they left him alone. But Lin's feet hurt so much that he could not sleep a wink. He tore at the ribbons with all his might, and after a great struggle succeeded in tearing them off. He stretched out his ten toes again, and luxuriating in their exquisite freedom, finally fell asleep.

The next morning, however, when the black-bearded maid discovered that he had torn off his foot-bandages, he immediately reported it to the "King," who ordered that Lin should be punished by receiving twenty strokes of the bamboo from the "Matron." Accordingly, a white-bearded "Matron" came in with a stick of bamboo about eight feet long, and when the others had stripped him and held him down, raised the stick and began to strike Lin's bottom and legs.

Before five strokes had been delivered, Lin's tender skin was bleeding, and the Matron did not have the heart to go on. "Look at her skin! Have you ever seen such white and tender and lovable skin? Why, I think indeed her looks are comparable to Pan An and Sung Yu!" the Matron thought to himself. "But what am I doing, comparing her bottom and not her face to them? Is that a compliment?"

The foot-binding maid came and asked Lin if he would behave from now on.

"Yes, I'll behave," Lin replied, and they stopped beating him. They wiped the blood from his wounds, and special ointment was sent by the "King" and ginseng soup was given him to drink.

Merchant Lin drank the soup, and fell on the bed for a rest. But the "King" had given orders that his feet must be bound again, and that he should be taught to walk on them. So with one maid supporting him on each side, Merchant Lin was marched up and down the room all day on his bound feet. When he lay down to sleep that night, he could not close his eyes for the excruciating pain.

But from now on, he was never left alone again. Maids took turns to sit with him. Merchant Lin knew that he was no longer in command of his destiny.

Before two weeks were over, Lin's feet had begun to assume a permanently arched form, and his toes begun to rot. Daily medical ablutions were given to them, and the pain persisted.

"I should have thought that Brother-in-law and Old Tuo would have come to my rescue by now," he thought one day as he was being led up and down his room. "I have endured all I can! I'd be better off dead!"

He sat down on the edge of the bed, and began to tear off his embroidered shoes and silk bandages. "Go tell your 'King' to put me to death at once, or let my feet loose," he told the Matron.

But when he returned, the Matron said, "The King said that if you don't obey his orders, you are to be hung upside down from the beam of the house."

"Then do it quickly! The quicker the better!" said Lin, impatient to have an end put to his agony.

Accordingly, they tied a rope around his feet and hung him upside down from the beam. Merchant Lin saw stars before his eyes. Sweat poured out of his body, and his legs became numb. He closed his eyes and waited for death to come to the rescue. But it did not come. At last he could stand it no longer, and began to scream like a pig being led to slaughter.

The order was given to cut him down.

From now on, Lin was completely in the power of the maids. Wanting to complete the task their "King" had assigned them as soon as possible, they tied the bandages around his feet tighter than ever. Several times, Lin thought of committing suicide, but with people watching him constantly, he had not a chance.

In due course, his feet lost much of their original shape. Blood and flesh were squeezed into a pulp and then little remained of his feet but dry bones and skin, shrunk, indeed, to a dainty size. Responding to daily anointing, his hair became shiny and smooth, and his body, after repeated ablutions of perfumed water, began to look very attractive indeed. His eyebrows were plucked to resemble a new moon. With blood-red lipstick and powder adorning his face, and jade and pearl adorning his coiffure and ears, Merchant Lin assumed, at last, a not unappealing appearance.

The "King" sent someone to watch his progress every day. One day, the Matron announced that the task of foot-binding had been completed. When the "King" herself came upstairs to have a look, she saw a Lin whose face was like a peach blossom, whose eyes were like autumn lakes, whose eyebrows suggested the lines of distant hills, and who stood before her in a willowy stance.

She was delighted. "What a beauty!" she thought to herself. "If I hadn't seen her hidden possibilities beneath her ridiculous man's costume, her beauty might never have come to light!"

She took a pearl bracelet and put it on Merchant Lin's wrist, and the maids persuaded him to sink down on his knees and give thanks. The "King" pulled him up and made him sit down beside her, and began to fondle his hands and smell them and look appreciatively at his dainty feet.

Lin went red with shame.

Extremely pleased, the "King" decided that Lin should enter her chambers the very next day. When Merchant Lin heard this, he saw his last hopes vanish. He was not even able to walk without someone to help him, and spent the whole night thinking about his wife and shedding tears.

In the morning, the "maids" came especially early to shave off the fine hairs from his face, and to powder him and comb him in preparation for his wedding. Supported by a pair of red embroidered high heeled shoes, his longer-than-ordinary "golden lotuses" became not obtrusively large. He wore a bridal crown and gown, and with jewels dangling and waves of perfume issuing from his person, was if not notably beautiful, at least a rather charming "bride."

After breakfast, "Imperial Concubines" came to congratulate him, and he was kept fully occupied until the afternoon, when maids came again to straighten his clothes and freshen up his appearance before escorting him to the Reception Hall.

Soon, palace attendants holding red lanterns came in and knelt before him and said, "The propitious hour has come. Would Madam please come to the Main Reception Hall to await His Majesty? The ceremonies will be conducted there."

Merchant Lin was stunned. His body and soul almost parted company.

The attendants seized him and escorted him downstairs. Countless officials and guests had come to witness the ceremony in the Main Reception Hall, which was brightly lighted with candles. As Lin walked toward "His Majesty," swaying on the arms of attendants, he was like a sprig of fresh flowers waving in the wind. When he was standing directly in front of the "King," he had no alternative but to tug at his sleeves and make a deep bow.

Congratulations were showered upon the "King" by the attendants.

As Lin was about to be ushered into the "King's" chambers, there came a great hubbub of noise from the outside. The "King" was startled.

It was Tang Ao, who had come to the rescue. If the reader wants to know what happened next, please turn to the next chapter.

7

Sarah M. Grimké
(1792–1873)

Letters on the Equality of the Sexes
(UNITED STATES, 1837)

In the early nineteenth century, the antislavery movement helped shift the "woman question" from education to politics. Inspired by Protestant religious revivals, social reformers in America and England campaigned to rid society of sins ranging from intemperance to slavery. In the United States, the sisters Sarah and Angelina Grimké, who were raised in a slave-holding southern family, converted to the Quaker faith and migrated to the North, embracing abolitionism. Through public speaking and writing they called on all women to oppose slavery. Conservative women and clergy condemned the sisters for speaking to mixed groups of men and women in public and for encouraging women to transcend their domestic and religious realms through the political act of petitioning the government to abolish slavery. In a series of published letters the Grimké sisters responded to their critics by defending women's rights. "The investigation of the rights of slaves," Angelina wrote, "has led me to a better understanding of my own." Their letters invoked Christian principles to reject the limitations on women's education, but they also protested the lesser value placed on women's labor and condemned the sexual vulnerability of female slaves. Soon after introducing these controversial topics, the sisters withdrew from public life. Other participants in the antislavery movement continued to debate women's roles as public reformers, providing a seedbed for the women's rights movement in the 1840s.

My Dear Sister,...

During the early part of my life, my lot was cast among the butterflies of the *fashionable* world; and of this class of women, I am constrained to say, both from experience and observation, that their education is miserably deficient; that they are taught to regard marriage as the one thing needful, the only avenue to distinction; hence to attract the notice and win the attentions of men, by their external charms, is the chief business of fashionable girls. They seldom think that men will be allured by intellectual acquirements, because they find, that where any mental superiority exists, a woman is generally shunned and regarded as stepping out of her "appropriate sphere," which, in their view, is to dress, to dance, to set out to the best possible advantage her person, to read the novels which inundate the press, and which do more to destroy her character as a rational creature, than any thing else. Fashionable women regard themselves, and are regarded by men, as pretty toys or as mere instruments of pleasure; and the vacuity of mind, the heartlessness, the frivolity which is the necessary result of this false and debasing estimate of women, can only be fully understood by those who have mingled in the folly and wickedness of fashionable life; and who have been called from such pursuits by the voice of the Lord Jesus, inviting their weary and heavy laden souls to come unto Him and learn of Him, that they may find something worthy of their immortal spirit, and their intellectual powers; that they may learn the high and holy purposes of their creation, and consecrate themselves unto the service of God; and not, as is now the case, to the pleasure of man.

There is another and much more numerous class in this country, who are withdrawn by education or circumstances from the circle of fashionable amusements, but who are brought up with the dangerous and absurd idea, that *marriage* is a kind of preferment; and that to be able to keep their husband's house, and render his situation comfortable, is the end of her being. Much that she does and says and thinks is done in reference to this situation; and to be married is too often held up to the view of girls as the sine qua non of human happiness and human existence. For this purpose more than for any other, I verily believe the majority of girls are trained. This is demonstrated by the imperfect education which is bestowed upon them, and the little pains taken to cultivate their minds, after they leave school, by the little time allowed them for reading, and by the idea being constantly inculcated, that although all household concerns should be attended to with scrupulous punctuality at particular seasons, the improvement of their intellectual capacities is only a secondary consideration, and may serve as an occupation to fill up the odds and ends of time....

Let no one think, from these remarks, that I regard a knowledge of housewifery as beneath the acquisition of women. Far from it: I believe that a complete knowledge of household affairs is an indispensable requisite in a woman's education,—that by the mistress of a family, whether married or single, doing her duty thoroughly and *understandingly*, the happiness of the family is increased to an incalculable degree, as well as a vast amount of time and money saved. All I complain of is, that our education consists so almost exclusively in culinary and other manual operations. I do long to see the time, when it will no longer be necessary for women to expend so many precious hours in furnishing "a well spread table," but that their husbands will forego some of their accustomed indulgences in this way, and encourage their wives to devote some portion of their time to mental cultivation, even at the expense of having to dine sometimes on baked potatoes, or bread and butter....

There is another way in which the general opinion, that women are inferior to men, is manifested, that bears with tremendous effect on the laboring class, and indeed on almost all who are obliged to earn a subsistence, whether it be by mental or physical exertion—I allude to the disproportionate value set on the time and labor of men and of women. A man who is engaged in teaching, can always, I believe, command a higher price for tuition than a woman—even when he teaches the same branches, and is not in any respect superior to the woman. This I know is the case in boarding and other schools with which I have been acquainted, and it is so in every occupation in which the sexes engage indiscriminately. As for example, in tailoring, a man has twice, or three times as much for making a waistcoat or pantaloons as a woman, although the work done by each may be equally good. In those employments which are peculiar to women, their time is estimated at only half the value of that of men. A woman who goes out to wash, works as hard in proportion as a wood sawyer, or a coal heaver, but she is not generally able to make more than half as much by a day's work.... There is yet another and more disastrous consequence arising from this unscriptural notion—women being educated, from earliest childhood, to regard themselves as inferior creatures, have not that self-respect which conscious equality would engender, and hence when their virtue is assailed, they yield to temptation with facility, under the idea that it rather exalts than debases them, to be connected with a superior being.

There is another class of women in this country, to whom I cannot refer, without feelings of the deepest shame and sorrow. I allude to our female slaves. Our southern cities are whelmed beneath a tide of pollution; the virtue of female slaves is wholly at the mercy of irresponsible tyrants, and women are bought and sold in our slave markets, to gratify the brutal lust of those who bear the name of Christians. In our slave States, if amid all her degradation and ignorance, a woman desires to preserve her virtue unsullied, she is either bribed or whipped into compliance, or if she dares resist her seducer, her life by the laws of some of the slave States may be, and has actually been sacrificed to the fury of disappointed passion. Where such laws do not exist, the power which is necessarily vested in the master over his property, leaves the defenceless slave entirely at his mercy, and the sufferings of some females on this account, both physical and mental, are intense....

Nor does the colored woman suffer alone: the moral purity of the white woman is deeply contaminated. In the daily habit of seeing the virtue of her enslaved sister sacrificed without hesitancy or remorse, she looks upon the crimes of seduction and illicit intercourse without horror, and although not personally involved in the guilt, she loses that value for innocence in her own, as well as the other sex, which is one of the strongest safeguards to virtue....

I cannot close this letter, without saying a few words on the benefits to be derived by men, as well as women, from the opinions I advocate relative to the equality of the sexes. Many women are now supported, in idleness and extravagance, by the industry of their husbands, fathers, or brothers, who are compelled to toil out their existence, at the counting house, or in the printing office, or some other laborious occupation, while the wife and daughters and sisters take no part in the support of the family, and appear to think that their sole business is to spend the hard bought earnings of their male friends. I deeply regret such a state of things, because I believe that if women felt their responsibility, for the support of themselves, or their families it would add strength and dignity to their characters, and teach them more true sympathy for their husbands, than is now generally manifested,—a sympathy which would be exhibited by actions as well as words. Our brethren may reject my doctrine, because it runs counter to common opinions, and because it wounds their pride; but I believe they would be "partakers of the benefit" resulting from the Equality of the Sexes, and would find that woman, as their equal, was unspeakably more valuable than woman as their inferior, both as a moral and an intellectual being.

Thine in the bonds of womanhood,

Sarah M. Grimké

8.

FLORA TRISTAN
(1803–44)

"The Emancipation of Working Class Women"
(FRANCE, 1843)

Early feminist writers justified education to improve middle-class motherhood, but as industrialism created a proletariat, socialist writers such as Flora Tristan addressed the particular concerns of women in the working class. Raised in Peru by her French mother, Tristan married young, left her husband, and worked as a governess to support her three children. In the 1830s she traveled to Europe, where she met utopian socialists such as Charles Fourier, who proclaimed that the progress of civilization depended on improving the status of women. Tristan petitioned the French government to reinstitute a Revolutionary-era law that had permitted divorce. She also questioned the socialization of girls to become servile wives. In addition to publishing accounts of her travels, in the 1840s Tristan wrote critiques of the condition of the working class. In the following selection, she invokes the memory of the French Revolution of 1789, when the common people proclaimed the rights of man. Proletarian women, she pointed out, still had to submit to their husbands as masters, bound to marriage because they could not support themselves. Tristan appealed to working men to affirm women's right to education as a way of improving the lot of their class, since educated women would become superior mothers and help their sons and daughters enjoy better lives.

These are the facts: until the present time, woman has been of no account in human societies. What has been the result? The priest, the legislator, the philosopher have treated her as a real pariah. Woman (who makes up half the human race) has been excluded from the Church, the law, and society. For her, there are no functions in the Church, no representation before the law, no functions in the State....

One must admit that what happened to the proletariat shows promise for women when their 1789 shall strike. From a very simple calculation, it is obvious that the wealth will increase indefinitely from the day when women (half the human race) are called to contribute their intelligence, strength, and capabilities to social activity. It is as easy to understand as "one plus one equals two." But, alas! We have not reached that stage yet. So while waiting for that happy 1789, let us examine what is going on in 1843.

The Church said woman was sin; the legislator, that by herself she was nothing, that she could not have any rights; the wise philosopher, that her constitution deprived her of any intelligence. The conclusion was that she was a poor being disinherited by God. So man and society treated her accordingly....

I demand rights for women because I am convinced that all the misfortunes in the world come from the neglect and contempt in which women's natural and inalienable rights have so far been held. I demand rights for women because that is the only way they will get an education, and because on their education depends the education of men in general, and men of the lower classes in particular. I demand rights for women because that is the only way to obtain their rehabilitation in the Church, under the law, and in society, and because this preliminary rehabilitation is necessary to arrive at the rehabilitation of the workers themselves. All working class woes can be summed up in two words: poverty and ignorance; ignorance and poverty. I see only one way to get out of this labyrinth: start by educating women, because women have the responsibility for educating male and female children....

A DECLARATION OF THE
RIGHTS OF WOMAN

Workers, I have barely outlined the conditions the proletarian class would enjoy if women were recognized as the equals of men. It should make you think about the existing evil and about the well-being that could exist. It should make you come to a decision.

Workers, you do not have the power to repeal old laws and make new ones. No, indeed, but you do have the power to protest against the inequity and the absurdity of laws which hinder humanity's progress and which make you suffer—you more than anyone. Thus you can—and it is even your sacred duty—you can protest strongly through your ideas, your speeches, and your writings, against all the laws which oppress you. Now, make sure that you understand this: The law that enslaves women and deprives them of an education also oppresses you, proletarian men.

To bring him up, educate him, and teach him the science of the world, the son of the rich has learned nurses and teachers, clever head-mistresses, and, finally, beautiful noble ladies—witty, elegant women—whose function consists of educating upper class youths when they get out of college. It is a very useful function for the well being of these high nobility gentlemen. These ladies teach them politeness and good manners so that they can become men who know how to live, men who behave in a genteel way. If a young man has any abilities, if he has the good luck to be under the protection of one of these lovely ladies, his fortune is made. At thirty-five, he is sure to be an ambassador or a minister. But meanwhile, you, poor workers, you have only your mothers to educate you and bring you up. To make of you men who know how to live, you have only the women of your class, your companions in ignorance and poverty.

Therefore, it is not in the name of the superiority of women (and I shall certainly be accused of that) that I tell you to demand rights for women. No, honestly. First, women must be recognized as full members of society before their superiority can be discussed. I take my stand on more solid grounds than that. It is in the name of your own interest, men, of your own improvement, men, and, lastly, it is in the name of the universal well being of all men and women that I urge you to demand rights for women and, in the meantime, to acknowledge them yourselves, at least in principle.

So, it is up to you, workers, victims of *de facto* inequality and injustice. It is up to you to establish, finally, on the earth, the reign of justice and absolute equality between women and men. Give a great example to the world, an example that will show your oppressors that you wish to triumph by your rights and not by brute force.

While demanding justice for yourselves, show that you are just and fair. You, the strong men, the men with bare arms, proclaim that you recognize women as your equals and that, as such, you recognize for women an equal right to the benefits of the universal union of working men and women....

Workers, in 1791, your fathers proclaimed the immortal Declaration of the Rights of Man. Because of this solemn declaration, you are today free and equal men before the law. Let your fathers be honored for this great work. But, proletarians, men of 1843, a work no less great awaits you. Set free the last slaves who remain in French society in your turn. Proclaim the rights of women in the same terms with which your fathers proclaimed your rights. Say:

> We, the French, proletarians, after fifty three years of experience, acknowledge that we are properly informed and convinced that the neglect and contempt of woman's natural rights are the only cause of the world's misfortunes. We have resolved to declare her sacred and inalienable rights in a solemn declaration written in our charter. We want women to be informed of our declaration, so that they will not let themselves be oppressed and demeaned by the injustice and tyranny of men. Men will grant the liberty and equality they enjoy to women, their mothers.

POINTS IN THE DECLARATION

1. The purpose of society being the common happiness of men and women, the Workers' Union guarantees to men and women their rights as working men and women.

2. These rights are: equality of admission in the Workers' Union palaces for children, the injured, and the elderly.

3. Since women are the equals of men as far as we are concerned, it is understood that girls will receive an education as rational, as broad in moral and professional sciences as the boys receive, although it will be varied.

4. As for the injured and the elderly, treatment will be the same in every way for women and men.

Workers, you can be sure that if you show enough equity and justice to inscribe in your charter the lines that I have just written, this Declaration of the Rights of Woman will soon be accepted in the mores, and eventually in the law. Within twenty years, you will see engraved on the front of the book of laws which will govern French society: Absolute Equality of Men and Women.

Then, brothers, and only then, human unity will be achieved.

Sons of '89, here is the task that your fathers have handed down to you.

9.

ELIZABETH CADY STANTON
(1815–1902)

"Declaration of Sentiments and Resolutions"
(UNITED STATES, 1848)

*Like the Grimké sisters, other women who participated in American re-
form movements chafed under restrictions that limited their right to speak
in public or to vote in temperance and antislavery meetings. When the
World Anti-Slavery Convention, held in London in 1840, refused to accept Americans Elizabeth Cady Stanton and Lucretia Mott as delegates
rather than as observers, the two women pledged that they would one day
address women's rights. Both were living near Seneca Falls, New York,
in 1848 when they issued a public invitation to a convention to discuss
"the civil and political rights of women." More than three hundred women
and men attended the two-day meeting, chaired by Mott's husband,
James. Stanton presented a document she had drafted modeled on the
Declaration of Independence, substituting for the colonists' grievances
against the king of England those of women against men. Sixty-eight
women and thirty-two men signed the Declaration of Sentiments, a historic articulation of equal rights feminism in its demands for women's access to education, property, jobs, and politics. Although not everyone present
supported the call for woman suffrage, another convention held several
weeks later did adopt suffrage as a goal of the fledgling women's rights
movement. Women themselves chaired the subsequent conventions that
met throughout the Northern states until the outbreak of the Civil War.
Stanton, who also raised seven children, devoted the rest of her life to
achieving women's rights to property, suffrage, and self-respect.*

When, in the course of human events, it becomes necessary for one portion of the family of man to assume among the people of the earth a position different from that which they have hitherto occupied, but one to which the laws of nature and of nature's God entitle them, a decent respect to the opinions of mankind requires that they should declare the causes that impel them to such a course.

We hold these truths to be self-evident: that all men and women are created equal; that they are endowed by their Creator with certain inalienable rights; that among these are life, liberty, and the pursuit of happiness; that to secure these rights governments are instituted, deriving their just powers from the consent of the governed. Whenever any form of government becomes destructive of these ends, it is the right of those who suffer from it to refuse allegiance to it, and to insist upon the institution of a new government, laying its foundation on such principles, and organizing its powers in such form, as to them shall seem most likely to effect their safety and happiness. Prudence, indeed, will dictate that governments long established should not be changed for light and transient causes; and accordingly all experience hath shown that mankind are more disposed to suffer, while evils are sufferable, than to right themselves by abolishing the forms to which they were accustomed. But when a long train of abuses and usurpations, pursuing invariably the same object evinces a design to reduce them under absolute despotism, it is their duty to throw off such government, and to provide new guards for their future security. Such has been the patient sufferance of the women under this government, and such is now the necessity which constrains them to demand the equal station to which they are entitled.

The history of mankind is a history of repeated injuries and usurpations on the part of man toward woman, having in direct object the establishment of an absolute tyranny over her. To prove this, let facts be submitted to a candid world.

He has never permitted her to exercise her inalienable right to the elective franchise.

He has compelled her to submit to laws, in the formation of which she had no voice.

He has withheld from her rights which are given to the most ignorant and degraded men—both natives and foreigners.

Having deprived her of this first right of a citizen, the elective franchise, thereby leaving her without representation in the halls of legislation, he has oppressed her on all sides.

He has made her, if married, in the eye of the law, civilly dead.

He has taken from her all right in property, even to the wages she earns.

He has made her, morally, an irresponsible being, as she can commit many crimes with impunity, provided they be done in the presence of her husband. In the covenant of marriage, she is compelled to promise obedience to her husband, he becoming, to all intents and purposes, her master—the law giving him power to deprive her of her liberty, and to administer chastisement.

He has so framed the laws of divorce, as to what shall be the proper causes, and in case of separation, to whom the guardianship of the children shall be given, as to be wholly regardless of the happiness of women—the law, in all cases, going upon a false supposition of the supremacy of man, and giving all power into his hands.

After depriving her of all rights as a married woman, if single, and the owner of property, he has taxed her to support a government which recognizes her only when her property can be made profitable to it.

He has monopolized nearly all the profitable employments, and from those she is permitted to follow, she receives but a scanty remuneration. He closes against her all the avenues to wealth and distinction which he considers most honorable to himself. As a teacher of theology, medicine, or law, she is not known.

He has denied her the facilities for obtaining a thorough education, all colleges being closed against her.

He allows her in Church, as well as State, but a subordinate position, claiming Apostolic authority for her exclusion from the ministry, and, with some exceptions, from any public participation in the affairs of the Church.

He has created a false public sentiment by giving to the world a different code of morals for men and women, by which moral delinquencies which exclude women from society, are not only tolerated, but deemed of little account in man.

He has usurped the prerogative of Jehovah himself, claiming it as his right to assign for her a sphere of action, when that belongs to her conscience and to her God.

He has endeavored, in every way that he could, to destroy her confidence in her own powers, to lessen her self-respect, and to make her willing to lead a dependent and abject life.

Now, in view of this entire disfranchisement of one-half the people of this country, their social and religious degradation—in view of the unjust laws above mentioned, and because women do feel themselves aggrieved, oppressed, and fraudulently deprived of their most sacred rights, we insist that they have immediate admission to all the rights and privileges which belong to them as citizens of the United States.

In entering upon the great work before us, we anticipate no small amount of misconception, misrepresentation, and ridicule; but we shall use every instrumentality within our power to effect our object. We shall employ agents, circulate tracts, petition the State and National legislatures, and endeavor to enlist the pulpit and the press in our behalf. We hope this Convention will be followed by a series of Conventions embracing every part of the country....

Whereas, The great precept of nature is conceded to be, that "man shall pursue his own true and substantial happiness." Blackstone in his Commentaries remarks, that this law of Nature being coeval with mankind, and dictated by God himself, is of course superior in obligation to any other. It is binding over all the globe, in all countries and at all times; no human laws are of any validity if contrary to this, and such of them as are valid, derive all their force, and all their validity, and all their authority, mediately and immediately, from this original; therefore,

Resolved, That such laws as conflict, in any way, with the true and substantial happiness of woman, are contrary to the great precept of nature and of no validity, for this is "superior in obligation to any other."

Resolved, That all laws which prevent woman from occupying such a station in society as her conscience shall dictate, or which place her in a position inferior to that of man, are contrary to the great precept of nature, and therefore of no force or authority.

Resolved, That woman is man's equal—was intended to be so by the Creator, and the highest good of the race demands that she should be recognized as such.

Resolved, That the women of this country ought to be enlightened in regard to the laws under which they live, that they may no longer publish their degradation by declaring themselves satisfied with their present position, nor their ignorance, by asserting that they have all the rights they want.

Resolved, That inasmuch as man, while claiming for himself intellectual superiority, does accord to woman moral superiority, it is preeminently his duty to encourage her to speak and teach, as she has an opportunity, in all religious assemblies.

Resolved, That the same amount of virtue, delicacy, and refinement of behavior that is required of woman in the social state, should also be required of man, and the same transgressions should be visited with equal severity on both man and woman.

Resolved, That the objection of indelicacy and impropriety, which is so often brought against woman when she addresses a public audience, comes with a very ill-grace from those who encourage, by their attendance, her appearance on the stage, in the concert, or in feats of the circus.

Resolved, That woman has too long rested satisfied in the circumscribed limits which corrupt customs and a perverted application of the Scriptures have marked out for her, and that it is time she should move in the enlarged sphere which her great Creator has assigned her.

Resolved, That it is the duty of the women of this country to secure to themselves their sacred right to the elective franchise.

Resolved, That the equality of human rights results necessarily from the fact of the identity of the race in capabilities and responsibilities.

Resolved, therefore, That, being invested by the Creator with the same capabilities, and the same consciousness of responsibility for their exercise, it is demonstrably the right and duty of woman, equally with man, to promote every righteous cause by every righteous means; and especially in regard to the great subjects of morals and religion, it is self-evidently her right to participate with her brother in teaching them, both in private and in public, by writing and by speaking, by any instrumentalities proper to be used, and in any assemblies proper to be held; and this being a self-evident truth growing out of the divinely implanted principles of human nature, any custom or authority adverse to it, whether modern or wearing the hoary sanction of antiquity, is to be regarded as a self-evident falsehood, and at war with mankind....

Resolved, That the speedy success of our cause depends upon the zealous and untiring efforts of both men and women, for the overthrow of the monopoly of the pulpit, and for the securing to woman an equal participation with men in the various trades, professions, and commerce.

10.

SOJOURNER TRUTH
(1797–1883)

Two Speeches
(UNITED STATES, 1851, 1867)

Born a slave named Isabella in upstate New York, later a domestic ser-
vant who married and who bore five children, Sojourner Truth chose her
name in 1843 when she became an itinerant Protestant preacher. She
soon joined the abolitionist and women's rights movements, earning a rep-
utation as an eloquent speaker for her biblically influenced, persuasive
rhetoric. One of the few orators to represent the experience of African
American women, her speeches have remained powerful reminders of the
racially specific meaning of womanhood. At a time when even social re-
formers replicated the racial discrimination of American culture, Truth
insisted that black women should have the same rights as white women.
Her speech at the 1851 Ohio Woman's Rights Convention has often been
reprinted in a stylized dialect based on the later recollections of white
participants. The following account was recorded at the time by African
American journalist Marius Robinson, who acknowledged that he could
not capture Truth's language in print. After emancipation, former aboli-
tionists split over whether to endorse black suffrage only or woman suf-
frage as well. At the May 1867 meeting of the American Equal Rights
Association, when she was more than eighty years old, Truth called for
equal rights for both former slaves and all women. She acknowledged the
rarity of her black suffragist voice, and she added to the political agenda
a call to improve women's earning power.

MAY 1851

May I say a few words? Receiving an affirmative answer, she proceeded; I want to say a few words about this matter. I am a woman's rights. I have as much muscle as any man, and can do as much work as any man. I have plowed and reaped and husked and chopped and mowed, and can any man do more than that? I have heard much about the sexes being equal; I can carry as much as any man, and can eat as much too, if I can get it. I am as strong as any man that is now. As for intellect, all I can say is, if woman have a pint and man a quart—why can't she have her little pint full? You need not be afraid to give us our rights for fear we will take too much, for we can't take more than our pint'll hold. The poor men seem to be all in confusion, and don't know what to do. Why children, if you have woman's rights give it to her and you will feel better. You will have your own rights, and they won't be so much trouble. I can't read, but I can hear. I have heard the bible and have learned that Eve caused man to sin. Well if woman upset the world, do give her a chance to set it right side up again. The Lady has spoken about Jesus, how he never spurned woman from him, and she was right. When Lazarus died, Mary and Martha came to him with faith and love and besought him to raise their brother. And Jesus wept—and Lazarus came forth. And how came Jesus into the world? Through God who created him and woman who bore him. Man, where is your part? But the women are coming up, blessed be God, and a few of the men are coming up with them. But man is in a right place, the poor slave is on him, woman is coming on him, and he is surely between a hawk and a buzzard.

MAY 1867

My friends, I am rejoiced that you are glad, but I don't know how you will feel when I get through. I come from another field—the country of the slave. They have got their liberty—so much good luck to have slavery partly destroyed; not entirely. I want it root and branch destroyed. Then we will all be free indeed. I feel that if I have to answer for the deeds done in my body just as much as a man, I have a right to have just as much as a man. There is a great stir about colored men getting their rights, but not a word about the colored women; and if colored men get their rights, and not colored women theirs, you see the colored men will be masters over the women, and it will be just as bad as it was before. So I am for keeping the thing going while things are stirring; because if we wait till it is still, it will take a great while to get it going again. White women are a great deal smarter, and know more than colored women, while colored women do not know scarcely anything. They go out washing, which is about as high as a colored woman gets, and their men go about idle, strutting up and down; and when the women come home, they ask for their money and take it all, and then scold because there is no food. I want you to consider on that, chil'n. I call you chil'n; you are somebody's chil'n, and I am old enough to be mother of all that is here. I want women to have their rights. In the Courts women have no right, no voice; nobody speaks for them. I wish woman to have her voice there among the pettifoggers. If it is not a fit place for women it is unfit for men to be there. I am above eighty years old; it is about time for me to be going. I have been forty years a slave and forty years free and would be here forty years more to have equal rights for all. I suppose I am kept here because something remains for me to do; I suppose I am yet to help to break the chain. I have done a great deal of work; as much as a man, but did not get so much pay. I used to work in the field and bind grain, keeping up with the cradler; but men doing no more, got twice as much pay; so with the German women. They work in the field and do as much work, but do not get the pay. We do as much, we eat as much, we want as much. I suppose I am about the only colored woman that goes about to speak for the rights of the colored woman. I want to keep the thing stirring, now that the ice is cracked.

What we want is a little money. You men know that you get as much again as women when you write, or for what you do. When we get our rights we shall not have to come to you for money, for then we shall have money enough in our own pockets; and may be you will ask us for money. But help us now until we get it. It is a good consolation to know that when we have got this battle once fought we shall not be coming to you any more. You have been having our right so long, that you think, like a slaveholder, that you own us. I know that it is hard for one who has held the reins for so long to give up; it cuts like a knife. It will feel all the better when it closes up again. I have been in

Washington about three years, seeing about these colored people. Now colored men have the right to vote; and what I want is to have colored women have the right to vote. There ought to be equal rights now more than ever, since colored people have got their freedom. I am going to talk several times while I am here; so now I will do a little singing. I have not heard any singing since I came here.

11.

HARRIET TAYLOR MILL
(1807–58)

"The Enfranchisement of Women"
(ENGLAND, 1851)

In the 1820s and 1830s, Harriet Taylor wrote essays emphasizing the importance of women's education and questioning marriage as woman's sole vocation. As transatlantic networks spread news of the women's rights conventions in the United States, she publicized the suffrage cause in the Westminster Review, *a reform journal that supported both the abolition of slavery and universal male suffrage (unlimited by the requirement of property ownership). She urged British liberals to support the enfranchisement of women as well as working men, and she called for equal access to education and the professions. Her views had a profound effect on the British philosopher John Stuart Mill, whom she met in the 1830s and married in 1851, after the death of her first husband. Both of the Mills wished to ensure the sovereignty of every individual by extending the rights of man to include women. John Stuart Mill, like Mary Wollstonecraft, expected most women would wish to be wives and mothers, but Harriet Taylor Mill recognized as well the importance of economic independence for single and married women. Her references to "Asiatic" women and "savages" reflected contemporary views about the superiority of European civilization. In modern times, she believed, human progress would inevitably involve democratic political systems that would ultimately include women's rights.*

Not only to the democracy of America, the claim of women to civil and political equality makes an irresistible appeal, but also to those Radicals and Chartists in the British islands, and democrats on the continent, who claim what is called universal suffrage as an inherent right, unjustly and oppressively withheld from them. For with what truth or rationality could the suffrage be termed universal, while half the human species remained excluded from it? To declare that a voice in the government is the right of all, and demand it only for a part—the part, namely, to which the claimant himself belongs—is to renounce even the appearance of principle. The Chartist who denies the suffrage to women, is a Chartist only because he is not a lord: he is one of those levellers who would level only down to themselves.

Even those who do not look upon a voice in the government as a matter of personal right, nor profess principles which require that it should be extended to all, have usually traditional maxims of political justice with which it is impossible to reconcile the exclusion of all women from the common rights of citizenship. It is an axiom of English freedom that taxation and representation should be co-extensive. Even under the laws which give the wife's property to the husband, there are many unmarried women who pay taxes. It is one of the fundamental doctrines of the British Constitution, that all persons should be tried by their peers: yet women, whenever tried, are by male judges and a male jury. To foreigners the law accords the privilege of claiming that half the jury should be composed of themselves; not so to women. Apart from maxims of detail, which represent local and national rather than universal ideas; it is an acknowledged dictate of justice to make no degrading distinctions without necessity. In all things the presumption ought to be on the side of equality. A reason must be given why anything should be permitted to one person and interdicted to another. But when that which is interdicted includes nearly everything which those to whom it is permitted most prize, and to be deprived of which they feel to be most insulting; when not only political liberty but personal freedom of action is the prerogative of a caste; when even in the exercise of industry, almost all employments which task the higher faculties in an important field, which lead to distinction, riches, or even pecuniary independence, are fenced round as the exclusive domain of the predominant section, scarcely any doors being left open to the dependent class, except such as all who can enter elsewhere disdainfully pass by; the miserable expediencies which are advanced as excuses for so grossly partial a dispensation, would not be sufficient, even if they were real, to render it other than a flagrant injustice. While, far from being expedient, we are firmly convinced that the division of mankind into two castes, one born to rule over the other, is in this case, as in all cases, an unqualified mischief; a source of perversion and demoralization, both to the favoured class and to those at whose expense they are favoured; producing none of the good which it is the custom to ascribe to it, and forming a bar, almost insuperable while it lasts, to any really vital improvement, either in the character or in the social condition of the human race....

We deny the right of any portion of the species to decide for another portion, or any individual for another individual, what is and what is not their "proper sphere." The proper sphere for all human beings is the largest and highest which they are able to attain to. What this is, cannot be ascertained, without complete liberty of choice. The speakers at the Convention in America have therefore done wisely and right, in refusing to entertain the question of the peculiar aptitudes either of women or of men, or the limits within this or that occupation may be supposed to be more adapted to the one or to the other. They justly maintain, that these questions can only be more adapted to the one or the other. They justly maintain, that these questions can only be satisfactorily answered by perfect freedom. Let every occupation be open to all, without favour or discouragement to any, and employments will fall into the hands of those men or women who are found by experience to be most capable of worthily exercising them. There need be no fear that women will take out of the hands of men any occupation which men perform better than they. Each individual will prove his or her capacities, in the only way in which capacities can be proved—by trial; and the world will have the benefit of the best faculties of all its inhabitants. But to interfere beforehand by an arbitrary limit, and declare that whatever be the genius, talent, energy, or force of mind of an individual of a certain sex or class, those faculties shall not be exerted, or shall be exerted only in some few of the many modes in which others are permitted to use theirs, is not only an injustice to the individual, and a detriment to society, which loses what it can ill spare, but is also the most effectual mode of providing that, in the sex or class so fettered, the qualities which are not permitted to be exercised shall not exist....

Concerning the fitness, then, of women for politics, there can be no question: but the dispute is more likely to turn upon the fitness of politics for women. When the reasons alleged for excluding women from active life in all its higher departments are stripped of their garb of declamatory phrases, and reduced to the simple expression of a meaning, they seem to be mainly three: first, the incompatibility of active life with maternity, and with the cares of a household; secondly, its alleged hardening effect on the character; and thirdly, the inexpediency of making an addition to the already excessive pressure of competition in every kind of professional or lucrative employment....

Our argument here brings us into collision with what may be termed the moderate reformers of the education of women; a sort of persons who cross the path of improvement on all great questions; those who would maintain the old bad principles, mitigating their consequences. These say, that women should be, not slaves, nor servants, but companions; and educated for that office (they do not say that men should be educated to be the companions of women). But since uncultivated women are not suitable companions for cultivated men, and a man who feels interest in things above and beyond the family circle wishes that his companion should sympathize with him in that interest; they therefore say, let women improve their understanding and taste, acquire general knowledge, cultivate poetry, art, even coquet with science, and some stretch their liberality so far as to say, inform themselves on politics; not as pursuits, but sufficiently to feel an interest in the subjects, and to be capable of holding a conversation on them with the husband, or at least of understanding and imbibing his wisdom. Very agreeable to him, no doubt, but unfortunately the reverse of improving. It is from having intellectual communion only with those to whom they can lay down the law, that so few men continue to advance in wisdom beyond the first stages. The most eminent men cease to improve, if they associate only with disciples. When they have overtopped those who immediately surround them, if they wish for further growth, they must seek for others of their own stature to consort with. The mental companionship which is improving, is communion between active minds, not mere contact between an active mind and a passive....

We have left behind a host of vulgar objections either as not worthy of an answer, or as answered by the general course of our remarks. A few words, however, must be said on one plea, which in England is made much use of for giving an unselfish air to the upholding of selfish privileges, and which, with unobserving, unreflecting people, passes for much more than it is worth. Women, it is said, do not desire—do not seek, what is called their emancipation. On the contrary, they generally disown such claims when made in their behalf, and fall with *acharnement* [rancor] upon any one of themselves who identifies herself with their common cause.

Supposing the fact to be true in the fullest extent ever asserted, if it proves that European women ought to remain as they are, it proves exactly the same with respect to Asiatic women; for they too, instead of murmuring at their seclusion, and at the restraint imposed upon them, pride themselves on it, and are astonished at the effrontery of women who receive visits from male acquaintances, and are seen in the streets unveiled. Habits of submission make men as well as women servile-minded. The vast population of Asia do not desire or value, probably would not accept, political liberty, nor the savage of the forest, civilization; which does not prove that either of those things is undesirable for them, or that they will not, at some future time, enjoy it. Custom hardens human beings to any kind of degradation, by deadening the part of their nature which would resist it. And the case of women is, in this respect, even a peculiar one, for no other inferior caste that we have heard of have been taught to regard degradation as their honour. The argument, however, implies a secret consciousness that the alleged preference of women for their dependent state is merely apparent; and arises from their being allowed no choice; for if the preference be natural, there can be no necessity for enforcing it by law....

12.

John Stuart Mill
(1806–73)

The Subjection of Women

(ENGLAND, 1869)

One of the major British philosophers of his era, John Stuart Mill wrote influential books on liberty, utilitarianism, and political economy. He credited Harriet Taylor Mill with inspiring his work in general and his ideas about women in particular. The Mills wrote essays supporting women's education and employment and condemning domestic violence. After his wife died, in 1858, Mill continued to agitate for women's rights. His 1869 book elaborated on her insights, including his rejection of any "natural" defense of women's subjection and his desire that equal education replace women's socialization to be "willing slaves" to their husbands. Mill applied John Locke's critique of absolute authority to the family. He supported not only property rights for married women but also the right to suffrage and freedom from unwanted sexual relations. As a member of the British House of Commons after 1865, Mill fought for the enfranchisement of women and rejected the antisuffrage rationale that husbands both represented their wives and protected their interests. Acknowledging the extent of family violence, Mill asked his colleagues rhetorically: "I should like to have a return laid before this House of the numbers of women who are annually beaten to death, kicked to death, or trampled to death by their male protectors."

Conquering races hold it to be Nature's own dictate that the conquered should obey the conquerors, or, as they euphoniously paraphrase it, that the feebler and more unwarlike races should submit to the braver and manlier. The smallest acquaintance with human life in the middle ages, shows how supremely natural the dominion of the feudal nobility over men of low condition appeared to the nobility themselves, and how unnatural the conception seemed, of a person of the inferior class claiming equality with them, or exercising authority over them. It hardly seemed less so to the class held in subjection. The emancipated serfs and burgesses, even in their most vigorous struggles, never made any pretension to a share of authority; they only demanded more or less of limitation to the power of tyrannizing over them. So true is it that unnatural generally means only uncustomary, and that everything which is usual appears natural. The subjection of women to men being a universal custom, any departure from it quite naturally appears unnatural. But how entirely, even in this case, the feeling is dependent on custom, appears by ample experience. Nothing so much astonishes the people of distant parts of the world, when they first learn anything about England, as to be told that it is under a queen: the thing seems to them so unnatural as to be almost incredible. To Englishmen this does not seem in the least degree unnatural, because they are used to it; but they do feel it unnatural that women should be soldiers or members of parliament. In the feudal ages, on the contrary, war and politics were not thought unnatural to women, because not unusual; it seemed natural that women of the privileged classes should be of manly character, inferior in nothing but bodily strength to their husbands and fathers. The independence of women seemed rather less unnatural to the Greeks than to other ancients, on account of the fabulous Amazons (whom they believed to be historical), and the partial example afforded by the Spartan women; who, though no less subordinate by law than in other Greek states, were more free in fact, and being trained to bodily exercises in the same manner with men, gave ample proof that they were not naturally disqualified for them. There can be little doubt that Spartan experience suggested to Plato, among many other of his doctrines, that of the social and political equality of the two sexes.

But, it will be said, the rule of men over women differs from all these others in not being a rule of force: it is accepted voluntarily; women make no complaint, and are consenting parties to it. In the first place, a great number of women do not accept it. Ever since there have been women able to make their sentiments known by their writings (the only mode of publicity which society permits to them), an increasing number of them have recorded protests against their present social condition: and recently many thousands of them, headed by the most eminent women known to the public, have petitioned Parliament for their admission to the Parliamentary Suffrage. The claim of women to be educated as solidly, and in the same branches of knowledge, as men, is urged with growing intensity, and with a great prospect of success; while the demand for their admission into professions and occupations hitherto closed against them, becomes every year more urgent. Though there are not in this country, as there are in the United States, periodical Conventions and an organized party to agitate for the Rights of Women, there is a numerous and active Society organized and managed by women, for the more limited object of obtaining the political franchise. Nor is it only in our own country and in America that women are beginning to protest, more or less collectively, against the disabilities under which they labour. France, and Italy, and Switzerland, and Russia now afford examples of the same thing. How many more women there are who silently cherish similar aspirations, no one can possibly know; but there are abundant tokens how many *would* cherish them, were they not so strenuously taught to repress them as contrary to the proprieties of their sex. It must be remembered, also, that no enslaved class ever asked for complete liberty at once.... It is a political law of nature that those who are under any power of ancient origin, never begin by complaining of the power itself, but only of its oppressive exercise. There is never any want of women who complain of ill usage by their husbands. There would be infinitely more, if complaint were not the greatest of all provocatives to a repetition and increase of the ill usage. It is this which frustrates all attempts to maintain the power but protect the woman against its abuses. In no other case (except that of a child) is the person who has been proved judicially to have suffered an injury, replaced under the physical power of the culprit who inflicted it. Accordingly wives, even in the most extreme and protracted cases of bodily ill usage, hardly ever dare avail themselves of the laws made for their protection: and if, in a moment of irrepressible indignation, or by the interference of neighbours, they are induced to do so, their whole effort afterwards is to disclose as little as they can, and to beg off their tyrant from his merited chastisement.

All causes, social and natural, combine to make it unlikely that women should be collectively rebellious to the power of men. They are so far in a position different from all other subject classes, that their masters require something more from them than actual service. Men do not want solely the obedience of women, they want their sentiments. All men, except the most brutish, desire to have, in the woman most nearly connected with them, not a forced slave but a willing one, not a slave merely, but a favourite. They have therefore put everything in practice to enslave their minds. The masters of all other slaves rely, for maintaining obedience, on fear; either fear of themselves, or religious fears. The masters of women wanted more than simple obedience, and they turned the whole force of education to effect their purpose. All women are brought up from the very earliest years in the belief that their ideal of character is the very opposite to that of men; not self-will, and government by self-control, but submission, and yielding to the control of others. All the moralities tell them that it is the duty of women, and all the current sentimentalities that it is their nature, to live for others; to make complete abnegation of themselves, and to have no life but in their affections. And by their affections are meant the only ones they are allowed to have—those to the men with whom they are connected, or to the children who constitute an additional and indefeasible tie between them and a man. When we put together three things—first, the natural attraction between opposite sexes; secondly, the wife's entire dependence on the husband, every privilege or pleasure she has being either his gift, or depending entirely on his will; and lastly, that the principal object of human pursuit, consideration, and all objects of social ambition, can in general be sought or obtained by her only through him, it would be a miracle if the object of being attractive to men had not become the polar star of feminine education and formation of character. And, this great means of influence over the minds of women having been acquired, an instinct of selfishness made men avail themselves of it to the utmost as a means of holding women in subjection, by representing to them meekness, submissiveness, and resignation of all individual will into the hands of a man, as an essential part of sexual attractiveness. . . .

The preceding considerations are amply sufficient to show that custom, however universal it may be, affords in this case no presumption, and ought not to create any prejudice, in favour of the arrangements which place women in social and political subjection to men. But I may go farther, and maintain that the course of history, and the tendencies of progressive human society, afford not only no presumption in favour of this system of inequality of rights, but a strong one against it; and that, so far as the whole course of human improvement up to this time, the whole stream of modern tendencies, warrants any inference on the subject, it is, that this relic of the past is discordant with the future, and must necessarily disappear.

For, what is the peculiar character of the modern world—the difference which chiefly distinguishes modern institutions, modern social ideas, modern life itself, from those of times long past? It is, that human beings are no longer born to their place in life, and chained down by an inexorable bond to the place they are born to, but are free to employ their faculties, and such favourable chances as offer, to achieve the lot which may appear to them most desirable. Human society of old was constituted on a very different principle. All were born to a fixed social position, and were mostly kept in it by law, or interdicted from any means by which they could emerge from it. As some men are born white and others black, so some were born slaves and others freemen and citizens; some were born patricians, others plebeians; some were born feudal nobles, others commoners and *roturiers*. A slave or serf could never make himself free, nor, except by the will of his master, become so. In most European countries it was not till towards the close of the middle ages, and as a consequence of the growth of regal power, that commoners could be ennobled.... In modern Europe, and most in those parts of it which have participated most largely in all other modern improvements, diametrically opposite doctrines now prevail. Law and government do not undertake to prescribe by whom any social or industrial operation shall or shall not be conducted, or what modes of conducting them shall be lawful. These things are left to the unfettered choice of individuals.... The old theory was, that the least possible should be left to the choice of the individual agent; that all he had to do should, as far as practicable, be laid down for him by superior wisdom. Left to himself he was sure to go wrong. The modern conviction, the fruit of a thousand years of experience, is, that things in which the individual is the person directly interested, never go right but as they are left to his own discretion; and that any regulation of them by authority, except to protect the rights of others, is sure to be mischievous.... It is not that all processes are supposed to be equally good, or all persons to be equally qualified for everything; but that freedom of individual choice is now known to be the only thing which procures the adoption of the best processes, and throws each operation into the hands of those who are best qualified for it....

If this general principle of social and economical science is not true; if individuals, with such help as they can derive from the opinion of those who know them, are not better judges than the law and the government, of their own capacities and vocation; the world cannot too soon abandon this principle, and return to the old system of regulations and disabilities. But if the principle is true, we ought to act as if we believed it, and not to ordain that to be born a girl instead of a boy, any more than to be born black instead of white, or a commoner instead of a nobleman, shall decide the person's position through all life—shall interdict people from all the more elevated social positions, and from all, except a few, respectable occupations.... In all things of any difficulty and importance, those who can do them well are fewer than the need, even with the most unrestricted latitude of choice: and any limitation of the field of selection deprives society of some chances of being served by the competent, without ever saving it from the incompetent....

... [T]he wife is the actual bond-servant of her husband: no less so, as far as legal obligation goes, than slaves commonly so called. She vows a lifelong obedience to him at the altar, and is held to it all through her life by law. Casuists may say that the obligation of obedience stops short of participation in crime, but it certainly extends to everything else. She can do no act whatever but by his permission, at least tacit. She can acquire no property but for him; the instant it becomes hers, even if by inheritance, it becomes *ipso facto* his. In this respect the wife's position under the common law of England is worse than that of slaves in the laws of many countries.... By means of settlements, the rich usually contrive to withdraw the whole or part of the inherited property of the wife from the absolute control of the husband: but they do not succeed in keeping it under her own control; the utmost they can do only prevents the husband from squandering it, at the same time debarring the rightful owner from its use. The property itself is out of the reach of both; and as to the income derived from it, the form of settlement most favourable to the wife (that called "to her separate use") only precludes the husband from receiving it instead of her: it must pass through her hands, but if he takes it from her by personal violence as soon as she receives it, he can neither be punished, nor compelled to restitution. This is the amount of the protection which, under the laws of this country, the most powerful nobleman can give to his own daughter as respects her husband. In the immense majority of cases there is no settlement: and the absorption of all rights, all property, as well as all freedom of action, is complete. The two are called "one person in law," for the purpose of inferring that whatever is hers is his, but the parallel inference is never drawn that whatever is his is hers; the maxim is not applied against the man, except to make him responsible to third parties for her acts, as a master is for the acts of his slaves or of his cattle. I am far from pretending that wives are in general no better treated than slaves; but no slave is a slave to the same lengths, and in so full a sense of the word, as a wife is. Hardly any slave, except one immediately attached to the master's person, is a slave at all hours and all minutes; in general he has, like a soldier, his fixed task, and when it is done, or when he is off duty, he disposes, within certain limits, of his own time, and has a family life into which the master rarely intrudes. "Uncle Tom" under his first master had his own life in his "cabin," almost as much as any man whose work takes him away from home, is able to have in his own family. But it cannot be so with the wife. Above all, a female slave has (in Christian countries) an admitted right, and is considered under a moral obligation, to refuse to her master the last familiarity. Not so the wife: however brutal a tyrant she may unfortunately be chained to—though she may know that he hates her, though it may be his daily pleasure to torture her, and though she may feel it impossible not to loathe him—he can claim from her and enforce the lowest degradation of a human being, that of being made the instrument of an animal function contrary to her inclinations. While she is held in this worst description of slavery as to her own person, what is her position in regard to the children in whom she and her master have a joint interest? They are by law *his* children. He alone has any legal rights over them. Not one act can she do towards or in relation to them, except by delegation from him.... This is her legal state. And from this state she has no means of withdrawing herself. If she leaves her husband, she can take nothing with her, neither her children nor anything which is rightfully her own. If he chooses, he can compel her to return, by law, or by physical force; or he may content himself with seizing for his own use anything which she may earn, or which may be given to her by her relations.... Surely, if a woman is denied any lot in life but that of being the personal body-servant of a despot, and is dependent for everything upon the chance of finding one who may be disposed to make a favourite of her instead of merely a drudge, it is a very cruel aggravation of her fate that she should be allowed to try this chance only once. The natural sequel and corollary from this state of things would be, that since her all in life depends upon obtaining a good master, she should be allowed to change again and again until she finds one. I am not saying that she ought to be allowed this privilege. That is a totally different consideration. The question of divorce, in the sense involving liberty of re-marriage, is one into which it is foreign to my purpose to enter. All I now say is, that to those to whom nothing but servitude is allowed, the free choice of servitude is the only, though a most insufficient, alleviation. Its refusal completes the assimilation of the wife to the slave—and the slave under not the mildest form of slavery: for in some slave codes the slave could, under certain circumstances of ill usage, legally compel the master to sell him. But no amount of ill usage, without adultery superadded, will in England free a wife from her tormentor....

When the support of the family depends, not on property, but on earnings, the common arrangement, by which the man earns the income and the wife superintends the domestic expenditure, seems to me in general the most suitable division of labour between the two persons. If, in addition to the physical suffering of bearing children, and the whole responsibility of their care and education in early years, the wife undertakes the careful and economical application of the husband's earnings to the general comfort of the family; she takes not only her fair share, but usually the larger share, of the bodily and mental exertion required by their joint existence. If she undertakes any additional portion, it seldom relieves her from this, but only prevents her from performing it properly. The care which she is herself disabled from taking of the children and the household, nobody else takes; those of the children who do not die, grow up as they best can, and the management of the household is likely to be so bad, as even in point of economy to be a great drawback from the value of the wife's earnings. In an otherwise just state of things, it is not, therefore, I think, a desirable custom, that the wife should contribute by her labour to the income of the family. In an unjust state of things, her doing so may be useful to her, by making her of more value in the eyes of the man who is legally her master; but, on the other hand, it enables him still farther to abuse his power, by forcing her to work, and leaving the support of the family to her exertions, while he spends most of his time in drinking and idleness. The *power* of earning is essential to the dignity of a woman, if she has not independent property. But if marriage were an equal contract, not implying the obligation of obedience; if the connexion were no longer enforced to the oppression of those to whom it is purely a mischief, but a separation, on just terms (I do not now speak of a divorce), could be obtained by any woman who was morally entitled to it; and if she would then find all honourable employments as freely open to her as to men; it would not be necessary for her protection, that during marriage she should make this particular use of her faculties....

On the other point which is involved in the just equality of women, their admissibility to all the functions and occupations hitherto retained as the monopoly of the stronger sex, I should anticipate no difficulty in convincing any one who has gone with me on the subject of the equality of women in the family. I believe that their disabilities elsewhere are only clung to in order to maintain their subordination in domestic life; because the generality of the male sex cannot yet tolerate the idea of living with an equal. Were it not for that, I think that almost every one, in the existing state of opinion in politics and political economy, would admit the injustice of excluding half the human race from the greater number of lucrative occupations, and from almost all high social functions; ordaining from their birth either that they are not, and cannot by any possibility become, fit for employments which are legally open to the stupidest and basest of the other sex, or else that however fit they may be, those employments shall be interdicted to them, in order to be preserved for the exclusive benefit of males.... The reason given in ... [the last two centuries] was not women's unfitness, but the interest of society, by which was meant the interest of men: just as the *raison d'état*, meaning the convenience of the government, and the support of existing authority, was deemed a sufficient explanation and excuse for the most flagitious crimes. In the present day, power holds a smoother language, and whomsoever it oppresses, always pretends to do so for their own good: accordingly, when anything is forbidden to women, it is thought necessary to say, and desirable to believe, that they are incapable of doing it, and that they depart from their real path of success and happiness when they aspire to it. But to make this reason plausible ... it is necessary to maintain that no women at all are fit for them, and that the most eminent women are inferior in mental faculties to the most mediocre of the men on whom those functions at present devolve....

In regard, however, to the larger question, the removal of women's disabilities—their recognition as the equals of men in all that belongs to citizenship—the opening to them of all honourable employments, and of the training and education which qualifies for those employments—there are many persons for whom it is not enough that the inequality has no just or legitimate defence; they require to be told what express advantage would be obtained by abolishing it.

To which let me first answer, the advantage of having the most universal and pervading of all human relations regulated by justice instead of injustice. The vast amount of this gain to human nature, it is hardly possible, by any explanation or illustration, to place in a stronger light than it is placed by the bare statement, to any one who attaches a moral meaning to words. All the selfish propensities, the self-worship, the unjust self-preference, which exist among mankind, have their source and root in, and derive their principal nourishment from, the present constitution of the relation between men and women. Think what it is to a boy, to grow up to manhood in the belief that without any merit or any exertion of his own, though he may be the most frivolous and empty or the most ignorant and stolid of mankind, by the mere fact of being born a male he is by right the superior of all and every one of an entire half of the human race: including probably some whose real superiority to himself he has daily or hourly occasion to feel....

The second benefit to be expected from giving to women the free use of their faculties, by leaving them the free choice of their employments, and opening to them the same field of occupation and the same prizes and encouragements as to other human beings, would be that of doubling the mass of mental faculties available for the higher service of humanity....

When we consider the positive evil caused to the disqualified half of the human race by their disqualification—first in the loss of the most inspiriting and elevating kind of personal enjoyment, and next in the weariness, disappointment, and profound dissatisfaction with life, which are so often the substitute for it; one feels that among all the lessons which men require for carrying on the struggle against the inevitable imperfections of their lot on earth, there is no lesson which they more need, than not to add to the evils which nature inflicts, by their jealous and prejudiced restrictions on one another. Their vain fears only substitute other and worse evils for those which they are idly apprehensive of: while every restraint on the freedom of conduct of any of their human fellow creatures, (otherwise than by making them responsible for any evil actually caused by it), dries up *pro tanto* the principal fountain of human happiness, and leaves the species less rich, to an inappreciable degree, in all that makes life valuable to the individual human being.

13.

Susan B. Anthony
(1820–1906)

"Social Purity"

(UNITED STATES, 1875)

One of the leading feminist strategists of the nineteenth century, Susan B.
Anthony formed her political views in upstate New York, in a region and
a family steeped in Quaker antislavery and temperance sentiments. In the
1850s she met Elizabeth Cady Stanton and the two began a lifelong fem-
inist collaboration. Anthony waged petition campaigns to gain both mar-
ried women's property rights and suffrage at the state level, and she
attempted to organize women factory workers. In the 1870s she claimed
the right of a citizen by voting, an act for which she was arrested. Stan-
ton and Anthony led the National Woman Suffrage Association, which
sought a federal constitutional amendment to enfranchise women. First
introduced into Congress in 1878, the "Anthony Amendment" did not be-
come law until 1920, in part because of opposition from the liquor indus-
try, which feared that women voters would enact prohibition. During the
1870s Anthony spoke throughout the United States on the theme of "So-
cial Purity," which referred to a single moral standard for both sexes, in-
cluding chastity before and fidelity within marriage. Like the members of
the Women's Christian Temperance Union, Anthony linked drunkenness
to the sexual abuse of women and called on men to adhere to the higher
standard of moral purity required of respectable women. Underlying this
critique of individual male vice was a structural analysis that blamed
prostitution on occupational and wage discrimination on women's subse-
quent economic dependence on men and on the denial of equal suffrage.

Though women, as a class, are much less addicted to drunkenness and licentiousness than men, it is universally conceded that they are by far the greater sufferers from these evils. Compelled by their position in society to depend on men for subsistence, for food, clothes, shelter, for every chance even to earn a dollar, they have no way of escape from the besotted victims of appetite and passion with whom their lot is cast. They must endure, if not endorse, these twin vices, embodied, as they so often are, in the person of father, brother, husband, son, employer. No one can doubt that the sufferings of the sober, virtuous woman, in legal subjection to the mastership of a drunken, immoral husband and father over herself and children, not only from physical abuse, but from spiritual shame and humiliation, must be such as the man himself can not possibly comprehend....

Forty years' efforts by men alone to suppress the evil of intemperance give us the following appalling figures: 600,000 common drunkards! Which, reckoning our population to be 40,000,000, gives us one drunkard to every seventeen moderate drinking and total-abstinence men. Granting to each of these 600,000 drunkards a wife and four children, we have 3,000,000 of the women and children of this nation helplessly, hopelessly bound to this vast army of irresponsible victims of appetite.

The roots of the giant evil, intemperance, are not merely moral and social; they extend deep and wide into the financial and political structure of the government; and whenever women, or men, shall intelligently and seriously set themselves about the work of uprooting the liquor traffic, they will find something more than tears and prayers needful to the task. Financial and political power must be combined with moral and social influence, all bound together in one earnest, energetic, persistent force.

The prosecutions in our courts for breach of promise, divorce, adultery, bigamy, seduction, rape; the newspaper reports every day of every year of scandals and outrages, of wife murders and paramour shootings, of abortions and infanticides, are perpetual reminders of men's incapacity to cope successfully with this monster evil of society.

The statistics of New York show the number of professional prostitutes in that city to be over twenty thousand. Add to these the thousands and tens of thousands of Boston, Philadelphia, Washington, New Orleans, St. Louis, Chicago, San Francisco, and all our cities, great and small, from ocean to ocean, and what a holocaust of the womanhood of this nation is sacrificed to the insatiate Moloch of lust. And yet more: those myriads of wretched women, publicly known as prostitutes, constitute but a small portion of the numbers who actually tread the paths of vice and crime. For, as the oft-broken ranks of the vast army of common drunkards are steadily filled by the boasted moderate drinkers, so are the ranks of professional prostitution continually replenished by discouraged, seduced, deserted unfortunates, who can no longer hide the terrible secret of their lives....

In 1869 the Catholics established a Foundling Hospital in New York City. At the close of the first six months Sister Irene reported thirteen hundred little waifs laid in the basket at her door. That meant thirteen hundred of the daughters of New York, with trembling hands and breaking hearts, trying to bury their sorrow and their shame from the world's cruel gaze. That meant thirteen hundred mothers' hopes blighted and blasted. Thirteen hundred Rachels weeping for their children because they were not!

Nor is it womanhood alone that is thus fearfully sacrificed. For every betrayed woman, there is always the betrayer, man. For every abandoned woman, there is always *one* abandoned man and oftener many more. It is estimated that there are 50,000 professional prostitutes in London, and Dr. Ryan calculates that there are 400,000 men in that city directly or indirectly connected with them, and that this vice causes the city an annual expenditure of $40,000,000.

All attempts to describe the loathsome and contagious disease which it engenders defy human language....

Man's legislative attempts to set back this fearful tide of social corruption have proved even more futile and disastrous than have those for the suppression of intemperance—as witness the Contagious Diseases Acts of England and the St. Louis experiment. And yet efforts to establish similar laws are constantly made in our large cities, New York and Washington barely escaping last winter.

To license certain persons to keep brothels and saloons is but to throw around them and their traffic the shield of law, and thereby to blunt the edge of all moral and social efforts against them. Nevertheless, in every large city, brothels are virtually licensed. When "Maggie Smith" is made to appear before the police court at the close of each quarter, to pay her fine of $10, $25 or $100, as an inmate or a keeper of a brothel, and allowed to continue her vocation, so long as she pays her fine, *that is license.* When a grand jury fails to find cause for indictment against a well-known keeper of a house of ill-fame, that, too, is *permission* for her and all of her class to follow their trade, against the statute laws of the State, and that with impunity.

The work of woman is not to lessen the severity or the certainty of the penalty for the violation of the moral law, but to prevent this violation by the removal of the causes which lead to it. These causes are said to be wholly different with the sexes. The acknowledged incentive to this vice on the part of man is his own abnormal passion; while on the part of woman, in the great majority of cases, it is conceded to be destitution—absolute want of the necessaries of life. Lecky, the famous historian of European morals, says: "The statistics of prostitution show that a great proportion of those women who have fallen into it have been impelled by the most extreme poverty, in many instances verging on starvation." All other conscientious students of this terrible problem, on both continents, agree with Mr. Lecky. Hence, there is no escape from the conclusion that, while woman's want of bread induces her to pursue this vice, man's love of the vice itself leads him into it and holds him there. While statistics show no lessening of the passional demand on the part of man, they reveal a most frightful increase of the temptations, the necessities, on the part of woman.

In the olden times, when the daughters of the family, as well as the wife, were occupied with useful and profitable work in the household, getting the meals and washing the dishes three times in every day of every year, doing the baking, the brewing, the washing and the ironing, the whitewashing, the butter and cheese and soap making, the mending and the making of clothes for the entire family, the carding, spinning and weaving of the cloth—when everything to eat, to drink and to wear was manufactured in the home, almost no young women "went out to work." But now, when nearly all these handicrafts are turned over to men and to machinery, tens of thousands, nay, millions, of the women of both hemispheres are thrust into the world's outer market of work to earn their own subsistence. Society, ever slow to change its conditions, presents to these millions but few and meager chances. Only the barest necessaries, and oftentimes not even those, can be purchased with the proceeds of the most excessive and exhausting labor.

Hence, the reward of virtue for the homeless, friendless, penniless woman is ever a scanty larder, a pinched, patched, faded wardrobe, a dank basement or rickety garret, with the colder, shabbier scorn and neglect of the more fortunate of her sex. Nightly, as weary and worn from her day's toil she wends her way through the dark alleys toward her still darker abode, where only cold and hunger await her, she sees on every side and at every turn the gilded hand of vice and crime outstretched, beckoning her to food and clothes and shelter; hears the whisper in softest accents, "Come with me and I will give you all the comforts, pleasures and luxuries that love and wealth can bestow." Since the vast multitudes of human beings, women like men, are not born to the courage or conscience of the martyr, can we wonder that so many poor girls fall, that so many accept material ease and comfort at the expense of spiritual purity and peace? Should we not wonder, rather, that so many escape the sad fate?

Clearly, then, the first step toward solving this problem is to lift this vast army of poverty-stricken women who now crowd our cities, above the temptation, the necessity, to sell themselves, in marriage or out, for bread and shelter. To do that, girls, like boys, must be educated to some lucrative employment; women, like men, must have equal chances to earn a living. If the plea that poverty is the cause of woman's prostitution be not true, perfect equality of chances to earn honest bread will demonstrate the falsehood by removing that pretext and placing her on the same plane with man. Then, if she is found in the ranks of vice and crime, she will be there for the same reason that man is and, from an object of pity, she, like him, will become a fit subject of contempt. From being the party sinned against, she will become an equal sinner, if not the greater of the two. Women, like men, must not only have "fair play" in the world of work and self-support, but, like men, must be eligible to all the honors and emoluments of society and government. Marriage, to women as to men, must be a luxury, not a necessity; an incident of life, not all of it. And the only possible way to accomplish this great change is to accord to women equal power in the making, shaping and controlling of the circumstances of life. That equality of rights and privileges is vested in the ballot, the symbol of power in a republic. Hence, our first and most urgent demand—that women shall be protected in the exercise of their inherent, personal, citizen's right to a voice in the government, municipal, state, national....

Whoever controls work and wages, controls morals. Therefore, we must have women employers, superintendents, committees, legislators; wherever girls go to seek the means of subsistence, there must be some woman. Nay, more; we must have women preachers, lawyers, doctors—that wherever women go to seek counsel—spiritual, legal, physical—there, too, they will be sure to find the best and noblest of their own sex to minister to them....

Now, why is it that man can hold woman to this high code of morals, like Cæsar's wife—not only pure but above suspicion—and so surely and severely punish her for every departure, while she is so helpless, so powerless to check him in his license, or to extricate herself from his presence and control? His power grows out of his right over her subsistence. Her lack of power grows out of her dependence on him for her food, her clothes, her shelter.

Marriage never will cease to be a wholly unequal partnership until the law recognizes the equal ownership in the joint earnings and possessions. The true relation of the sexes never can be attained until woman is free and equal with man. Neither in the making nor executing of the laws regulating these relations has woman ever had the slightest voice. The statutes for marriage and divorce, for adultery, breach of promise, seduction, rape, bigamy, abortion, infanticide—all were made by men. They, alone, decide who are guilty of violating these laws and what shall be their punishment, with judge, jury and advocate all men, with no woman's voice heard in our courts, save as accused or witness, and in many cases the married woman is denied the poor privilege of testifying as to her own guilt or innocence of the crime charged against her....

If the divine law visits the sins of the fathers upon the children, equally so does it transmit to them their virtues. Therefore, if it is through woman's ignorant subjection to the tyranny of man's appetites and passions that the life-current of the race is corrupted, then must it be through her intelligent emancipation that the race shall be redeemed from the curse, and her children and children's children rise up to call her blessed. When the mother of Christ shall be made the true model of womanhood and motherhood, when the office of maternity shall be held sacred and the mother shall consecrate herself, as did Mary, to the one idea of bringing forth the Christ-child, then, and not till then, will this earth see a new order of men and women, prone to good rather than evil....

As the fountain can rise no higher than the spring that feeds it, so a legislative body will enact or enforce no law above the average sentiment of the people who created it. Any and every reform work is sure to lead women to the ballot-box. It is idle for them to hope to battle successfully against the monster evils of society until they shall be armed with weapons equal to those of the enemy—votes and money. Archimedes said, "Give to me a fulcrum on which to plant my lever, and I will move the world." And I say, give to woman the ballot, the political fulcrum, on which to plant her moral lever, and she will lift the world into a nobler and purer atmosphere.

Two great necessities forced this nation to extend justice and equality to the negro:

First, Military necessity, which compelled the abolition of the crime and curse of slavery, before the rebellion could be overcome.

Second, Political necessity, which required the enfranchisement of the newly-freed men, before the work of reconstruction could begin.

The third is now pressing, Moral necessity—to emancipate woman, before Social Purity, the nation's safeguard, ever can be established.

14.

HENRIK IBSEN
(1828–1906)

The Doll's House
(NORWAY, 1879)

In the late nineteenth century, the character of Nora Helmer became an icon of the "new woman." At a time when wives owed obedience to husbands and service to children, Ibsen's Nora rejected her stultifying middle-class life and infantilization within a "doll house" and declared her independence from men. Ibsen had been influenced by discussions of the "woman question" in Norway, particularly by the work of the novelist Camilla Collett, a founder of the Norwegian women's movement. He had written an earlier feminist play, Pillars of Society *(1877), and he supported women's property rights and suffrage. First produced in Italy,* The Doll's House *soon reached audiences in Germany, London, and New York. The character of Nora Helmer enjoyed the privileges of middle-class married life, but by incurring a debt she endangered her family's economic position. The play's resolution—her rejection of paternalism in the final scene, excerpted here—shocked critics. Conservatives condemned Nora's selfish disregard for familial duty, but feminists from Italy to Japan began to cite the play as an inspiration for their own quest for independence. The "new woman" epitomized by Nora came to symbolize the individualism of modern society, as well as female emancipation.*

HELMER. You loved me just as a wife should love her husband. It was only the means you could not judge rightly about. But do you think you are less dear to me for not knowing how to act alone? No, indeed; only lean on me; I will advise and guide you. I should be no true man if it were not just this woman's helplessness that makes you doubly attractive in my eyes. You must not dwell on the harsh words I spoke in my first moment of terror, when I believed ruin was about to crush my very life out. I have forgiven you, Nora; I swear to you I have forgiven you.

NORA. I thank you for your forgiveness (*goes through the left door*).

HELMER. No, stay (*looks in*). What are you doing in the alcove?

NORA (*inside*). Taking off my masquerade dress.

HELMER (*in the open door*). Yes, do, dear; try to rest and restore your mind to its balance, my scared little song-bird. You may go to rest in comfort; I have broad wings to protect you (*walks round by the door*). Oh, how beautiful and cozy our home is, Nora! Here you are safe; here I can shelter you like a hunted dove, whom I have saved from the claws of the hawk. I shall soon quiet your poor beating heart. Believe me, Nora, gradually peace will return. To-morrow all this will look quite different to you; I shall not need to repeat over and over again that I forgive you: you will feel for yourself that it is true. How can you think I could ever bring my heart to drive you away, or even so much as reproach you? Oh, you don't know what a true man's heart is made of, Nora! A man feels there is something indescribably sweet and soothing in his having forgiven his wife, that he has honestly forgiven her from the bottom of his heart. She becomes his property in a double sense, as it were. She is as though born again; she has become to a certain extent at once his wife and his child. And that is what you shall really be to me henceforth, you ill-advised and helpless darling. Don't be anxious about anything, Nora: only open your heart to me, and I will be both will and conscience to you. Why, what's this? Not gone to bed? You have changed your dress.

NORA (*entering in her every-day dress*). Yes, Torvald; now I have changed my dress.

HELMER. But why, now it is so late?

NORA. I shall not sleep to-night.

HELMER. But, Nora dear…

NORA (*looking at her watch*). It is not so very late. Sit down here, Torvald. We two have much to say to each other (*she sits on one side of the table*).

HELMER. Nora, what does that mean? Your cold, set face!

NORA. Sit down; it will take some time. I have to talk over many things with you.

HELMER. (*sitting opposite to her at the table*). Nora, you make me anxious…I don't in the least understand you.

NORA. Just so. You don't understand me. And in the same way I have never understood you, till to-night. No, don't interrupt me. Only listen to what I say…. This is a breaking off, Torvald.

HELMER. How do you mean?

NORA (*after a short silence*). Does not one thing strike you as we sit here?

HELMER. What should strike me?

NORA. We have now been married eight years. Does it not strike you that to-night for the first time we two, you and I, husband and wife, are speaking together seriously?

HELMER. Well; "seriously," what does that mean?

NORA. During eight whole years and more, since the day we first made each other's acquaintance, we have never exchanged one serious word about serious things.

HELMER. Ought I, then, to have persistently initiated you into difficulties you could not help me by sharing?

NORA. I am not talking of difficulties. All I am saying is, that we have never yet seriously talked any one thing over together.

HELMER. But, dearest Nora, would it have been any good to you if we had?

NORA. That is the very point. You have never understood me…. I have been greatly wronged, Torvald. First by father and then by you.

HELMER. What! by us two, by us two—who have loved you more deeply than all others have?

NORA (*shakes her head*). You two have never loved me. You only thought it was pleasant to be in love with me.

HELMER. But, Nora, these are strange words.

NORA. Yes; it is just so, Torvald. While I was still at home with father, he used to tell me all his views, and so of course I held the same views; if at any time I had a different view I concealed it, because he would not have liked people with opinions of their own. He used to call me his little doll, and play with me, as I in my turn used to play with my dolls. Then I came to live in your house.

HELMER. What expressions you do use to describe our marriage!

NORA (*undisturbed*). I mean—then I passed over from father's hands into yours. You settled everything according to your taste; or I did only what you liked; I don't exactly know. I think it was both ways, first one and then the other. When I look back on it now it seems to me as if I had been living here like a poor man, only from hand to mouth. I lived by performing tricks for you, Torvald. But you would have it so. You and father have sinned greatly against me. It is the fault of you two that nothing has been made of me.

HELMER. How senseless and ungrateful you are.... Haven't you been happy here?

NORA. No, never; I thought I was, but I never was.

HELMER. Not...not happy?

NORA. No; only merry. And you were always so friendly and kind to me. But our house has been nothing but a nursery. Here I have been your doll-wife, just as at home I used to be papa's doll-child. And my children were, in their turn, my dolls. I was exceedingly delighted when you played with me, just as the children were whenever I played with them. That has been our marriage, Torvald.

HELMER. There is some truth in what you say, exaggerated and overdrawn though it may be. But henceforth it shall be different. The time for play is gone by; now comes the time for education.

NORA. Whose education—mine or the children's?

HELMER. Yours, as well as the children's, dear Nora.

NORA. Oh, Torvald, you are not the man to educate me into being the right wife for you.

HELMER. And *you* say that?

NORA. And I—how have I been prepared to educate the children?

HELMER. Nora!

NORA. Did you not say just now yourself that *that* was a task you dared not intrust to me?

HELMER. In a moment of excitement. How can you lay any stress upon that?

NORA. No; you were perfectly right. For that task I am not ready. There is another which must be performed first. I must first try to educate myself. In that you are not the man to help me. I must set to work alone: you are not the man to help me with it. I must do it alone. And that is why I am going away from you now.

HELMER (*jumping up*). What—what are you saying?

NORA. I must be thrown entirely upon myself if I am to come to any understanding as to what I am and what the things around me are: so I can not stay with you any longer.

HELMER. Nora, Nora!

NORA. I shall now leave your house at once. Christina will, I am sure, take me in for tonight. . . .

HELMER. You are insane. I shall not allow that; I forbid it.

NORA. From this time it is useless for you to forbid me things. Whatever belongs to me I shall take with me. I will have nothing from you either now or later on.

HELMER. What utter madness this is!

NORA. To-morrow I shall go home—I mean to my birthplace. There it will be easier for me to get something to do of one sort or another.

HELMER. Oh, you blind, inexperienced creature!

NORA. I must try to gain experience, Torvald.

HELMER. To forsake your home, your husband, and your children! And only think what people will say about it.

NORA. I can not take that into consideration. I only know that to go is necessary for me.

HELMER. Oh, it drives one wild! Is this the way you can evade your holiest duties?

NORA. What do you consider my holiest duties?

HELMER. Do I need to tell you that? Are they not your duties to your husband and your children?

NORA. I have other duties equally sacred.

HELMER. No, you have not. What duties do you mean?

NORA. Duties toward myself.

HELMER. Before all else you are a wife and mother.

NORA. I no longer think so. I think that before all else I am a human being just as you are, or at least I will try to become one. I know very well that most people agree with you, Torvald, and what is to be found in books. But I can not be satisfied any longer with what most people say, and with what is in books. I must think over things for myself, and try to get clear about them.

...

HELMER. Oh, you think and talk like a silly child.

NORA. Very likely. But you neither think nor speak like the man I could be one with. When your terror was over—not for what threatened *me*, but for what involved *you*—and when there was nothing more to fear, then it was in your eyes as though nothing whatever had happened. I was just as much as ever your lark, your doll, whom you would take twice as much care of in future because she was so weak and frail (*stands up*). Torvald, in that moment it became clear to me that I had been living here all these years with a strange man and had borne him three children. Oh, I can not bear to think of it. I could tear myself to pieces!

HELMER (*sadly*). I see it, I see it: a chasm has opened between us.... But, Nora, can it never be filled up?

NORA. As I now am I am no wife for you.

HELMER. I am strong enough to become another man.

NORA. Perhaps, when your doll is taken away from you.

HELMER. Part—part from you! No, Nora, no; I can not grasp it.

NORA (*going into the right room*). The more reason for it to happen. (*She comes in with her walking things, and a small traveling bag, which she puts on the chair by the table.*)

HELMER. Nora, Nora, not now. Wait till tomorrow.

NORA (*putting on her cloak*). I can not spend the night in the house of a man who is a stranger to me.

HELMER. But can't we live here as brother and sister?

NORA (*tying her bonnet tightly*). You know quite well that would not last long (*puts her shawl on*). Good-by, Torvald. I will not see the children before I go. I know they are in better hands than mine. As I now am I can be nothing to them.

HELMER. But later, Nora—later on?

NORA. How can I tell? I have no idea what will become of me.

HELMER. But you are my wife—both as you are now and as you will become.

NORA. Listen, Torvald. When a wife leaves her husband's house, as I am doing, then I have heard he is free from all duties toward her in the eyes of the law. At any rate, I release you from all duties. You must feel yourself no more bound by anything than I feel. There must be perfect freedom on both sides. There, there is your ring back. Give me mine.

HELMER. That too?

NORA. That too.

HELMER. Here it is.

NORA. Very well. Yes; now it is all past and gone. Here, I lay the keys down. The maids know how to manage everything in the house far better than I do. To-morrow, when I have started on my journey, Christina will come, in order to pack up the few things that are my own. They will be sent after me.

HELMER. Past and gone! Nora, will you never think of me again?

NORA. Certainly. I shall think very often of you and the children and this house.

HELMER. May I write to you, Nora?

NORA. No, never. You must not.

HELMER. But I may send you what...

NORA. Nothing, nothing.

HELMER. Help you when you are in need?

NORA. No, I say. I take nothing from strangers.

HELMER. Nora, can I never become to you anything but a stranger?

NORA (*taking her traveling bag sadly*). The greatest miracle of all would have to happen then, Torvald.

HELMER. Tell me what the greatest miracle is.

NORA. We both should need to change so, you as well as I, that— Oh, Torvald, I no longer believe in anything miraculous.

HELMER. But I believe in it. Tell me. We must so change that...

NORA. That our living together could be a marriage. Good-by. (*She goes out through the hall.*)

HELMER (*sinks in a chair by the door with his hands before his face*). Nora, Nora! (*He looks round and stands up.*) Empty. She isn't here now. (*A hope inspires him.*) The greatest miracle! (*Below-stairs a door is heard shutting ominously in the lock.*)

15.

KISHIDA TOSHIKO
(1863–1901)

"Daughters in Boxes"

(JAPAN, 1883)

Resentment about the constraints of familial duty recurred in feminist writing in the late nineteenth century. In Japan, where Western political ideas circulated after 1868, women involved in popular-rights movements questioned the limitations on their marital choices and called for female education and citizenship. Kishida Toshiko had been a tutor for the empress, but she rejected life at court for being "far from the real world." In 1882, when she was only nineteen years old, she gave her first public speech, "The Way for Women," in which she criticized the Japanese family. Like Wollstonecraft, Kishida stressed the compatibility of education and marriage. Thousands of Japanese women flocked to her talks when she toured the country and some formed women's groups to achieve her goals. After delivering "Daughters in Boxes" in 1883, Kishida was arrested, tried, and fined for having made a political speech without a permit. (The transcription of this speech survives because it was recorded by a police officer.) The government soon suppressed the liberal movement in which Kishida participated and during the 1890s banned women's political participation. Nonetheless, women's magazines, girls' schools, and female workers' societies sustained interest in feminist ideas. Kishida married a political colleague, taught in a women's seminary, and wrote poetry, fiction, and essays in support of women's rights.

[T]o turn to the topic of this evening's lecture, the expression "daughters in boxes" is a popular one, heard with frequency in the regions of Kyoto and Osaka. It is the daughters of middle-class families and above who are often referred to as such. Why such an expression? Because these girls are like creatures kept in a box. They may have hands and feet and a voice—but all to no avail, because their freedom is restricted. Unable to move, their hands and feet are useless. Unable to speak, their voice has no purpose. Hence the expression.

It is only for daughters that such boxes are constructed. Parents who make these boxes do not mean to restrict their daughters' freedom. Rather, they hope to guide their daughters along the correct path toward acquiring womanly virtues. Therefore, it is out of love for their daughters that these parents construct these boxes. Or so we are told, but if we look at the situation more closely, we cannot but question whether or not it is truly love that these parents have for their daughters. For do they not cause their daughters to suffer? I should like to gather a few students—perhaps only two or three—and make of them true daughters in a box. But the box I would construct would not be a box with walls. Rather, it would be a formless box. For a box with walls visible to the human eye is cramped and does not allow one to cultivate truly bright and healthy children. Sisters crowd each other, competing for space, and end up developing warped personalities. And so I intend to create a box without walls.

A box without walls is one that allows its occupants to tread wherever their feet might lead and stretch their arms as wide as they wish. Some may object and say: is your box not one that encourages dissipation and willfulness? No, it is not so at all. My box without walls is made of heaven and earth—its lid I would fashion out of the transparent blue of the sky and at its bottom would be the fathomless depths of the earth upon which we stand. My box would not be cramped, allowing its occupants such a tiny space that whenever they attempt to move, their arms and legs strike against one another, causing them to suffer. It may seem biased to say so, but constructing this box is above all a woman's task and an important task at that. A hastily made box will not do. A woman should carry with her into marriage a box filled with a good education. Upon giving birth to a daughter, she should raise her in the box she has herself carefully constructed. Thus she will nurture a bright daughter of good character. But if she forces her daughter into a box she has hastily constructed, the child will chafe at the narrowness of the structure and resent being placed inside. Far better to build the box before the birth of the child, for indeed a woman's ability to produce good children for the propagation of the family and to encourage domestic harmony depends on how carefully she has built this box.

I do not know anything about the world beyond my own small frame of reference, but I think it safe to say that all Japanese families raise their daughters in boxes. Certainly the kind of boxes we create and the way we raise our daughters in them varies in degree from household to household. Among these, I can identify approximately three different types of boxes. Of these three, which one would I select? I would select the one in which the parents value the teachings of the wise and holy men of the past and, through the lessons imparted in classics such as the *Great Learning for Women* and the *Small Learning for Women*, pass on to their daughters an appreciation for knowledge. Compared to the other two boxes, this one is far more cultivated. But then, which box comes next? Next we have a box that upon the birth of a daughter is fitted with a secluded room deep in its interior; this is where the daughter is kept. The entrance to this room is barricaded by a long blind, and she must not leave the room. Nor may she lift the blind. And so she stays deep in her room behind her blind. The parents of the daughter in this box treat her not with affection; rather, they bring her only harm. And then, as for the third: in this box the parents refuse to recognize their responsibility to their daughter and teach her naught. They make no effort to shower her with love, and instead expect her to obey their every word without complaint. The mother abusively wields her power over her daughter and otherwise is hateful in her treatment of her child. Such is the third box. Of the three boxes I have just introduced this evening, I consider the first commendable in its cultivation. But the second and third are not satisfactory and are not to be recommended.

Next, I would like to take up an extremely practical matter, and that is the way mothers today raise their daughters. There are some who argue, with exceedingly boorish logic, that learning is an obstacle to a woman's successful marriage. This argument is particularly specious. Women need learning. But if you think by learning that I am referring only to the *Four Books* and the *Five Classics* or the eight great writers of the Tang and Song—Han Yü in particular—or recitations of the great Chinese poets, then you are greatly mistaken. Nor am I advocating the composition of *waka* poetry or the extemporaneous recitation of short verses. A romantic ramble while enjoying the elegant diversions of moon- or flower-viewing do not to my mind constitute learning, either. Now, a daughter might display a natural talent for letters and be able to gladden her readers with her many compositions. Then let her become a writer. But those without talent should not waste their time in elegant diversions with moon and flowers or in dabbling with mountains and streams as though they were some revered recluse. No, what I call learning requires that a woman recognize, at least, the responsibility that she must shoulder as a woman; so long as she lives in this precious country of ours, she should refrain from squandering her talents. What I desire most is for a woman to prepare herself for marriage by assembling appropriate knowledge as the most essential item in her trousseau.

Eight or nine out of ten mothers in our society today believe that they have accomplished their duty if their daughters, once married, are not sent home in divorce. It does not even occur to them that their daughters might deserve higher goals. How can these mothers successfully accomplish their tasks when their expectations for their daughters are so low? What then is the appropriate way to raise a daughter?

What I deem appropriate is to allow daughters to study first, and then have them marry. Education is the most essential item in a woman's wedding trousseau. And what are the subjects she should study? Economics and ethics. Although a woman lives under her husband's protection for most of her life, the day may come when he should die. Then she should fortify herself with her moral training and plan her future with her financial knowledge. Thus these subjects, when taken together, form the most important item a woman will bring to her marriage. Her kimono cabinet and bedding chest are vulnerable to theft and easily lost to fire. They cannot be trusted to last with absolute certainty. Even so, those who do not appreciate the fact that a daughter too should be educated, dismiss their maids and servants as soon as their daughter comes of age. Their rationale for this is that their daughter will soon be sent in marriage to a stranger's house, where she must know the ins-and-outs of cleaning. What better time to learn than now? And so they set her to work in the absence of the servants and maids. Truly, can we say that these parents know how to raise a daughter?

... But to return to the subject at hand, we humans are like these flowers. Therefore, we cannot cultivate the human spirit to its full and brilliant potential if we restrict its freedom as would a gardener his flowers. To take the analogy further, let us compare these flowers to humanity and more particularly to daughters. If we enclose them in boxes; if we capture them when they try to escape and bind them in place, then just as the petals of the bound flower will scatter and fall, so too the bounty of the human mind will wither. And so I say to you, before you put your daughters in a box, try to imagine how she will feel once inside, and thus construct the box to be as broad as the world is wide so that she might feel free. Should you do so, I guarantee that you will produce a true and virtuous daughter. But if you do not—if you force your daughter inside a narrow box and restrict her freedom—I have no doubt that your daughter will either escape or elope and you will have to send your servants and maids out to search high and low to find her and drag her back. On the contrary, if the daughters in boxes today are allowed to feel as free as those outside the box then the need to keep them tucked away in restrictive boxes loses its currency. And if we no longer need restrictive boxes, then daughters will no longer need to escape them and servants and maids will no longer need to spend their time chasing after them. Their energy can be more appropriately applied to the management of the house, thus better utilizing household resources!

16.

FRIEDRICH ENGELS
(1820–95)

The Origin of the Family, Private Property,
and the State
(GERMANY, 1884)

In The Communist Manifesto *(1848), Karl Marx and Friedrich Engels called for proletarian revolutions to replace capitalism with worker-run state socialism. They believed that wage labor and trade unions—rather than mere legal rights—would lead to women's emancipation. But Marxists also acknowledged that women in the working class faced a dual exploitation, in the family as well as the workplace. In his treatise on the origins of inequality, Engels compared the husband to the bourgeoisie and the wife to the proletariat. Drawing on contemporary ethnographic observers, such as Johann Bachofen, he suggested that women had enjoyed higher status within the matrilineal clans of primitive communistic societies. Settled agriculture, surplus wealth, and private property, however, introduced patrilineal inheritance and led to "the world historical defeat of the female sex" and their degradation to the status of slaves to men. Only the abolition of capitalism, Engels concluded, would liberate women; the proletarian family would lead the way to undermining male supremacy. Along with August Bebel, whose* Woman and Socialism *(1879) also compared matriarchal and patriarchal systems, Engels laid the groundwork for a Marxian analysis of gender inequality that influenced socialist and communist politics for more than a century.*

The communistic household, in which most or all of the women belong to one and the same gens [clan], while the men come from various gentes, is the material foundation of that supremacy of the women which was general in primitive times, and which it is Bachofen's third great merit to have discovered. The reports of travelers and missionaries, I may add, to the effect that women among savages and barbarians are overburdened with work in no way contradict what has been said. The division of labor between the two sexes is determined by quite other causes than by the position of woman in society. Among peoples where the women have to work far harder than we think suitable, there is often much more real respect for women than among our Europeans. The lady of civilization, surrounded by false homage and estranged from all real work, has an infinitely lower social position than the hard-working woman of barbarism, who was regarded among her people as a real lady (lady, *frowa*, *Frau*—mistress) and who was also a lady in character....

Bachofen is also perfectly right when he consistently maintains that the transition from what he calls "hetærism" or "*Sumpfzeugung*" to monogamy was brought about primarily through the women. The more the traditional sexual relations lost the naïve primitive character of forest life, owing to the development of economic conditions with consequent undermining of the old communism and growing density of population, the more oppressive and humiliating must the women have felt them to be, and the greater their longing for the right of chastity, of temporary or permanent marriage with one man only, as a way of release. This advance could not in any case have originated with the men, if only because it has never occurred to them, even to this day, to renounce the pleasures of actual group marriage. Only when the women had brought about the transition to pairing marriage were the men able to introduce strict monogamy—though indeed only for women....

We now leave America, the classic soil of the pairing family. No sign allows us to conclude that a higher form of family developed here, or that there was ever permanent monogamy anywhere in America prior to its discovery and conquest. But not so in the Old World.

Here the domestication of animals and the breeding of herds had developed a hitherto unsuspected source of wealth and created entirely new social relations. Up to the lower stage of barbarism, permanent wealth had consisted almost solely of house, clothing, crude ornaments and the tools for obtaining and preparing food—boat, weapons, and domestic utensils of the simplest kind. Food had to be won afresh day by day. Now, with their herds of horses, camels, asses, cattle, sheep, goats, and pigs, the advancing pastoral peoples—the Semites on the Euphrates and the Tigris, and the Aryans in the Indian country of the Five Streams (Punjab), in the Ganges region, and in the steppes then much more abundantly watered of the Oxus and the Jaxartes—had acquired property which only needed supervision and the rudest care to reproduce itself in steadily increasing quantities and to supply the most abundant food in the form of milk and meat. All former means of procuring food now receded into the background; hunting, formerly a necessity, now became a luxury.

But to whom did this new wealth belong? Originally to the gens, without a doubt. Private property in herds must have already started at an early period, however. It is difficult to say whether the author of the so-called first book of Moses regarded the patriarch Abraham as the owner of his herds in his own right as head of a family community or by right of his position as actual hereditary head of a gens. What is certain is that we must not think of him as a property owner in the modern sense of the word. And it is also certain that at the threshold of authentic history we already find the herds everywhere separately owned by heads of families, as are the artistic products of barbarism—metal implements, luxury articles and, finally, the human cattle—the slaves.

For now slavery had also been invented. To the barbarian of the lower stage, a slave was valueless. Hence the treatment of defeated enemies by the American Indians was quite different from that at a higher stage. The men were killed or adopted as brothers into the tribe of the victors; the women were taken as wives or otherwise adopted with their surviving children. At this stage human labor-power still does not produce any considerable surplus over and above its maintenance costs. That was no longer the case after the introduction of cattle-breeding, metalworking, weaving and, lastly, agriculture. Just as the wives whom it had formerly been so easy to obtain had now acquired an exchange value and were bought, so also with the forces of labor, particularly since the herds had definitely become family possessions. The family did not multiply so rapidly as the cattle. More people were needed to look after them; for this purpose use could be made of the enemies captured in war, who could also be bred just as easily as the cattle themselves.

Once it had passed into the private possession of families and there rapidly begun to augment, this wealth dealt a severe blow to the society founded on pairing marriage and the matriarchal gens. Pairing marriage had brought a new element into the family. By the side of the natural mother of the child it placed its natural and attested father, with a better warrant of paternity, probably, than that of many a "father" today. According to the division of labor within the family at that time, it was the man's part to obtain food and the instruments of labor necessary for the purpose. He therefore also owned the instruments of labor, and in the event of husband and wife separating, he took them with him, just as she retained her household goods. Therefore, according to the social custom of the time, the man was also the owner of the new source of subsistence, the cattle, and later of the new instruments of labor, the slaves. But according to the custom of the same society, his children could not inherit from him. . . .

The children of the dead man, however, did not belong to his gens, but to that of their mother; it was from her that they inherited, at first conjointly with her other blood-relations, later perhaps with rights of priority; they could not inherit from their father, because they did not belong to his gens, within which his property had to remain. When the owner of the herds died, therefore, his herds would go first to his brothers and sisters and to his sister's children, or to the issue of his mother's sisters. But his own children were disinherited.

Thus, on the one hand, in proportion as wealth increased, it made the man's position in the family more important than the woman's, and on the other hand created an impulse to exploit this strengthened position in order to overthrow, in favor of his children, the traditional order of inheritance. This, however, was impossible so long as descent was reckoned according to mother-right. Mother-right, therefore, had to be overthrown, and overthrown it was. This was by no means so difficult as it looks to us today. For this revolution—one of the most decisive ever experienced by humanity—could take place without disturbing a single one of the living members of a gens. All could remain as they were. A simple decree sufficed that in the future the offspring of the male members should remain within the gens, but that of the female should be excluded by being transferred to the gens of their father. The reckoning of descent in the female line and the matriarchal law of inheritance were thereby overthrown, and the male line of descent and the paternal law of inheritance were substituted for them. As to how and when this revolution took place among civilized peoples, we have no knowledge. It falls entirely within prehistoric times....

The result was hopeless confusion, which could only be remedied and to a certain extent was remedied by the transition to father-right....

The overthrow of mother-right was the *world historical defeat of the female sex*. The man took command in the home also; the woman was degraded and reduced to servitude, she became the slave of his lust and a mere instrument for the production of children. This degraded position of the woman, especially conspicuous among the Greeks of the heroic and still more of the classical age, has gradually been palliated and glozed over, and sometimes clothed in a milder form; in no sense has it been abolished....

[The monogamous family] develops out of the pairing family, as previously shown, in the transitional period between the upper and middle stages of barbarism; its decisive victory is one of the signs that civilization is beginning. It is based on the supremacy of the man, the express purpose being to produce children of undisputed paternity; such paternity is demanded because these children are later to come into their father's property as his natural heirs. It is distinguished from pairing marriage by the much greater strength of the marriage tie, which can no longer be dissolved at either partner's wish. As a rule, it is now only the man who can dissolve it, and put away his wife. The right of conjugal infidelity also remains secured to him, at any rate by custom (the *Code*

Napoléon explicitly accords it to the husband as long as he does not bring his concubine into the house), and as social life develops he exercises his right more and more; should the wife recall the old form of sexual life and attempt to revive it, she is punished more severely than ever....

This is the origin of monogamy as far as we can trace it back among the most civilized and highly developed people of antiquity. It was not in any way the fruit of individual sex-love, with which it had nothing whatever to do; marriages remained as before marriages of convenience. It was the first form of the family to be based, not on natural, but on economic conditions—on the victory of private property over primitive, natural communal property. The Greeks themselves put the matter quite frankly: the sole exclusive aims of monogamous marriage were to make the man supreme in the family, and to propagate, as the future heirs to his wealth, children indisputably his own. Otherwise, marriage was a burden, a duty which had to be performed, whether one liked it or not, to gods, state, and one's ancestors. In Athens the law exacted from the man not only marriage but also the performance of a minimum of so-called conjugal duties.

Thus when monogamous marriage first makes its appearance in history, it is not as the reconciliation of man and woman, still less as the highest form of such a reconciliation. Quite the contrary. Monogamous marriage comes on the scene as the subjugation of the one sex by the other; it announces a struggle between the sexes unknown throughout the whole previous prehistoric period. In an old unpublished manuscript, written by Marx and myself in 1846, I find the words: "The first division of labor is that between man and woman for the propagation of children." And today I can add: The first class opposition that appears in history coincides with the development of the antagonism between man and woman in monogamous marriage, and the first class oppression coincides with that of the female sex by the male. Monogamous marriage was a great historical step forward; nevertheless, together with slavery and private wealth, it opens the period that has lasted until today in which every step forward is also relatively a step backward, in which prosperity and development for some is won through the misery and frustration of others....

As regards the legal equality of husband and wife in marriage, the position is no better. The legal inequality of the two partners, bequeathed to us from earlier social conditions, is not the cause but the effect of the economic oppression of the woman. In the old communistic household, which comprised many couples and their children, the task entrusted to the women of managing the household was as much a public and socially necessary industry as the procuring of food by the men. With the patriarchal family, and still more with the single monogamous family, a change came. Household management lost its public character. It no longer concerned society. It became a *private service*; the wife became the head servant, excluded from all participation in social production. Not until the coming of modern large-scale industry was the road to social production opened to her again—and then only to the proletarian wife. But it was opened in such a manner that, if she carries out her duties in the private service of her family, she remains excluded from public production and unable to earn; and if she wants to take part in public production and earn independently, she cannot carry out family duties. And the wife's position in the factory is the position of women in all branches of business, right up to medicine and the law. The modern individual family is founded on the open or concealed domestic slavery of the wife, and modern society is a mass composed of these individual families as its molecules.

In the great majority of cases today, at least in the possessing classes, the husband is obliged to earn a living and support his family, and that in itself gives him a position of supremacy, without any need for special legal titles and privileges. Within the family he is the bourgeois and the wife represents the proletariat. In the industrial world, the specific character of the economic oppression burdening the proletariat is visible in all its sharpness only when all special legal privileges of the capitalist class have been abolished and complete legal equality of both classes established. The democratic republic does not do away with the opposition of the two classes; on the contrary, it provides the clear field on which the fight can be fought out. And in the same way, the peculiar character of the supremacy of the husband over the wife in the modern family, the necessity of creating real social equality between them, and the way to do it, will only be seen in the clear light of day when both possess legally complete equality of rights. Then it will be plain that the first condition for the liberation of the wife is to bring the whole female sex back into public industry, and that this in turn demands the abolition of the monogamous family as the economic unit of society....

Full freedom of marriage can therefore only be generally established when the abolition of capitalist production and of the property relations created by it has removed all the accompanying economic considerations which still exert such a powerful influence on the choice of a marriage partner. For then there is no other motive left except mutual inclination....

17.

FRANCISCA DINIZ
(Nineteenth century)

"Equality of Rights"
(BRAZIL, 1890)

Liberal feminist ideas circulated internationally, particularly during periods of democratic reform. Ten years after Brazil became an independent nation in 1822, a translation of Wollstonecraft's Vindication of the Rights of Woman *appeared there. In the 1850s educated, urban women produced the first Brazilian feminist journals, in which they questioned men's tyranny in marriage. As Brazil became industrialized in the late nineteenth century, the movement for women's education expanded. In 1873, schoolteacher Francisca Diniz began to publish* O sexo feminino (The Female Sex), *a journal that supported the emancipation of slaves along with women's rights to education and property. At a time when even the few Brazilian women who were literate had no access to higher education, Diniz and her daughters founded a private school to offer an advanced curriculum to girls. In 1889, when Brazil extended suffrage from property owners to all literate males, Diniz invoked the language of natural rights to argue that women should also be able to vote. Brazilian women eventually gained suffrage in 1932, after an extended political campaign initiated in 1918 by Bertha Lutz, who also represented Brazil in international feminist organizations and contributed to the inclusion of women's rights in the charter of the United Nations after World War II.*

Like a Columbus at the prow of his ship, like an eagle with his eyes fixed on the sun of the future, the nineteenth century proceeds toward a new world, a new paradise, where women shall have their thrones of honor and receive their radiant queens' crowns not from the sacrilegious hands of an Alcibiades but from the sacred hands of Justice and Right, the true sovereigns, who will depose the false kings seated on their thrones of injustice and iniquity brandishing their scepters of despotism. Yes, we believe that the prophecy of the immortal Victor Hugo will be achieved. We have faith that this century will triumph through the radiant ideal of justice that surrounds it.

We believe, with the strong faith noble causes inspire, that an ideal state will soon be here, when educated women free from traditional prejudices and superstitions will banish from their education the oppression and false beliefs besetting them and will fully develop their physical, moral, and intellectual attributes. Then, linked arm in arm with virtuous, honest, and just men in the garden of spiritual civilization, women will climb the steps of light to have their ephemeral physical beauty crowned with the immortal diadem of true beauty, of science and creativity. In the full light of the new era of redemption we shall battle for the restoration of equal rights and our cause—the Emancipation of Women.

We women do not wish to be the Venus de Milo, but rather the Venus Urania, so that we can brilliantly traverse all the orbits that human endeavor traces at the dawn of humanity and society.

We do not wish to play the role of ornaments in the palaces of the stronger sex. Nor do we wish to continue in the semislavery in which we languish, mutilated in our personalities through laws decreed by men. This is no different from the old days of slave labor when the enslaved could not protest their enslavement.

We are not daunted by such hypocrisy as men's treating us like queens only to give us the scepter of the kitchen, or the procreation machine, etc. We are considered nothing but objects of indispensable necessity! We are cactus flowers and nothing more.

Women's emancipation through education is the bright torch which can dispel the darkness and bring us to the august temple of science and to a proper life in a civilized society.

Moral advancement, which can best lead us to understand our rights and duties, will guide our hearts toward the paradise of goodness and of domestic, social, and human happiness. The union of fine arts with literature, a star in the soul's beautiful sky, will make women men's worthy companions in the struggle for social progress and in the labors of family life.

In short, we want women to be fully aware of their own worth and of what they can achieve with their bodies as well as through their moral beauty and the force of their intellects. We want the lords of the stronger sex to know that although under their laws they can execute us for our political ideas, as they did such ill-fated women as Charlotte Corday and many others, they owe us the justice of equal rights. And that includes the right to vote and to be elected to office.

By right we should not be denied expression in Parliament. We should not continue to be mutilated in our moral and mental personality. The right to vote is an attribute of humanity because it stems from the power of speech. Women are human beings, too.

We Brazilian, Italian, French, and other women of diverse nationalities do not request the vote under the restrictions currently imposed on Englishwomen, but with the full rights of republican citizens. We live in a generous and marvelous country recognized as a world leader in liberal ideas and in the ability to throw off old prejudices.

What we ask is a right never demanded before, and therefore ignored. But it was never deleted from natural law.

Women must publicly plead their cause, which is the cause of right, justice, and humanity. No one should forget that women as mothers represent the sanctity of infinite love. As daughters they represent angelic tenderness. As wives, immortal fidelity. As sisters, the purest dedication and friendship. Moreover, these qualities the Supreme Creator bestowed on them prove their superiority, not their inferiority, and show that equality of action should be put into practice by those men who proclaim the principle of equality.

We Brazilians, Portuguese, French, English, Italian, German, etc., women, like noble Aspasias, side by side with the Hypatiases and

Semiramises, etc., are asking for what is due us and what, by natural right, cannot be denied us.

Our ideas are not utopian but instead great and noble, and they will induce humanity to advance toward justice.

This is our political program.

18.

ANNA JULIA COOPER
(1858–1964)

A Voice from the South

(UNITED STATES, 1892)

The African American educator Anna Julia Cooper published her collection of essays on womanhood and race during an era when segregation, black disfranchisement, and vigilante violence enforced white supremacy in the American South. Born into slavery, Cooper longed for education. She graduated from Oberlin College, one of the first schools to admit women and blacks, and she eventually earned a doctorate from the University of Paris. Like other African American female reformers who established schools, opposed lynching, and provided community service, Cooper refused to accept the constraints of either gender or race. She insisted that the women's movement must include women of all races, and she directly addressed Southern white fears of "social equality," a code for interracial relationships that whites invoked to justify segregation. Like Elizabeth Cady Stanton, Cooper argued that equal opportunity would allow women's unique influences to benefit all people, although her emphasis on gender difference contrasted with Stanton's equal rights philosophy. Both writers shared the view that humanity lost valuable resources when it restricted or ignored women's contributions.

Only the BLACK WOMAN can say "when and where I enter, in the quiet, undisputed dignity of my womanhood, without violence and without suing or special patronage, then and there the whole *Negro race enters with me.*" Is it not evident then that as individual workers for this race we must address ourselves with no half-hearted zeal to this feature of our mission. The need is felt and must be recognized by all. There is a call for workers, for missionaries, for men and women with the double consecration of a fundamental love of humanity and a desire for its melioration through the Gospel; but superadded to this we demand an intelligent and sympathetic comprehension of the interests and special needs of the Negro.... We need men who can let their interest and gallantry extend outside the circle of their aesthetic appreciation; men who can be a father, a brother, a friend to every weak, struggling unshielded girl. We need women who are so sure of their own social footing that they need not fear leaning to lend a hand to a fallen or falling sister. We need men and women who do not exhaust their genius splitting hairs on aristocratic distinctions and thanking God they are not as others; but earnest, unselfish souls, who can go into the highways and byways, lifting up and leading, advising and encouraging with the truly catholic benevolence of the Gospel of Christ....

There is, then, a real and special influence of woman. An influence subtle and often involuntary, an influence so intimately interwoven in, so intricately interpenetrated by the masculine influence of the time that it is often difficult to extricate the delicate meshes and analyze and identify the closely clinging fibers. And yet, without this influence—so long as woman sat with bandaged eyes and manacled hands, fast bound in the clamps of ignorance and inaction, the world of thought moved in its orbit like the revolutions of the moon; with one face (the man's face) always out, so that the spectator could not distinguish whether it was disc or sphere.

Now I claim that it is the prevalence of the Higher Education among women, the making it a common everyday affair for women to reason and think and express their thought, the training and stimulus which enable and encourage women to administer to the world the bread it needs as well as the sugar it cries for; in short it is the transmitting the potential forces of her soul into dynamic factors that has given symmetry and completeness to the world's agencies. So only could it be consummated that Mercy, the lesson she teaches, and Truth, the task man has set himself, should meet together: that righteousness, or *rightness*, man's ideal,—and *peace*, its necessary 'other half,' should kiss each other.

We must thank the general enlightenment and independence of woman (which we may now regard as a *fait accompli*) that both these forces are now at work in the world, and it is fair to demand from them for the twentieth century a higher type of civilization than any attained in the nineteenth. Religion, science, art, economics, have all needed the feminine flavor; and literature, the expression of what is permanent and best in all of these, may be gauged at any time to measure the strength of the feminine ingredient. You will not find theology consigning infants to lakes of unquenchable fire long after women have had a chance to grasp, master, and wield its dogmas. You will not find science annihilating personality from the government of the Universe and making of God an ungovernable, unintelligible, blind, often destructive physical force; you will not find jurisprudence formulating as an axiom the absurdity that man and wife are one, and that one the man—that the married woman may not hold or bequeath her own property save as subject to her husband's direction; you will not find political economists declaring that the only possible adjustment between laborers and capitalists is that of selfishness and rapacity—that each must get all he can and keep all that he gets, while the world cries *laissez faire* and the lawyers explain, "it is the beautiful working of the law of supply and demand"; in fine, you will not find the law of love shut out from the affairs of men after the feminine half of the world's truth is completed....

Now please understand me. I do not ask you to admit that these benefactions and virtues are the exclusive possession of women, or even that women are their chief and only advocates. It may be a man who formulates and makes them vocal. It may be, and often is, a man who weeps over the wrongs and struggles for the amelioration: but that man has imbibed those impulses from a mother rather than from a father and is simply materializing and giving back to the world in tangible form the ideal love and tenderness, devotion and care that have cherished and nourished the helpless period of his own existence.

All I claim is that there is a feminine as well as a masculine side to truth; that these are related not as inferior and superior, not as better and worse, not as weaker and stronger, but as complements—complements in one necessary and symmetric whole. That as the man is more noble in reason, so the woman is more quick in sympathy. That as he is indefatigable in pursuit of abstract truth, so is she in caring for the interests by the way—striving tenderly and lovingly that not one of the least of these 'little ones' should perish. That while we not unfrequently see women who reason, we say, with the coolness and precision of a man, and men as considerate of helplessness as a woman, still there is a general consensus of mankind that the one trait is essentially masculine and the other as peculiarly feminine. That both are needed to be worked into the training of children, in order that our boys may supplement their virility by tenderness and sensibility, and our girls may round out their gentleness by strength and self-reliance. That, as both are alike necessary in giving symmetry to the individual, so a nation or a race will degenerate into mere emotionalism on the one hand, or bullyism on the other, if dominated by either exclusively; lastly, and most emphatically, that the feminine factor can have its proper effect only through woman's development and education so that she may fitly and intelligently stamp her force on the forces of her day, and add her modicum to the riches of the world's thought....

Lately a great national and international movement characteristic of this age and country, a movement based on the inherent right of every soul to its own highest development, I mean the movement making for Woman's full, free, and complete emancipation, has, after much courting, obtained the gracious smile of the Southern woman— I beg her pardon—the Southern *lady.*

She represents blood, and of course could not be expected to leave that out; and firstly and foremostly she must not, in any organization she may deign to grace with her presence, be asked to associate with "these people who were once her slaves."

Now the Southern woman (I may be pardoned, being one myself) was never renowned for her reasoning powers, and it is not surprising that just a little picking will make her logic fall to pieces even here.

In the first place she imagines that because her grandfather had slaves who were black, all the blacks in the world of every shade and tint were once in the position of her slaves. This is as bad as the Irishman who was about to kill a peaceable Jew in the streets of Cork,—having just learned that Jews slew his Redeemer. The black race constitutes one-seventh the known population of the globe; and there are representatives of it here as elsewhere who were never in bondage at any time to any man,—whose blood is as blue and lineage as noble as any, even that of the white lady of the South. That her slaves were black and she despises her slaves, should no more argue antipathy to all dark people and peoples, than that Guiteau, an assassin, was white, and I hate assassins, should make me hate all persons more or less white. The objection shows a want of clear discrimination.

The second fallacy in the objection grows out of the use of an ambiguous middle, as the logicians would call it, or assigning a double signification to the term "*Social equality.*" ...

The "social equality" implied by civility to the Negro is a very different thing from forced association with him socially. Indeed it seems to me that the mere application of a little cold common sense would show that uncongenial social environments could by no means be forced on any one. I do not, and cannot be made to associate with all dark persons, simply on the ground that I am dark; and I presume the Southern lady can imagine some whose faces are white, with whom she would no sooner think of chatting unreservedly than, were it possible, with a veritable "darkey." Such things must and will always be left to individual election. No law, human or divine, can legislate for or against them. Like seeks like; and I am sure with the Southern lady's antipathies at their present temperature, she might enter ten thousand organizations besprinkled with colored women without being any more deflected by them than by the proximity of a stone. The social equality scare then is all humbug, conscious or unconscious, I know not which. And were it not too bitter a thought to utter here, I might add that the overtures for forced association in the past history of these two races were not made by the manacled black man, nor by *the silent and suffering black woman*! ...

The cause of freedom is not the cause of a race or a sect, a party or a class,—it is the cause of human kind, the very birthright of humanity. Now unless we are greatly mistaken the Reform of our day, known as the Woman's Movement, is essentially such an Embodiment, if its pioneers could only realize it, of the universal good. And specially important is it that there be no confusion of ideas among its leaders as to its scope and universality. All mists must be cleared from the eyes of woman if she is to be a teacher of morals and manners: the former strikes its roots in the individual and its training and pruning may be accomplished by classes; but the latter is to lubricate the joints and minimize the friction of society, and it is important and fundamental that there be no chromatic or other aberration when the teacher is settling the point, "Who is my neighbor?"

It is not the intelligent woman vs. the ignorant woman; nor the white woman vs. the black, the brown, and the red,—it is not even the cause of woman vs. man. Nay, 'tis woman's strongest vindication for speaking that *the world needs to hear her voice*. It would be subversive of every human interest that the cry of one-half the human family be stifled.

19.

ELIZABETH CADY STANTON
(1815–1902)

"The Solitude of Self"
(UNITED STATES, 1892)

The preeminent feminist political writer in nineteenth-century America, Elizabeth Cady Stanton had proselytized for women's rights since the 1840s (see her "Declaration of Sentiments," page 58). Toward the end of her life, resistance to women's higher education and suffrage remained powerful. To refute deeply entrenched views that women depended on men for protection and political representation, Stanton told the National American Woman Suffrage Association (N.A.W.S.A.) that women possessed the same right to self-sovereignty that American men enjoyed. Written on the occasion of her resignation as president of N.A.W.S.A., and subsequently presented before U.S. congressional committees, her speech clearly articulates the individualism that characterized equal rights feminism in the United States. Yet it also echoes the instrumental arguments of Mary Wollstonecraft and Anna Julia Cooper in its insistence that education and political representation enable women to perform their familial duties and to contribute to the "general good."

The point I wish plainly to bring before you on this occasion is the individuality of each human soul; our Protestant idea, the right of individual conscience and judgment; our republican idea, individual citizenship. In discussing the rights of woman, we are to consider, first, what belongs to her as an individual, in a world of her own, the arbiter of her own destiny, an imaginary Robinson Crusoe, with her woman Friday on a solitary island. Her rights under such circumstances are to use all her faculties for her own safety and happiness.

Secondly, if we consider her a citizen, as a member of a great nation, she must have the same rights as all other members, according to the fundamental principles of our government.

Thirdly, viewed as a woman, an equal factor in civilization, her rights and duties are still the same; individual happiness and development.

Fourthly, it is only the incidental relations of life, such as mother, wife, sister, daughter, that may involve some special duties and training. It is the usual discussion in regard to woman's sphere; such men as Herbert Spencer, Frederic Harrison and Grant Allen, uniformly subordinate her rights and duties as an individual, as a citizen, as a woman, to the necessities of these incidental relations, neither of which a large class of women may ever assume. In discussing the sphere of man, we do not decide his rights as an individual, as a citizen, as a man, by his duties as a father, a husband, or a brother, relations he may never fill. Moreover, he would be better fitted for these very relations, and whatever special work he might choose to do to earn his bread, by the complete development of all his faculties as an individual.

Just so with woman. The education that will fit her to discharge the duties in the largest sphere of human usefulness will best fit her for whatever special work she may be compelled to do.

The isolation of every human soul, and the necessity of self-dependence, must give each individual the right to choose his own surroundings.

The strongest reason for giving woman all the opportunities for higher education, for the full development of her faculties, forces of mind and body; for giving her the most enlarged freedom of thought and action; a complete emancipation from all forms of bondage, of custom, dependence, superstition; from all the crippling influences of fear—is the solitude and personal responsibility of her own individual life. The strongest reason why we ask for woman a voice in the government under which she lives; in the religion she is asked to believe; equality in social life, where she is the chief factor; a place in the trades and professions, where she may earn her bread, is because of her birthright to self-sovereignity; because as an individual she must rely on herself. No matter how much women prefer to lean, to be protected and supported, nor how much men desire to have them do so, they must make the voyage of life alone, and for safety in an emergency, they must know something of the laws of navigation. To guide our own craft, we must be captain, pilot, engineer; with chart and compass to stand at the wheel; to watch the winds and waves, and know when to take in the sail, and to read the signs in the firmament over all. It matters not whether the solitary voyager is man or woman; nature, having endowed them equally, leaves them to their own skill and judgment in the hour of danger, and, if not equal to the occasion, alike they perish.

To appreciate the importance of fitting every human soul for independent action, think for a moment of the immeasurable solitude of self. We come into the world alone, unlike all who have gone before us; we leave it alone, under circumstances peculiar to ourselves. No mortal ever has been, no mortal ever will be like the soul just launched on the sea of life. There can never again be just such a combination of prenatal influences; never again just such environments as make up the infancy, youth and manhood of this one. Nature never repeats herself, and the possibilities of one human soul will never be found in another. No one has ever found two blades of ribbon grass alike, and no one will ever find two human beings alike. Seeing, then, what must be the infinite diversity in human character, we can in a measure appreciate the loss to a nation when any large class of the people is uneducated and unrepresented in the government.

We ask for the complete development of every individual, first, for his own benefit and happiness. In fitting out an army, we give each soldier his own knapsack, arms, powder, his blanket, cup, knife, fork and spoon. We provide alike for all their individual necessities; then each man bears his own burden.

Again, we ask complete individual development for the general good; for the consensus of the competent on the whole round of human interests, on all questions of national life; and here each man must bear his share of the general burden....

To throw obstacles in the way of a complete education is like putting out the eyes; to deny the rights of property like cutting off the hands. To deny political equality is to rob the ostracised of all self-respect; of credit in the market place; of recompense in the world of work; of a voice in selecting those who make and administer the law; a choice in the jury before whom they are tried, and in the judge who decides their punishment. Shakespeare's play of "Titus Andronicus" contains a terrible satire on woman's position in the 19th century. Rude men (the play tells us) seized the king's daughter, cut out her tongue, cut off her hands, and then bade her go call for water and wash her hands. What a picture of woman's position! Robbed of her natural rights; handicapped by law and custom at every turn, yet compelled to fight her own battles, and in the emergencies of life to fall back on herself for protection.

The girl of sixteen, thrown on the world to support herself, to make her own place in society, to resist the temptations that surround her and maintain a spotless integrity, must do all this by native force or superior education. She does not acquire this power by being trained to trust others and distrust herself. If she wearies of the struggle, finding it hard work to swim up stream, and allows herself to drift with the current, she will find plenty of company, but not one to share her misery in the hour of her deepest humiliation. If she tries to retrieve her position, to conceal the past, her life is hedged about with fears lest willing hands should tear the veil from what she fain would hide. Young and friendless, *she* knows the bitter solitude of self.

How the little courtesies of life on the surface of society, deemed so important from man towards woman, fade into utter insignificance in view of the deeper tragedies in which she must play her part alone, where no human aid is possible!

The young wife and mother, at the head of some establishment, with a kind husband to shield her from the adverse winds of life, with wealth, fortune and position, has a certain harbor of safety, secure against the ordinary ills of life. But to manage a household, have a desirable influence in society, keep her friends and the affections of her husband, train her children and servants well, she must have rare common sense, wisdom, diplomacy, and a knowledge of human nature. To do all this, she needs the cardinal virtues and the strong points of character that the most successful statesman possesses. An uneducated woman, trained to dependence, with no resources in herself, must make a failure of any position in life.

Whatever the theories may be of woman's dependence on man, in the supreme moments of her life, he cannot bear her burdens. Alone she goes to the gates of death to give life to every man that is born into the world; no one can share her fears, no one can mitigate her pangs; and if her sorrow is greater than she can bear, alone she passes beyond the gates into the vast unknown....

We may have many friends, love, kindness, sympathy and charity, to smooth our pathway in everyday life, but in the tragedies and triumphs of human experience, each mortal stands alone.

But when all artificial trammels are removed, and women are recognized as individuals, responsible for their own environments, thoroughly educated for all positions in life they may be called to fill; with all the resources in themselves that liberal thought and broad culture can give; guided by their own conscience and judgment, trained to self-protection, by healthy development of the muscular system, and skill in the use of weapons of defence; and stimulated to self-support by a knowledge of the business world and the pleasure that pecuniary independence must ever give; when women are trained in this way, they will in a measure be fitted for those hours of solitude that come alike to all, whether prepared or otherwise. As in our extremity we must depend on ourselves, the dictates of wisdom point to complete individual development.

Whatever may be said of man's protecting power in ordinary conditions, amid all the terrible disasters by land and sea, in the supreme moments of danger, alone woman must ever meet the horrors of the situation. The Angel of Death even makes no royal pathway for her. Man's love and sympathy enter only into the sunshine of our lives. In that solemn solitude of self, that links us with the immeasurable and the eternal, each soul lives alone forever....

[T]here is a solitude which each and every one of us has always carried with him, more inaccessible than the ice-cold mountains, more profound than the midnight sea; the solitude of self. Our inner being which we call ourself, no eye nor touch of man or angel has ever pierced. It is more hidden than the caves of the gnome; the sacred adytum of the oracle; the hidden chamber of Eleusinian mystery, for to it only Omniscience is permitted to enter.

Such is individual life. Who, I ask you, can take, dare take on himself the rights, the duties, the responsibilities of another human soul?

20.

CHARLOTTE PERKINS GILMAN
(1860–1935)

"The Yellow Wallpaper"
(UNITED STATES, 1892)

Charlotte Perkins Gilman published several of the most important works of feminist theory in the United States in the early twentieth century. Her short story "The Yellow Wallpaper" has become a classic of American feminist fiction. Gilman drew on her own experience of the disease then known as neuresthenia and her rejection of the "rest cure" prescribed by a prominent physician S. Weir Mitchell. Foreshadowing later feminist critiques of men's monopoly of medical care, the story details the morbid effects of the infantilization of women patients and, more generally, the societal constraints on women's creativity. Gilman's own mental state improved only when she rejected the claims of familial duty—leaving her husband and child—and embraced the life of the mind. In addition to writing Women and Economics *(1898),* The Home, Its Work and Influence *(1903), and* The Man-Made World; or, Our Androcentric Culture *(1911), she published a feminist journal, the* Forerunner *(1909–16), and wrote fiction, including a utopian feminist novel,* Herland *(1915). Although she supported woman suffrage, Gilman emphasized the economic basis of inequality and incorporated socialist principles of communal responsibility for familial tasks. Like other progressive reformers of her generation, she adopted eugenic ideas about white superiority even as she criticized biological theories about women's inferiority.*

It is very seldom that mere ordinary people like John and myself secure ancestral halls for the summer.

A colonial mansion, a hereditary estate, I would say a haunted house and reach the height of romantic felicity—but that would be asking too much of fate!

Still I will proudly declare that there is something queer about it.

Else, why should it be let so cheaply? And why have stood so long untenanted?

John laughs at me, of course, but one expects that.

John is practical in the extreme. He has no patience with faith, an intense horror of superstition, and he scoffs openly at any talk of things not to be felt and seen and put down in figures.

John is a physician, and *perhaps*—(I would not say it to a living soul, of course, but this is dead paper and a great relief to my mind)—*perhaps* that is one reason I do not get well faster.

You see, he does not believe I am sick! And what can one do?

If a physician of high standing, and one's own husband, assures friends and relatives that there is really nothing the matter with one but temporary nervous depression—a slight hysterical tendency—what is one to do?

My brother is also a physician, and also of high standing, and he says the same thing.

So I take phosphates or phosphites—whichever it is—and tonics, and air and exercise, and journeys, and am absolutely forbidden to "work" until I am well again.

Personally, I disagree with their ideas.

Personally, I believe that congenial work, with excitement and change, would do me good.

But what is one to do?

I did write for a while in spite of them; but it *does* exhaust me a good deal—having to be so sly about it, or else meet with heavy opposition.

I sometimes fancy that in my condition, if I had less opposition and more society and stimulus—but John says the very worst thing I can do is to think about my condition, and I confess it always makes me feel bad.

So I will let it alone and talk about the house.

The most beautiful place! It is quite alone, standing well back from the road, quite three miles from the village. It makes me think of English places that you read about, for there are hedges and walls and gates that lock, and lots of separate little houses for the gardeners and people.

There is a *delicious* garden! I never saw such a garden—large and shady, full of box-bordered paths, and lined with long grape-covered arbors with seats under them.

There were greenhouses, but they are all broken now.

There was some legal trouble, I believe, something about the heirs and co-heirs; anyhow, the place has been empty for years.

That spoils my ghostliness, I am afraid, but I don't care—there is something strange about the house—I can feel it.

I even said so to John one moonlight evening, but he said what I felt was a draught, and shut the window.

I get unreasonably angry with John sometimes. I'm sure I never used to be so sensitive. I think it is due to this nervous condition.

But John says if I feel so I shall neglect proper self-control; so I take pains to control myself—before him, at least, and that makes me very tired.

I don't like our room a bit. I wanted one downstairs that opened onto the piazza and had roses all over the window, and such pretty old-fashioned chintz hangings! But John would not hear of it.

He said there was only one window and not room for two beds, and no near room for him if he took another.

He is very careful and loving, and hardly lets me stir without special direction.

I have a schedule prescription for each hour in the day; he takes all care from me, and so I feel basely ungrateful not to value it more.

He said he came here solely on my account, that I was to have perfect rest and all the air I could get. "Your exercise depends on your strength, my dear," said he, "and your food somewhat on your appetite; but air you can absorb all the time." So we took the nursery at the top of the house.

It is a big, airy room, the whole floor nearly, with windows that look all ways, and air and sunshine galore. It was nursery first, and then playroom and gymnasium, I should judge, for the windows are barred for little children, and there are rings and things in the walls.

The paint and paper look as if a boys' school had used it. It is stripped off—the paper—in great patches all around the head of my bed, about as far as I can reach, and in a great place on the other side of the room low down. I never saw a worse paper in my life. One of those sprawling, flamboyant patterns committing every artistic sin.

It is dull enough to confuse the eye in following, pronounced enough constantly to irritate and provoke study, and when you follow the lame uncertain curves for a little distance they suddenly commit suicide— plunge off at outrageous angles, destroy themselves in unheard-of contradictions.

The color is repellent, almost revolting: a smouldering unclean yellow, strangely faded by the slow-turning sunlight. It is a dull yet lurid orange in some places, a sickly sulphur tint in others.

No wonder the children hated it! I should hate it myself if I had to live in this room long.

There comes John, and I must put this away—he hates to have me write a word.

We have been here two weeks, and I haven't felt like writing before, since that first day.

I am sitting by the window now, up in this atrocious nursery, and there is nothing to hinder my writing as much as I please, save lack of strength.

John is away all day, and even some nights when his cases are serious.

I am glad my case is not serious!

But these nervous troubles are dreadfully depressing.

John does not know how much I really suffer. He knows there is no reason to suffer, and that satisfies him.

Of course it is only nervousness. It does weigh on me so not to do my duty in any way!

I meant to be such a help to John, such a real rest and comfort, and here I am a comparative burden already!

Nobody would believe what an effort it is to do what little I am able—to dress and entertain, and order things.

It is fortunate Mary is so good with the baby. Such a dear baby!

And yet I *cannot* be with him, it makes me so nervous.

I suppose John never was nervous in his life. He laughs at me so about this wallpaper!

At first he meant to repaper the room, but afterward he said that I was letting it get the better of me, and that nothing was worse for a nervous patient than to give way to such fancies.

He said that after the wallpaper was changed it would be the heavy bedstead, and then the barred windows, and then that gate at the head of the stairs, and so on.

"You know the place is doing you good," he said, "and really, dear, I don't care to renovate the house just for a three months' rental."

"Then do let us go downstairs," I said. "There are such pretty rooms there."

Then he took me in his arms and called me a blessed little goose, and said he would go down cellar, if I wished, and have it white-washed into the bargain.

But he is right enough about the beds and windows and things.

It is as airy and comfortable a room as anyone need wish, and, of course, I would not be so silly as to make him uncomfortable just for a whim.

I'm really getting quite fond of the big room, all but that horrid paper.

Out of one window I can see the garden—those mysterious deep-shaded arbors, the riotous old-fashioned flowers, and bushes and gnarly trees.

Out of another I get a lovely view of the bay and a little private wharf belonging to the estate. There is a beautiful shaded lane that runs down there from the house. I always fancy I see people walking in these numerous paths and arbors, but John has cautioned me not to give way to fancy in the least. He says that with my imaginative power and habit of story-making, a nervous weakness like mine is sure to lead to all manner of excited fancies, and that I ought to use my will and good sense to check the tendency. So I try.

I think sometimes that if I were only well enough to write a little it would relieve the press of ideas and rest me.

But I find I get pretty tired when I try.

It is so discouraging not to have any advice and companionship about my work. When I get really well, John says we will ask Cousin Henry and Julia down for a long visit; but he says he would as soon put fireworks in my pillow-case as to let me have those stimulating people about now.

I wish I could get well faster.

But I must not think about that. This paper looks to me as if it *knew* what a vicious influence it had!

There is a recurrent spot where the pattern lolls like a broken neck and two bulbous eyes stare at you upside down.

I get positively angry with the impertinence of it and the ever-lastingness. Up and down and sideways they crawl, and those absurd unblinking eyes are everywhere. There is one place where two breadths didn't match, and the eyes go all up and down the line, one a little higher than the other.

I never saw so much expression in an inanimate thing before, and we all know how much expression they have! I used to lie awake as a child and get more entertainment and terror out of blank walls and plain furniture than most children could find in a toy-store.

I remember what a kindly wink the knobs of our big old bureau used to have, and there was one chair that always seemed like a strong friend.

I used to feel that if any of the other things looked too fierce I could always hop into that chair and be safe.

The furniture in this room is no worse than inharmonious, however, for we had to bring it all from downstairs. I suppose when this was used as a playroom they had to take the nursery things out, and no wonder! I never saw such ravages as the children have made here.

The wallpaper, as I said before, is torn off in spots, and it sticketh closer than a brother—they must have had perseverance as well as hatred.

Then the floor is scratched and gouged and splintered, the plaster itself is dug out here and there, and this great heavy bed, which is all we found in the room, looks as if it had been through the wars.

But I don't mind it a bit—only the paper.

There comes John's sister. Such a dear girl as she is, and so careful of me! I must not let her find me writing.

She is a perfect and enthusiastic housekeeper, and hopes for no better profession. I verily believe she thinks it is the writing which made me sick!

But I can write when she is out, and see her a long way off from these windows.

There is one that commands the road, a lovely shaded winding road, and one that just looks off over the country. A lovely country, too, full of great elms and velvet meadows.

This wallpaper has a kind of sub-pattern in a different shade, a particularly irritating one, for you can only see it in certain lights, and not clearly then.

But in the places where it isn't faded and where the sun is just so—I can see a strange, provoking, formless sort of figure that seems to skulk about behind that silly and conspicuous front design.

There's sister on the stairs!

Well, the Fourth of July is over! The people are all gone, and I am tired out. John thought it might do me good to see a little company, so we just had Mother and Nellie and the children down for a week.

Of course I didn't do a thing. Jennie sees to everything now.

But it tired me all the same.

John says if I don't pick up faster he shall send me to Weir Mitchell in the fall.

But I don't want to go there at all. I had a friend who was in his hands once, and she says he is just like John and my brother, only more so!

Besides, it is such an undertaking to go so far.

I don't feel as if it was worthwhile to turn my hand over for anything, and I'm getting dreadfully fretful and querulous.

I cry at nothing, and cry most of the time.

Of course I don't when John is here, or anybody else, but when I am alone.

And I am alone a good deal just now. John is kept in town very often by serious cases, and Jennie is good and lets me alone when I want her to.

So I walk a little in the garden or down that lovely lane, sit on the porch under the roses, and lie down up here a good deal.

I'm getting really fond of the room in spite of the wallpaper. Perhaps *because* of the wallpaper.

It dwells in my mind so!

I lie here on this great immovable bed—it is nailed down, I

believe—and follow that pattern about by the hour. It is as good as gymnastics, I assure you. I start, we'll say, at the bottom, down in the corner over there where it has not been touched, and I determine for the thousandth time that I *will* follow that pointless pattern to some sort of a conclusion.

I know a little of the principle of design, and I know this thing was not arranged on any laws of radiation, or alternation, or repetition, or symmetry, or anything else that I ever heard of.

It is repeated, of course, by the breadths, but not otherwise.

Looked at in one way, each breadth stands alone; the bloated curves and flourishes—a kind of "debased Romanesque" with delirium tremens—go waddling up and down in isolated columns of fatuity.

But, on the other hand, they connect diagonally, and the sprawling outlines run off in great slanting waves of optic horror, like a lot of wallowing sea-weeds in full chase.

The whole thing goes horizontally, too, at least it seems so, and I exhaust myself trying to distinguish the order of its going in that direction.

They have used a horizontal breadth for a frieze, and that adds wonderfully to the confusion.

There is one end of the room where it is almost intact, and there, when the crosslights fade and the low sun shines directly upon it, I can almost fancy radiation after all—the interminable grotesque seems to form around a common center and rush off in headlong plunges of equal distraction.

It makes me tired to follow it. I will take a nap, I guess.

I don't know why I should write this.

I don't want to.

I don't feel able.

And I know John would think it absurd. But I *must* say what I feel and think in some way—it is such a relief!

But the effort is getting to be greater than the relief.

Half the time now I am awfully lazy, and lie down ever so much. John says I mustn't lose my strength, and has me take cod liver oil and lots of tonics and things, to say nothing of ale and wine and rare meat.

Dear John! He loves me very dearly, and hates to have me sick. I tried to have a real earnest reasonable talk with him the other day, and tell him how I wish he would let me go and make a visit to Cousin Henry and Julia.

But he said I wasn't able to go, nor able to stand it after I got there; and I did not make out a very good case for myself, for I was crying before I had finished.

It is getting to be a great effort for me to think straight. Just this nervous weakness, I suppose.

And dear John gathered me up in his arms, and just carried me upstairs and laid me on the bed, and sat by me and read to me till it tired my head.

He said I was his darling and his comfort and all he had, and that I must take care of myself for his sake, and keep well.

He says no one but myself can help me out of it, that I must use my will and self-control and not let any silly fancies run away with me.

There's one comfort—the baby is well and happy, and does not have to occupy this nursery with the horrid wallpaper.

If we had not used it, that blessed child would have! What a fortunate escape! Why, I wouldn't have a child of mine, an impressionable little thing, live in such a room for worlds.

I never thought of it before, but it is lucky that John kept me here after all; I can stand it so much easier than a baby, you see.

Of course I never mention it to them any more—I am too wise—but I keep watch for it all the same.

There are things in that wallpaper that nobody knows about but me, or ever will.

Behind that outside pattern the dim shapes get clearer every day.

It is always the same shape, only very numerous.

And it is like a woman stooping down and creeping about behind that pattern. I don't like it a bit. I wonder—I begin to think—I wish John would take me away from here!

It is so hard to talk with John about my case, because he is so wise, and because he loves me so.

But I tried it last night.

It was moonlight. The moon shines in all around just as the sun does.

I hate to see it sometimes, it creeps so slowly, and always comes in by one window or another.

John was asleep and I hated to waken him, so I kept still and watched the moonlight on that undulating wallpaper till I felt creepy.

The faint figure behind seemed to shake the pattern, just as if she wanted to get out.

I got up softly and went to feel and see if the paper *did* move, and when I came back John was awake.

"What is it, little girl?" he said. "Don't go walking about like that—you'll get cold."

I thought it was a good time to talk, so I told him that I really was not gaining here, and that I wished he would take me away.

"Why, darling!" said he. "Our lease will be up in three weeks, and I can't see how to leave before.

"The repairs are not done at home, and I cannot possibly leave town just now. Of course, if you were in any danger, I could and would, but you really are better, dear, whether you can see it or not. I am a doctor, dear, and I know. You are gaining flesh and color, your appetite is better, I feel really much easier about you."

"I don't weigh a bit more," said I, "nor as much; and my appetite may be better in the evening when you are here but it is worse in the morning when you are away!"

"Bless her little heart!" said he with a big hug. "She shall be as sick as she pleases! But now let's improve the shining hours by going to sleep, and talk about it in the morning!"

"And you won't go away?" I asked gloomily.

"Why, how can I, dear? It is only three weeks more and then we will take a nice little trip of a few days while Jennie is getting the house ready. Really, dear, you are better!"

"Better in body perhaps—" I began, and stopped short, for he sat up straight and looked at me with such a stern, reproachful look that I could not say another word.

"My darling," said he, "I beg of you, for my sake and for our child's sake, as well as for your own, that you will never for one instant let that idea enter your mind! There is nothing so dangerous, so fascinating, to a temperament like yours. It is a false and foolish fancy. Can you not trust me as a physician when I tell you so?"

So of course I said no more on that score, and we went to sleep before long. He thought I was asleep first, but I wasn't, and lay there for hours trying to decide whether that front pattern and the back pattern really did move together or separately.

On a pattern like this, by daylight, there is a lack of sequence, a defiance of law, that is a constant irritant to a normal mind.

The color is hideous enough, and unreliable enough, and infuriating enough, but the pattern is torturing.

You think you have mastered it, but just as you get well under way in following, it turns a back-somersault and there you are. It slaps you in the face, knocks you down, and tramples upon you. It is like a bad dream.

The outside pattern is a florid arabesque, reminding one of a fungus. If you can imagine a toadstool in joints, an interminable string of toadstools, budding and sprouting in endless convolutions—why, that is something like it.

That is, sometimes!

There is one marked peculiarity about this paper, a thing nobody seems to notice but myself, and that is that it changes as the light changes.

When the sun shoots in through the east window—I always watch for that first long, straight ray—it changes so quickly that I never can quite believe it.

That is why I watch it always.

By moonlight—the moon shines in all night when there is a moon—I wouldn't know it was the same paper.

At night in any kind of light, in twilight, candlelight, lamplight, and worst of all by moonlight, it becomes bars! The outside pattern, I mean, and the woman behind it is as plain as can be.

I didn't realize for a long time what the thing was that showed behind, that dim sub-pattern, but now I am quite sure it is a woman.

By daylight she is subdued, quiet. I fancy it is the pattern that keeps her so still. It is so puzzling. It keeps me quiet by the hour.

I lie down ever so much now. John says it is good for me, and to sleep all I can.

Indeed he started the habit by making me lie down for an hour after each meal.

It is a very bad habit, I am convinced, for you see, I don't sleep.

And that cultivates deceit, for I don't tell them I'm awake—oh, no!

The fact is I am getting a little afraid of John.

He seems very queer sometimes, and even Jennie has an inexplicable look.

It strikes me occasionally, just as a scientific hypothesis, that perhaps it is the paper!

I have watched John when he did not know I was looking, and come into the room suddenly on the most innocent excuses, and I've caught him several times *looking at the paper*! And Jennie too. I caught Jennie with her hand on it once.

She didn't know I was in the room, and when I asked her in a quiet, a very quiet voice, with the most restrained manner possible, what she was doing with the paper, she turned around as if she had been caught stealing, and looked quite angry—asked me why I should frighten her so!

Then she said that the paper stained everything it touched, that she had found yellow smooches on all my clothes and John's and she wished we would be more careful!

Did not that sound innocent? But I know she was studying that pattern, and I am determined that nobody shall find it out but myself!

Life is very much more exciting now than it used to be. You see, I have something more to expect, to look forward to, to watch. I really do eat better, and am more quiet than I was.

John is so pleased to see me improve! He laughed a little the other day, and said I seemed to be flourishing in spite of my wallpaper.

I turned it off with a laugh. I had no intention of telling him it was *because* of the wallpaper—he would make fun of me. He might even want to take me away.

I don't want to leave now until I have found it out. There is a week more, and I think that will be enough.

I'm feeling so much better!

I don't sleep much at night, for it is so interesting to watch developments; but I sleep a good deal during the daytime.

In the daytime it is tiresome and perplexing.

There are always new shoots on the fungus, and new shades of yellow all over it. I cannot keep count of them, though I have tried conscientiously.

It is the strangest yellow, that wallpaper! It makes me think of all the yellow things I ever saw—not beautiful ones like buttercups, but old, foul, bad yellow things.

But there is something else about that paper—the smell! I noticed it the moment we came into the room, but with so much air and sun it was not bad. Now we have had a week of fog and rain, and whether the windows are open or not, the smell is here.

It creeps all over the house.

I find it hovering in the dining-room, skulking in the parlor, hiding in the hall, lying in wait for me on the stairs.

It gets into my hair.

Even when I go to ride, if I turn my head suddenly and surprise it—there is that smell!

Such a peculiar odor, too! I have spent hours in trying to analyze it, to find what it smelled like.

It is not bad—at first—and very gentle, but quite the subtlest, most enduring odor I ever met.

In this damp weather it is awful. I wake up in the night and find it hanging over me.

It used to disturb me at first. I thought seriously of burning the house—to reach the smell.

But now I am used to it. The only thing I can think of that it is like is the *color* of the paper! A yellow smell.

There is a very funny mark on this wall, low down, near the mop-board. A streak that runs round the room. It goes behind every piece of furniture, except the bed, a long, straight, even *smooch,* as if it had been rubbed over and over.

I wonder how it was done and who did it, and what they did it for. Round and round and round—round and round and round—it makes me dizzy!

I really have discovered something at last.

Through watching so much at night, when it changes so, I have finally found out.

The front pattern *does* move—and no wonder! The woman behind shakes it!

Sometimes I think there are a great many women behind, and sometimes only one, and she crawls around fast, and her crawling shakes it all over.

Then in the very bright spots she keeps still, and in the very shady spots she just takes hold of the bars and shakes them hard.

And she is all the time trying to climb through. But nobody could climb through that pattern—it strangles so; I think that is why it has so many heads.

They get through, and then the pattern strangles them off and turns them upside down, and makes their eyes white!

If those heads were covered or taken off it would not be half so bad.

I think that woman gets out in the daytime!

And I'll tell you why—privately—I've seen her!

I can see her out of every one of my windows!

It is the same woman, I know, for she is always creeping, and most women do not creep by daylight.

I see her in that long shaded lane, creeping up and down. I see her in those dark grape arbors, creeping all around the garden.

I see her on that long road under the trees, creeping along, and when a carriage comes she hides under the blackberry vines.

I don't blame her a bit. It must be very humiliating to be caught creeping by daylight!

I always lock the door when I creep by daylight. I can't do it at night, for I know John would suspect something at once.

And John is so queer now that I don't want to irritate him. I wish he would take another room! Besides, I don't want anybody to get that woman out at night but myself.

I often wonder if I could see her out of all the windows at once.

But, turn as fast as I can, I can only see out of one at one time.

And though I always see her, she *may* be able to creep faster than I can turn! I have watched her sometimes away off in the open country, creeping as fast as a cloud shadow in a wind.

If only that top pattern could be gotten off from the under one! I mean to try it, little by little.

I have found out another funny thing, but I shan't tell it this time! It does not do to trust people too much.

There are only two more days to get this paper off, and I believe John is beginning to notice. I don't like the look in his eyes.

And I heard him ask Jennie a lot of professional questions about me. She had a very good report to give.

She said I slept a good deal in the daytime.

John knows I don't sleep very well at night, for all I'm so quiet!

He asked me all sorts of questions, too, and pretended to be very loving and kind.

As if I couldn't see through him!

Still, I don't wonder he acts so, sleeping under this paper for three months.

It only interests me, but I feel sure John and Jennie are affected by it.

Hurrah! This is the last day, but it is enough. John is to stay in town over night, and won't be out until this evening.

Jennie wanted to sleep with me—the sly thing; but I told her I should undoubtedly rest better for a night all alone.

That was clever, for really I wasn't alone a bit! As soon as it was moonlight and that poor thing began to crawl and shake the pattern, I got up and ran to help her.

I pulled and she shook. I shook and she pulled, and before morning we had peeled off yards of that paper.

A strip about as high as my head and half around the room.

And then when the sun came and that awful pattern began to laugh at me, I declared I would finish it today!

We go away tomorrow, and they are moving all my furniture down again to leave things as they were before.

Jennie looked at the wall in amazement, but I told her merrily that I did it out of pure spite at the vicious thing.

She laughed and said she wouldn't mind doing it herself, but I must not get tired.

How she betrayed herself that time!

But I am here, and no person touches this paper but Me—not *alive*!

She tried to get me out of the room—it was too patent! But I said it was so quiet and empty and clean now that I believed I would lie down again and sleep all I could, and not to wake me even for dinner—I would call when I woke.

So now she is gone, and the servants are gone, and the things are gone, and there is nothing left but that great bedstead nailed down, with the canvas mattress we found on it.

We shall sleep downstairs tonight, and take the boat home tomorrow.

I quite enjoy the room, now it is bare again.

How those children did tear about here!

This bedstead is fairly gnawed!

But I must get to work.

I have locked the door and thrown the key down into the front path.

I don't want to go out, and I don't want to have anybody come in, till John comes.

I want to astonish him.

I've got a rope up here that even Jennie did not find. If that woman does get out, and tries to get away, I can tie her!

But I forgot I could not reach far without anything to stand on!

This bed will *not* move!

I tried to lift and push it until I was lame, and then I got so angry I bit off a little piece at one corner—but it hurt my teeth.

Then I peeled off all the paper I could reach standing on the floor. It sticks horribly and the pattern just enjoys it! All those strangled heads and bulbous eyes and waddling fungus growths just shriek with derision!

I am getting angry enough to do something desperate. To jump out of the window would be admirable exercise, but the bars are too strong even to try.

Besides I wouldn't do it. Of course not. I know well enough that a step like that is improper and might be misconstrued.

I don't like to *look* out of the windows even—there are so many of those creeping women, and they creep so fast.

I wonder if they all come out of that wallpaper as I did?

But I am securely fastened now by my well-hidden rope—you don't get *me* out in the road there!

I suppose I shall have to get back behind the pattern when it comes night, and that is hard!

It is so pleasant to be out in this great room and creep around as I please!

I don't want to go outside. I won't, even if Jennie asks me to.

For outside you have to creep on the ground, and everything is green instead of yellow.

But here I can creep smoothly on the floor, and my shoulder just fits in that long smooch around the wall, so I cannot lose my way.

Why, there's John at the door!

It is no use, young man, you can't open it!

How he does call and pound!

Now he's crying to Jennie for an axe.

It would be a shame to break down that beautiful door!

"John, dear!" said I in the gentlest voice. "The key is down by the front steps, under a plantain leaf!"

That silenced him for a few moments.

Then he said, very quietly indeed, "Open the door, my darling!"

"I can't," said I. "The key is down by the front door under a plantain leaf!" And then I said it again, several times, very gently and slowly, and said it so often that he had to go and see, and he got it of course, and came in. He stopped short by the door.

"What is the matter?" he cried. "For God's sake, what are you doing!"

I kept on creeping just the same, but I looked at him over my shoulder.

"I've got out at last," said I, "in spite of you and Jane. And I've pulled off most of the paper, so you can't put me back!"

Now why should that man have fainted? But he did, and right across my path by the wall, so that I had to creep over him every time!

21

QASIM AMIN
(1863–1908)

"The Liberation of Women"
(EGYPT, 1899)

In the late nineteenth century, intellectuals who wished to modernize their countries or free them from colonial rule often championed the education of women. One such reformer, the Egyptian judge Qasim Amin, initiated a debate over the status of women in Islamic cultures that continues to the present. Amin, who had studied in France in the 1880s, defended Egyptian culture from European detractors, but at the same time he questioned the practices of polygamy, veiling, and female seclusion. He favored women's education as a superior path to female virtue. Although Amin valued European principles of human rights, he believed firmly that Islamic law, if properly interpreted, had equal or greater potential for the emancipation of women. Egyptian critics of his 1899 treatise on the liberation of women condemned Amin for imitating European society and endangering Islam. In response, he published The New Woman *(1900), in which he reiterated the importance of women's emancipation to the progress of the nation. In subsequent decades Egyptian women themselves would elaborate on his themes and seek political rights as well as education. Throughout the world, Muslim feminists continue to argue that the Koran requires women's equality.*

I call on every lover of truth to examine with me the status of women in Egyptian society. I am confident that such individuals will arrive independently at the same conclusion I have, namely the necessity of improving the status of Egyptian women. The truth I am presenting today has preoccupied me for a long time; I have considered it, examined it, and analyzed it. When it was eventually stripped of all confounding errors, it occupied an important place in my thinking, rivaled other ideas, overcame them, and finally reached the point where it became my dominant thought, alerting me to its advantages and reminding me of its necessity. I became aware of the absence of a platform from which this truth could be elevated from reflection to the unlimited space of appeal and attention....

This is the basis of our observations. This evidence of history confirms and demonstrates that the status of women is inseparably tied to the status of a nation. When the status of a nation is low, reflecting an uncivilized condition for that nation, the status of women is also low, and when the status of a nation is elevated, reflecting the progress and civilization of that nation, the status of women in that country is also elevated. We have learned that women in the first human societies were treated as slaves. The ancient Greeks and Romans, for example, considered a woman to be under the power of her father, then her husband, and after him his eldest son. The head of the family had the absolute right of ownership over her life. He could dispose of her through trade, donation, or death, whenever and in whatever way he wished. His heirs eventually inherited her and with her all the rights that were given to the owner. Prior to Islam, it was acceptable for Arab fathers to kill their daughters and for men to gratify themselves with women with no legal bonds or numerical limits. This authority still prevails among uncivilized African and American tribes. Some Asians even believe that a woman has no immortal soul and that she should not live after her husband dies. Other Asians present her to their guests as a sign of hospitality, just as one would present a guest with the best of his possessions.

These traits are present among emerging societies, which are based on familial and tribal bonds rather than on formal structures. Force is the only law with which such societies are familiar. The use of force is also the medium of control for governments run by autocratic structures.

On the other hand, we find that women in nations with a more advanced civilization have gradually advanced from the low status to which they have been relegated and have started to overcome the gap that has separated them from men. One woman is crawling while the other is taking steps; one is walking while the other is running. These discrepancies reflect the different societies to which these women belong and the level of civilization of these societies. The American woman is in the forefront, followed by the British, the German, the French, the Austrian, the Italian, and the Russian woman, and so on. Women in all these societies have felt that they deserve their independence, and are searching for the means to achieve it. These women believe that they are human beings and that they deserve freedom, and they are therefore striving for freedom and demanding every human right.

Westerners, who like to associate all good things with their religion, believe that the Western woman has advanced because her Christian religion helped her achieve freedom. This belief, however, is inaccurate. Christianity did not set up a system which guarantees the freedom of women; it does not guarantee her rights through either specific or general rules; and it does not prescribe any guiding principles on this topic. In every country where Christianity has been introduced and spread it has left no tangible impact on the normative structure affecting women's status. On the contrary, Christianity has been molded by the traditions and manners of the specific nations in which it was introduced. If there were a religion which could have had power and influence over local traditions, then the Muslim women today should have been at the forefront of free women on earth.

The Islamic legal system, the Shari'a, stipulated the equality of women and men before any other legal system. Islam declared women's freedom and emancipation, and granted women all human rights during a time when women occupied the lowest status in all societies. According to Islamic law, women are considered to possess the same legal capabilities in all civil cases pertaining to buying, donating, trusteeship, and disposal of goods, unhindered by requirements of permission from either their father or their husband. These advantages have not yet been attained by some contemporary Western women, yet they demonstrate that respect for women and for their equality with men were basic to the principles of the liberal Shari'a. In fact, our legal system went so far in its kindness to women that it rid them of the burden of earning a living and freed them from the obligation of participating in household and child-rearing expenses. This is unlike some Western laws, which equate men and women only with regard to their duties, giving preference to men with regard to societal rights.

Within the Shari'a, the tendency to equate men's and women's rights is obvious, even in the context of divorce. Islam has created for women mechanisms worthy of consideration and contrary to what Westerners and some Muslims imagine or believe. These will be discussed later.

Islamic law favors men in one area only—polygamy. The reason is obvious and is related to the issue of lineage, without which marriage is meaningless. This topic too will be addressed later. In summary, nothing in the laws of Islam or in its intentions can account for the low status of Muslim women. The existing situation is contrary to the law, because originally women in Islam were granted an equal place in human society.

What a pity! Unacceptable customs, traditions, and superstitions inherited from the countries in which Islam spread have been allowed to permeate this beautiful religion. Knowledge in these countries had not developed to the point of giving women the status already given them by the Shari'a....

Despising the woman, a man filled his home with slaves, white or black, or with numerous wives, satisfying himself with any of them whenever his passion and lust drove him. He ignored the prescribed religious obligations, which required good intentions for his actions and justice in his dealings....

An observer might think that I now maintain the veil should be completely dispensed with—but this is not the case. I still defend the use of the veil and consider it one of the PERMANENT CORNERSTONES OF MORALITY. I would recommend, however, that we adhere to its use according to Islamic law, which differs from our present popular traditions. Our people are ostentatious in their caution and in their interpretations of what they believe to be the application of the law, to the extent that they presently exceed the limits of the Shari'a and have harmed the nation's interests.

My observations on this topic also indicate that Westerners have gone too far in the exposure of their women so that it is difficult for a Western woman to guard herself from sensuous desires and unacceptable shameful feelings. We, on the other hand, have gone to extremes in veiling our women and prohibiting them from appearing unveiled before men, to such an extent that we turn women into objects or goods we own. We have deprived them of the mental and cultural advantages that are their natural due as human beings. The legal veil, however, is somewhere between these two extremes....

God created this world and gave human beings mastery over it so that they could enjoy the benefits according to what they can achieve. God granted human beings privileges for administering this world, but He also placed limitations on them. Thus God established equality between men and women regarding their obligations and privileges. God did not divide the universe, making one part of it to be enjoyed by women alone and another to be enjoyed by men, working in it segregated from women. In fact, He created the burdens of life to be shared and controlled by both men and women. How can a woman enjoy all the pleasures, feelings, and power that God created for her, and how can she work in the universe if she is banned from the sight of any man except a blood relative or some other man to whom she cannot be married according to Islamic law? Undoubtedly, this is not what the Shari'a meant, and it should not be allowed by either law or reason. Thus we see that necessity has changed the use of the veil among most classes of Muslims. This is apparent among maids, working women, villagers, and even among Bedouin women. All these women are Muslim—indeed they may be more religious than the city-dwellers....

Furthermore, I do not believe that the veil is a necessary part of desirable behavior for women. There is no basis for such a claim. What is the relation between desirable behavior and exposing or veiling the face of a woman? What is the basis for discriminating against women?

Is not good behavior in reality the same for both men and women? Is it not a product of an individual's intentions and work rather than of external appearances and clothes?

The fear of temptation, addressed by almost every line written on the subject, is a matter close to the hearts of distrustful men. Women should not concern themselves with it nor ask to know anything about it. Whoever fears temptation, whether man or woman, should avert his or her glance. The instructions that appear in the precious verses about averting one's gaze apply to both men and women. This proves clearly that it is no more appropriate for a woman to cover her face than for a man to cover his.

How strange! If men feared that women would be tempted, why were not men ordered to wear the veil and conceal their faces from women? Is a man's will considered weaker than a woman's? Are men to be regarded as weaker than women in controlling their desires? Is a woman considered so much stronger than a man that men have been allowed to show their faces to the eyes of women, regardless of how handsome or attractive they are, while women are forbidden to show their faces to men, from the fear that men's desires may escape the control of their minds, and they may thus be tempted by any woman they see, however ugly or disfigured she be? Any man who claims this viewpoint must then admit that women have a more perfect disposition than men; why then should women always be placed under the protection of men? If however, this viewpoint is incorrect, what justifies this traditional control over women's lives?

The veil and the gauze face-cover actually increase the risk of temptation. The thin, white, gauze face-cover reveals the good features and hides the blemishes; the veil conceals the tip of the nose, the mouth, and the jaws, and reveals the forehead, temples, eyebrows, eyes, cheeks, and sides of the neck. These two coverings are in reality part of the ornaments worn by women that incite an onlooker's desires. They prompt him to wish to discover more of what is concealed after he has been tempted by the large area exposed. If a woman's face were uncovered, it is possible that her total appearance might turn glances away from her.

Temptation is not provoked by exposing some parts of a woman's body. In fact, the main causes of temptation are the revealing movements of a woman's body as she walks and the actions that reflect what is in her mind. The gauze face-cover and the veil, which hide a woman's identity, allow her to reveal what she wishes to reveal and to act in a manner that incites desire. She need not be concerned that anyone might identify her and report that so-and-so, or the wife of so-and-so, was doing such-and-such. She can accomplish whatever she desires under the protection of her veil. If her face were uncovered, her family status or her own honor would restrain her from initiating any provocative behavior that might attract attention to herself.

In truth, the gauze face-cover and the veil are not part of the Shari'a, in terms either of piety or of morality. They have been handed down to us from ancient traditions that preceded Islam and have continued to survive. The proof is that this tradition is unknown in many other Islamic countries, and it is still a custom in many Eastern countries that do not claim Islam as their religion. Covering the bosom is part of Islamic law—there are clear admonitions about this—but nothing is mentioned about covering the face....

Our task now is to identify a remedy for the problems that we anticipate in relaxing women's seclusion. The most effective remedy, in our opinion, is a type of upbringing that will itself become an impenetrable veil and fortress protecting a woman from all forms of corruption at each stage of her liberation.

It may be argued that while a proper upbringing and education will improve a woman's behavior, her independence increases her vulnerability to corruption. I would respond by saying that the freedom we seek is limited and that it still prohibits a woman from being alone with a stranger. This prohibition is sufficient safeguard against corruption, which results primarily from a man and a woman being alone together. Freedom itself can never be harmful, especially when supported by a proper upbringing, which results in strong, independent, and self-directed individuals. A person with an inadequate upbringing becomes dependent on others for every need. Independence for both men and women elevates them from all that is contemptible and despicable. The proper upbringing of women needs to become our primary objective.

A proper upbringing and an independent will are the two universally necessary factors for the progress of men. They are the desired goals of every nation in pursuit of happiness, and they are among the most noble means for attaining the perfection for which a nation is destined. How then can a rational person claim that these two factors would have a negative effect on women? Whoever claims that a proper education and an independent will would corrupt women is shortsighted. Such people do not consider the benefits of these qualities, and have not realized that all good things, when misused, can have flaws!...

Before concluding this discussion, I must state that with the present status of women, I am unable to recommend the total and immediate elimination of seclusion. The reason for this cautious approach is that such a sudden revolution could lead to an increase in the behavior that we consider corrupt and would therefore not achieve the desired goals. What I do recommend, however, is the preparation of our daughters for this change, starting in their childhood. This early preparation will gradually accustom them to independence and to the belief that chastity is an inner spiritual quality, not the result of a garment which hides the body. They will also become accustomed to interacting with men—whether relatives or strangers—while respecting the limits of the Shari'a and conforming to accepted moral principles. These changes, I hope, will take place under the supervision of their guardians. This preparation will eventually facilitate the integration of women with men, with the least negative consequences, except in such unusual cases as spare neither the secluded nor the unsecluded woman!

22.

ROKEYA SAKHAWAT HOSSAIN
(1880–1932)

"Sultana's Dream"
(INDIA, 1905)

In British-ruled India during the nineteenth century, both male and female reformers, such as Rammohun Roy and Pandita Ramabai, drew on Mary Wollstonecraft's ideas to advocate education and property rights for women. The Bengali writer Rokeya Sakhawat Hossain continued this tradition in the early twentieth century. In her elite Muslim family, women lived in the seclusion of purdah and only sons merited schooling. Hossain defied the limits on female education through the tutelage of a brother and the encouragement of her husband, who bequeathed funds so that his young widow could establish a school for girls. In addition to writing a series of articles about the harmful effects of seclusion on Muslim women, in 1905 Hossain published a short story, "Sultana's Dream," in the English-language The Indian Ladies Magazine. *In her utopian world, Ladyland, men rather than women endured purdah (zenana), while women moved freely in a gardenlike society ruled by a queen. A more benign gender reversal than the dystopian fantasy of Li Ju-chen a century earlier, the story predated by a decade Charlotte Perkins Gilman's utopian novel* Herland. *In Hossain's vision, women could make major scientific advances, including control of the climate and the use of solar power to avert war, once they obtained educational opportunities. In addition to her writing, Hossain taught at the girls's school she founded in Calcutta, and in 1916 she established the Muslim Women's Association.*

One evening I was lounging in an easy chair in my bedroom and thinking lazily of the condition of Indian womanhood. I am not sure whether I dozed off or not. But, as far as I remember, I was wide awake. I saw the moonlit sky sparkling with thousands of diamond-like stars, very distinctly.

All on a sudden a lady stood before me; how she came in, I do not know. I took her for my friend, Sister Sara.

"Good morning," said Sister Sara. I smiled inwardly as I knew it was not morning, but starry night. However, I replied to her, saying, "How do you do?"

"I am all right, thank you. Will you please come out and have a look at our garden?"

I looked again at the moon through the open window, and thought there was no harm in going out at that time. The men-servants outside were fast asleep just then, and I could have a pleasant walk with Sister Sara.

I used to have my walks with Sister Sara, when we were at Darjeeling. Many a time did we walk hand in hand and talk light-heartedly in the botanical gardens there. I fancied, Sister Sara had probably come to take me to some such garden and I readily accepted her offer and went out with her.

When walking I found to my surprise that it was a fine morning. The town was fully awake and the streets alive with bustling crowds. I was feeling very shy, thinking I was walking in the street in broad daylight, but there was not a single man visible.

Some of the passers-by made jokes at me. Though I could not understand their language, yet I felt sure they were joking. I asked my friend, "What do they say?"

"The women say that you look very mannish."

"Mannish?" said I, "What do they mean by that?"

"They mean that you are shy and timid like men."

"Shy and timid like men?" It was really a joke. I became very nervous, when I found that my companion was not Sister Sara, but a stranger. Oh, what a fool had I been to mistake this lady for my dear old friend, Sister Sara.

She felt my fingers tremble in her hand, as we were walking hand in hand.

"What is the matter, dear?" she said affectionately. "I feel somewhat awkward," I said in a rather apologizing tone, "as being a purdahnishin woman I am not accustomed to walking about unveiled."

"You need not be afraid of coming across a man here. This is Lady-land, free from sin and harm. Virtue herself reigns here."

By and by I was enjoying the scenery. Really it was very grand. I mistook a patch of green grass for a velvet cushion. Feeling as if I were walking on a soft carpet, I looked down and found the path covered with moss and flowers.

"How nice it is," said I.

"Do you like it?" asked Sister Sara. (I continued calling her "Sister Sara," and she kept calling me by my name.)

"Yes, very much; but I do not like to tread on the tender and sweet flowers."

"Never mind, dear Sultana; your treading will not harm them; they are street flowers."

"The whole place looks like a garden," said I admiringly. "You have arranged every plant so skillfully."

"Your Calcutta could become a nicer garden than this if only your countrymen wanted to make it so."

"They would think it useless to give so much attention to horticulture, while they have so many other things to do."

"They could not find a better excuse," said she with smile.

I became very curious to know where the men were. I met more than a hundred women while walking there, but not a single man.

"Where are the men?" I asked her.

"In their proper places, where they ought to be."

"Pray let me know what you mean by 'their proper places.'"

"O, I see my mistake, you cannot know our customs, as you were never here before. We shut our men indoors."

"Just as we are kept in the zenana?"

"Exactly so."

"How funny," I burst into a laugh. Sister Sara laughed too.

"But dear Sultana, how unfair it is to shut in the harmless women and let loose the men."

"Why? It is not safe for us to come out of the zenana, as we are naturally weak."

"Yes, it is not safe so long as there are men about the streets, nor is it so when a wild animal enters a marketplace."

"Of course not."

"Suppose, some lunatics escape from the asylum and begin to do all sorts of mischief to men, horses and other creatures; in that case what will your countrymen do?"

"They will try to capture them and put them back into their asylum."

"Thank you! And you do not think it wise to keep sane people inside an asylum and let loose the insane?"

"Of course not!" said I laughing lightly.

"As a matter of fact, in your country this very thing is done! Men, who do or at least are capable of doing no end of mischief, are let loose and the innocent women, shut up in the zenana! How can you trust those untrained men out of doors?"

"We have no hand or voice in the management of our social affairs. In India man is lord and master, he has taken to himself all powers and privileges and shut up the women in the zenana."

"Why do you allow yourselves to be shut up?"

"Because it cannot be helped as they as stronger than women."

"A lion is stronger than a man, but it does not enable him to dominate the human race. You have neglected the duty you owe to yourselves and you have lost your natural rights by shutting your eyes to your own interests."

"But my dear sister Sara, if we do everything by ourselves, what will the men do then?"

"They should not do anything, excuse me; they are fit for nothing. Only catch them and put them into the zenana."

"But would it be very easy to catch and put them inside the four walls?" said I. "And even if this were done, would all their business, political and commercial—also go with them into the zenana?"

Sister Sara made no reply. She only smiled sweetly. Perhaps she thought it useless to argue with one who was no better than a frog in a well.

By this time we reached sister Sara's house. It was situated in a beautiful heart-shaped garden. It was a bungalow with a corrugated iron roof. It was cooler and nicer than any of our rich buildings. I cannot describe how neat and how nicely furnished and how tastefully decorated it was.

We sat side by side. She brought out of the parlour a piece of embroidery work and began putting on a fresh design.

"Do you know knitting and needle work?"

"Yes; we have nothing else to do in our zenana."

"But we not trust our zenana members with embroidery!" she said laughing, "as a man has not patience enough to pass thread through a needle hole even!"

"Have you done all this work yourself?" I asked her pointing to the various pieces of embroidered teapoy cloths.

"Yes."

"How can you find time to do all these? You have to do the office work as well? Have you not?"

"Yes. I do not stick to the laboratory all day long. I finish my work in two hours."

"In two hours! How do you manage? In our land the officers, magistrates—for instance, work seven hours daily."

"I have seen some of them doing their work. Do you think they work all the seven hours?"

"Certainly they do!"

"No, dear Sultana, they do not. They dawdle away their time in smoking. Some smoke two or three choroots during the office time. They talk much about their work, but do little. Suppose one choroot takes half an hour to burn off, and a man smokes twelve choroots daily; then you see, he wastes six hours every day in sheer smoking."

We talked on various subjects, and I learned that they were not subject to any kind of epidemic disease, nor did they suffer from mosquito bites as we do. I was very much astonished to hear that in Ladyland no one died in youth except by rare accident.

"Will you care to see our kitchen?" she asked me.

"With pleasure," said I, and we went to see it. Of course the men had been asked to clear off when I was going there. The kitchen was situated in a beautiful vegetable garden. Every creeper, every tomato plant was itself an ornament. I found no smoke, nor any chimney either in the kitchen—it was clean and bright; the windows were decorated with flower gardens. There was no sign of coal or fire.

"How do you cook?" I asked.

"With solar heat," she said, at the same time showing me the pipe, through which passed the concentrated sunlight and heat. And she cooked something then and there to show me the process.

"How did you manage to gather and store up the sun heat?" I asked her in amazement.

"Let me tell you a little of our past history then. Thirty years ago, when our present Queen was thirteen years old, she inherited the throne. She was Queen in name only, the Prime Minister really ruling the country.

"Our good Queen liked science very much. She circulated an order that all the women in her country should be educated. Accordingly a number of girls' schools were founded and supported by the government. Education was spread far and wide among women. And early marriage also was stopped. No woman was to be allowed to marry before she was twenty-one. I must tell you that, before this change we had been kept in strict purdah."

"How the tables are turned," I interposed with a laugh.

"But the seclusion is the same," she said. "In a few years we had separate universities, where no men were admitted."

"In the capital, where our Queen lives, there are two universities. One of these invented a wonderful balloon, to which they attached a number of pipes. By means of this captive balloon which they managed to keep afloat above the cloud-land, they could draw as much water from the atmosphere as they pleased. As the water was incessantly being drawn by the university people no cloud gathered and the ingenious Lady Principal stopped rain and storms thereby."

"Really! Now I understand why there is no mud here!" said I. But I could not understand how it was possible to accumulate water in the pipes. She explained to me how it was done, but I was unable to understand her, as my scientific knowledge was very limited. However, she went on.

"When the other university came to know of this, they became exceedingly jealous and tried to do something more extraordinary still. They invented an instrument by which they could collect as much sun-heat as they wanted. And they kept the heat stored up to be distributed among others as required.

"While the women were engaged in scientific research, the men of this country were busy increasing their military power. When they came to know that the female universities were able to draw water from the atmosphere and collect heat from the sun, they only laughed at the members of the universities and called the whole thing 'a sentimental nightmare'!"

"Your achievements are very wonderful indeed! But tell me, how you managed to put the men of your country into the zenana. Did you entrap them first?"

"No."

"It is not likely that they would surrender their free and open air life of their own accord and confine themselves within the four walls of the zenana! They must have been overpowered."

"Yes, they have been!"

"By whom? By some lady warriors, I suppose?"

"No, not by arms."

"Yes, it cannot be so. Men's arms are stronger than women's. Then?"

"By brain."

"Even their brains are bigger and heavier than women's. Are they not?"

"Yes, but what of that? An elephant also has got a bigger and heavier brain than a man has. Yet man can enchain elephants and employ them, according to their own wishes."

"Well said, but tell me please, how it all actually happened. I am dying to know it!"

"Women's brains are somewhat quicker than men's. Ten years ago, when the military officers called our scientific discoveries 'a sentimental nightmare,' some of the young ladies wanted to say something in reply to those remarks. But both the Lady Principals restrained them and said, they should reply not by word, but by deed, if ever they got the opportunity. And they had not long to wait for that opportunity."

"How marvelous!" I heartily clapped my hands. "And now the proud gentlemen are dreaming sentimental dreams themselves."

"Soon afterwards certain persons came from a neighbouring

country and took shelter in ours. They were in trouble having committed some political offense. The king who cared more for power than for good government asked our kind-hearted Queen to hand them over to his officers. She refused, as it was against her principle to turn out refugees. For this refusal the king declared war against our country.

"Our military officers sprang to their feet at once and marched out to meet the enemy.

"The enemy however, was too strong for them. Our soldiers fought bravely, no doubt. But in spite of all their bravery the foreign army advanced step by step to invade our country.

"Nearly all the men had gone out to fight; even a boy of sixteen was not left home. Most of our warriors were killed, the rest driven back and the enemy came within twenty-five miles of the capital.

"A meeting of a number of wise ladies was held at the Queen's palace to advise as to what should be done to save the land.

"Some proposed to fight like soldiers; others objected and said that women were not trained to fight with swords and guns, nor were they accustomed to fighting with any weapons. A third party regretfully remarked that they were hopelessly weak of body.

" 'If you cannot save your country for lack of physical strength,' said the Queen, 'try to do so by brain power.'

"There was a dead silence for a few minutes. Her Royal Highness said again, 'I must commit suicide if the land and my honour are lost.'

"Then the Lady Principal of the second university (who had collected sun-heat), who had been silently thinking during the consultation, remarked that they were all but lost, and there was little hope left for them. There was, however, one plan which she would like to try, and this would be her first and last efforts; if she failed in this, there would be nothing left but to commit suicide. All present solemnly vowed that they would never allow themselves to be enslaved, no matter what happened.

"The Queen thanked them heartily, and asked the Lady Principal to try her plan.

"The Lady Principal rose again and said, 'before we go out the men must enter the zenanas. I make this prayer for the sake of purdah.' 'Yes, of course,' replied Her Royal Highness.

"On the following day the Queen called upon all men to retire into zenanas for the sake of honour and liberty.

"Wounded and tired as they were, they took that order rather for a boon! They bowed low and entered the zenanas without uttering a single word of protest. They were sure that there was no hope for this country at all.

"Then the Lady Principal with her two thousand students marched to the battle field, and arriving there directed all the rays of the concentrated sunlight and heat towards the enemy.

"The heat and light were too much for them to bear. They all ran away panic-stricken, not knowing in their bewilderment how to counteract that scorching heat. When they fled away leaving their guns and other ammunitions of war, they were burnt down by means of the same sun heat.

"Since then no one has tried to invade our country any more."

"And since then your countrymen never tried to come out of the zenana?"

"Yes, they wanted to be free. Some of the police commissioners and district magistrates sent word to the Queen to the effect that the military officers certainly deserved to be imprisoned for their failure; but they never neglected their duty and therefore they should not be punished and they prayed to be restored to their respective offices.

"Her Royal Highness sent them a circular letter intimating to them that if their services should ever be needed they would be sent for, and that in the meanwhile they should remain where they were.

"Now that they are accustomed to the purdah system and have ceased to grumble at their seclusion, we call the system 'Murdana' instead of 'zenana.'"

"But how do you manage," I asked Sister Sara, "to do without the police or magistrates in case of theft or murder?"

"Since the 'Murdana' system has been established, there has been no more crime or sin; therefore we do not require a policeman to find out a culprit, nor do we want a magistrate to try a criminal case."

"That is very good, indeed. I suppose if there was any dishonest person, you could very easily chastise her. As you gained a decisive victory without shedding a single drop of blood, you could drive off crime and criminals too without much difficulty!"

"Now, dear Sultana, will you sit here or come to my parlour?" she asked me.

"Your kitchen is not inferior to a queen's boudoir!" I replied with a pleasant smile, "but we must leave it now; for the gentlemen may be cursing me for keeping them away from their duties in the kitchen so long." We both laughed heartily.

"How my friends at home will be amused and amazed, when I go back and tell them that in the far-off Ladyland, ladies rule over the country and control all social matters, while gentlemen are kept in the Murdanas to mind babies, to cook and to do all sorts of domestic work; and that cooking is so easy a thing that it is simply a pleasure to cook!"

"Yes, tell them about all that you see here."

"Please let me know, how you carry on land cultivation and how you plough the land and do other hard manual work."

"Our fields are tilled by means of electricity, which supplies motive power for other hard work as well, and we employ it for our aerial conveyances too. We have no rail road nor any paved streets here."

"Therefore neither street nor railway accidents occur here," said I. "Do not you ever suffer from want of rainwater?" I asked.

"Never since the 'water balloon' has been set up. You see the big balloon and pipes attached thereto. By their aid we can draw as much rainwater as we require. Nor do we ever suffer from flood or thunderstorms. We are all very busy making nature yield as much as she can. We do not find time to quarrel with one another as we never sit idle. Our noble Queen is exceedingly fond of botany; it is her ambition to convert the whole country into one grand garden."

"The idea is excellent. What is your chief food?"

"Fruits."

"How do you keep your country cool in hot weather? We regard the rainfall in summer as a blessing from heaven."

"When the heat becomes unbearable, we sprinkle the ground with plentiful showers drawn from the artificial fountains. And in cold weather we keep our room warm with sun heat."

She showed me her bathroom, the roof of which was removable. She could enjoy a shower bath whenever she liked, by simply removing the roof (which was like the lid of a box) and turning on the tap of the shower pipe.

"You are a lucky people!" ejaculated I. "You know no want. What is you religion, may I ask?"

"Our religion is based on Love and Truth. It is our religious duty to love one another and to be absolutely truthful. If any person lies, she or he is...."

"Punished with death?"

"No, not with death. We do not take pleasure in killing a creature of God, especially a human being. The liar is asked to leave this land for good and never to come to it again."

"Is an offender never forgiven?"

"Yes, if that person repents sincerely."

"Are you not allowed to see any man, except your own relations?"

"No one except sacred relations."

"Our circle of sacred relations is very limited; even first cousins are not sacred."

"But ours is very large; a distant cousin is as sacred as a brother."

"That is very good. I see purity itself reigns over your land. I should like to see the good Queen, who is so sagacious and far-sighted and who has made all these rules."

"All right," said Sister Sara.

Then she screwed a couple of seats onto a square piece of plank. To this plank she attached two smooth and well-polished balls. When I asked her what the balls were for, she said they were hydrogen balls and they were used to overcome the force of gravity. The balls were of different capacities to be used according to the different weights desired to be overcome. She then fastened to the air-car two wing-like blades, which, she said, were worked by electricity. After we were comfortably seated she touched a knob and the blades began to whirl, moving faster and faster every moment. At first we were raised to the height of about six or seven feet and then off we flew. And before I could realize that we had commenced moving, we reached the garden of the Queen.

My friend lowered the air-car by reversing the action of the machine, and when the car touched the ground the machine was stopped and we got out.

I had seen from the air-car the Queen walking on a garden path with her little daughter (who was four years old) and her maids of honour.

"Halloo! You here!" cried the Queen addressing Sister Sara. I was introduced to Her Royal Highness and was received by her cordially without any ceremony.

I was very much delighted to make her acquaintance. In the course of the conversation I had with her, the Queen told me that she had no objection to permitting her subjects to trade with other countries. "But," she continued, "no trade was possible with countries where the women were kept in the zenanas and so unable to come and trade with us. Men, we find, are rather of lower morals and so we do not like dealing with them. We do not covet other people's land, we do not fight for piece of diamond though it may be a thousand-fold brighter than the Koh-i-Noor, nor do we grudge a ruler his peacock throne. We dive deep into the ocean of knowledge and try to find out the precious gems, which Nature has kept in store for us. We enjoy Nature's gifts as much as we can."

After taking leave of the Queen, I visited the famous universities, and was shown some of their manufactories, laboratories and observatories.

After visiting the above places of interest we got again into the aircar, but as soon as it began moving, I somehow slipped down and the fall startled me out of my dream. And on opening my eyes, I found myself in my own bed lounging in the easy chair!

23.

QIU JIN
(1875–1907)

Stones of the Jingwei Bird
(CHINA, 1905–07)

Just as earlier democratic revolutions and abolitionist campaigns in-
spired demands for women's rights, twentieth-century nationalist move-
ments stimulated feminism. One of the revolutionaries who wished to free
China from foreign domination, Qiu Jin believed that liberating women
from social constraints would further the nationalist project. From her
childhood she had rebelled against female socialization and embraced in-
tellectual over domestic pursuits. Although she married and had two chil-
dren, in 1904 Qiu Jin left her family to study in Japan, where she joined
a women's political group and began publishing her revolutionary views.
When she returned to China she published a short-lived women's news
journal and began writing in a form of vernacular fiction known as tanci
(storyteller's tales) about heroines who sought to end women's oppression.
Stones of the Jingwei Bird *mixed story and song to reach the masses*
of women, most of whom were illiterate. In the preface Qiu Jin expressed
her goals of elevating women from servility to men and replacing their
slavish devotion to beauty with intellectual aspirations, invoking strong
women of the past as models. The title of the narrative refers to a mythi-
cal bird that tried to fill the ocean with pebbles. Qiu Jin could only begin
to contribute to this formidable task. Before completing her tale she was
arrested for participating in a failed uprising against the Chinese gov-
ernment and was executed at age thirty-two.

I live in an era of transition. Taking advantage of the light of the dawning civilization and the paltry knowledge I possess, I have thrown off the yokes of the past. Yet I am often pained that my sister compatriots remain in a World of Darkness, as though drunk or dreaming, oblivious to the changes around them. Even though there are now schools for women, few enroll in them. Let me ask you, of our twenty million women, how many still grovel at the feet of tyrannical men? Alas, today they continue to powder and paint themselves, chatter about their hairdos and bind their feet, adorn their heads with gold and pearls, and drape their bodies in brocade. Toadying for favor, they ingratiate themselves to men—obeying their commands like horses or cows. They are no more than the servile and shameless playthings of men. But though they are subjected to immeasurable oppression, they are unaware of their pain; though suffer abuse and humiliation, they have no shame. They are completely blind and ignorant, saying with idiotic serenity: this is our fate. They feel no disgrace in begging like slaves and groveling on their knees. Instead of supporting their compatriots, they stand on the sidelines obeying their husbands and sons and opposing those who build schools and factories for women. Then there are those delicate ladies of noble families, with their fancy houses and fine appearances, their piles of pearls and gold, who willingly worship stupid temple idols and fatten the Buddhist monks and nuns to pray for their happiness, yet when they see other women who are engulfed in suffering, they don't even offer a helping hand. Alas! Do they feel no compassion?

I continued to be baffled by this situation until, after long reflection, I suddenly awoke. Now I declare: wherever there are women, are there not also heroines, philanthropists, and exceptional individuals to be found? I am not referring to those women in scholarly circles, for they have already been nurtured by civilization. But are there not also heroines even within the World of Darkness? Unfortunately, women suffer from ignorance and limited experience, and thus no matter how many books they may have in their possession, they have a hard time understanding what they mean. For this reason, I have composed this *tanci* in plain language, hoping that all women will comprehend its content and that it will enable them to leave the darkness behind and ascend to the civilized realm. I have tried my best to write systematically about the demeaning realities of women's existence, about their suffering and shame, in hopes of startling my readers, making them aware of their own shortcomings, and rousing them to further enlighten our women's world.

Every day I burn incense, praying that women will emancipate themselves from their slavish confines and arise as heroines and female gallants on the stage of liberty, following in the footsteps of Madame Roland, Anita, Sophia Perofskaya, Harriet Beecher Stowe, and Joan of Arc. With all my heart, I beseech and beg my twenty million female compatriots to assume their responsibility as citizens. Arise! Arise! Chinese women, arise!

I lament that the Chinese motherland has descended into darkness. How can we bear to have our magnificent rivers and mountains swallowed up by foreign races? We forty million heirs of the Chinese motherland are but slaves, useless to the bone. We willingly cower before others and seek glory by ingratiating ourselves to them. Fortunately, among us loyal subjects have been reincarnated who will rebuild this entire nation from scratch.

But the pathetic world of women remains without glory, complacently awaiting death amid these seas of sorrow, these cities of sadness. Forgotten are the unwavering courage of Mulan and the heroic spirit of Hongyu. However, the winds of Europe and the rains of America are suddenly surging forth and are beginning to revive such spirits. Chinese women will throw off their shackles and stand up with passion; they will all become heroines. They will ascend the stage of the new world, where the heavens have mandated that they reconsolidate the nation.

24

EMMA GOLDMAN
(1869–1940)

"The Tragedy of Woman's Emancipation"
(UNITED STATES, 1906)

A leading anarchist and feminist, Emma Goldman emigrated from Lithuania to the United States in 1886, inspired by the lives of Russian revolutionaries of the late nineteenth century to escape from her authoritarian father. Like other young Jewish women she earned low wages in a garment factory, but unlike most of her peers she rejected marital life for political activism. After 1900 Goldman earned a national reputation as an effective anarchist writer and speaker, drawing large crowds to her lectures on topics including free speech, modern drama, and contraception. Goldman championed the freedom of the individual and rejected state or corporate control. At a time when most women reformers concentrated on education, employment, and suffrage, Goldman considered these goals far too narrow. She demanded sexual and reproductive emancipation as well, including access to contraceptive information. The Red Scare in the United States after World War I cut short her influence in her adopted country. Arrested for her anticonscription activities during World War I, in 1919 she was deported to Russia but chose to live in exile in France. Goldman's critique of established institutions, as well as her insights into the "internal tyrants" of social convention that inhibited women, foreshadowed the politics of personal life articulated by feminists after the 1960s.

I begin my article with an admission: Regardless of all political and economic theories, treating of the fundamental differences between the various groups within the human race, regardless of class and race distinctions, regardless of all artificial boundary lines between woman's rights and man's rights, I hold that there is a point where these differentiations may meet and grow into one perfect whole.

With this I do not mean to propose a peace treaty. The general social antagonism which has taken hold of our entire public life to-day, brought about through the force of opposing and contradictory interests, will crumble to pieces when the reorganization of our social life, based upon the principles of economic justice, shall have become a reality.

Peace and harmony between the sexes and individuals does not necessarily depend on a superficial equalization of human beings; nor does it call for the elimination of individual traits or peculiarities. The problem that confronts us to-day, and which the nearest future is to solve, is how to be oneself, and yet in oneness with others, to feel deeply with all human beings and still retain one's own innate qualities. This seems to me the basis upon which the mass and the individual, the true democrat and the true individuality, man and woman can meet without antagonism and opposition. The motto should not be forgive one another; it should be, understand one another. The oft-quoted sentence of Mme. de Staël: "To understand everything means to forgive everything," has never particularly appealed to me; it has the odor of the confessional; to forgive one's fellow being conveys the idea of pharisaical superiority. To understand one's fellow being suffices. This admission partly represents the fundamental aspect of my views on the emancipation of woman and its effect upon the entire sex.

Emancipation should make it possible for her to be human in the truest sense. Everything within her that craves assertion and activity should reach its fullest expression; and all artificial barriers should be broken and the road towards greater freedom cleared of every trace of centuries of submission and slavery.

This was the original aim of the movement for woman's emancipation. But the results so far achieved have isolated woman and have robbed her of the fountain springs of that happiness which is so essential to her. Merely external emancipation has made of the modern woman an artificial being who reminds one of the products of French arboriculture with its arabesque trees and shrubs—pyramids, wheels and wreaths; anything except the forms which would be reached by the expression of their own inner qualities. Such artificially grown plants of the female sex are to be found in large numbers, especially in the so-called intellectual sphere of our life.

Liberty and equality for woman! What hopes and aspirations these words awakened when they were first uttered by some of the noblest and bravest souls of those days. The sun in all its light and glory was to rise upon a new world; in this world woman was to be free to direct her own destiny, an aim certainly worthy of the great enthusiasm, courage, perseverance and ceaseless effort of the tremendous host of pioneer men and women, who staked everything against a world of prejudice and ignorance.

My hopes also move towards that goal, but I insist that the emancipation of woman, as interpreted and practically applied to-day, has failed to reach that great end. Now, woman is confronted with the necessity of emancipating herself from emancipation, if she really desires to be free. This may sound paradoxical, but is, nevertheless, only too true.

What has she achieved through her emancipation? Equal suffrage in a few states. Has that purified our political life, as many well-meaning advocates have predicted? Certainly not. Incidentally it is really time that persons with plain, sound judgment should cease to talk about corruption in politics in a boarding-school tone. Corruption of politics has nothing to do with the morals or the laxity of morals of various political personalities. Its cause is altogether a material one. Politics is the reflex of the business and industrial world, the mottoes of which are: "to take is more blessed than to give"; "buy cheap and sell dear"; "one soiled hand washes the other." There is no hope that even woman, with her right to vote, will ever purify politics.

Emancipation has brought woman economic equality with man;

that is, she can choose her own profession and trade, but as her past and present physical training have not equipped her with the necessary strength to compete with man, she is often compelled to exhaust all her energy, use up her vitality and strain every nerve in order to reach the market value. Very few ever succeed, for it is a fact that women doctors, lawyers, architects and engineers are neither met with the same confidence, nor do they receive the same remuneration. And those that do reach that enticing equality generally do so at the expense of their physical and psychical well-being. As to the great mass of working girls and women, how much independence is gained if the narrowness and lack of freedom of the home is exchanged for the narrowness and lack of freedom of the factory, sweatshop, department store, or office? In addition is the burden which is laid on many women of looking after a "home, sweet home"—cold, dreary, disorderly, uninviting—after a day's hard work. Glorious independence! No wonder that hundreds of girls are so willing to accept the first offer of marriage, sick and tired of their independence behind the counter, or at the sewing or typewriting machine. They are just as ready to marry as girls of middle class people who long to throw off the yoke of parental dependence. A so-called independence which leads only to earning the merest subsistence is not so enticing, not so ideal that one can expect woman to sacrifice everything for it. Our highly praised independence is, after all, but a slow process of dulling and stifling woman's nature, her love instinct and her mother instinct.

Nevertheless, the position of the working girl is far more natural and human than that of her seemingly more fortunate sister in the more cultured professional walk of life. Teachers, physicians, lawyers, engineers, etc., who have to make a dignified, straightened and proper appearance, while the inner life is growing empty and dead.

The narrowness of the existing conception of woman's independence and emancipation; the dread of love for a man who is not her social equal; the fear that love will rob her of her freedom and independence; the horror that love or the joy of motherhood will only hinder her in the full exercise of her profession—all these together make of the emancipated modern woman a compulsory vestal, before whom life, with its great clarifying sorrows and its deep, entrancing joys, rolls on without touching or gripping her soul.

Emancipation as understood by the majority of its adherents and exponents, is of too narrow a scope to permit the boundless joy and ecstasy contained in the deep emotion of the true woman, sweetheart, mother, in freedom.

The tragic fate of the self-supporting or economically free woman does not consist of too many, but of too few experiences. True, she surpasses her sister of past generations in knowledge of the world and human nature; and it is because of that that she feels deeply the lack of life's essence, which alone can enrich the human soul and without which the majority of women have become mere professional automatons....

True, the movement for woman's rights has broken many old fetters, but it has also established new ones. The great movement of true emancipation has not met with a great race of women, who could look liberty in the face. Their narrow puritanical vision banished man as a disturber and doubtful character out of their emotional life. Man was not to be tolerated at any price, except perhaps as the father of a child, since a child could not very well come to life without a father. Fortunately, the most rigid puritanism never will be strong enough to kill the innate craving for motherhood. But woman's freedom is closely allied to man's freedom, and many of my so-called emancipated sisters seem to overlook the fact that a child born in freedom needs the love and devotion of each human being about him, man as well as woman. Unfortunately, it is this narrow conception of human relations that has brought about a great tragedy in the lives of the modern man and woman....

Time and again it has been conclusively proven that the old matrimonial relation restricted woman to the function of man's servant and the bearer of his children. And yet we find many emancipated women who prefer marriage with all its deficiencies to the narrowness of an unmarried life; narrow and unendurable because of the chains of moral and social prejudice that cramp and bind her nature.

The cause for such inconsistency on the part of many advanced women is to be found in the fact that they never truly understood the meaning of emancipation. They thought that all that was needed was independence from external tyrannies; the internal tyrants, far more harmful to life and growth, such as ethical and social conventions, were left to take care of themselves; and they have taken care of themselves. They seem to get along beautifully in the heads and hearts of the most active exponents of woman's emancipation, as in the heads and hearts of our grandmothers.

These internal tyrants, whether they be in the form of public opinion or what will mother say, or brother, father, aunt or relative of any sort; what will Mrs. Grundy, Mr. Comstock, the employer, the Board of Education say? All these busybodies, moral detectives, jailers of the human spirit, what will they say? Until woman has learned to defy them all, to stand firmly on her own ground and to insist upon her own unrestricted freedom, to listen to the voice of her nature, whether it call for life's greatest treasure, love for a man, or her most glorious privilege, the right to give birth to a child, she cannot call herself emancipated. How many emancipated women are brave enough to acknowledge that the voice of love is calling, wildly beating against their breasts demanding to be heard, to be satisfied....

Salvation lies in an energetic march onward towards a brighter and clearer future. We are in need of unhampered growth out of old traditions and habits. The movement for woman's emancipation has so far made but the first step in that direction. It is to be hoped that it will gather strength to make another. The right to vote, equal civil rights, are all very good demands, but true emancipation begins neither at the polls nor in courts. It begins in woman's soul. History tells us that every oppressed class gained its true liberation from its masters through its own efforts. It is necessary that woman learn that lesson, that she realize that her freedom will reach as far as her power to achieve her freedom reaches. It is therefore far more important for her to begin with her inner regeneration, to cut loose from the weight of prejudices, traditions, and customs. The demand for various equal rights in every vocation in life is just and fair, but, after all, the most vital right is the right to love and be loved. Indeed if the partial emancipation is to become a complete and true emancipation of woman, it will have to do away with the ridiculous notion that to be loved, to be sweetheart and mother, is synonymous with being slave or subordinate. It will have to do away with the absurd notion of the dualism of the sexes, or that man and woman represent two antagonistic worlds.

Pettiness separates, breadth unites. Let us be broad and big. Let us not overlook vital things, because of the bulk of trifles confronting us. A true conception of the relation of the sexes will not admit of conqueror and conquered; it knows of but one great thing: to give of one's self boundlessly in order to find oneself richer, deeper, better. That alone can fill the emptiness and replace the tragedy of woman's emancipation with joy, limitless joy.

25.

Alexandra Kollontai
(1872–1952)

"The Social Basis of the Woman Question"
(RUSSIA, 1909)

Although they differed in their evaluations of free love, Emma Goldman and Alexandra Kollontai both questioned the limitations of bourgeois feminism. Kollontai echoed the Marxist view of the woman question first articulated by August Bebel and Friedrich Engels. Like her mentor Clara Zetkin, who led the German Social Democratic women's movement, Kollontai differentiated the politics of working-class women from those who sought equal rights and suffrage. She argued that only a socialist revolution against capitalism could provide the economic security and state support for child care that would enable working women to be emancipated. In this essay Kollontai questions whether socialists, who offer a materialist explanation of women's oppression, can find common cause with bourgeois feminists, who seek mere legal reforms. After the Bolshevik Revolution of 1917, Vladimir Lenin appointed Kollontai to the post of commissar for social welfare. She decreed free maternity care as well as equal work responsibilities for women in the USSR and fostered communal child rearing in schools and nurseries. Kollontai also supported abortion and divorce. Her influence was short-lived, however. After Lenin's death the Soviets reversed most of her policies. As in other communist nations, Soviet women worked for wages, some in professional jobs, but they remained responsible for child and family care, with minimal social support.

The followers of historical materialism reject the existence of a special woman question separate from the general social question of our day. Specific economic factors were behind the subordination of women; natural qualities have been a secondary factor in this process. Only the complete disappearance of these factors, only the evolution of those forces which at some point in the past gave rise to the subjection of women, is able in a fundamental way to influence and change their social position. In other words, women can become truly free and equal only in a world organised along new social and productive lines....

However apparently radical the demands of the feminists, one must not lose sight of the fact that the feminists cannot, on account of their class position, fight for that fundamental transformation of the contemporary economic and social structure of society without which the liberation of women cannot be complete.

If in certain circumstances the short-term tasks of women of all classes coincide, the final aims of the two camps, which in the long term determine the direction of the movement and the tactics to be used, differ sharply. While for the feminists the achievement of equal rights with men in the framework of the contemporary capitalist world represents a sufficiently concrete end in itself, equal rights at the present time are, for the proletarian women, only a means of advancing the struggle against the economic slavery of the working class. The feminists see men as the main enemy, for men have unjustly seized all rights and privileges for themselves, leaving women only chains and duties. For them a victory is won when a prerogative previously enjoyed exclusively by the male sex is conceded to the "fair sex." Proletarian women have a different attitude. They do not see men as the enemy and the oppressor; on the contrary, they think of men as their comrades, who share with them the drudgery of the daily round and fight with them for a better future. The woman and her male comrade are enslaved by the same social conditions; the same hated chains of capitalism oppress their will and deprive them of the joys and charms of life. It is true that several specific aspects of the contemporary system lie with double weight upon women, as it is also true that the conditions of hired labour sometimes turn working women into competitors and rivals to men. But in these unfavourable situations, the working class knows who is guilty....

In face of the growing social difficulties, the sincere fighter for the cause must stop in sad bewilderment. She cannot but see how little the general women's movement has done for proletarian women, how incapable it is of improving the working and living conditions of the working class. The future of humanity must seem grey, drab and uncertain to those women who are fighting for equality but who have not adopted the proletarian world outlook or developed a firm faith in the coming of a more perfect social system. While the contemporary capitalist world remains unchanged, liberation must seem to them incomplete and impartial. What despair must grip the more thoughtful and sensitive of these women. Only the working class is capable of maintaining morale in the modern world with its distorted social relations. With firm and measured step it advances steadily towards its aim. It draws the working women to its ranks. The proletarian woman bravely starts out on the thorny path of labour. Her legs sag; her body is torn. There are dangerous precipices along the way, and cruel beasts of prey are close at hand.

But only by taking this path is the woman able to achieve that distant but alluring aim—her true liberation in a new world of labour. During this difficult march to the bright future the proletarian woman, until recently a humiliated, downtrodden slave with no rights, learns to discard the slave mentality that has clung to her; step by step she transforms herself into an independent worker, an independent personality, free in love. It is she, fighting in the ranks of the proletariat, who wins for women the right to work; it is she, the "younger sister," who prepares the ground for the "free" and "equal" woman of the future.

For what reason, then, should the woman worker seek a union with the bourgeois feminists? Who, in actual fact, would stand to gain in the event of such an alliance? Certainly not the woman worker. She is her own saviour; her future is in her own hands. The working woman guards her class interests and is not deceived by great speeches about the "world all women share." The working woman must not and does not forget that while the aim of bourgeois women is to secure their own welfare in the framework of a society antagonistic to us, our aim is to build, in the place of the old, outdated world, a bright temple of universal labour, comradely solidarity and joyful freedom....

The struggle for political rights, for the right to receive doctorates and other academic degrees, and for equal pay for equal work, is not the full sum of the fight for equality. To become really free woman has to throw off the heavy chains of the current forms of the family, which are outmoded and oppressive. For women, the solution of the family question is no less important than the achievement of political equality and economic independence.

In the family of today, the structure of which is confirmed by custom and law, woman is oppressed not only as a person but as a wife and mother. In most of the countries of the civilised world the civil code places women in a greater or lesser dependence on her husband, and awards the husband not only the right to dispose of her property but also the right of moral and physical dominance over her....

The feminists are struggling for freer forms of marriage and for the "right to maternity"; they are raising their voices in defence of the prostitute, the human being persecuted by all. See how rich feminist literature is in the search for new forms of relationships and in enthusiastic demands for the "moral equality" of the sexes. Is it not true that while in the sphere of economic liberation the bourgeois women lag behind the many-million-strong army of proletarian women who are pioneering the way for the "new woman," in the fight for the solution of the family question the laurels go to the feminists?...

The heroic struggle of individual young women of the bourgeois world, who fling down the gauntlet and demand of society the right to "dare to love" without orders and without chains, ought to serve as an example for all women languishing in family chains—this is what is preached by the more emancipated feminists abroad and our progressive equal righters at home. The marriage question, in other words, is solved in their view without reference to the external situation; it is solved independently of changes in the economic structure of society. The isolated, heroic efforts of individuals is enough. Let a woman simply "dare," and the problem of marriage is solved.

But less heroic women shake their heads in distrust. "It is all very well for the heroines of novels blessed by the prudent author with great independence, unselfish friends and extraordinary qualities of charm, to throw down the gauntlet. But what about those who have no capital, insufficient wages, no friends and little charm?" And the question of maternity preys on the mind of the woman who strives for freedom. Is "free love" possible? Can it be realised as a common phenomenon, as the generally accepted norm rather than the individual exception, given the economic structure of our society? Is it possible to ignore the element of private property in contemporary marriage? Is it possible, in an individualistic world, to ignore the formal marriage contract without damaging the interests of women? For the marital contract is the only guarantee that all the difficulties of maternity will not fall on the woman alone. Will not that which once happened to the male worker now happen to the woman? The removal of guild regulations, without the establishment of new rules governing the conduct of the masters, gave capital absolute power over the workers. The tempting slogan "freedom of contract for labour and capital" became a means for the naked exploitation of labour by capital. "Free love," introduced consistently into contemporary class society, instead of freeing woman from the hardships of family life, would surely shoulder her with a new burden—the task of caring, alone and unaided, for her children.

Only a whole number of fundamental reforms in the sphere of social relations—reforms transposing obligations from the family to society and the state—could create a situation where the principle of "free love" might to some extent be fulfilled. But can we seriously expect the modern class state, however democratic it may be, to take upon itself the duties towards mothers and children which at present are undertaken by that individualistic unit, the modern family? Only the fundamental transformation of all productive relations could create the social prerequisites to protect women from the negative aspects of the "free love" formula. Are we not aware of the depravity and abnormalities that in present conditions are anxious to pass themselves off under this convenient label? Consider all those gentlemen owning and administering industrial enterprises who force women among their workforce and clerical staff to satisfy their sexual whims, using the threat of dismissal to achieve their ends. Are they not, in their own way, practising "free love"? All those "masters of the house" who rape their servants and throw them out pregnant on to the street, are they not adhering to the formula of "free love"?

"But we are not talking of that kind of 'freedom,'" object the advocates of free marriage. "On the contrary, we demand the acceptance of a 'single morality' equally binding for both sexes. We oppose the sexual licence that is current, and view as moral only the free union that is based on true love." But, my dear friends, do you not think that your ideal of "free marriage," when practised in the conditions of present society, might produce results that differ little from the distorted practice of sexual freedom? Only when women are relieved of all those material burdens which at the present time create a dual dependence, on capital and on the husband, can the principle of "free love" be implemented without bringing new grief for women in its wake....

The feminists declare themselves to be on the side of social reform, and some of them even say they are in favour of socialism—in the far distant future, of course—but they are not intending to struggle in the ranks of the working class for the realisation of these aims. The best of them believe, with a naive sincerity, that once the deputies' seats are within their reach they will be able to cure the social sores which have in their view developed because men, with their inherent egoism, have been masters of the situation. However good the intentions of individual groups of feminists towards the proletariat, whenever the question of class struggle has been posed they have left the battlefield in a fright. They find that they do not wish to interfere in alien causes, and prefer to retire to their bourgeois liberalism which is so comfortably familiar.

No, however much the bourgeois feminists try to repress the true aim of their political desires, however much they assure their younger sisters that involvement in political life promises immeasurable benefits for the women of the working class, the bourgeois spirit that pervades the whole feminist movement gives a class colouring even to the demand for equal political rights with men, which would seem to be a general women's demand. Different aims and understandings of how political rights are to be used create an unbridgeable gulf between bourgeois and proletarian women. This does not contradict the fact that the immediate tasks of the two groups of women coincide to a certain degree, for the representatives of all classes which have received access to political power strive above all to achieve a review of the civil code, which in every country, to a greater or lesser extent, discriminates against women. Women press for legal changes that create more favourable conditions of labour for themselves; they stand together against the regulations legalising prostitution etc. However, the coincidence of these immediate tasks is of a purely formal nature. For class interest determines that the attitude of the two groups to these reforms is sharply contradictory....

Thus, when the feminists talk to working women about the need for a common struggle to realise some "general women's" principle, women of the working class are naturally distrustful.

26

THREE POEMS

The theme of women breaking free from old constraints in order to assert newfound energies recurs across international borders in the early twentieth century, particularly within the contexts of democratic, revolutionary, and labor movements. In the southwestern United States, women of Mexican origin, such as Sara Estela Ramírez, supported the Mexican revolution, published newspapers, plays, and poems, and formed feminist organizations. Ramírez's poem "Rise Up! To Woman" invokes powerful female figures but urges women to transcend the roles of goddess and queen in order to engage actively in the world. In Japan, Yosano Akiko rejected the traditional authority of the emperor and contributed to the feminist periodical Bluestocking, *a term earlier used to describe educated European women. A major modern Japanese poet, in 1911 she captured the spirit of women's uprising in "The Day the Mountains Move," which inspired feminists internationally throughout the twentieth century. The same year, moved by the strikes staged in northeastern American cities by women factory workers, the journalist James Oppenheim wrote "Bread and Roses." The refrain expresses a socialist feminist vision of a full life for all workers. The poem originally appeared in a popular magazine, but the title phrase soon adorned the picket signs of women strikers and, when set to music, the song became an anthem of the American labor movement.*

Sara Estela Ramírez
(1881–1910)

"Rise Up! To Woman"

(UNITED STATES, 1910)

Rise up! Rise up to life, to activity, to
the beauty of truly living; but rise up radiant
and powerful, beautiful with qualities, splendid
with virtues, strong with energies.

You, the queen of the world, Goddess of
universal adoration; you, the sovereign to whom
homage is paid, do not confine yourself so to
your temple of God, nor to your triumphant
courtesan's chamber.

That is unworthy of you, before Goddess
or Queen, be a mother, be a woman.

One who is truly a woman is more than
a goddess or queen. Do not let the incense on
the altar, or the applause in the audience
intoxicate you, there is something more noble
and more grand than all of that.

Gods are thrown out of temples; kings
are driven from their thrones, woman is
always woman.

Gods live what their followers want.
Kings live as long as they are not dethroned;
woman always lives and this is the secret of
her happiness, to live.

Only action is life; to feel that one lives
is the most beautiful sensation.

Rise up, then, to the beauties of life;
but rise up so, beautiful with qualities,
splendid with virtues, strong with energies.

Yosano Akiko

(1878–1942)

"The Day the Mountains Move"

(JAPAN, 1911)

The day the mountains move has come.
I speak, but no one believes me.
For a time the mountains have been asleep,
But long ago they all danced with fire.
It doesn't matter if you believe this,
My friends, as long as you believe:
All the sleeping women
Are now awake and moving.

James Oppenheim
(1882–1932)

"Bread and Roses"
(UNITED STATES, 1911)

As we come marching, marching, in the beauty of the day,
A million darkened kitchens, a thousand mill lofts gray
Are touched with all the radiance that a sudden sun discloses
For the people hear us singing, "Bread and Roses, Bread and Roses."

As we come marching, marching, we battle too for men—
For they are women's children, and we mother them again.
Our lives shall not be sweated from our birth until life closes—
Hearts starve as well as bodies: Give us Bread but give us Roses.

As we come marching, marching, unnumbered women dead
Go crying through our singing their ancient song of Bread;
Small art and love and beauty their drudging spirits knew—
Yes it is bread we fight for—but we fight for Roses, too.

As we come marching, marching, we bring the Greater Days—
The rising of the women means the rising of the race—
No more the drudge and idler—ten that toil while one reposes—
But a sharing of life's glories: Bread and Roses, Bread and Roses.

27.

Luisa Capetillo
(1879–1922)

Mi opinión

(PUERTO RICO, 1911)

Incorporating both liberal calls for women's education and socialist analyses of class oppression, Luisa Capetillo envisioned a universal liberation across the lines of gender and class. Born in Puerto Rico to a working-class family that valued education highly, she labored in cigar factories in Puerto Rico, Florida, and New York, becoming a valued "reader" of news and fiction to her co-workers. Along with organizing factory and farm workers and supporting woman suffrage, Capetillo wrote for the labor press. She published a magazine for working-class women as well as several books expounding her political ideas. While she linked women's emancipation to the fate of the working class, like Emma Goldman she recognized as well the unique constraints on women's sexual and reproductive lives. Capetillo advocated free love and bore three children outside marriage. Reflecting the views of her generation, however, she devalued lesbianism as inferior to heterosexual relationships. Out of print between 1913 and 2004, Mi opinión *was one of the first feminist texts to appear in the Caribbean.*

Nowadays, all this talk about the "silence and seclusion of woman" is unacceptable because today the European woman aspires to public office, to government, to administering towns, without losing her feminine personality, nor her motherly and wifely duties.

The author of "Modern Women in the Family" believes "that it is good that the modern woman prove that she knows how to study on par with men in order to acquire an academic degree, that she knows how to handle the surgeon's scalpel, the naturalist's microscope, and the engraver's burin, all of which demonstrates how erroneous is the theory of female mental inferiority. It is good that a woman demonstrates that she knows how to carry out the duties of public office with as much skill as a man; that one's capacity, consciousness, and loyalty in fulfilling obligations are not the sole privilege of the stronger sex, and that she knows how to support herself and also her husband."

It is has been said countless times, that women in the public sphere and workplace would lose ground, jeopardizing their home, their family and their children!

But those who think in this way forget that the lady of high and well-off position goes to the stores, visits friends, museums and theaters, and dressmakers and the home is left alone, her children with the servants or their nannies only. The mothers see their children for only a moment, they give them a kiss, and go out again, and this is their daily routine.

There is never enough time for their boudoir, or for courtesy calls, for the dressmaker, and for strolls along the Pardo or the Prado, the Bois de Boulogne, or the Champs Elysées. All those strolls are done at just the right time so that the woman can be seen there and satisfy their vanity and follow the fashion. How is it that the husbands of these elegant ladies neither care nor bother to find out if their home and children are jeopardized left in this continual solitude? The children don't see the mother at any moment. In these cases it would be more useful if she would devote herself to studying or choose a job that would give her the means to be more useful. Women possess a high degree of sagacious insight, promptness, and good administrative sense. Why not perform some administrative positions?

Why should one think that home life will be in jeopardy by women working?

Is home life not jeopardized when a woman does not want to breast feed her child, or when she doesn't want to accompany her husband to the theater, because she went to church to confess? And isn't the family jeopardized when she occupies her day in church, social visits, and strolls? But the home is not jeopardized when the woman contributes with her talent and activities to the development of nations.

And the working class woman who leaves her children at home in order to tend those of the rich, and who works in factories and workshops, doesn't she jeopardize her home?

The working-class home, the peasant and his wife, who abandons her home and has no one to leave behind to care for the children, and who returns home to find her child burned in an accident, this home is not in jeopardy?

So they say it endangers the household! It endangers the family! Women are confused, mistaken for men! But this is the home of the wealthy, the family of the aristocrat! It is the highborn lady!

But what about the poor home, the working class family, does it not harm itself? The unhappy servant or peasant woman who rents herself out to breastfeed the son of the wealthy and who must abandon her own children, doesn't she suffer? Doesn't she have natural feelings? The poor woman who must push a cart in the mines, mixed in with male workers, who goes and comes back alone, does not become a man. And neither do the women who go off to work the land. No way! These people are made of bronze, and are tempered by adversity! The poor wife of a sugar mill or road worker, who only makes 50 or 60 cents a day and who does not make enough to look after four or six children whom she has to dress and cannot, so to help out she washes others' clothes and does odd jobs, and thus leaves her children unattended, doesn't she bring harm on herself? . . .

A woman whose husband owns a sugar mill or hacienda and calls herself a Spiritist or Christian should not seek to load herself down with jewelry, nor make useless purchases. She should visit the families of her peons, who produce the wealth she and her husband possess and who continue increasing it, and observe how they live, if they lack items that are useful or necessary, like chairs, beds, and other utensils. And she should notice if their roof doesn't leak, and if the inhabitants can live in the the house in sanitary conditions, that it is sufficiently clean so that she would want to live there herself.

After visiting their peons, she should explain to her husband the state and conditions of these unfortunate souls that produce her family's capital and obtain a salary increase for them, and she should do so discreetly and frugally instead of using fancy garments and other useless adornments on her body or in her home. She should go to them consoling and healing the sad homes of those victims of exploitation. Take them clothes, footwear, books and attempt to instruct them by reading to them and by making sure that there are schools in the neighborhood to educate the children of these employees.

How beautiful and comely she would be, woman sowing goodness, fulfilling her obligation to humanity!

What brilliant flashes of light would illuminate her soul!

How sweet and free of vexation would be her life!

The woman who begins to practice these actions and establish a modicum of fraternity and social equality, would elevate herself to a level so far above human mean-spiritedness and egotism, that her name would be inscribed in everyone's consciousness and she would occupy a sacred place in every heart that worshipped her. And in her future, what would await her? Her deeds of love and justice would blaze a shining path would lead her to enjoy the fruits of the good she had sown.

Woman, you are able to sow justice and are willing to do so; do not be upset, nor get upset, do not become restless, do not flee; move forward! And for the good of future generations place the first stone of the edifice for social equality serenely and resolutely, with all the rights that pertain to you, without bowing your head, since you are no longer the material and intellectual slave you once were. Your initiative will be crowned by success, being achieved by your own efforts, and your soul will be luminous and beautiful like a sun of truth and justice.

Woman of wealth! You can redeem your exploited brothers. Redeem them and the glory of heaven will be yours!

And if you find opposition from your husband, if he is cruel and egotistical and becomes an obstacle to your great and just aspirations, do not blame him and do not fear him; because in him, you will see the symbol of ignorance, trying to hold on to its power.

Do not fear him and continue marching forward because, like Isabel of Hungary, your contributions will become beautiful and perfumed roses that will lighten your step and will save you the displeasure of contradicting your tyrant.

Oh woman! you will set a great and dignified example by breaking all traditional customs, which are unjust and tyrannical, the symbols of ignorance, in order to establish the realm of Freedom, Equality, and Fraternity, symbols of truth and justice!

Do not fear criticism, nor mockery and scorn, they are the howls of impotence, rise up, rise up, higher, higher! Like Jesus at Calvary and seek the redemption of the Puerto Rican proletariat, which will be the preface to universal redemption!...

I cannot explain why a man always feels he has rights over a woman. For example, a young man, regardless of age, always aspires to form a bond with a young virgin without life experience. Although he has tasted and enjoyed all types of pleasures and knows of all types of vices, he thinks it perfectly natural to form a bond with a young woman who is temperate and honest.

This is what has been allowed by social formulas. Rather, this is what we women have tolerated, because of our supposed weakness that we have always been accused of.

When I have time to contemplate a young man wooing a young woman, and I focus on their respective physiognomies, I marvel and protest that this man dare do to court her when he is not of the same moral stature as she. He is all withered and worn, she is beautiful, enticing, and chaste, and even so, he finds that he bestows a great favor on the woman in marrying her.

We women have to change this system, we have to transform these customs. No woman should accept a man who is not up to her moral stature; and if men do not want give up these practices, they will have to agree in bestowing upon us the same liberties.

It is ridiculous, stupid that a couple in love with each other cannot belong to each other physically because decrepit formulisms call it immoral, or that when they separate, the man goes off to satiate his pent-up passion with another woman, and the girl masturbates or has sexual "relations" with another woman, thereby atrophying her mind and jeopardizing her beauty. This is criminal, odious, and shameful, against nature, and the parents are responsible. What is natural is that this man and this woman fulfill their love by making use of the rights that nature has given them, without stupid fears.

What would be natural is that when the man develops fully and feels the need to search for a companion, he choose someone pleasing to him and, if she accepts him, the two make their nest and create a family, without preambles or silliness. This would be ideal, the sublime and correct thing, what nature ordains. Man and woman belong to each other as virgins, and in this manner there would be no fears of prostitution or adultery.

A man should not make use of his sexual urges until he has reached full development, and then he searches for a beloved, takes her home and creates a family.

With this kind of practice we would have a healthy, strong, robust, and happy generation.

No man should be with a woman other than she whom he will choose to create a family. Then we could speak of good manners, of morality, but in the shape we are in, all of us prostituted, speaking of morality is ironic, idiotic, and useless. . . .

28.

EMMELINE PANKHURST
(1858–1928)

Suffrage Speech at the Old Bailey
(ENGLAND, 1912)

Even as middle-class women in western Europe and the United States gained access to education and equal property rights, the suffrage movement continued to elicit strong resistance. Both men and women feared that enfranchising women would lead to family disorder and political instability. In the early twentieth century, after decades of lobbying male legislators, suffragists escalated their campaigns. In England, the Women's Social and Political Union (WSPU), founded in 1903 by Emmeline Pankhurst, attracted large crowds at suffrage demonstrations and adopted the militant tactics of the Irish independence movement. Under the creed "Deeds, Not Words" they destroyed property, went to prison, endured forced feeding, and gained media attention for their cause. Their methods influenced young feminists from the United States, such as Alice Paul, who introduced militance into the American suffrage movement after 1914. During her 1912 trial for conspiracy to incite destruction of property, Emmeline Pankhurst used her address at the Old Bailey criminal court to publicize the history of British women's political exclusion and to justify militance as a last resort. Although they convicted Pankhurst, along with her codefendants Frederick and Emmeline Pethick-Lawrence, the jurors unanimously added a rider to the verdict asking the court to exercise clemency, given the "undoubtedly pure motives that underlie the agitation that has led to this trouble."

I will try to make you understand what it is that has brought a woman no longer young into this dock.... After the passing of the Reform Act of 1867 women imagined—and, I think, had good reason to imagine—that that enfranchising Act would entitle women to register as Parliamentary voters. The great Reform Act of 1832, which has been referred to in this case because it was characteristic of very great violence on the part of men, enfranchised a great many men, but, at the same time, excluded women from the franchise because the word "male" was used for the first time in history. In regard to the word "male," it made it impossible for the woman to be registered, and women maintained that while it was enfranchisement for men it was disenfranchisement for women....

So, gentlemen, in this Court, Mrs. Pethick Lawrence and I are persons to be punished, but we are not persons to have any voice in making the laws which we may break, and which we may be punished for breaking. That was the decision—the final decision—that we must pay our taxes, we must obey laws; but when it comes to choosing the men who impose the taxes and make the laws, we have no legal existence; we have no right to help choose these men.... It has an intimate bearing upon this question of violence on the part of the members of the Women's Social and Political Union.

The year before last I was convicted with other women for having gone to the House of Commons with a petition in my hand, insisting upon going to the door of the House of Commons, and insisting on my right to remain there until my petition was received.... It was decided, as in 1867 ... that we had not the right to insist upon presenting this petition. We had the right to petition, and we had the right to present petitions, but if the person to whom we wished to present them would not receive them, we could not present them. So we were acting illegally in insisting upon the right to present. I want to say here, my lord, that had these judges in 1909 decided that women had the right to petition there would have been no organised violence, there would have been no stone-throwing in this agitation. It was because the women were made to feel that they had no hope in the law—in the consciences of specious politicians—that there was no one to whom to appeal, that the women said, "Well, this is a belated agitation; it is the twentieth century, when these things were supposed to be settled; but we have got to fight out the weary fight as women, and get this question settled somehow as best we can. . . ."

A very great many women have tried to do this useful public work to show that they were fit for the rights and responsibilities of citizenship—as fit as some drunken loafer who neglects his family, but who, because he is a man and has the necessary qualification, is entitled to decide not only his own fate and the fate of other men, but the fate of women and children as well. All this I did, and at the end of it— since there is no distinction in sex where brains are concerned—at the end of it all I was forced to the conclusion that so far as our enfranchisement was concerned, we had been wasting time. I found that men would say that you were not unfit for the vote, and that if all women were like you they would have no objection to giving you the vote. Oh! we women, who have done the dirty work of the political parties, have never had any reason to complain that our services have not been appreciated personally. But some of us came to realise that after all this appreciation we were blacklegs, as the working men call it— blacklegs to our own sex, and so some of us decided that a time had come when this became a sort of reproach to us, which we could not endure any longer. . . .

We founded the Women's Social and Political Union in 1903. Our first intention was to try and influence the particular political Party, which was then coming into power, to make this question of the enfranchisement of women their own question and to push it. It took some little time to convince us—and I need not weary you with the history of all that has happened—but it took some little time to convince us that that was no use; that we could not secure things in that way. Then in 1905 we faced the hard facts. We realised that there was a Press boycott against Women's Suffrage. Our speeches at public meetings were not reported, our letters to the editors were not published, even if we implored the editors; even the things relating to Women's Suffrage in Parliament were not recorded. They said the subject was not of sufficient public interest to be reported in the Press, and they were not prepared to report it. Then with regard to the men politicians in 1905: we realised how shadowy were the fine phrases about democracy, about human equality, used by the gentlemen who were then coming into power. They meant to ignore the women—there was no doubt whatever about that. For in the official documents coming from the Liberal party on the eve of the 1905 election, there were sentences like this: "What the country wants is a simple measure of Manhood Suffrage." There was no room for the inclusion of women. We knew perfectly well that if there was to be franchise reform at all, the Liberal party which was then coming into power did not mean Votes for Women, in spite of all the pledges of members; in spite of the fact that a majority of the House of Commons, especially on the Liberal side, was pledged to it—it did not mean that they were going to put it into practice. And so we found some way of forcing their attention to this question.

Now I come to the facts with regard to militancy. We realised that the plans we had in our minds would involve great sacrifice on our part, that it might cost us all we had. We were at that time a little organisation, composed in the main of working women, the wives and daughters of working men. And my daughters and I took a leading part, naturally, because we thought the thing out, and, to a certain extent, because we were of better social position than most of our members, and we felt a sense of responsibility....

Then came the election of 1905, and the first of the acts which, my lord, can by any stretch of imagination be described as militant.... The first act was the going to a great Liberal demonstration in the Free Trade Hall, Manchester, of two girls with a little banner, made on my dining-room table, with the inscription, "Votes for Women," and asking Sir Edward Grey, the speaker, not "Are you in favour of Woman's Suffrage?" but, "Will the Liberal Government when it takes office give women the Vote?" For asking that question, just as men would have asked it, but with more respect for order than men would have shown ... for insisting upon an answer to that question when the speech was finished, these girls were treated with violence and flung out of the meeting; and when they held a protest meeting in the street they were arrested, and were sent to prison, one for a week as a common criminal, and the other for three days. That was the so-called militancy. I ask you, gentlemen, whether, if that had been done by men, the word militant would have borne any construction but one of determination and earnestness and insistence upon having that question answered. As long as they had a chance of putting questions, even if they were thrown out after having asked them, women were content to do nothing more. Then, these gentlemen developed a desire to catch trains; they rushed away from their meetings directly their speeches were finished, and the women got no opportunity of putting their questions. . . .

The next step the women took was to ask questions during the course of meetings, because, as I told you, these gentlemen gave them no opportunity of asking them afterwards. And then began the interjections of which we have heard, the interference with the right to hold public meetings, the interference with the right of free speech, of which we have heard, for which these women, these hooligan women, as they have been called—have been denounced. I ask you, gentlemen, to imagine the amount of courage which it needs for a woman to undertake that kind of work. When men come to interrupt women's meetings, they come in gangs, with noisy instruments, and sing and shout together, and stamp their feet. But when women have gone to Cabinet Ministers' meetings—only to interrupt Cabinet Ministers and nobody else—they have gone singly. . . .

[In 1908 I] addressed that meeting in the Caxton Hall, and then, as on many other occasions, I explained why I was hoping that the Prime Minister would receive us. I said there comes a time when movements may outgrow the people who start them. There comes a time when people who desire that everything shall be orderly, suddenly may fail, and I felt so seriously that day that that time was rapidly coming, my lord, that I earnestly hoped, and I put it in my speech, that members of the Government, although we were only women, would see us, would hear us, and would look for themselves, and not merely look to the columns of the newspapers which excluded all references to the magnitude of this agitation.

What was the result? I only got a few yards from the Caxton Hall when I was arrested. I had a petition in one hand; I had a little bunch of lilies in the other hand. And the other women who were with me were no more armed than I was. We were arrested. Next day we were taken before the magistrate, and in consequence of that act I suffered my first imprisonment of six weeks in Holloway Gaol. . . .

Now it has been stated in this Court that it is not the Women's So-

cial and Political Union that is in the Court, but that it is certain defendants. The action of the Government, gentlemen, is certainly
against the defendants who are before you here to-day, but it is also
against the Women's Social and Political Union. The intention is to
crush that organisation....

They thought that if they put out of the way the influential members of the organisation they, as one member of the Cabinet, I believe,
said, would crush the movement and get it "on the run." Well, Governments have many times been mistaken, gentlemen, and I venture
to suggest to you that Governments are mistaken again. I think the answer to the Government was given at the Albert Hall meeting held
immediately after our arrest. Within a few minutes, without the elo-
quence of Mrs. Pethick Lawrence, without the appeals of the people
who have been called the leaders of this movement, in a very few minutes ten thousand pounds was subscribed for the carrying on of this
movement....

I may, as a woman, say one word more. We say in England that
every man is tried by his peers. I might have been justified as a woman,
if at the opening of this case I had said you are not entitled to try me
for this offence. What right have you, as men, to judge women? Who
gave you that right, women having no voice in deciding the legal system of this country, no voice in saying what is a crime and what is not
a crime? But in this Court I have not made that plea, and I have consented to be tried by this Court, and I think you will agree with me
that the right of judgment of a Court depends upon consent. I have
consented, and consented merely because I believe this trial marks the
last in this hard struggle women are making for recognition. I feel that
women, who have now, as they always have had, to perform the ordinary duties of citizenship are now going to win some power to fix the
condition of their sex and decide their duties, and I feel it all the more
because this Government, which has instituted proceedings against
us, is a Government dealing more with the lives of mankind than any
Government which ever ruled this country. Year by year, and month
by month, the fate of women is decided. How they are to live, their relationships with children, the marriage laws under which they are
joined in union and pledge their affections—these great questions are
being settled, and also will be settled. And so, my lord, I feel it is a
great advantage, though it is at the risk of our liberty, that we are un-

dergoing this trial. And referring, gentlemen, to what I said about your right to try me, I might tell you of a case—and that is my last word—of a young girl who was put on her trial for her life before a great Irish judge not long ago. And the judge said to those who were responsible for her being there, Where was the man? There was nothing in the law to make the father of that child responsible for the murder of the child for which the girl was being tried. But the judge said: "I will not try that child till the participator of her guilt is in the dock with her," and that case was never tried by that jury at all; but was adjourned till the father of the child also stood in the dock. If we are guilty of this of-fence, this conspiracy, other people, some of the members of His Majesty's Government, should be in the dock by our side. But I do not ask you to say that you will not sentence us until they are by our side, though I do suggest that members of His Majesty's Government and Opposition have used language at least as inflammatory and danger-ous as ourselves, and I think in justice, while these people set us such an example, the verdict of this Court in our case should be one of Not Guilty.

29

Women's International League for Peace and Freedom

Resolutions of the Zurich Conference

(1919)

With the outbreak of World War I in 1914, international suffrage and reform organizations, which had been meeting since the late 1880s, suspended their annual conferences. In 1915, Aletta Jacobs of Holland, along with pacifists from Germany, England, and the United States, convened an International Congress of Women at The Hague to work for world peace. Women, they believed, shared an aversion to war and favored alternatives to violence. More than a thousand delegates pledged to resist and prevent war and to urge their governments to seek reconciliation. American social reformer Jane Addams presided over the congress and the new organization that emerged, the Women's International League for Peace and Freedom (WILPF). Meeting in Zurich in 1919, WILPF condemned the Treaty of Versailles, which ended World War I, for imposing punitive reparations that would "only lead to future wars." The group also criticized the newly established League of Nations for failing to address the underlying causes of war. In resolutions presented to "the powers in Paris" who negotiated the Treaty, WILPF advocated the rights of women, workers, Jews, and racial minorities. Although largely ignored at the time, their resolutions presage many of the doctrines adopted at the founding of the United Nations after World War II. Two WILPF leaders were awarded the Nobel Prize for Peace, Jane Addams in 1931 and Emily Greene Balch in 1946.

The Peace Conference is urged to insert in the Peace Treaty the following Women's Charter:

The Contracting Parties recognize that the status of women, social, political and economic, is of supreme international importance.

They hold that the natural relation between men and women is that of interdependence and cooperation and that it is injurious to the community to restrict women to a position of dependence, to discourage their education or development, or to limit their opportunities.

They hold that the recognition of women's service to the world not only as wage earners but as mothers and homemakers is an essential factor in the building up of the world's peace.

They recognize that differences in social development and tradition make strict uniformity with respect to the status of women difficult of immediate attainment. But, holding as they do, that social progress is dependent upon the status of the women in the community, they think that there are certain principles which all communities should endeavor to apply.

Among these principles the following seem to the Contracting Parties to be of special and urgent importance:

a. That suffrage should be granted to women and their equal status with men upon legislative and administrative bodies, both national and international, recognized.

b. That women, equally with men, should have the protection of the law against slavery such as still exists in some parts of Eastern Europe, Asia and Africa.

c. That on marriage a woman should have full personal and civil rights, including the right to use and disposal of her own earnings and property, and should not be under the tutelage of her husband.

d. That the mother should have the same right of guardianship of her children as the father.

e. That a married woman should have the same right to retain and change her nationality as a man.

f. That all opportunities for education should be open to both sexes.

g. That women should have the same opportunity for training and for entering industries and profession as men.

h. That women should receive the same pay as men for the same work.

i. That the traffic in women should be suppressed, the regulation of vice abolished and the equal moral standard recognized.

j. That the responsibility not only of the mother, but also of the father, of a child born out of wedlock should be recognized.

k. That there should be adequate economic provision for the service of motherhood.

l. That no political or industrial quarrel should deprive the mother of food for her children.

Without claiming that these principles are complete, the Contracting Parties are of opinion, that they are well fitted to guide the policy of the League of Nations, and that if adopted by the communities which are Members of the League, they will confer lasting benefits upon the whole world....

PEACE AND LIBERTY

Consent and Coercion.

Since the test of the civilization of a State is the extent to which it relies upon moral appeal and consent rather than coercion, the International Congress of Women affirms that it should be the aim of all government to replace coercion by consent and cooperation, and with this object in view to educate and strengthen the free will of the people by democratic institutions, the safeguarding of the rights of minorities, and the strict limitation of the power of the States.

Peaceful Methods in Revolutionary Movements.

The world is facing wide-spread revolutionary changes at a time when the habit of violence has been fostered by a world war.

This International Congress of Women recognizes that there is a fundamentally just demand underlying most of these revolutionary movements and declares its sympathy with the purpose of the workers who are rising up everywhere to make an end of exploitation and to claim their world. Nevertheless the women of the Congress reassert their faith in methods of peace and believe it is their special part in this revolutionary age to counsel against violence from any side. . . .

Race Equality.

We believe no human being should be deprived of an education, prevented from earning a living, debarred from any legitimate pursuit in which he wishes to engage, or be subjected to any humiliation, on account of race or colour. We recommend that members of this Congress should do everything in their power to abrogate laws and change customs which lead to discrimination against human beings on account of race or colour.

The Jews.

We hold that no restriction should be placed on the civil or political rights of the Jews because of their race.

Deportations.

Mass deportations have become a world-wide phenomenon since 1914, and inflict suffering and death in many forms upon innocent people. The Women's International League for Peace and Freedom recommends that this subject should receive attention at the earliest possible moment. The expulsion of thousands of innocent people cannot be treated as an internal affair of any of the nations concerned.

Rights of Asylum.

Several freedom-loving nations, which had for centuries distinguished themselves by affording asylum to refuges and exile have, since 1914, reversed their age-long enlightened policy. We therefore recommend to our National Sections that they urge upon their Governments the re-establishment of the rights of asylum, and the repeal of all laws which endanger or abolish it.

Rejection of War as a Means of Settling Differences between Peoples.

This International Congress of Women abides by the principle laid down by the Women's Congress at the Hague in 1915, that we do not admit war as a means of settling differences between peoples.

International Organisation of Women Against War.

This International Congress of Women, recognizing that a strike of women against war of all kinds can only be effective if taken up internationally, urges the National Sections to work for an international agreement between women to refuse their support of war in money, work, or propaganda.

30.

W.E.B. Du Bois
(1868–1963)

"The Damnation of Women"
(UNITED STATES, 1919)

The leading African American intellectual of the twentieth century, W.E.B. Du Bois was raised in the North and educated at Harvard and in Europe. As a historian and sociologist he explored black social and cultural life in America, while as an activist he helped found the National Association for the Advancement of Colored People in 1909 and edited its journal, The Crisis. *After World War I Du Bois increasingly embraced a pan-African politics and Marxian analysis. In 1908 he was one of the first black male intellectuals to publicly support the revived woman suffrage movement. In this 1919 essay, which builds on the earlier ideas of Anna Julia Cooper, Du Bois recognizes the particular burdens faced by African American women and insists that they have a right to both economic independence and motherhood. He also extols their inherent beauty and criticizes internal hierarchies of lightness in terms that anticipate the cultural movements of the 1960s.*

The world wants healthy babies and intelligent workers. Today we refuse to allow the combination and force thousands of intelligent workers to go childless at a horrible expenditure of moral force, or we damn them if they break our idiotic conventions. Only at the sacrifice of intelligence and the chance to do their best work can the majority of modern women bear children. This is the damnation of women.

All womanhood is hampered today because the world on which it is emerging is a world that tries to worship both virgins and mothers and in the end despises motherhood and despoils virgins.

The future woman must have a life work and economic independence. She must have knowledge. She must have the right of motherhood at her own discretion. The present mincing horror at free womanhood must pass if we are ever to be rid of the bestiality of free manhood; not by guarding the weak in weakness do we gain strength, but by making weakness free and strong.

The world must choose the free woman or the white wraith of the prostitute. Today it wavers between the prostitute and the nun. Civilization must show two things: the glory and beauty of creating life and the need and duty of power and intelligence. This and this only will make the perfect marriage of love and work.

> God is Love,
> Love is God;
> There is no God but Love
> And Work is His Prophet!

All this of woman,—but what of black women?

The world that wills to worship womankind studiously forgets its darker sisters. They seem in a sense to typify that veiled Melancholy:

> "Whose saintly visage is too bright
> To hit the sense of human sight,
> And, therefore, to our weaker view
> O'er-laid with black." ...

As I look about me today in this veiled world of mine, despite the noisier and more spectacular advance of my brothers, I instinctively feel and know that it is the five million women of my race who really count. Black women (and women whose grandmothers were black) are today furnishing our teachers; they are the main pillars of those social settlements which we call churches; and they have with small doubt raised three-fourths of our church property. If we have today, as seems likely, over a billion dollars of accumulated goods, who shall say how much of it has been wrung from the hearts of servant girls and washerwomen and women toilers in the fields? As makers of two million homes these women are today seeking in marvelous ways to show forth our strength and beauty and our conception of the truth.

In the United States in 1910 there were 4,931,882 women of Negro descent; over twelve hundred thousand of these were children, another million were girls and young women under twenty, and two and a half-million were adults. As a mass these women were unlettered,— a fourth of those from fifteen to twenty-five years of age were unable to write. These women are passing through, not only a moral, but an economic revolution. Their grandmothers married at twelve and fifteen, but twenty-seven per cent of these women today who have passed fifteen are still single.

Yet these black women toil and toil hard. There were in 1910 two and a half million Negro homes in the United States. Out of these homes walked daily to work two million women and girls over ten years of age,—over half of the colored female population as against a fifth in the case of white women. These, then, are a group of workers, fighting for their daily bread like men; independent and approaching economic freedom! They furnished a million farm laborers, 80,000 farmers, 22,000 teachers, 600,000 servants and washerwomen, and 50,000 in trades and merchandizing.

The family group, however, which is the ideal of the culture with which these folk have been born, is not based on the idea of an economically independent working mother. Rather its ideal harks back to the sheltered harem with the mother emerging at first as nurse and homemaker, while the man remains the sole breadwinner. What is the inevitable result of the clash of such ideals and such facts in the colored group? Broken families.

Among native white women one in ten is separated from her husband by death, divorce, or desertion. Among Negroes the ratio is one in seven. Is the cause racial? No, it is economic, because there is the same high ratio among the white foreign-born. The breaking up of the present family is the result of modern working and sex conditions and it hits the laborers with terrible force. The Negroes are put in a peculiarly difficult position, because the wage of the male breadwinner is below the standard, while the openings for colored women in certain lines of domestic work, and now in industries, are many. Thus while toil holds the father and brother in country and town at low wages, the sisters and mothers are called to the city. As a result the Negro women outnumber the men nine or ten to eight in many cities, making what Charlotte Gilman bluntly calls "cheap women."

What shall we say to this new economic equality in a great laboring class? Some people within and without the race deplore it. "Back to the homes with the women," they cry, "and higher wage for the men." But how impossible this is has been shown by war conditions. Cessation of foreign migration has raised Negro men's wages, to be sure—but it has not only raised Negro women's wages, it has opened to them a score of new avenues of earning a living. Indeed, here, in microcosm and with differences emphasizing sex equality, is the industrial history of labor in the 19th and 20th centuries. We cannot abolish the new economic freedom of women. We cannot imprison women again in a home or require them all on pain of death to be nurses and housekeepers.

What is today the message of these black women to America and to the world? The uplift of women is, next to the problem of the color line and the peace movement, our greatest modern cause. When, now, two of these movements—woman and color—combine in one, the combination has deep meaning.

In other years women's way was clear: to be beautiful, to be petted, to bear children. Such has been their theoretic destiny and if perchance they have been ugly, hurt, and barren, that has been forgotten with studied silence. In partial compensation for this narrowed destiny the white world has lavished its politeness on its womankind,—its chivalry and bows, its uncoverings and courtesies—all the accumulated homage disused for courts and kings and craving exercise. The revolt of white women against this preordained destiny has in these latter days reached splendid proportions, but it is the revolt of an aristocracy of brains and ability,—the middle class and rank and file still plod on in the appointed path, paid by the homage, the almost mocking homage, of men.

From black women of America, however, (and from some others, too, but chiefly from black women and their daughters' daughters) this gauze has been withheld and without semblance of such apology they have been frankly trodden under the feet of men. They are and have been objected to, apparently for reasons peculiarly exasperating to reasoning human beings. When in this world a man comes forward with a thought, a deed, a vision, we ask not, how does he look,—but what is his message? It is of but passing interest whether or not the messenger is beautiful or ugly,—the *message* is the thing. This, which is axiomatic among men, has been in past ages but partially true if the messenger was a woman. The world still wants to ask that a woman primarily be pretty and if she is not, the mob pouts and asks querulously, "What else are women for?" Beauty "is its own excuse for being," but there are other excuses, as most men know, and when the white world objects to black women because it does not consider them beautiful, the black world of right asks two questions: "What is beauty?" and, "Suppose you think them ugly, what then? If ugliness and unconventionality and eccentricity of face and deed do not hinder men from doing the world's work and reaping the world's reward, why should it hinder women?"

Other things being equal, all of us, black and white, would prefer to be beautiful in face and form and suitably clothed; but most of us are not so, and one of the mightiest revolts of the century is against the devilish decree that no woman is a woman who is not by present standards a beautiful woman. This decree the black women of America have in large measure escaped from the first. Not being expected to be merely ornamental, they have girded themselves for work, instead of adorning their bodies only for play. Their sturdier minds have concluded that if a woman be clean, healthy, and educated, she is as pleasing as God wills and far more useful than most of her sisters. If in addition to this she is pink and white and straight-haired, and some of her fellow-men prefer this, well and good; but if she is black or brown and crowned in curled mists (and this to us is the most beautiful thing on earth), this is surely the flimsiest excuse for spiritual incarceration or banishment.

The very attempt to do this in the case of Negro Americans has strangely over-reached itself. By so much as the defective eyesight of the white world rejects black women as beauties, by so much the more it needs them as human beings,—an enviable alternative, as many a white woman knows. Consequently, for black women alone, as a group, "handsome is that handsome does" and they are asked to be no more beautiful than God made them, but they are asked to be efficient, to be strong, fertile, muscled, and able to work. If they marry, they must as independent workers be able to help support their children, for their men are paid on a scale which makes sole support of the family often impossible....

Out of a sex freedom that today makes us shudder will come in time a day when we will no longer pay men for work they do not do, for the sake of their harem; we will pay women what they earn and insist on their working and earning it; we will allow those persons to vote who know enough to vote, whether they be black or female, white or male; and we will ward race suicide, not by further burdening the over-burdened, but by honoring motherhood, even when the sneaking father shirks his duty.

"Wait till the lady passes," said a Nashville white boy.

"She's no lady; she's a nigger," answered another.

So some few women are born free, and some amid insult and scarlet letters achieve freedom; but our women in black had freedom thrust contemptuously upon them. With that freedom they are buying an untrammeled independence and dear as is the price they pay for it, it will in the end be worth every taunt and groan. Today the dreams of the mothers are coming true. We have still our poverty and degradation, our lewdness and our cruel toil; but we have, too, a vast group of women of Negro blood who for strength of character, cleanness of soul, and unselfish devotion of purpose, is today easily the peer of any group of women in the civilized world. And more than that, in the great rank and file of our five million women we have the up-working of new revolutionary ideals, which must in time have vast influence on the thought and action of this land.

For this, their promise, and for their hard past, I honor the women of my race. Their beauty,—their dark and mysterious beauty of midnight eyes, crumpled hair, and soft, full-featured faces—is perhaps more to me than to you, because I was born to its warm and subtle spell; but their worth is yours as well as mine. No other women on earth could have emerged from the hell of force and temptation which once engulfed and still surrounds black women in America with half the modesty and womanliness that they retain. I have always felt like bowing myself before them in all abasement, searching to bring some tribute to these long-suffering victims, these burdened sisters of mine, whom the world, the wise, white world, loves to affront and ridicule and wantonly to insult. I have known the women of many lands and nations,—I have known and seen and lived beside them, but none have I known more sweetly feminine, more unswervingly loyal, more desperately earnest, and more instinctively pure in body and in soul than the daughters of my black mothers. This, then,—a little thing—to their memory and inspiration.

31

Margaret Sanger
(1879–1966)

Woman and the New Race

(UNITED STATES, 1920)

Margaret Sanger devoted her life to the cause of "birth control," a term she coined in 1916. Raised in a large Irish American family, she had trained as a nurse and married before she became involved in socialist and labor movements in New York City. Sanger decried the physical toll that constant childbearing took among working-class women. In defiance of a U.S. law banning the circulation of contraceptive information, Sanger published pamphlets and then a newspaper, The Woman Rebel, *advocating access to birth control. In 1916, she opened the first birth control clinic and went to jail when it was raided. American women had long used contraception to curtail fertility, but Sanger's articles and books helped shatter the public silence about both contraception and female sexuality. Although she invoked women's health and personal freedom as grounds for birth control, Sanger also emphasized the passion of motherhood, if voluntary. After World War I Sanger turned away from radical politics and courted the medical profession and middle-class supporters through the American Birth Control League. Her views on the elimination of the "unfit" as a solution to social problems reflected the eugenic theories of human betterment that Sanger embraced. During the 1930s and 1940s, when Planned Parenthood clinics increasingly made birth control accessible, Sanger supported both population control in the developing world and the medical research that led to the development of oral contraception.*

The most far-reaching social development of modern times is the revolt of woman against sex servitude. The most important force in the remaking of the world is a free motherhood. Beside this force, the elaborate international programmes of modern statesmen are weak and superficial. Diplomats may formulate leagues of nations and nations may pledge their utmost strength to maintain them, statesmen may dream of reconstructing the world out of alliances, hegemonies and spheres of influence, but woman, continuing to produce explosive populations, will convert these pledges into the proverbial scraps of paper; or she may, by controlling birth, lift motherhood to the plane of a voluntary, intelligent function, and remake the world. When the world is thus remade, it will exceed the dream of statesman, reformer and revolutionist.

Only in recent years has woman's position as the gentler and weaker half of the human family been emphatically and generally questioned. Men assumed that this was woman's place; woman herself accepted it. It seldom occurred to anyone to ask whether she would go on occupying it forever.

Upon the mere surface of woman's organized protests there were no indications that she was desirous of achieving a fundamental change in her position. She claimed the right of suffrage and legislative regulation of her working hours, and asked that her property rights be equal to those of the man. None of these demands, however, affected directly the most vital factors of her existence. Whether she won her point or failed to win it, she remained a dominated weakling in a society controlled by men.

Woman's acceptance of her inferior status was the more real because it was unconscious. She had chained herself to her place in society and the family through the maternal functions of her nature, and only chains thus strong could have bound her to her lot as a brood animal for the masculine civilizations of the world. In accepting her role as the "weaker and gentler half," she accepted that function. In turn, the acceptance of that function fixed the more firmly her rank as an inferior.

Caught in this "vicious circle," woman has, through her reproductive ability, founded and perpetuated the tyrannies of the Earth. Whether it was the tyranny of a monarchy, an oligarchy or a republic, the one indispensable factor of its existence was, as it is now, hordes of human beings—human beings so plentiful as to be cheap, and so cheap that ignorance was their natural lot. Upon the rock of an unenlightened, submissive maternity have these been founded; upon the product of such a maternity have they flourished.

No despot ever flung forth his legions to die in foreign conquest, no privilege-ruled nation ever erupted across its borders, to lock in death embrace with another, but behind them loomed the driving power of a population too large for its boundaries and its natural resources.

No period of low wages or of idleness with their want among the workers, no peonage or sweatshop, no child-labor factory, ever came into being, save from the same source. Nor have famine and plague been as much "acts of God" as acts of too prolific mothers. They, also, as all students know, have their basic causes in over-population.

The creators of over-population are the women, who, while wringing their hands over each fresh horror, submit anew to their task of producing the multitudes who will bring about the *next* tragedy of civilization.

While unknowingly laying the foundations of tyrannies and providing the human tinder for racial conflagrations, woman was also unknowingly creating slums, filling asylums with insane, and institutions with other defectives. She was replenishing the ranks of the prostitutes, furnishing grist for the criminal courts and inmates for prisons. Had she planned deliberately to achieve this tragic total of human waste and misery, she could hardly have done it more effectively.

Woman's passivity under the burden of her disastrous task was almost altogether that of ignorant resignation. She knew virtually nothing about her reproductive nature and less about the consequences of her excessive childbearing. It is true that, obeying the inner urge of their natures, *some* women revolted. They went even to the extreme of infanticide and abortion. Usually their revolts were not general enough. They fought as individuals, not as a mass. In the mass they sank back into blind and hopeless subjection. They went on breeding with staggering rapidity those numberless, undesired children who become the clogs and the destroyers of civilizations.

To-day, however, woman is rising in fundamental revolt. Even her efforts at mere reform are, as we shall see later, steps in that direction. Underneath each of them is the feminine urge to complete freedom. Millions of women are asserting their right to voluntary motherhood. They are determined to decide for themselves whether they shall become mothers, under what conditions and when. This is the fundamental revolt referred to. It is for woman the key to the temple of liberty....

War, famine, poverty and oppression of the workers will continue while woman makes life cheap. They will cease only when she limits her reproductivity and human life is no longer a thing to be wasted.

Two chief obstacles hinder the discharge of this tremendous obligation. The first and the lesser is the legal barrier. Dark-Age laws would still deny to her the knowledge of her reproductive nature. Such knowledge is indispensable to intelligent motherhood and she must achieve it, despite absurd statutes and equally absurd moral canons.

The second and more serious barrier is her own ignorance of the extent and effect of her submission. Until she knows the evil her subjection has wrought to herself, to her progeny and to the world at large, she cannot wipe out that evil.

To get rid of these obstacles is to invite attack from the forces of reaction which are so strongly entrenched in our present-day society. It means warfare in every phase of her life. Nevertheless, at whatever cost, she must emerge from her ignorance and assume her responsibility.

She can do this only when she has awakened to a knowledge of herself and of the consequences of her ignorance. The first step is birth control. Through birth control she will attain to voluntary motherhood. Having attained this, the basic freedom of her sex, she will cease to enslave herself and the mass of humanity. Then, through the understanding of the intuitive forward urge within her, she will not stop at patching up the world; she will remake it....

The sex life of women has been clouded in darkness, restrictive, repressive and morbid. Women have not had the opportunity to know themselves, nor have they been permitted to give play to their inner natures, that they might create a morality practical, idealistic and high for their own needs.

On the other hand, church and state have forbidden women to leave their legal mates, or to refuse to submit to the marital embrace, no matter how filthy, drunken, diseased or otherwise repulsive the man might be—no matter how much of a crime it might be to bring to birth a child by him.

Woman was and is condemned to a system under which the lawful rapes exceed the unlawful ones a million to one. She has had nothing to say as to whether she shall have strength sufficient to give a child a fair physical and mental start in life; she has had as little to do with determining whether her own body shall be wrecked by excessive child-bearing. She has been adjured not to complain of the burden of caring for children she has not wanted. Only the married woman who has been constantly loved by the most understanding and considerate of husbands has escaped these horrors. Besides the wrongs done to women in marriage, those involved in promiscuity, infidelities and rapes become inconsequential in nature and in number.

Out of woman's inner nature, in rebellion against these conditions, is rising the new morality. Let it be realized that this creation of new sex ideals is a challenge to the church. Being a challenge to the church, it is also, in less degree, a challenge to the state. The woman who takes a fearless stand for the incoming sex ideals must expect to be assailed by reactionaries of every kind. Imperialists and exploiters will fight hardest in the open, but the ecclesiastic will fight longest in the dark. He understands the situation best of all; he best knows what reaction he has to fear from the morals of women who have attained liberty. For, be it repeated, the church has always known and feared the spiritual potentialities of woman's freedom.

And in this lies the answer to the question why the opponent of birth control raises the moral issue. Sex morals for women have been one-sided; they have been purely negative, inhibitory and repressive. They have been fixed by agencies which have sought to keep women enslaved; which have been determined, even as they are now, to use woman solely as an asset to the church, the state and the man. Any means of freedom which will enable women to live and think for themselves first, will be attacked as immoral by these selfish agencies.

What effect will the practice of birth control have upon woman's moral development? As we have seen in other chapters, it will break her bonds. It will free her to understand the cravings and soul needs of herself and other women. It will enable her to develop her love nature separate from and independent of her maternal nature.

It goes without saying that the woman whose children are desired and are of such number that she can not only give them adequate care but keep herself mentally and spiritually alive, as well as physically fit, can discharge her duties to her children much better than the overworked, broken and querulous mother of a large, unwanted family.

Thus the way is open to her for a twofold development; first, through her own full rounded life, and next, through her loving, unstrained, full-hearted relationship with her offspring. The bloom of mother love will have an opportunity to infuse itself into her soul and make her, indeed, the fond, affectionate guardian of her offspring that sentiment now pictures her but hard facts deny her the privilege of being. She will preserve also her love life with her mate in its ripening perfection. She will want children with a deeper passion, and will love them with a far greater love.

In spite of the age-long teaching that sex life in itself is unclean, the world has been moving to a realization that a great love between a man and woman is a holy thing, freighted with great possibilities for spiritual growth. The fear of unwanted children removed, the assurance that she will have a sufficient amount of time in which to develop her love life to its greatest beauty, with its comradeship in many fields—these will lift woman by the very soaring quality of her innermost self to spiritual heights that few have attained. Then the coming of eagerly desired children will but enrich life in all its avenues, rather than enslave and impoverish it as do unwanted ones to-day....

This situation implies in turn a number of conditions. Foremost among them is woman's knowledge of her sexual nature, both in its physiology and its spiritual significance. She must not only know her own body, its care and its needs, but she must know the power of the sex force, its use, its abuse, as well as how to direct it for the benefit of the race. Thus she can transmit to her children an equipment that will enable them to break the bonds that have held humanity enslaved for ages....

32

SHAREEFEH HAMID ALI
(twentieth century)

"East and West in Cooperation"
(INDIA, 1935)

Since the 1840s, European and North American feminists corresponded, met, and, after 1880, built international organizations to promote suffrage and peace. As European world domination declined after World War I, women in Latin America, Asia, and Africa increasingly took part in these international groups. The suffragist International Alliance of Women (IAW), founded in 1904, included more than fifty countries by the 1930s. The leadership, however, remained dominated by elite, white, Christian women, many of whom sought to uplift women of the "East" by assimilating them to Western values and styles. At the IAW meeting in Istanbul in 1935, Shareefeh Hamid Ali of India explained to women "of the West" that cooperation in the quest for improving women's lives required respect for the unique cultural backgrounds of constituent nations. In contrast to writers who rejected practices such as veiling as a sign of inferiority, Ali insisted on preserving national dress. She rejected the patronizing attitudes of "enforced guides" and counseled Western women to learn as well as teach in reciprocal exchanges of knowledge. Like the Egyptian feminist Huda Shaarawi, Ali called on Western women to support the anticolonial movements for independence from British rule. A participant in the Women's International League for Peace and Freedom, Ali was one of the original members of the U.N. Commission on the Status of Women.

I shall leave it to my Western sisters to tell us in what manner and in which way we can help them by our cooperation. As far as we are concerned we are desirous of seeking remedial measures against ill health, illiteracy, poverty, unemployment, underpayment of labour, [and] maternal and infantile mortality. We want new laws of equality of marriage, divorce, inheritance and guardianship.

What we want to preserve in our Oriental Civilisation is simplicity of life: philosophy, art, the cult of the family, veneration of motherhood, and spiritual consciousness.

(Incidentally, we must preserve our dress at all costs. A costume is the index of the growth of one's inner self, it is a hallmark of the individuality of each nation. Sartorial imitation to our mind is a sign of acceptance of an inferior position which Europe is only too ready to impose in Asia and Africa.)

We desire your help in friendliness and fellowship, we need your moral support and your vast organising capacities to enable us to discard hampering customs and traditions which have been strangling us. We wish to gain a position worthy of womanhood. If you help us in obtaining our object, you will have allies in Asia and Africa who will in their turn help you to attain your vision of a better world. Our unity of thought and ideals will go far in influencing the thought of the world. Our object will be gained by uniting our forces, by strengthening one another, [and] by exchange of data and experience concerning the condition of women in our respective countries, which will enable us to attain civic, economic, and political equal status for our sex. Our one aim and object in life must be to promote peace—peace in the continent and peace in the world.

We seek your cooperation in attaining this ideal—common to all countries and to all civilisations—but we of the East must warn you of the west that any arrogant assumption of superiority or of patronage on the part of Europe or America, [and] any undue pressure of enforcement of religion or government or of trade or economic "spheres of influence," will alienate Asia and Africa [and] with it the woman-hood of Asia and Africa.

We women of the East are now aware [of the] strength which sol-idarity and unity will bring to us. We are also aware of our manifold weaknesses, [though] we see the road straight in front of us which will lead us to our goal.

May we hope to have you with us as friendly and not enforced guides—that we shall have from you cordiality and human fellowship—and not "tutelage and patronage"?

I assure you as a representative from India in Asia that your help and friendship given in this manner will be far more effective and will be cordially reciprocated.

We in Asia have also our own contributions to make to the civilisa-tion of the world. For centuries Asia has been the cradle of religions—of spiritual knowledge—of philosophy which gives life a deeper significance. Perhaps your complexities of life will be influenced and eased by our simplicities. Let us try and give of our[selves] to each other.

33

VIRGINIA WOOLF
(1882–1941)

Three Guineas
(ENGLAND, 1938)

*In the context of the rise of European fascism in the 1930s, the British nov-
elist Virginia Woolf contemplated how women could help prevent tyranny
and war. Best known for her modernist fiction, including* Mrs. Dalloway
(1925) and To the Lighthouse *(1927), Woolf's classic feminist essay,*
A Room of One's Own *(1929), argued that women could become authors if they had adequate incomes and a place in which to write. In*
Three Guineas *she moved beyond the liberal feminist goals of education
and employment to link gender hierarchy in the home to tyranny within the
state. The essay takes the form of responses to letters requesting financial
contributions from three societies: one to prevent war, one to promote
women's education, and one to support women in the professions. In granting one guinea each to organizations to promote women's entry into the
public sphere, Woolf insisted that educated women not perpetuate a society
that promulgated social inequalities and waged war. Her views foreshadowed later radical feminists who criticized women's adoption of male values and who created separate women's institutions. In the postcolonial
era, however, feminists would reappraise Woolf's statement that "[A]s a
woman I have no country. . . . As a woman my country is the whole world."*

Three years is a long time to leave a letter unanswered, and your letter has been lying without an answer even longer than that. I had hoped that it would answer itself, or that other people would answer it for me. But there it is with its question—How in your opinion are we to prevent war?—still unanswered....

It is now that the first difficulty of communication between us appears. Let us rapidly indicate the reason. We both come of what, in this hybrid age when, though birth is mixed, classes still remain fixed, it is convenient to call the educated class. When we meet in the flesh we speak with the same accent; use knives and forks in the same way; expect maids to cook dinner and wash up after dinner; and can talk during dinner without much difficulty about politics and people; war and peace; barbarism and civilization—all the questions indeed suggested by your letter. Moreover, we both earn our livings. But...those three dots mark a precipice, a gulf so deeply cut between us that for three years and more I have been sitting on my side of it wondering whether it is any use to try to speak across it. Let us then ask someone else—it is Mary Kingsley—to speak for us. "I don't know if I ever revealed to you the fact that being allowed to learn German was *all* the paid-for education I ever had. Two thousand pounds was spent on my brother's, I still hope not in vain." Mary Kingsley is not speaking for herself alone; she is speaking, still, for many of the daughters of educated men. And she is not merely speaking for them; she is also pointing to a very important fact about them, a fact that must profoundly influence all that follows: the fact of Arthur's Education Fund. You, who have read *Pendennis,* will remember how the mysterious letters A.E.F. figured in the household ledgers. Ever since the thirteenth century English families have been paying money into that account. From the Pastons to the Pendennises, all educated families from the thirteenth century to the present moment have paid money into that account. It is a voracious receptacle. Where there were many sons to educate it required a great effort on the part of the family to keep it full. For your education was not merely in book-learning; games educated your body; friends taught you more than books or games. Talk with them broadened your outlook and enriched your mind. In the holidays you travelled; acquired a taste for art; a knowledge of foreign politics; and then, before you could earn your own living, your father made you an allowance upon which it was possible for you to live while you learnt the profession which now entitles you to add the letters K.C. to your name. All this came out of Arthur's Education Fund. And to this your sisters, as Mary Kingsley indicates, made their contribution. Not only did their own education, save for such small sums as paid the German teacher, go into it; but many of those luxuries and trimmings which are, after all, an essential part of education—travel, society, solitude, a lodging apart from the family house—they were paid into it too. It was a voracious receptacle, a solid fact—Arthur's Education Fund—a fact so solid indeed that it cast a shadow over the entire landscape. And the result is that though we look at the same things, we see them differently. What is that congregation of buildings there, with a semi-monastic look, with chapels and halls and green playing-fields? To you it is your old school, Eton or Harrow; your old university, Oxford or Cambridge; the source of memories and of traditions innumerable. But to us, who see it through the shadow of Arthur's Education Fund, it is a schoolroom table; an omnibus going to a class; a little woman with a red nose who is not well educated herself but has an invalid mother to support; an allowance of £50 a year with which to buy clothes, give presents and take journeys on coming to maturity. Such is the effect that Arthur's Education Fund has had upon us. So magically does it change the landscape that the noble courts and quadrangles of Oxford and Cambridge often appear to educated men's daughters like petticoats with holes in them, cold legs of mutton, and the boat train starting for abroad while the guard slams the door in their faces....

You, of course, could once more take up arms—in Spain, as before in France—in defence of peace. But that presumably is a method that having tried you have rejected. At any rate that method is not open to us; both the Army and the Navy are closed to our sex. We are not allowed to fight. Nor again are we allowed to be members of the Stock Exchange. Thus we can use neither the pressure of force nor the pressure of money. The less direct but still effective weapons which our brothers, as educated men, possess in the diplomatic service, in the

Church, are also denied to us. We cannot preach sermons or negoti-
ate treaties. Then again although it is true that we can write articles
or send letters to the Press, the control of the Press—the decision
what to print, what not to print—is entirely in the hands of your sex.
It is true that for the past twenty years we have been admitted to the
Civil Service and to the Bar; but our position there is still very pre-
carious and our authority of the slightest. Thus all the weapons with
which an educated man can enforce his opinions are either beyond
our grasp or so nearly beyond it that even if we used them we could
scarcely inflict one scratch. If the men in your profession were to unite
in any demand and were to say: "If it is not granted we will stop work,"
the laws of England would cease to be administered. If the women in
your profession said the same thing it would make no difference to the
laws of England whatever. Not only are we incomparably weaker than
the men of our own class; we are weaker than the women of the working class. If the working women of the country were to say: "If you go
to war, we will refuse to make munitions or to help in the production
of goods," the difficulty of war-making would be seriously increased.
But if all the daughters of educated men were to down tools tomorrow, nothing essential either to the life or to the war-making of the
community would be embarrassed. Our class is the weakest of all the
classes in the state. We have no weapon with which to enforce our
will.

The answer to that is so familiar that we can easily anticipate it.
The daughters of educated men have no direct influence, it is true; but
they possess the greatest power of all; that is, the influence that they
can exert upon educated men. If this is true, if, that is, influence is still
the strongest of our weapons and the only one that can be effective in
helping you to prevent war, let us, before we sign your manifesto or
join your society, consider what that influence amounts to....

[T]here was of course one political cause which the daughters of
educated men had much at heart during the past 150 years: the franchise. But when we consider how long it took them to win that cause,
and what labour, we can only conclude that influence has to be
combined with wealth in order to be effective as a political weapon,
and that influence of the kind that can be exerted by the daughters of
educated men is very low in power, very slow in action, and very
painful in use. Certainly the one great political achievement of the

educated man's daughter cost her over a century of the most exhausting and menial labour; kept her trudging in processions, working in offices, speaking at street corners; finally, because she used force, sent her to prison, and would very likely still keep her there, had it not been, paradoxically enough, that the help she gave her brothers when they used force at last gave her the right to call herself, if not a full daughter, still a step-daughter of England....

[The right to earn one's living] was conferred upon us less than twenty years ago, in the year 1919, by an Act which unbarred the professions. The door of the private house was thrown open. In every purse there was, or might be, one bright new sixpence in whose light every thought, every sight, every action looked different. Twenty years is not, as time goes, a long time; nor is a sixpenny bit a very important coin; nor can we yet draw upon biography to supply us with a picture of the lives and minds of the new-sixpenny owners. But in imagination perhaps we can see the educated man's daughter, as she issues from the shadow of the private house, and stands on the bridge which lies between the old world and the new, and asks, as she twirls the sacred coin in her hand, "What shall I do with it? What do I see with it?" ...

What real influence can we bring to bear upon law or business, religion or politics—we to whom many doors are still locked, or at best ajar, we who have neither capital nor force behind us? It seems as if our influence must stop short at the surface. When we have expressed an opinion upon the surface we have done all that we can do. It is true that the surface may have some connection with the depths, but if we are to help you to prevent war we must try to penetrate deeper beneath the skin. Let us then look in another direction—in a direction natural to educated men's daughters, in the direction of education itself.

Here, fortunately, the year, the sacred year 1919, comes to our help. Since that year put it into the power of educated men's daughters to earn their livings they have at last some real influence upon education. They have money. They have money to subscribe to causes. Honorary treasurers invoke their help. To prove it, here, opportunely, cheek by jowl with your letter, is a letter from one such treasurer asking for money with which to rebuild a women's college. And when honorary treasurers invoke help, it stands to reason that they can be bargained with. We have the right to say to her, "You shall only have our guinea with which to help you to rebuild your college if you will help this gentleman whose letter also lies before us to prevent war." We can say to her, "You must educate the young to hate war. You must teach them to feel the inhumanity, the beastliness, the insupportability of war." But what kind of education shall we bargain for? What sort of education will teach the young to hate war?...

At Cambridge, in the year 1937, the women's colleges—you will scarcely believe it, Sir, but once more it is the voice of fact that is speaking, not of fiction—the women's colleges are not allowed to be members of the university, and the number of educated men's daughters who are allowed to receive a university education is still strictly limited; though both sexes contribute to the university funds. As for poverty, *The Times* newspaper supplies us with figures; any ironmonger will provide us with a foot-rule; if we measure the money available for scholarships at the men's colleges with the money available for their sisters at the women's colleges, we shall save ourselves the trouble of adding up; and come to the conclusion that the colleges for the sisters of educated men are, compared with their brothers' colleges, unbelievably and shamefully poor....

Let us then discuss as quickly as we can the sort of education that is needed. Now since history and biography—the only evidence available to an outsider—seem to prove that the old education of the old colleges breeds neither a particular respect for liberty nor a particular hatred of war it is clear that you must rebuild your college differently. It is young and poor; let it therefore take advantage of those qualities and be founded on poverty and youth. Obviously, then, it must be an experimental college, an adventurous college. Let it be built on lines of its own. It must be built not of carved stone and stained glass, but of some cheap, easily combustible material which does not hoard dust and perpetrate traditions. Do not have chapels. Do not have museums and libraries with chained books and first editions under glass cases. Let the pictures and the books be new and always changing. Let it be decorated afresh by each generation with their own hands cheaply....

For, to repeat, if those daughters are not going to be educated they are not going to earn their livings; if they are not going to earn their livings, they are going once more to be restricted to the education of the private house; and if they are going to be restricted to the education of the private house they are going, once more, to exert all their influence both consciously and unconsciously in favour of war. Of that there can be little doubt....

So, Sir, if you want us to help you to prevent war the conclusion seems to be inevitable; we must help to rebuild the college which, imperfect as it may be, is the only alternative to the education of the private house. We must hope that in time that education may be altered. That guinea must be given before we give you the guinea that you ask for your own society. But it is contributing to the same cause—the prevention of war....

Now that we have given one guinea towards rebuilding a college we must consider whether there is not more that we can do to help you to prevent war. And it is at once obvious, if what we have said about influence is true, that we must turn to the professions, because if we could persuade those who can earn their livings, and thus actually hold in their hands this new weapon, our only weapon, the weapon of independent opinion based upon independent income, to use that weapon against war, we should do more to help you than by appealing to those who must teach the young to earn their livings;...

This conclusion then bring us back to the...letter asking for a subscription to the society for helping the daughters of educated men to obtain employment in the professions. You will agree, Sir, that we have strong selfish motives for helping her—there can be no doubt about that. For to help women to earn their livings in the professions is to help them to possess that weapon of independent opinion which is still their most powerful weapon. It is to help them to have a mind of their own and a will of their own with which to help you to prevent war. But...—here again, in those dots, doubts and hesitations assert themselves. Can we, considering the facts given above, send her our guinea without laying down very stringent terms as to how that guinea shall be spent?

For the facts which we have discovered in checking her statement as to her financial position have raised questions which make us wonder whether we are wise to encourage people to enter the professions if we wish to prevent war. You will remember that we are using our psychological insight (for that is our only qualification) to decide what kind of qualities in human nature are likely to lead to war. And the facts disclosed above are of a kind to make us ask, before we write our cheque, whether if we encourage the daughters of educated men to enter the professions we shall not be encouraging the very qualities that we wish to prevent? Shall we not be doing our guinea's worth to ensure that in two or three centuries not only the educated men in the professions but the educated women in the professions will be asking—oh, of whom? as the poet says—the very question that you are asking us now: How can we prevent war? If we encourage the daughters to enter the professions without making any conditions as to the way in which the professions are to be practised shall we not be doing our best to stereotype the old tune which human nature, like a gramophone whose needle has stuck, is now grinding out with such disastrous unanimity? "Here we go round the mulberry tree, the mulberry tree, the mulberry tree. Give it all to me, give it all to me, all to me. Three hundred millions spent upon war." With that song, or something like it, ringing in our ears we cannot send our guinea to the honorary treasurer without warning her that she shall only have it on condition that she shall swear that the professions in future shall be practised so that they lead to a different song and a different conclusion. She shall only have it if she can satisfy us that our guinea shall be spent in the cause of peace....

Therefore this guinea, which is to help you to help women to enter the professions, has this condition as a first condition attached to it. You shall swear that you will do all in your power to insist that any woman who enters any profession shall in no way hinder any other human being, whether man or woman, white or black, provided that he or she is qualified to enter that profession, from entering it; but shall do all in her power to help them....

Here then is your own letter. In that, as we have seen, after asking for an opinion as to how to prevent war, you go on to suggest certain practical measures by which we can help you to prevent it. These are it appears that we should sign a manifesto, pledging ourselves "to protect culture and intellectual liberty"; that we should join a certain society, devoted to certain measures whose aim is to preserve peace; and, finally, that we should subscribe to that society which like the others is in need of funds....

That request then for a guinea answered, and the cheque signed, only one further request of yours remains to be considered—it is that we should fill up a form and become members of your society. On the face of it that seems a simple request, easily granted. For what can be simpler than to join the society to which this guinea has just been contributed? On the face of it, how easy, how simple; but in the depths, how difficult, how complicated.... What possible doubts, what possible hesitations can those dots stand for? What reason or what emotion can make us hesitate to become members of a society whose aims we approve, to whose funds we have contributed? It may be neither reason nor emotion, but something more profound and fundamental than either. It may be difference. Different we are, as facts have proved, both in sex and in education. And it is from that difference, as we have already said, that our help can come, if help we can, to protect liberty, to prevent war. But if we sign this form which implies a promise to become active members of your society, it would seem that we must lose that difference and therefore sacrifice that help. To explain why this is so is not easy, even though the gift of a guinea has made it possible (so we have boasted) to speak freely without fear or flattery....

The very word "society" sets tolling in memory the dismal bells of a harsh music: shall not, shall not, shall not. You shall not learn; you shall not earn; you shall not own; you shall not—such was the society relationship of brother to sister for many centuries. And though it is possible, and to the optimistic credible, that in time a new society may ring a carillon of splendid harmony, and your letter heralds it, that day is far distant. Inevitably we ask ourselves, is there not something in the conglomeration of people into societies that releases what is most selfish and violent, least rational and humane in the individuals themselves? Inevitably we look upon society, so kind to you, so harsh to us, as an ill-fitting form that distorts the truth; deforms the mind; fetters the will. Inevitably we look upon societies as conspiracies that sink the private brother, whom many of us have reason to respect, and inflate in his stead a monstrous male, loud of voice, hard of fist, childishly intent upon scoring the floor of the earth with chalk marks, within whose mystic boundaries human beings are penned, rigidly, separately, artificially; where, daubed red and gold, decorated like a savage with feathers he goes through mystic rites and enjoys the dubious pleasures of power and dominion while we, "his" women, are locked in the private house without share in the many societies of which his society is composed. For such reasons compact as they are of many memories and emotions—for who shall analyse the complexity of a mind that holds so deep a reservoir of time past within it?—it seems both wrong for us rationally and impossible for us emotionally to fill up your form and join your society. For by so doing we should merge our identity in yours; follow and repeat and score still deeper the old worn ruts in which society, like a gramophone whose needle has stuck, is grinding out with intolerable unanimity "Three hundred millions spent upon arms." We should not give effect to a view which our own experience of "society" should have helped us to envisage. Thus, Sir, while we respect you as a private person and prove it by giving you a guinea to spend as you choose, we believe that we can help you most effectively by refusing to join your society; by working for our common ends—justice and equality and liberty for all men and women—outside your society, not within....

Let us then draw rapidly in outline the kind of society which the daughters of educated men found and join outside your society but in co-operation with its ends. In the first place, this new society, you will be relieved to learn, would have no honorary treasurer, for it would need no funds. It would have no office, no committee, no secretary; it would call no meetings; it would hold no conferences. If name it must have, it could be called the Outsiders' Society. That is not a resonant name, but it has the advantage that it squares with facts—the facts of history, of law, of biography; even, it may be, with the still hidden facts of our still unknown psychology. It would consist of educated men's daughters working in their own class—how indeed can they work in any other?—and by their own methods for liberty, equality and peace. Their first duty, to which they would bind themselves not by oath, for oaths and ceremonies have no part in a society which must be anonymous and elastic before everything, would be not to fight with arms.... [I]f you insist upon fighting to protect me, or 'our' country, let it be understood, soberly and rationally between us, that you are fighting to gratify a sex instinct which I cannot share; to procure benefits which I have not shared and probably will not share; but not to gratify my instincts, or to protect myself or my country. For, the outsider will say, "in fact, as a woman, I have no country. As a woman I want no country. As a woman my country is the whole world." And if, when reason has said its say, still some obstinate emotion remains, some love of England dropped into a child's ears by the cawing of rooks in an elm tree, by the splash of waves on a beach, or by English voices murmuring nursery rhymes, this drop of pure, if irrational, emotion she will make serve her to give to England first what she desires of peace and freedom for the whole world....

To return then to the form that you have sent and ask us to fill up: for the reasons given we will leave it unsigned. But in order to prove as substantially as possible that our aims are the same as yours, here is the guinea, a free gift, given freely, without any other conditions than you choose to impose upon yourself. It is the third of three guineas; but the three guineas, you will observe, though given to three different treasurers are all given to the same cause, for the causes are the same and inseparable.

Now, since you are pressed for time, let me make an end; apologising three times over to the three of you, first for the length of this letter, second for the smallness of the contribution, and thirdly for writing at all. The blame for that however rests upon you, for this letter would never have been written had you not asked for an answer to your own.

34.

ALVA MYRDAL
(1902–86)

Nation and Family

(SWEDEN, 1941)

The social scientist, writer, and politician Alva Myrdal began to address social welfare policies in a 1934 book, coauthored with her husband, Gunnar Myrdal, that addressed the decline in Swedish birthrates. In contrast to Depression-era efforts to remove women from the labor force, the Myrdals called for equal economic opportunity, along with state-sponsored day care and housing, to make it easier for women to combine wage labor with childrearing. Within a few years a group of twenty-five women's organizations issued "A Call to Sweden's Women," insisting on the right to work, paid vacations for housewives, legalized contraception, support for single mothers, and greater political representation for women. In Nation and Family, *Alva Myrdal explained why women's work had shifted from the household to the paid labor force and stressed the economic value of women's productivity. She also predicted the psychological dilemmas facing women who chose to remain homemakers. Sweden implemented many of the reforms feminists recommended, supporting not only working mothers but working fathers as well. In addition to shaping future social welfare policies, Alva Myrdal anticipated the movement of women into politics. She served the Swedish government as an ambassador, a delegate to United Nations disarmament conferences, a member of parliament, and as minister for disarmament. In 1982 she won a Nobel Peace Prize for her work to end the international arms race.*

In Sweden as elsewhere popular attitudes toward women's problems are still chaotic in most groups. Traditional thinking is enmeshed in an accumulation of vague interests, confused emotions, and pure nonsense, involving the whole question of women's status. They are inherited from the epoch of early industrialism and focused in the doctrine that women's place is in the home and not on the labor market. At bottom there lies a set of real and harassing problems. How is women's scheme of life to be determined by their function as childbearers? In how far should young women's work and life plans be geared to the future eventuality of marriage and motherhood? How are the relations within the triangle of work-support-marriage to be organized in order to avoid an unreasonable degree of economic and personal waste? A final answer to these questions has not been worked out in any modern country.

Meanwhile women are in the peculiar situation that work and economic support, otherwise depending upon productive contributions in an economic market and regulated by impersonal contracts, are also offered by the choice of marriage. This involves a very personal type of contract. Remuneration is only slightly related to efficiency of work and is largely determined by the good will and capability of the husband. Woman's work in the home has acquired a high value and traditionally involves social status. The value, however, is not determined by the quantity and quality of her own labor but is derived from the status the husband has acquired in his field. The highest esteem is, therefore, most often the reward of the housewife who presides over a home in which there is practically no work at all for her to do....

Housework is becoming less labor consuming....

Much of the routine work in all homes, rural and urban, has been gradually absorbed by industry, leaving housework increasingly in the position of involving merely preparation of finished or semifinished products instead of their manufacture. For understanding the movement for the emancipation of women as it actually developed it should be noted also that the growth of commerce and the professions was eliminating housework.... It is thus only logical that the movement for women's emancipation, which is to be seen mainly as a thrust not for conquering new territory but rather for regaining their part of an old one, had as its first goals the attainment of professional education and legal rights in personal and economic matters....

In the past the energy of the women's movement was for the most part geared to fighting for these legal rights. It should be understood that this century-long fight for emancipation did not cause the underlying changes in social structure but accompanied them, symbolizing adjustment difficulties along with the general process of democratization. The right to inherit, the right to education, the right to have a vocation, the right to enter economic contracts, and the right to vote all had to be exacted by political appeal and won in the Riksdag. It is thus also understandable that when the last issue, that of work versus marriage, was finally raised it was carried on by the feminists as a fight for preserving a human right, the married woman's right to work. No important legal barriers existed any more although there were many institutional ones, and the adversaries of women's rights were demanding that even legal barriers again be erected. Society at large was slow in attaining a wholehearted understanding of this right of married women to work outside their homes....

The situation became more explosive when the population crisis focused attention on married women as deficient propagators. To understand fully how dangerous this constellation was it is only necessary to recall that the population and family argument had for several decades been effectively utilized against job-seeking married women. The principal reason why their work was considered unwholesome for society was that it was supposed to break up the family and particularly to prevent the bearing and rearing of children. In this situation anything could have happened. The remarkable thing is that in this crucial moment the population argument was wrenched out of the hands of the antifeminists and instead used as a new and formidable weapon for the emancipation ideals. The old debate on married women's right to work was turned into a fight for the working woman's right to marry and have children. The change in public opinion concerning women's problems brought about by this reformulation of the issue was tremendous. It should be noted that in the beginning the feminists themselves were merely bewildered, as their past experiences had made them suspicious of the very term "population policy." The gain was purely a gift to them. Only gradually did they come to appreciate their new strategic situation....

The economic irrationality from a national point of view of not utilizing the productive resources available, often invested with costly training, was first pointed out. Also, it was shown that remunerative work for the wife, sometimes only for a few stabilizing years in the beginning of marriage, must be thought of as a precondition for marriage in many cases, particularly among young people. The fertility of working wives might be low but nobody should think that these wives would bear more children if they were compelled to stay at home and the families were deprived of part of their incomes. From a population point of view the demand should rather be greater security for working women against dismissal because of marriage or childbirth and in addition organizational devices which would make it easier for them to bear and rear children....

The general conclusions of [an] investigation, demanded by the Swedish Parliament because of repeated private bills to restrict women's right to work, were summarized by the Committee in the following uncompromising terms:

> Even if married women in some regards are a relatively new phenomenon on the labor market, our investigation has not found any support for the hypothesis that this factor should fall outside the ordinary framework for the present social and economic organization of cultural progress. After having gone into intensive factual studies of the matter, it seems far more evident to this Committee that the gainful work of married women can neither be spared nor ought to be restricted. The organization of society will instead have to adjust itself to the new situation which is caused by the more general participation of women in work outside the home. At the same time, however, the possibility for mothers to devote time to children during their infancy ought to be regained through social reorganization.

> With regard to various proposals suggested for investigation the Committee wants to give the following summarization of its opinions:
> 1. All attempts legally to restrict married women's right to retain or obtain gainful employment, just as all other restrictive measures against such work, must be firmly rejected.

2. Gratuities, marriage loans, bulk payment of earned pensions, premature pensioning and similar economic encouragements for voluntary retirement on marriage cannot be considered as serving any social aim.

3. Possibilities for obtaining part-time work and temporary positions ought increasingly to be provided both for married women and other persons who for approved reasons want shorter work hours.

4. Possibilities for married couples to get positions in the same locality ought, if they do not damage legitimate interests of other persons, to be provided to some extent.

5. The question of the legal right for married women to retain their own surname ought to be given renewed consideration.

6. Social measures for alleviating the mother's care of small children ought to be instituted and given economic support, but they ought to the same extent to satisfy the needs of mothers engaged both in employment and in homework....

The victories for Swedish women have been won on that one ideological alignment which alone can make the position of the working mother accepted by all as a matter of course, that her marrying and her childbearing are to be encouraged and not discouraged by society. So expressed, her rights coincide with the interests of society. In other words, what is protected is women's right to have those very children that society also wants....

The most disquieting questions as to psychological satisfaction are not those concerning the working mothers. Given time, a practical will to reform less important details in life and some adaptation to the new partnership marriages will probably result in the emergence of a fairly stable organization for family life. What is more puzzling to the young woman considering her future married life is her status if a homemaker. What was called the economic dilemma of the homemaker also has a psychological aspect. When the homemaker chooses the lot of dependence, she chooses dependence on some one individual. How will that dependence work out in terms of mental tensions and satisfactions? How long is a woman going to accept the fact that when young so much of her life is organized just to "catch" a man and become married? Could her life be rearranged so as to give her a more clearly definable status? Could marriage be made to require real "man-sized" tasks of women? How are women to endure the lack of a schematic network of daily work routine, such as characterizes other strata of life? How are they going to stand that time distribution which scatters much of their work when the rest of the world is at leisure and gives them leisure at odd hours when nobody else has it? ...

Summarizing what may be expected from these women themselves in regard to the future of Swedish population, it is believed that the reforms called into being in Sweden will help them better to combine motherhood and remunerative work. The practical difficulties are so numerous, however, that there will probably be a long transitional period when women will either have to shun too heavy maternal responsibilities or give up their gainful work. The risk is great that society will proceed so slowly in solving these problems of women's existence that new and even more desperate crises may invade the whole field of women, family, and population.

35

DING LING
(1904–86)

"Thoughts on March 8"
(CHINA, 1942)

Women active within twentieth-century communist movements typically accepted the Marxist view that women's emancipation would follow from the revolutionary success of the proletariat. In China, Ding Ling (born Jiang Bingzhi), a highly respected writer associated with the May Fourth (1919) cultural and political reform movement, later joined the Communist party and dared to question the limitations on women within the revolutionary left. She attended a socialist-run girls' school in the 1920s, published fiction exploring the problems of modern women, and married a poet who was executed for his political activities. After joining the party in the 1930s, Ding Ling was imprisoned, but she escaped to the Communist-controlled Yan'an region. The title of her essay, written in August 1941, refers to the date of International Women's Day, when socialists and communists celebrated women workers. Published in the Communist party newspaper, the controversial essay criticized the view of women as "backwards" and pointed out the pressures on them to marry and have children at the sacrifice of their own careers. After invoking the specter of Ibsen's Nora returning home in defeat and descending into misery, Ding Ling urged women to remain intellectually active through meaningful work. She continued to write influential revolutionary literature and remained loyal to the Communist party that ruled China after 1949, but her critical views led to her expulsion from the party in the 1950s and her imprisonment for five years during the Cultural Revolution.

When will it no longer be necessary to attach special weight to the word "woman" and raise it specially?

Each year this day comes round. Every year on this day, meetings are held all over the world where women muster their forces. Even though things have not been as lively these last two years in Yan'an as they were in previous years, it appears that at least a few people are busy at work here. And there will certainly be a congress, speeches, circular telegrams, and articles.

Women in Yan'an are happier than women elsewhere in China. So much so that many people ask enviously: "How come the women comrades get so rosy and fat on millet?" It doesn't seem to surprise anyone that women make up a big proportion of the staff in the hospitals, sanatoria, and clinics, but they are inevitably the subject of conversation, as a fascinating problem, on every conceivable occasion.

Moreover, all kinds of women comrades are often the target of deserved criticism. In my view these reproaches are serious and justifiable.

People are always interested when women comrades get married, but that is not enough for them. It is virtually impossible for women comrades to get onto friendly terms with a man comrade, and even less likely for them to become friendly with more than one. Cartoonists ridicule them: "A departmental head getting married too?" The poets say, "All the leaders in Yan'an are horsemen, and none of them are artists. In Yan'an it's impossible for an artist to find a pretty sweetheart." But in other situations, they are lectured: "Damn it, you look down on us old cadres and say we're country bumpkins. But if it weren't for us country bumpkins, you wouldn't be coming to Yan'an to eat millet!" But women invariably want to get married. (It's even more of a sin not to be married, and single women are even more of a target for rumors and slanderous gossip.) So they can't afford to be choosy, anyone will do: whether he rides horses or wears straw sandals, whether he's an artist or a supervisor. They inevitably have children. The fate of such children is various. Some are wrapped in soft baby wool and patterned felt and looked after by governesses. Others are wrapped in soiled cloth and left crying in their parents' beds, while their parents consume much of the child allowance. But for this allowance (twenty-five yuan a month, or just over three pounds of pork), many of them would probably never get a taste of meat. Whoever they marry, the fact is that those women who are compelled to bear children will probably be publicly derided as "Noras who have returned home." Those women comrades in a position to employ governesses can go out once a week to a prim get-together and dance. Behind their backs there will also be the most incredible gossip and whispering campaigns, but as soon as they go somewhere, they cause a great stir and all eyes are glued to them. This has nothing to do with our theories, our doctrines, and the speeches we make at meetings. We all know this to be a fact, a fact that is right before our eyes, but it is never mentioned.

It is the same with divorce. In general there are three conditions to pay attention to when getting married: (1) political purity; (2) both parties should be more or less the same age and comparable in looks; (3) mutual help. Even though everyone is said to fulfill these conditions—as for point 1, there are no open traitors in Yan'an; as for point 3, you can call anything "mutual help," including darning socks, patching shoes, and even feminine comfort—everyone nevertheless makes a great show of giving thoughtful attention to them. And yet the pretext for divorce is invariably the wife's political backwardness. I am the first to admit that it is a shame when a man's wife is not progressive and retards his progress. But let us consider to what degree they are backward. Before marrying, they were inspired by the desire to soar in the heavenly heights and lead a life of bitter struggle. They got married partly because of physiological necessity and partly as a response to sweet talk about "mutual help." Thereupon they are forced to toil away and become "Noras returned home." Afraid of being thought "backward," those who are a bit more daring rush around begging nurseries to take their children. They ask for abortions and risk punishment and even death by secretly swallowing potions to produce abortions. But the answer comes back: "Isn't giving birth to children also work? You're just after an easy life; you want to be in the limelight. After all, what indispensable political work have you performed? Since you are so frightened of having children and are not willing to take responsibility once you have had them, why did you get married in the first place? No one forced you to." Under these conditions, it is impossible for women to escape this destiny of "backwardness." When women capable of working sacrifice their careers for the joys of motherhood, people always sing their praises. But after ten years or so, they have no way of escaping the tragedy of "backwardness." Even from my point of view, as a woman, there is nothing attractive about such "backward" elements. Their skin is beginning to wrinkle, their hair is growing thin, and fatigue is robbing them of their last traces of attractiveness. It should be self-evident that they are in a tragic situation. But whereas in the old society they would probably have been pitied and considered unfortunate, nowadays their tragedy is seen as something self-inflicted, as their just deserts. Is it not so that there is a discussion going on in legal circles as to whether divorces should be granted simply on the petition of one party or on the basis of mutual agreement? In the great majority of cases, it is the husband who petitions for divorce. For the wife to do so, she must be leading an immoral life, and then of course she deserves to be cursed.

I myself am a woman, and I therefore understand the failings of women better than others. But I also have a deeper understanding of what they suffer. Women are incapable of transcending the age they live in, of being perfect, or of being hard as steel. They are incapable of resisting all the temptations of society or all the silent oppression they suffer here in Yan'an. They each have their own past written in blood and tears; they have experienced great emotions—in elation as in depression, whether engaged in the lone battle of life or drawn into the humdrum stream of life. This is even truer of the women comrades who come to Yan'an, and I therefore have much sympathy for those fallen and classified as criminals. What is more, I hope that men, especially those in top positions, as well as women themselves, will consider the mistakes women commit in their social context. It would be better if there were less empty theorizing and more talk about real problems, so that theory and practice would not be divorced, and better if all Communist Party members were more responsible for their own moral conduct. But we must also hope for a little more from our women comrades, especially those in Yan'an. We must urge ourselves on and develop our comradely feeling.

People without ability have never been in a position to seize everything. Therefore, if women want equality, they must first strengthen

themselves. There is no need to stress this point, since we all understand it. Today there are certain to be people who make fine speeches
bragging about the need to acquire political power first. I would simply mention a few things that any frontliner, whether a proletarian, a
fighter in the war of resistance, or a woman, should pay attention to in
his or her everyday life:

1. Don't allow yourself to fall ill. A wild life can at times appear romantic,
   poetic, and attractive, but in today's conditions it is inappropriate. You
   are the best keeper of your life. There is nothing more unfortunate
   nowadays than to lose your health. It is closest to your heart. The only
   thing to do is keep a close watch on it, pay careful attention to it, and
   cherish it.

2. Make sure you are happy. Only when you are happy can you be youth-
   ful, active, fulfilled in your life, and steadfast in the face of all difficulties; only then will you see a future ahead of you and know how to
   enjoy yourself. This sort of happiness is not a life of contentment, but a
   life of struggle and of advance. Therefore we should all do some meaningful work each day and some reading, so that each of us is in a position to give something to others. Loafing about simply encourages the
   feeling that life is hollow, feeble, and in decay.

3. Use your brain, and make a habit of doing so. Correct any tendency not
   to think and ponder, or to swim with the current. Before you say or do
   anything, think whether what you are saying is right, whether that is
   the most suitable way of dealing with the problem, whether it goes
   against your own principles, whether you feel you can take responsibility for it. Then you will have no cause to regret your actions later. This
   is what is known as acting rationally. It is the best way of avoiding the
   pitfalls of sweet words and honeyed phrases, of being sidetracked by
   petty gains, of wasting our emotions and wasting our lives.

4. Resolution in hardship, perseverance to the end. Aware, modern women
   should identify and cast off all their rosy illusions. Happiness is to take
   up the struggle in the midst of the raging storm and not to pluck the
   lute in the moonlight or recite poetry among the blossoms. In the absence of the greatest resolution, it is very easy to falter in mid-path. Not
   to suffer is to become degenerate. The strength to carry on should be
   nurtured through the quality of "perseverance." People without great
   aims and ambitions rarely have the firmness of purpose that does not
   covet petty advantages or seek a comfortable existence. But only those
   who have aims and ambitions for the benefit, not of the individual, but
   of humankind as a whole can persevere to the end.

August 3, dawn

Postscript. On rereading this article, it seems to me that there is much room for improvement in the passage on what we should expect from women, but because I have to meet a deadline with the manuscript, I have no time to revise it. But I also feel that there are some things that, if said by a leader before a big audience, would probably evoke satisfaction. But when they are written by a woman, they are more than likely to be demolished. But since I have written it, I offer it as I always intended, for the perusal of those people who have similar views.

36

HUDA SHAARAWI
(1879–1947)

Speeches, Arab Feminist Conference
(EGYPT, 1944)

*For upper-class women in Egypt, where the British ruled from 1882 to
1923, European ideas converged with anticolonial politics to encourage
feminism. Huda Shaarawi grew up within the protected realm of her family, entered an arranged marriage at age thirteen, and wore a veil. She
began to question whether Islam required female seclusion when she participated in a salon run by a French-born mentor. Shaarawi helped found
a charity for poor women and, after traveling to France, she adopted the
goals of educational and political rights for women. She also became active
in the Egyptian independence movement, organizing women's mass
protests against British occupation. In the 1920s, Shaarawi established a
high school for girls and successfully campaigned for women's access to
Egyptian universities. In 1923, then a widow, she publicly unveiled after
her return to Cairo from a meeting of the International Alliance of Women,
an act that inspired urban women in the Middle East to follow her example. The same year she founded the Egyptian Feminist Union (EFU), serving as its president until 1947. In 1944 the EFU organized a pan-Arab
women's conference, from which the Arab Feminist Union emerged. As
Shaawari explained at the founding conference, Islamic law (Sharia),
if properly interpreted, granted women full equality with men, including
rights to education and political participation as well as responsibilities for
religious practice. She appealed to Arab men to recognize women as full
partners in the project of national advancement.*

Ladies and Gentlemen, The Arab woman who is equal to the man in duties and obligations will not accept, in the twentieth century, the distinctions between the sexes that the advanced countries have done away with. The Arab woman will not agree to be chained in slavery and to pay for the consequences of men's mistakes with respect to her country's rights and the future of her children. The woman also demands with her loudest voice to be restored her political rights, rights granted to her by the *Sharia* and dictated to her by the demands of the present. The advanced nations have recognised that the man and the woman are to each other like the brain and heart are to the body; if the balance between these two organs is upset the system of the whole body will be upset. Likewise, if the balance between the two sexes in the nation is upset it will disintegrate and collapse. The advanced nations, after careful examination into the matter, have come to believe in the equality of sexes in all rights even though their religious and secular laws have not reached the level Islam has reached in terms of justice towards the woman. Islam has given her the right to vote for the ruler and has allowed her to give opinions on questions of jurisprudence and religion. The woman, given by the Creator the right to vote for the successor of the Prophet, is deprived of the right to vote for a deputy in a circuit or district election by a (male) being created by God. At the same time, this right is enjoyed by a man who might have less education and experience than the woman. And she is the mother who has given birth to the man and has raised him and guided him. The *Sharia* gave her the right to education, to take part in the *hijra* (referring to the time of the Prophet Muhammad and his flight from Mecca to Medina), and to fight in the ranks of warriors and has made her equal to the man in all rights and responsibilities, even in the crimes that either sex can commit. However, the man who alone distributes rights, has kept for himself the right to legislate and rule, generously turning over to his partner his own share of responsibilities and sanctions without seeking her opinion about the division. The woman today demands to regain her share of rights that have been taken from her and gives back to the man the responsibilities and sanctions he has given to her. Gentlemen, this is justice and I do not believe that the Arab man who demands that the others give him back his usurped rights would be avaricious and not give the woman back her own lawful rights, all the more so since he himself has tasted the bitterness of deprivation and usurped rights.

Whenever the woman has demanded her rights in legislation and ruling to participate with the man in all things that bring good and benefit to her nation and her children, he claims he wants to spare the woman the perils of election battles, forgetting that she is more zealous about the election of deputies than men and that she already participates in election battles, quite often influencing the results. It is strange that in these cases she becomes the subject of his respect and kindness but when the election battle subsides he denies her what she has brought about.

If the man is sincere in what he says let him prove this by first giving the woman her political rights without her having to go through cruel political battles. In our parliamentary life there is wide opportunity for that in the elections of the governorates and municipality councils, and family affairs councils and in being appointed a member of the senate. Gentlemen, I leave room for the conferees to defend the rights of the woman in all areas.

THE CLOSING SPEECH

In this final session of the conference please allow me, on behalf of myself and the conference organisers, to thank you for honouring us with your sustained presence during the four days of this conference despite the length of the sessions dealing with issues men are often ill at ease with. I thank you for the concern you have expressed on these matters and for the attention you have given to our objectives, a successful step on the road towards realising our demands. We are proud of this step which signals, thanks be to God, that we have gained the confidence of male intellectuals and reformers in the demonstrated abilities of women in effectively carrying out different kinds of work in the service of country and nation. There are some who still hesitate to give us this confidence and do not understand the benefits that accrue to the nation when women enjoy their political rights. Others fear that the women will compete with them in work. Let me assure you all that if depriving women of the political and civil rights they demand, and that men oppose, would benefit the country, or would increase men's rights, we would relinquish them with pleasure, but, unfortunately, they would be lost rights that men could not use for themselves or for the country. These rights, buried alive, are of no benefit to society. Every woman who does not stand up for her legitimate rights would be considered as not standing up for the rights of her country and the future of her children and society. Every man who is pushed by his selfishness to trespass on the legitimate rights of women is robbing the rights of others and bringing harm to his country. He is an obstacle preventing the country from benefiting from the abilities and efforts of half the nation or more. He is impeding the advancement of his country and preventing it from being placed in the position it deserves—among the advanced nations whose civilisation was built on the shoulders of women and men together, just as Arab civilisation at the beginning of Islam was built on the co-operation and equality of the two sexes. Now after this feminist conference and the presentation of the cause of women to the public and the placing of its documents in a historical archive, it is incumbent upon man to record on his own page in the historical record that which will honour him and justify his stand before God, the nation, and future generations.

37.

FUNMILAYO RANSOME-KUTI
(1900–78)

"We Had Equality till Britain Came"
(NIGERIA, 1947)

When Funmilayo Ransome-Kuti of Nigeria visited England in 1947, she, like many other African women living under colonial rule, questioned the idea of European progress. Born in a Yoruba province where women had long been active in trade and shared some political authority with men, Ransome-Kuti studied at a girls' school in England, became a teacher, married a Nigerian Christian clergyman, and raised four children. In the 1940s the local women's union she formed offered literacy classes for poor women and then evolved into a national women's movement to improve schools and health care and to end unfair taxation of women. After refusing to pay taxes herself, Ransome-Kuti led mass demonstrations of women, helping to bring about the abdication of the Nigerian king. She was instrumental in forming the Nigerian Women's Union in 1949, which advocated women's enfranchisement and their representation in government. Active in transnational women's movements, Ransome-Kuti worked with the Women's International League for Peace and Freedom. Although not a communist herself, she agreed to write an article about the condition of women in Nigeria for the British Communist Party newspaper, the Daily Worker. *Along with detailing the "appalling" conditions of life for Nigerian women, she called on British women to take responsibility for the plight of colonial subjects. After Nigerian independence in 1960, Ransome-Kuti became a critic of the government.*

Before the British advent in Nigeria, life there was mainly agricultural, and there was division of labour between men and women. The men cultivated the land and sowed, and it was chiefly the duty of women to reap. Women owned property, traded and exercised considerable political and social influence in society. They were responsible for crowning the Kings on Coronation days. Whatever disabilities there were then endured both by men and women alike. With the advent of British rule, slavery was abolished, and Christianity introduced into many parts of the country, but instead of the women being educated and assisted to live like human beings their condition has deteriorated.

The women of Nigeria are poverty-stricken, disease ridden, superstitious and badly nourished, although they are the main producers of their country's wealth. They make palm-oil, ground-nut oil, pottery; they spin and weave clothing; they haul rice, prepare cocoa and coffee beans, and so on. The men sow and hoe, and women do the rest of the work. Yet they hardly realise an appreciable income—7s. 6d. to 15s a month is the normal rate of pay and this has not come up while the cost of living is now very high. The reason is that most of their producers are bought by the Combined Mercantile Firms which dictate the buying prices.

FOUR SCHOOLS

Not more than one per cent of the women of Nigeria can read or write. Throughout Nigeria, which is 372,674 square miles, there are only four secondary schools for girls, three in the colony of Lagos, and one in the protectorate at Ibadan. The Union of Women has tried to run voluntary schools for adult education but the women, who start work at four in the morning are, by evening, too tired to learn.

The health of Nigerian women is appalling. Most of them are disease-ridden. Malaria, hookworm disease, guinea-worm, tuberculosis and diseases of pregnancy take an annual high percentage in mortality rate. Yaws, gonorrhoea [sic], syphillis and leprosy constitute major problems which must be immediately tackled. There is no free treatment for women and children in publicly-owned institutions, for the medical officers, both European and African, demand fees before attending to the sick who come there.

DEVOTED NURSE

Maternity and Child Welfare Services are still in their experimental stages where they exist at all. Child Welfare Centres are very few, poorly staffed and ill-organized. In one of the child welfare centres in Abeokuta, in the Western Province, an old nurse, about 80 years of age, is in charge, with a few un-trained girls, straight from school to help her, without the help of a qualified medical practitioner. She is a Britisher of the type of Florence Nightingale or Mary Slessor. She prefers to die in Nigeria among the people she loves so well.

STRIPPED NAKED

Taxation of women is unknown in the Colony and Protectorate of Nigeria, with the singular exception of the Abeokuta and Ijebu Provinces of Western Nigeria. Here poll tax and income tax are forcibly demanded of women. The method of collecting and assessing taxes is abominable. Young girls are sometimes stripped naked in the street by the men officially designated collectors in order to ascertain whether they are mature enough to pay tax or not. Income tax is assessed arbitrarily. The members of the assessment committee work on commission basis: the more money they are able to collect, the greater their commission, so they relentlessly extort money from those who can ill-afford to pay.

WE APPEAL . . .

This is why the people of Nigeria and the Cameroons have sent a delegation of protest to Britain under the auspices of their National

Council. As the only woman on the deputation, I have been charged with the duty—"to appeal fervently to the women of Great Britain, in the name of the women of Nigeria and the Cameroons under British Mandate, to help free us from slavery, political, social and economic, in order that we may be able to take our rightful place amidst the Commonwealth of Nations."

Your country is responsible for the state of ours. Can you let this state of things continue?

Finally, I would like to make it clear that we are neither anti-British nor desire to drive the British from our country. But we are definitely anti-oppression and anti-exploitation.

38

SIMONE DE BEAUVOIR
(1908–86)

The Second Sex
(FRANCE, 1949)

One of the most important feminist texts of the twentieth century, The
Second Sex *carries on the centuries-long project of refuting myths of female inferiority and rejecting biological explanations of women's secondary status. A major force in French intellectual life and a prize-winning
novelist, Simone de Beauvoir applied her extensive knowledge of philosophical, historical, and psychological theory to analyze the problem of
modern woman. De Beauvoir drew on both existentialist and Marxist
ideas when she conceptualized woman as an immanent "Other," unable to
achieve human freedom, who was produced in opposition to a transcen-
dent male, who could choose liberty.* The Second Sex *documents a range
of female experiences to show how women are constrained by culture, rejecting Freudian views and favoring the historical materialism of Marx.
De Beauvoir argued that economic independence, along with birth control,
abortion, and child care, would enable women to choose freely their own
individual destinies. She herself chose not to marry, although she had a
lifelong relationship with the philosopher Jean-Paul Sartre as well as relationships with women. At the time she wrote* The Second Sex, *de
Beauvoir did not identify as a feminist, but the book (first translated into
English in 1953) had a profound influence on American feminists. Asked
in the 1970s about her views, de Beauvoir stated that she no longer believed that socialism would emancipate women; rather, she embraced feminism as a potentially revolutionary force that would benefit all.*

For a long time I have hesitated to write a book on woman. The subject is irritating, especially to women; and it is not new. Enough ink has been spilled in the quarreling over feminism, now practically over, and perhaps we should say no more about it. It is still talked about, however, for the voluminous nonsense uttered during the last century seems to have done little to illuminate the problem. After all, is there a problem? And if so, what is it? Are there women, really? Most assuredly the theory of the eternal feminine still has its adherents who will whisper in your ear: "Even in Russia women still are *women*"; and other erudite persons—sometimes the very same—say with a sigh: "Woman is losing her way, woman is lost." One wonders if women still exist, if they will always exist, whether or not it is desirable that they should, what place they occupy in this world, what their place should be. "What has become of women?" was asked recently in an ephemeral magazine.

But first we must ask: what is a woman? *"Tota mulier in utero,"* says one, "woman is a womb." But in speaking of certain women, connoisseurs declare that they are not women, although they are equipped with a uterus like the rest. All agree in recognizing the fact that females exist in the human species; today as always they make up about one half of humanity. And yet we are told that femininity is in danger; we are exhorted to be women, remain women, become women. It would appear, then, that every female human being is not necessarily a woman; to be so considered she must share in that mysterious and threatened reality known as femininity. Is this attribute something secreted by the ovaries? Or is it a Platonic essence, a product of the philosophic imagination? Is a rustling petticoat enough to bring it down to earth? Although some women try zealously to incarnate this essence, it is hardly patentable. It is frequently described in vague and dazzling terms that seem to have been borrowed from the vocabulary of the seers, and indeed in the times of St. Thomas it was considered an essence as certainly defined as the somniferous virtue of the poppy.

But conceptualism has lost ground. The biological and social sciences no longer admit the existence of unchangeably fixed entities that determine given characteristics, such as those ascribed to woman, the Jew, or the Negro. Science regards any characteristic as a reaction dependent in part upon a *situation*. If today femininity no longer exists, then it never existed. But does the word *woman*, then, have no specific content? This is stoutly affirmed by those who hold to the philosophy of the enlightenment, of rationalism, of nominalism; women, to them, are merely the human beings arbitrarily designated by the word *woman*. Many American women particularly are prepared to think that there is no longer any place for woman as such; if a backward individual still takes herself for a woman, her friends advise her to be psychoanalyzed and thus get rid of this obsession. In regard to a work, *Modern Woman: The Lost Sex*, which in other respects has its irritating features, Dorothy Parker has written: "I cannot be just to books which treat of woman as woman.... My idea is that all of us, men as well as women, should be regarded as human beings." But nominalism is a rather inadequate doctrine, and the antifemininists have had no trouble in showing that women simply *are not* men. Surely woman is, like man, a human being; but such a declaration is abstract. The fact is that every concrete human being is always a singular, separate individual. To decline to accept such notions as the eternal feminine, the black soul, the Jewish character, is not to deny that Jews, Negroes, women exist today—this denial does not represent a liberation for those concerned, but rather a flight from reality. Some years ago a well-known woman writer refused to permit her portrait to appear in a series of photographs especially devoted to women writers; she wished to be counted among the men. But in order to gain this privilege she made use of her husband's influence! Women who assert that they are men lay claim none the less to masculine consideration and respect. I recall also a young Trotskyite standing on a platform at a boisterous meeting and getting ready to use her fists, in spite of her evident fragility. She was denying her feminine weakness; but it was for love of a militant male whose equal she wished to be. The attitude of defiance of many American women proves that they are haunted by a sense of their femininity. In truth, to go for a walk with one's eyes open is enough to demonstrate that humanity is divided into two classes of individuals whose clothes, faces, bodies, smiles, gaits, interests, and occupations are manifestly different. Perhaps these differences are superficial, perhaps they are destined to disappear. What is certain is that right now they do most obviously exist.

If her functioning as a female is not enough to define woman, if we decline also to explain her through "the eternal feminine," and if nevertheless we admit, provisionally, that women do exist, then we must face the question: what is a woman?

To state the question is, to me, to suggest, at once, a preliminary answer. The fact that I ask it is in itself significant. A man would never get the notion of writing a book on the peculiar situation of the human male. But if I wish to define myself, I must first of all say: "I am a woman"; on this truth must be based all further discussion. A man never begins by presenting himself as an individual of a certain sex; it goes without saying that he is a man. The terms *masculine* and *feminine* are used symmetrically only as a matter of form, as on legal papers. In actuality the relation of the two sexes is not quite like that of two electrical poles, for man represents both the positive and the neutral, as is indicated by the common use of *man* to designate human beings in general; whereas woman represents only the negative, defined by limiting criteria, without reciprocity. In the midst of an abstract discussion it is vexing to hear a man say: "You think thus and so because you are a woman"; but I know that my only defense is to reply: "I think thus and so because it is true," thereby removing my subjective self from the argument. It would be out of the question to reply: "And you think the contrary because you are a man," for it is understood that the fact of being a man is no peculiarity. A man is in the right in being a man; it is the woman who is in the wrong. It amounts to this: just as for the ancients there was an absolute vertical with reference to which the oblique was defined, so there is an absolute human type, the masculine. Woman has ovaries, a uterus; these peculiarities imprison her in her subjectivity, circumscribe her within the limits of her own nature. It is often said that she thinks with her glands. Man superbly ignores the fact that his anatomy also includes glands, such as the testicles, and that they secrete hormones. He thinks of his body as a direct and normal connection with the world, which he believes he apprehends objectively, whereas he regards the body of woman as a hindrance, a prison, weighed down by everything peculiar to it. "The female is a female by virtue of a certain *lack* of qualities," said Aristotle; "we

should regard the female nature as afflicted with a natural defective-
ness." And St. Thomas for his part pronounced woman to be an "imperfect man," an "incidental" being. This is symbolized in Genesis
where Eve is depicted as made from what Bossuet called "a supernu-
merary bone" of Adam.

Thus humanity is male and man defines woman not in herself
but as relative to him; she is not regarded as an autonomous being.
Michelet writes: "Woman, the relative being...." And Benda is most
positive in his *Rapport d'Uriel:* "The body of man makes sense in itself
quite apart from that of woman, whereas the latter seems wanting in
significance by itself.... Man can think of himself without woman. She
cannot think of herself without man." And she is simply what man decrees; thus she is called "the sex," by which is meant that she appears
essentially to the male as a sexual being. For him she is sex—absolute
sex, no less. She is defined and differentiated with reference to man
and not he with reference to her; she is the incidental, the inessential
as opposed to the essential. He is the Subject, he is the Absolute—she
is the Other.

The category of the *Other* is as primordial as consciousness itself.
In the most primitive societies, in the most ancient mythologies, one
finds the expression of a duality—that of the Self and the Other. This
duality was not originally attached to the division of the sexes; it was
not dependent upon any empirical facts. It is revealed in such works
as that of Granet on Chinese thought and those of Dumézil on the
East Indies and Rome. The feminine element was at first no more involved in such pairs as Varuna-Mitra, Uranus-Zeus, Sun-Moon, and
Day-Night than it was in the contrasts between Good and Evil, lucky
and unlucky auspices, right and left, God and Lucifer. Otherness is a
fundamental category of human thought.

Thus it is that no group ever sets itself up as the One without at
once setting up the Other over against itself. If three travelers chance
to occupy the same compartment, that is enough to make vaguely hostile "others" out of all the rest of the passengers on the train. In small-
town eyes all persons not belonging to the village are "strangers" and
suspect; to the native of a country all who inhabit other countries are
"foreigners"; Jews are "different" for the anti-Semite, Negroes are "inferior" for American racists, aborigines are "natives" for colonists, proletarians are the "lower class" for the privileged....

But the other consciousness, the other ego, sets up a reciprocal claim. The native traveling abroad is shocked to find himself in turn regarded as a "stranger" by the natives of neighboring countries. As a matter of fact, wars, festivals, trading, treaties, and contests among tribes, nations, and classes tend to deprive the concept *Other* of its absolute sense and to make manifest its relativity; willy-nilly, individuals and groups are forced to realize the reciprocity of their relations. How is it, then, that this reciprocity has not been recognized between the sexes, that one of the contrasting terms is set up as the sole essential, denying any relativity in regard to its correlative and defining the latter as pure otherness? Why is it that women do not dispute male sovereignty? No subject will readily volunteer to become the object, the inessential; it is not the Other who, in defining himself as the Other, establishes the One. The Other is posed as such by the One in defining himself as the One. But if the Other is not to regain the status of being the One, he must be submissive enough to accept this alien point of view. Whence comes this submission in the case of woman?

There are, to be sure, other cases in which a certain category has been able to dominate another completely for a time. Very often this privilege depends upon inequality of numbers—the majority imposes its rule upon the minority or persecutes it. But women are not a minority, like the American Negroes or the Jews; there are as many women as men on earth. Again, the two groups concerned have often been originally independent; they may have been formerly unaware of each other's existence, or perhaps they recognized each other's autonomy. But a historical event has resulted in the subjugation of the weaker by the stronger. The scattering of the Jews, the introduction of slavery into America, the conquests of imperialism are examples in point. In these cases the oppressed retained at least the memory of former days; they possessed in common a past, a tradition, sometimes a religion or a culture.

The parallel drawn by Bebel between women and the proletariat is valid in that neither ever formed a minority or a separate collective unit of mankind. And instead of a single historical event it is in both cases a historical development that explains their status as a class and accounts for the membership of *particular individuals* in that class. But proletarians have not always existed, whereas there have always been women. They are women in virtue of their anatomy and physiology.

Throughout history they have always been subordinated to men, and hence their dependency is not the result of a historical event or a social change—it was not something that *occurred*. The reason why otherness in this case seems to be an absolute is in part that it lacks the contingent or incidental nature of historical facts. A condition brought about at a certain time can be abolished at some other time, as the Negroes of Haiti and others have proved; but it might seem that a natural condition is beyond the possibility of change. In truth, however, the nature of things is no more immutably given, once for all, than is historical reality. If woman seems to be the inessential which never becomes the essential, it is because she herself fails to bring about this change. Proletarians say "We"; Negroes also. Regarding themselves as subjects, they transform the bourgeois, the whites, into "others." But women do not say "We," except at some congress of feminists or similar formal demonstration; men say "women," and women use the same word in referring to themselves. They do not authentically assume a subjective attitude. The proletarians have accomplished the revolution in Russia, the Negroes in Haiti, the Indo-Chinese are battling for it in Indo-China; but the women's effort has never been anything more than a symbolic agitation. They have gained only what men have been willing to grant; they have taken nothing, they have only received.

The reason for this is that women lack concrete means for organizing themselves into a unit which can stand face to face with the correlative unit. They have no past, no history, no religion of their own; and they have no such solidarity of work and interest as that of the proletariat. They are not even promiscuously herded together in the way that creates community feeling among the American Negroes, the ghetto Jews, the workers of Saint-Denis, or the factory hands of Renault. They live dispersed among the males, attached through residence, housework, economic condition, and social standing to certain men—fathers or husbands—more firmly than they are to other women. If they belong to the bourgeoisie, they feel solidarity with men of that class, not with proletarian women; if they are white, their allegiance is to white men, not to Negro women. The proletariat can propose to massacre the ruling class, and a sufficiently fanatical Jew or Negro might dream of getting sole possession of the atomic bomb and making humanity wholly Jewish or black; but woman cannot even dream of exterminating the males. The bond that unites her to her oppressors is not comparable to any other. The division of the sexes is a biological fact, not an event in human history. Male and female stand opposed within a primordial *Mitsein*, and woman has not broken it. The couple is a fundamental unity with its two halves riveted together, and the cleavage of society along the line of sex is impossible. Here is to be found the basic trait of woman: she is the Other in a totality of which the two components are necessary to one another....

But it will be asked at once: how did all this begin? It is easy to see that the duality of the sexes, like any duality, gives rise to conflict. And doubtless the winner will assume the status of absolute. But why should man have won from the start? It seems possible that women could have won the victory; or that the outcome of the conflict might never have been decided. How is it that this world has always belonged to the men and that things have begun to change only recently? Is this change a good thing? Will it bring about an equal sharing of the world between men and women?

These questions are not new, and they have often been answered. But the very fact that woman *is the Other* tends to cast suspicion upon all the justifications that men have ever been able to provide for it. These have all too evidently been dictated by men's interest. A little-known feminist of the seventeenth century, Poulain de la Barre, put it this way: "All that has been written about women by men should be suspect, for the men are at once judge and party to the lawsuit." Everywhere, at all times, the males have displayed their satisfaction in feeling that they are the lords of creation. "Blessed be God ... that He did not make me a woman," say the Jews in their morning prayers, while their wives pray on a note of resignation: "Blessed be the Lord, who created me according to His will." The first among the blessings for which Plato thanked the gods was that he had been created free, not enslaved; the second, a man, not a woman. But the males could not enjoy this privilege fully unless they believed it to be founded on the absolute and the eternal; they sought to make the fact of their supremacy into a right. "Being men, those who have made and compiled the laws have favored their own sex, and jurists have elevated these laws into principles," to quote Poulain de la Barre once more.

Legislators, priests, philosophers, writers, and scientists have striven to show that the subordinate position of woman is willed in heaven and advantageous on earth. [...]

It was only later, in the eighteenth century, that genuinely democratic men began to view the matter objectively. Diderot, among others, strove to show that woman is, like man, a human being. Later John Stuart Mill came fervently to her defense. But these philosophers displayed unusual impartiality. In the nineteenth century the feminist quarrel became again a quarrel of partisans. One of the consequences of the industrial revolution was the entrance of women into productive labor, and it was just here that the claims of the feminists emerged from the realm of theory and acquired an economic basis, while their opponents became the more aggressive. Although landed property lost power to some extent, the bourgeoisie clung to the old morality that found the guarantee of private property in the solidity of the family. Woman was ordered back into the home the more harshly as her emancipation became a real menace. Even within the working class the men endeavored to restrain woman's liberation, because they began to see the women as dangerous competitors—the more so because they were accustomed to work for lower wages.

In proving woman's inferiority, the antifeminists then began to draw not only upon religion, philosophy, and theology, as before, but also upon science—biology, experimental psychology, etc. At most they were willing to grant "equality in difference" to the *other* sex. That profitable formula is most significant; it is precisely like the "equal but separate" formula of the Jim Crow laws aimed at the North American Negroes. As is well known, this so-called equalitarian segregation has resulted only in the most extreme discrimination.... [T]here are deep similarities between the situation of woman and that of the Negro. Both are being emancipated today from a like paternalism, and the former master class wishes to "keep them in their place"—that is, the place chosen for them. In both cases the former masters lavish more or less sincere eulogies, either on the virtues of "the good Negro" with his dormant, childish, merry soul—the submissive Negro—or on the merits of the woman who is "truly feminine"—that is, frivolous, infantile, irresponsible—the submissive woman. In both cases the dominant class bases its argument on a state of affairs that it has itself created.... Yes, women on the whole *are* today inferior to men; that is, their situation affords them fewer possibilities. The question is: should that state of affairs continue?

Many men hope that it will continue; not all have given up the battle. The conservative bourgeoisie still see in the emancipation of women a menace to their morality and their interests. Some men dread feminine competition. Recently a male student wrote in the *Hebdo-Latin:* "Every woman student who goes into medicine or law robs us of a job." He never questioned his rights in this world. And economic interests are not the only ones concerned. One of the benefits that oppression confers upon the oppressors is that the most humble among them is made to *feel* superior; thus, a "poor white" in the South can console himself with the thought that he is not a "dirty nigger"—and the more prosperous whites cleverly exploit this pride.

Similarly, the most mediocre of males feels himself a demigod as compared with women....

It is, in point of fact, a difficult matter for man to realize the extreme importance of social discriminations which seem outwardly insignificant but which produce in woman moral and intellectual effects so profound that they appear to spring from her original nature. The most sympathetic of men never fully comprehend woman's concrete situation. And there is no reason to put much trust in the men when they rush to the defense of privileges whose full extent they can hardly measure. We shall not, then, permit ourselves to be intimidated by the number and violence of the attacks launched against women, nor to be entrapped by the self-seeking eulogies bestowed on the "true woman," nor to profit by the enthusiasm for woman's destiny manifested by men who would not for the world have any part of it.

We should consider the arguments of the feminists with no less suspicion, however, for very often their controversial aim deprives them of all real value. If the "woman question" seems trivial, it is because masculine arrogance has made of it a "quarrel"; and when quarreling one no longer reasons well. People have tirelessly sought to prove that woman is superior, inferior, or equal to man. Some say that, having been created after Adam, she is evidently a secondary being; others say on the contrary that Adam was only a rough draft and that God succeeded in producing the human being in perfection when He created Eve. Woman's brain is smaller; yes, but it is relatively larger.

Christ was made a man; yes, but perhaps for his greater humility. Each argument at once suggests its opposite, and both are often fallacious. If we are to gain understanding, we must get out of these ruts; we must discard the vague notions of superiority, inferiority, equality which have hitherto corrupted every discussion of the subject and start afresh....

If we survey some of the works on woman, we note that one of the points of view most frequently adopted is that of the public good, the general interest; and one always means by this the benefit of society as one wishes it to be maintained or established. For our part, we hold that the only public good is that which assures the private good of the citizens; we shall pass judgment on institutions according to their effectiveness in giving concrete opportunities to individuals. But we do not confuse the idea of private interest with that of happiness, although that is another common point of view. Are not women of the harem more happy than women voters? Is not the housekeeper happier than the working-woman? It is not too clear just what the word *happy* really means and still less what true values it may mask. There is no possibility of measuring the happiness of others, and it is always easy to describe as happy the situation in which one wishes to place them.

In particular those who are condemned to stagnation are often pronounced happy on the pretext that happiness consists in being at rest. This notion we reject, for our perspective is that of existentialist ethics. Every subject plays his part as such specifically through exploits or projects that serve as a mode of transcendence; he achieves liberty only through a continual reaching out toward other liberties. There is no justification for present existence other than its expansion into an indefinitely open future. Every time transcendence falls back into immanence, stagnation, there is a degradation of existence into the *"en-soi"*—the brutish life of subjection to given conditions—and of liberty into constraint and contingence. This downfall represents a moral fault if the subject consents to it; if it is inflicted upon him, it spells frustration and oppression. In both cases it is an absolute evil. Every individual concerned to justify his existence feels that his existence involves an undefined need to transcend himself, to engage in freely chosen projects.

Now, what peculiarly signalizes the situation of woman is that she— a free and autonomous being like all human creatures—nevertheless finds herself living in a world where men compel her to assume the status of the Other. They propose to stabilize her as object and to doom her to immanence since her transcendence is to be overshadowed and forever transcended by another ego (*conscience*) which is essential and sovereign. The drama of woman lies in this conflict between the fundamental aspirations of every subject (ego)—who always regards the self as the essential—and the compulsions of a situation in which she is the inessential. How can a human being in woman's situation attain fulfillment? What roads are open to her? Which are blocked? How can independence be recovered in a state of dependency? What circumstances limit woman's liberty and how can they be overcome? These are the fundamental questions on which I would fain throw some light. This means that I am interested in the fortunes of the individual as defined not in terms of happiness but in terms of liberty.

Quite evidently this problem would be without significance if we were to believe that woman's destiny is inevitably determined by physiological, psychological, or economic forces. Hence I shall discuss first of all the light in which woman is viewed by biology, psychoanalysis, and historical materialism. Next I shall try to show exactly how the concept of the "truly feminine" has been fashioned—why woman has been defined as the Other—and what have been the consequences from man's point of view. Then from woman's point of view I shall describe the world in which women must live; and thus we shall be able to envisage the difficulties in their way as, endeavoring to make their escape from the sphere hitherto assigned them, they aspire to full membership in the human race.

39

FEDERATION OF SOUTH AFRICAN WOMEN

Women's Charter and Aims

(SOUTH AFRICA, 1954)

In South Africa, the minority of whites descended from British and Dutch colonial rulers maintained a system of racial control known as apartheid. In response, African women and men protested constraints on their liberties. In the early twentieth century, traditional women's organizations employed passive resistance to protest laws requiring African women to carry passes in order to move about, resulting in women's exclusion from the laws. In the 1940s a Women's League formed within the African National Congress (ANC), which opposed white minority rule. When the white government reinstituted the pass system, women again defied the law. In 1954, women active in the anti-apartheid movement, including white women from the Communist Party, created the Federation of South African Women (FSAW). The federation addressed discrimination against women both in society and within the antiapartheid movement. Like other feminist documents, their charter recognized that social attitudes lagged behind the economic transformations in women's lives; only with women's freedom, the charter insisted, would national liberation be complete. The FSAW gathered more than ten thousand women at a 1956 march to protest pass laws and mobilized non-violent resistance for another decade. The anti-apartheid movement culminated in a 1996 democratic constitution that ensured women's full citizenship.

PREAMBLE: We, the women of South Africa, wives and mothers, working women and housewives, African, Indians, European and Coloured, hereby declare our aim of striving for the removal of all laws, regulations, conventions and customs that discriminate against us as women, and that deprive us in any way of our inherent right to the advantages, responsibilities and opportunities that society offers to any one section of the population.

A SINGLE SOCIETY: We women do not form a society separate from the men. There is only one society, and it is made up of both women and men. As women we share the problems and anxieties of our men, and join hands with them to remove social evils and obstacles to progress.

TEST OF CIVILISATION: The level of civilisation which any society has reached can be measured by the degree of freedom that its members enjoy. The status of women is a test of civilisation. Measured by that standard, South Africa must be considered low in the scale of civilised nations.

WOMEN'S LOT: We women share with our menfolk the cares and anxieties imposed by poverty and its evils. As wives and mothers, it falls upon us to make small wages stretch a long way. It is we who feel the cries of our children when they are hungry and sick. It is our lot to keep and care for the homes that are too small, broken and dirty to be kept clean. We know the burden of looking after children and land when our husbands are away in the mines, on the farms, and in the towns earning our daily bread.

We know what it is to keep family life going in pondokkies and shanties, or in overcrowded one-room apartments. We know the bitterness of children taken to lawless ways, of daughters becoming unmarried mothers whilst still at school, of boys and girls growing up without education, training or jobs at a living wage.

POOR AND RICH: These are evils that need not exist. They exist because the society in which we live is divided into poor and rich, into non-European and European. They exist because there are privileges for the few, discrimination and harsh treatment for the many. We women have stood and will stand shoulder to shoulder with our menfolk in a common struggle against poverty, race and class discrimination, and the evils of the colour-bar.

NATIONAL LIBERATION: As members of the National Liberatory movements and Trade Unions, in and through our various organisations, we march forward with our men in the struggle for liberation and the defence of the working people. We pledge ourselves to keep high the banner of equality, fraternity and liberty. As women there rests upon us also the burden of removing from our society all the social differences developed in past times between men and women, which have the effect of keeping our sex in a position of inferiority and subordination.

EQUALITY FOR WOMEN: We resolve to struggle for the removal of laws and customs that deny African women the right to own, inherit or alienate property. We resolve to work for a change in the laws of marriage such as are found amongst our African, Malay and Indian people, which have the effect of placing wives in the position of legal subjection to husbands, and giving husbands the power to dispose of wives' property and earnings, and dictate to them in all matters affecting them and their children.

We recognise that the women are treated as minors by these marriage and property laws because of ancient and revered traditions and customs which had their origin in the antiquity of the people and no doubt served purposes of great value in bygone times.

There was a time in the African society when every woman reaching marriageable stage was assured of a husband, home, land and security.

Then husbands and wives with their children belonged to families and clans that supplied most of their own material needs and were largely self-sufficient. Men and women were partners in a compact and closely integrated family unit.

WOMEN WHO LABOUR: Those conditions have gone. The tribal and kinship society to which they belonged has been destroyed as a result of the loss of tribal land, migration of men away from the tribal home, the growth of towns and industries, and the rise of a great body of wage-earners on the farms and in the urban areas, who depend wholly or mainly on wages for a livelihood.

Thousands of African women, like Indians, Coloured and European women, are employed today in factories, homes, offices, shops, on farms, in professions as nurses, teachers and the like. As unmarried women, widows or divorcees they have to fend for themselves, often without the assistance of a male relative. Many of them are responsible not only for their own livelihood but also that of their children.

Large numbers of women today are in fact the sole breadwinners and heads of their families.

FOREVER MINORS: Nevertheless, the laws and practices derived from an earlier and different state of society are still applied to them. They are responsible for their own person and their children. Yet the law seeks to enforce upon them the status of a minor.

Not only are African, Coloured and Indian women denied political rights, but they are also in many parts of the Union denied the same status as men in such matters as the right to enter into contracts, to own and dispose of property, and to exercise guardianship over their children.

OBSTACLE TO PROGRESS: The law has lagged behind the development of society; it no longer corresponds to the actual social and economic position of women. The law has become an obstacle to progress of the women, and therefore a brake on the whole of society.

This intolerable condition would not be allowed to continue were it not for the refusal of a large section of our menfolk to concede to us women the rights and privileges which they demand for themselves.

We shall teach the men that they cannot hope to liberate themselves from the evils of discrimination and prejudice as long as they fail to extend to women complete and unqualified equality in law and in practice.

NEED FOR EDUCATION: We also recognise that large numbers of our womenfolk continue to be bound by traditional practices and conventions, and fail to realise that these have become obsolete and a brake on progress. It is our duty and privilege to enlist all women in our struggle for emancipation and to bring to them all realisation of the intimate relationship that exists between their status of inferiority as women and the inferior status to which their people are subjected by discriminatory laws and colour prejudices.

It is our intention to carry out a nation-wide programme of education that will bring home to the men and women of all national groups the realisation that freedom cannot be won for any one section or for the people as a whole as long as we women are kept in bondage.

AN APPEAL: We women appeal to all progressive organisations, to members of the great National Liberatory movements, to the trade unions and working class organisations, to the churches, educational and welfare organisations, to all progressive men and women who have the interests of the people at heart, to join with us in this great and noble endeavour.

OUR AIMS: We declare the following aims:

This organisation is formed for the purpose of uniting women in common action for the removal of all political, legal, economic and social disabilities. We shall strive for women to obtain:

1. The right to vote and to be elected to all State bodies, without restriction or discrimination.
2. The right to full opportunities for employment with equal pay and possibilities of promotion in all spheres of work.
3. Equal rights with men in relation to property, marriage and children, and for the removal of all laws and customs that deny women such equal rights.
4. For the development of every child through free compulsory education for all; for the protection of mother and child through maternity homes, welfare clinics, creches and nursery schools, in countryside and towns; through proper homes for all, and through the provision of water, light, transport, sanitation, and other amenities of modern civilisation.

5. For the removal of all laws that restrict free movement, that prevent or hinder the right of free association and activity in democratic organisations, and the right to participate in the work of these organisations.

6. To build and strengthen women's sections in the National Liberatory movements, the organisation of women in trade unions, and through the peoples' varied organisation.

7. To cooperate with all other organisations that have similar aims in South Africa as well as throughout the world.

8. To strive for permanent peace throughout the world.

40.

BETTY FRIEDAN
(1921–2006)

The Feminine Mystique
(UNITED STATES, 1963)

The daughter of a Russian Jewish immigrant and a former newspaper-woman, Bettye Goldstein graduated from Smith College and worked as a journalist in the labor movement before marrying and raising children in a post–World War II American suburb. Her 1963 bestselling critique of the "mystique of feminine fulfillment" helped revive liberal feminism in the United States after a period of quiescence. Like other American social critics of Cold War–era conformity, Friedan called attention to the limits of affluence and the importance of individualism. She particularly faulted psychologists, educators, and the media for constructing an unrewarding feminine ideal, and she skillfully used women's personal stories to expose the limits of suburban motherhood. Friedan's book struck a chord among white, middle-class, and educated women in the 1960s, many of whom claimed that it "changed my life." She inspired these women to reject the dominant stereotypes of neurotic career women and to seek creative and rewarding work outside the home. A highly visible leader of American feminism, Friedan helped found the National Organization for Women (1966), which sought equal rights legislation, the National Association for the Repeal of Abortion Laws (1969), and the National Women's Political Caucus (1971).

The problem lay buried, unspoken, for many years in the minds of American women. It was a strange stirring, a sense of dissatisfaction, a yearning that women suffered in the middle of the twentieth century in the United States. Each suburban wife struggled with it alone. As she made the beds, shopped for groceries, matched slipcover material, ate peanut butter sandwiches with her children, chauffeured Cub Scouts and Brownies, lay beside her husband at night—she was afraid to ask even of herself the silent question—"Is this all?"

For over fifteen years there was no word of this yearning in the millions of words written about women, for women, in all the columns, books and articles by experts telling women their role was to seek fulfillment as wives and mothers. Over and over women heard in voices of tradition and of Freudian sophistication that they could desire no greater destiny than to glory in their own femininity. Experts told them how to catch a man and keep him, how to breastfeed children and handle their toilet training, how to cope with sibling rivalry and adolescent rebellion; how to buy a dishwasher, bake bread, cook gourmet snails, and build a swimming pool with their own hands; how to dress, look, and act more feminine and make marriage more exciting; how to keep their husbands from dying young and their sons from growing into delinquents. They were taught to pity the neurotic, unfeminine, unhappy women who wanted to be poets or physicists or presidents. They learned that truly feminine women do not want careers, higher education, political rights—the independence and the opportunities that the old-fashioned feminists fought for. Some women, in their forties and fifties, still remembered painfully giving up those dreams, but most of the younger women no longer even thought about them. A thousand expert voices applauded their femininity, their adjustment, their new maturity. All they had to do was devote their lives from earliest girlhood to finding a husband and bearing children.

By the end of the nineteen-fifties, the average marriage age of women in America dropped to 20, and was still dropping, into the teens. Fourteen million girls were engaged by 17. The proportion of women attending college in comparison with men dropped from 47 per cent in 1920 to 35 per cent in 1958. A century earlier, women had fought for higher education; now girls went to college to get a husband. By the mid-fifties, 60 per cent dropped out of college to marry, or because they were afraid too much education would be a marriage bar. Colleges built dormitories for "married students," but the students were almost always the husbands. A new degree was instituted for the wives—"Ph.T." (Putting Husband Through).

Then American girls began getting married in high school. And the women's magazines, deploring the unhappy statistics about these young marriages, urged that courses on marriage, and marriage counselors, be installed in the high schools. Girls started going steady at twelve and thirteen, in junior high. Manufacturers put out brassieres with false bosoms of foam rubber for little girls of ten. And an advertisement for a child's dress, sizes 3–6x, in the *New York Times* in the fall of 1960, said: "She Too Can Join the Man-Trap Set."

By the end of the fifties, the United States birthrate was overtaking India's. The birth-control movement, renamed Planned Parenthood, was asked to find a method whereby women who had been advised that a third or fourth baby would be born dead or defective might have it anyhow. Statisticians were especially astounded at the fantastic increase in the number of babies among college women. Where once they had two children, now they had four, five, six. Women who had once wanted careers were now making careers out of having babies. So rejoiced *Life* magazine in a 1956 paean to the movement of American women back to the home.

In a New York hospital, a woman had a nervous breakdown when she found she could not breastfeed her baby. In other hospitals, women dying of cancer refused a drug which research had proved might save their lives: its side effects were said to be unfeminine. "If I have only one life, let me live it as a blonde," a larger-than-life-sized picture of a pretty, vacuous woman proclaimed from newspaper, magazine, and drugstore ads. And across America, three out of every ten women dyed their hair blonde. They ate a chalk called Metrecal, instead of food, to shrink to the size of the thin young models. Department-store buyers reported that American women, since 1939, had become three and four sizes smaller. "Women are out to fit the clothes, instead of vice-versa," one buyer said.

Interior decorators were designing kitchens with mosaic murals and original paintings, for kitchens were once again the center of women's lives. Home sewing became a million-dollar industry. Many women no longer left their homes, except to shop, chauffeur their children, or attend a social engagement with their husbands. Girls were growing up in America without ever having jobs outside the home. In the late fifties, a sociological phenomenon was suddenly remarked: a third of American women now worked, but most were no longer young and very few were pursuing careers. They were married women who held part-time jobs, selling or secretarial, to put their husbands through school, their sons through college, or to help pay the mortgage. Or they were widows supporting families. Fewer and fewer women were entering professional work. The shortages in the nursing, social work, and teaching professions caused crises in almost every American city. Concerned over the Soviet Union's lead in the space race, scientists noted that America's greatest source of unused brainpower was women. But girls would not study physics: it was "unfeminine." A girl refused a science fellowship at Johns Hopkins to take a job in a real-estate office. All she wanted, she said, was what every other American girl wanted—to get married, have four children and live in a nice house in a nice suburb.

The suburban housewife—she was the dream image of the young American women and the envy, it was said, of women all over the world. The American housewife—freed by science and labor-saving appliances from the drudgery, the dangers of childbirth and the illnesses of her grandmother. She was healthy, beautiful, educated, concerned only about her husband, her children, her home. She had found true feminine fulfillment. As a housewife and mother, she was respected as a full and equal partner to man in his world. She was free to choose automobiles, clothes, appliances, supermarkets; she had everything that women ever dreamed of.

In the fifteen years after World War II, this mystique of feminine fulfillment became the cherished and self-perpetuating core of contemporary American culture. Millions of women lived their lives in the image of those pretty pictures of the American suburban housewife, kissing their husbands goodbye in front of the picture window, depositing their stationwagonsful of children at school, and smiling as they ran the new electric waxer over the spotless kitchen floor. They baked their own bread, sewed their own and their children's clothes, kept their new washing machines and dryers running all day. They changed the sheets on the beds twice a week instead of once, took the rug-hooking class in adult education, and pitied their poor frustrated mothers, who had dreamed of having a career. Their only dream was to be perfect wives and mothers; their highest ambition to have five children and a beautiful house, their only fight to get and keep their husbands. They had no thought for the unfeminine problems of the world outside the home; they wanted the men to make the major decisions. They gloried in their role as women, and wrote proudly on the census blank: "Occupation: housewife."

For over fifteen years, the words written for women, and the words women used when they talked to each other, while their husbands sat on the other side of the room and talked shop or politics or septic tanks, were about problems with their children, or how to keep their husbands happy, or improve their children's school, or cook chicken or make slipcovers. Nobody argued whether women were inferior or superior to men; they were simply different. Words like "emancipation" and "career" sounded strange and embarrassing; no one had used them for years. When a Frenchwoman named Simone de Beauvoir wrote a book called *The Second Sex*, an American critic commented that she obviously "didn't know what life was all about," and besides, she was talking about French women. The "woman problem" in America no longer existed.

If a woman had a problem in the 1950's and 1960's, she knew that something must be wrong with her marriage, or with herself. Other women were satisfied with their lives, she thought. What kind of a woman was she if she did not feel this mysterious fulfillment waxing the kitchen floor? She was so ashamed to admit her dissatisfaction that she never knew how many other women shared it. If she tried to tell her husband, he didn't understand what she was talking about. She did not really understand it herself. For over fifteen years women in America found it harder to talk about this problem than about sex. Even the psychoanalysts had no name for it. When a woman went to a psychiatrist for help, as many women did, she would say, "I'm so ashamed," or "I must be hopelessly neurotic." "I don't know what's wrong with women today," a suburban psychiatrist said uneasily. "I only know something is wrong because most of my patients happen to be women. And their problem isn't sexual." Most women with this problem did not go to see a psychoanalyst, however. "There's nothing wrong really," they kept telling themselves. "There isn't any problem."

But on an April morning in 1959, I heard a mother of four, having coffee with four other mothers in a suburban development fifteen miles from New York, say in a tone of quiet desperation, "the problem." And the others knew, without words, that she was not talking about a problem with her husband, or her children, or her home. Suddenly they realized they all shared the same problem, the problem that has no name. They began, hesitantly, to talk about it. Later, after they had picked up their children at nursery school and taken them home to nap, two of the women cried, in sheer relief, just to know they were not alone.

Gradually I came to realize that the problem that has no name was shared by countless women in America. As a magazine writer I often interviewed women about problems with their children, or their marriages, or their houses, or their communities. But after a while I began to recognize the telltale signs of this other problem. I saw the same signs in suburban ranch houses and split-levels on Long Island and in New Jersey and Westchester County; in colonial houses in a small Massachusetts town; on patios in Memphis; in suburban and city apartments; in living rooms in the Midwest. Sometimes I sensed the problem, not as a reporter, but as a suburban housewife, for during this time I was also bringing up my own three children in Rockland County, New York. I heard echoes of the problem in college dormitories and semiprivate maternity wards, at PTA meetings and luncheons of the League of Women Voters, at suburban cocktail parties, in station wagons waiting for trains, and in snatches of conversation overheard at Schrafft's. The groping words I heard from other women, on quiet afternoons when children were at school or on quiet evenings when husbands worked late, I think I understood first as a woman long before I understood their larger social and psychological implications.

Just what was this problem that has no name? What were the words women used when they tried to express it? Sometimes a woman would say "I feel empty somehow...incomplete." Or she would say, "I feel as if I don't exist." Sometimes she blotted out the feeling with a tranquilizer. Sometimes she thought the problem was with her husband, or her children, or that what she really needed was to redecorate her house, or move to a better neighborhood, or have an affair, or another baby. Sometimes, she went to a doctor with symptoms she could hardly describe: "A tired feeling... I get so angry with the children it scares me... I feel like crying without any reason." (A Cleveland doctor called it "the housewife's syndrome.") A number of women told me about great bleeding blisters that break out on their hands and arms. "I call it the housewife's blight," said a family doctor in Pennsylvania. "I see it so often lately in these young women with four, five and six children who bury themselves in their dishpans. But it isn't caused by detergent and it isn't cured by cortisone."

Sometimes a woman would tell me that the feeling gets so strong she runs out of the house and walks through the streets. Or she stays inside her house and cries. Or her children tell her a joke, and she doesn't laugh because she doesn't hear it. I talked to women who had spent years on the analyst's couch, working out their "adjustment to the feminine role," their blocks to "fulfillment as a wife and mother." But the desperate tone in these women's voices, and the look in their eyes, was the same as the tone and the look of other women, who were sure they had no problem, even though they did have a strange feeling of desperation....

In 1960, the problem that has no name burst like a boil through the image of the happy American housewife. In the television commercials the pretty housewives still beamed over their foaming dishpans and *Time*'s cover story on "The Suburban Wife, an American Phenomenon" protested: "Having too good a time... to believe that they should be unhappy." But the actual unhappiness of the American housewife was suddenly being reported—from the *New York Times* and *Newsweek* to *Good Housekeeping* and CBS Television ("The Trapped Housewife"), although almost everybody who talked about it found some superficial reason to dismiss it....

Home economists suggested more realistic preparation for housewives, such as high-school workshops in home appliances. College educators suggested more discussion groups on home management and the family, to prepare women for the adjustment to domestic life.

A spate of articles appeared in the mass magazines offering "Fifty-eight Ways to Make Your Marriage More Exciting." No month went by without a new book by a psychiatrist or sexologist offering technical advice on finding greater fulfillment through sex.

A male humorist joked in *Harper's Bazaar* (July 1960) that the problem could be solved by taking away woman's right to vote. ("In the pre-19th Amendment era, the American woman was placid, sheltered and sure of her role in American society. She left all the political decisions to her husband and he, in turn, left all the family decisions to her. Today a woman has to make both the family *and* the political decisions, and it's too much for her.")

A number of educators suggested seriously that women no longer be admitted to the four-year colleges and universities: in the growing college crisis, the education which girls could not use as housewives was more urgently needed than ever by boys to do the work of the atomic age....

The alternative offered was a choice that few women would contemplate. In the sympathetic words of the *New York Times:* "All admit to being deeply frustrated at times by the lack of privacy, the physical burden, the routine of family life, the confinement of it. However, none would give up her home and family if she had the choice to make again." *Redbook* commented: "Few women would want to thumb their noses at husbands, children and community and go off on their own. Those who do may be talented individuals, but they rarely are successful women."...

By 1962 the plight of the trapped American housewife had become a national parlor game. Whole issues of magazines, newspaper columns, books learned and frivolous, educational conferences and television panels were devoted to the problem....

If the secret of feminine fulfillment is having children, never have so many women, with the freedom to choose, had so many children, in so few years, so willingly. If the answer is love, never have women searched for love with such determination. And yet there is a growing suspicion that the problem may not be sexual, though it must somehow be related to sex. I have heard from many doctors evidence of new sexual problems between man and wife—sexual hunger in wives so great their husbands cannot satisfy it. "We have made woman a sex creature," said a psychiatrist at the Margaret Sanger marriage counseling clinic. "She has no identity except as a wife and mother. She does not know who she is herself. She waits all day for her husband to come home at night to make her feel alive. And now it is the husband who is not interested. It is terrible for the women, to lie there, night after night, waiting for her husband to make her feel alive." Why is there such a market for books and articles offering sexual advice? The kind of sexual orgasm which Kinsey found in statistical plenitude in the recent generations of American women does not seem to make this problem go away....

Can the problem that has no name be somehow related to the domestic routine of the housewife? When a woman tries to put the problem into words, she often merely describes the daily life she leads. What is there in this recital of comfortable domestic detail that could possibly cause such a feeling of desperation? Is she trapped simply by the enormous demands of her role as modern housewife: wife, mistress, mother, nurse, consumer, cook, chauffeur; expert on interior decoration, child care, appliance repair, furniture refinishing, nutrition, and education? ...

This terrible tiredness took so many women to doctors in the 1950's that one decided to investigate it. He found, surprisingly, that his patients suffering from "housewife's fatigue" slept more than an adult needed to sleep—as much as ten hours a day—and that the actual energy they expended on housework did not tax their capacity. The real problem must be something else, he decided—perhaps boredom. Some doctors told their women patients they must get out of the house for a day, treat themselves to a movie in town. Others prescribed tranquilizers. Many suburban housewives were taking tranquilizers like cough drops. "You wake up in the morning, and you feel as if there's no point in going on another day like this. So you take a tranquilizer because it makes you not care so much that it's pointless."

It is easy to see the concrete details that trap the suburban housewife, the continual demands on her time. But the chains that bind her in her trap are chains in her own mind and spirit. They are chains made up of mistaken ideas and misinterpreted facts, of incomplete truths and unreal choices. They are not easily seen and not easily shaken off.

How can any woman see the whole truth within the bounds of her own life? How can she believe that voice inside herself, when it denies the conventional, accepted truths by which she has been living? And yet the women I have talked to, who are finally listening to that inner voice, seem in some incredible way to be groping through to a truth that has defied the experts....

If I am right, the problem that has no name stirring in the minds of so many American women today is not a matter of loss of femininity or too much education, or the demands of domesticity. It is far more important than anyone recognizes. It is the key to these other new and old problems which have been torturing women and their husbands and children, and puzzling their doctors and educators for years. It may well be the key to our future as a nation and a culture. We can no longer ignore that voice within women that says: "I want something more than my husband and my children and my home."...

"Easy enough to say," the woman inside the housewife's trap remarks, "but what can I do, alone in the house, with the children yelling and the laundry to sort and no grandmother to babysit?" It is easier to live through someone else than to become complete yourself. The freedom to lead and plan your own life is frightening if you have never faced it before. It is frightening when a woman finally realizes that there is no answer to the question "who am I" except the voice inside herself. She may spend years on the analyst's couch, working out her "adjustment to the feminine role," her blocks to "fulfillment as a wife and mother." And still the voice inside her may say, "That's not it." Even the best psychoanalyst can only give her the courage to listen to her own voice. When society asks so little of women, every woman has to listen to her own inner voice to find her identity in this changing world. She must create, out of her own needs and abilities, a new life plan, fitting in the love and children and home that have defined femininity in the past with the work toward a greater purpose that shapes the future....

[Once she realizes] neither her husband nor her children, nor the things in her house, nor sex, nor being like all the other women, can give her a self—she often finds the solution much easier than she anticipated.

Of the many women I talked to in the suburbs and cities, some were just beginning to face the problem, others were well on their way to solving it, and for still others it was no longer a problem. In the stillness of an April afternoon with all her children in school, a woman told me:

I put all my energies into the children, carting them around, worrying about them, teaching them things. Suddenly, there was this terrible feeling of emptiness. All that volunteer work I'd taken on—Scouts, PTA, the League, just didn't seem worth doing all of a sudden. As a girl, I wanted to be an actress. It was too late to go back to that. I stayed in the house all day, cleaning things I hadn't cleaned in years. I spent a lot of time just crying. My husband and I talked about its being an American woman's problem, how you give up a career for the children, and then you reach a point where you can't go back. I felt so envious of the few women I know who had a definite skill and kept working at it. My dream of being an actress wasn't real—I didn't work at it. Did I have to throw my whole self into the children? I've spent my whole life just immersed in other people, and never even knew what kind of a person I was myself. Now I think even having another baby wouldn't solve that emptiness long. You can't go back—you have to go on. There must be some real way I can go on myself.

This woman was just beginning her search for identity. Another woman had made it to the other side, and could look back now and see the problem clearly. Her home was colorful, casual, but technically she was no longer "just a housewife." She was paid for her work as a professional painter. She told me that when she stopped conforming to the conventional picture of femininity she finally began to *enjoy* being a woman. She said:

I used to work so hard to maintain this beautiful picture of myself as a wife and mother. I had all of my children by natural childbirth. I breastfed them all. I got mad once at an older woman at a party when I said childbirth is the most important thing in life, the basic animal, and she said, "Don't you want to be more than an animal?" ...

The first step in that plan is to see housework for what it is—not a career, but something that must be done as quickly and efficiently as possible. Once a woman stops trying to make cooking, cleaning, washing, ironing, "something more," she can say "no, I don't want a stove with rounded corners, I don't want four different kinds of soap." She can say "no" to those mass daydreams of the women's magazines and television, "no" to the depth researchers and manipulators who are trying to run her life. Then, she can use the vacuum cleaner and the dishwasher and all the automatic appliances, and even the instant mashed potatoes for what they are truly worth—to save time that can be used in more creative ways.

The second step, and perhaps the most difficult for the products of sex-directed education, is to see marriage as it really is, brushing aside the veil of over-glorification imposed by the feminine mystique. Many women I talked to felt strangely discontented with their husbands, continually irritated with their children, when they saw marriage and motherhood as the final fulfillment of their lives. But when they began to use their various abilities with a purpose of their own in society, they not only spoke of a new feeling of "aliveness" or "completeness" in themselves, but of a new, though hard to define, difference in the way they felt about their husbands and children....

The only way for a woman, as for a man, to find herself, to know herself as a person, is by creative work of her own. There is no other way. But a job, any job, is not the answer—in fact, it can be part of the trap. Women who do not look for jobs equal to their actual capacity, who do not let themselves develop the lifetime interests and goals which require serious education and training, who take a job at twenty or forty to "help out at home" or just to kill extra time, are walking, almost as surely as the ones who stay inside the housewife trap, to a nonexistent future....

What is needed now is a national educational program, similar to the GI bill, for women who seriously want to continue or resume their education—and who are willing to commit themselves to its use in a profession. The bill would provide properly qualified women with tuition fees, plus an additional subsidy to defray other expenses—books, travel, even, if necessary, some household help. Such a measure would cost far less than the GI bill. It would permit mothers to use existing educational facilities on a part-time basis and carry on individual study and research projects at home during the years when regular classroom attendance is impossible. The whole concept of women's education would be regeared from four-year college to a life plan under which a woman could continue her education, without conflict with her marriage, her husband and her children....

In the light of woman's long battle for emancipation, the recent sexual counterrevolution in America has been perhaps a final crisis, a strange breath-holding interval before the larva breaks out of the shell into maturity—a moratorium during which many millions of women put themselves on ice and stopped growing. They say that one day science will be able to make the human body live longer by freezing its growth. American women lately have been living much longer than men—walking through their leftover lives like living dead women. Perhaps men may live longer in America when women carry more of the burden of the battle with the world, instead of being a burden themselves. I think their wasted energy will continue to be destructive to their husbands, to their children, and to themselves until it is used in their own battle with the world. But when women as well as men emerge from biological living to realize their human selves, those leftover halves of life may become their years of greatest fulfillment.

Then the split in the image will be healed, and daughters will not face that jumping-off point at twenty-one or forty-one. When their mothers' fulfillment makes girls sure they want to be women, they will not have to "beat themselves down" to be feminine; they can stretch and stretch until their own efforts will tell them who they are. They will not need the regard of boy or man to feel alive. And when women do not need to live through their husbands and children, men will not fear the love and strength of women, nor need another's weakness to prove their own masculinity. They can finally see each other as they are. And this may be the next step in human evolution.

Who knows what women can be when they are finally free to become themselves? Who knows what women's intelligence will contribute when it can be nourished without denying love? Who knows of the possibilities of love when men and women share not only children, home, and garden, not only the fulfillment of their biological roles, but the responsibilities and passions of the work that creates the human future and the full human knowledge of who they are? It has barely begun, the search of women for themselves. But the time is at hand when the voices of the feminine mystique can no longer drown out the inner voice that is driving women on to become complete.

41

PAULI MURRAY
(1910–85)

Testimony, House Committee on
Education and Labor
(UNITED STATES, 1970)

Pauli Murray called attention to the intersections of race and gender when she coined the term "Jane Crow" to refer to the sexism that she considered the "twin evil" of "Jim Crow" racial segregation. Murray grew up in the segregated southern United States but went to college in the North during the 1930s, where she traveled in progressive circles. In the 1940s, years before Rosa Parks helped spark mass civil rights protests, Murray was jailed for refusing to give up her "white" seat on a public bus. She later earned law degrees at both Howard and Yale universities and, while working on civil rights cases during the 1960s, she elaborated on the parallels between race and gender discrimination. Although the Civil Rights Act of 1964 banned gender bias as well as race bias in employment, the government largely failed to respond to working women's complaints. To address this problem, Betty Friedan called a meeting in 1966, at which Pauli Murray helped draft the statement of purpose that established the National Organization for Women. As Congress considered further laws against sex discrimination in education and employment, Murray testified to their need, particularly for African American women. She was then a professor at Brandeis University, but several years later she entered an Episcopal theological seminary and in 1977 Murray became the first African American woman to be ordained as an Episcopal priest.

[I]n my view it is only as we recognize and hold sacred the uniqueness of each individual that we come to see clearly the moral and social evil of locking this individual into a group stereotype, whether favorable or unfavorable. I have learned this lesson, in part, because I am both a Negro and a woman whose experience embodies the conjunction of race and sex discrimination.

This experience also embodies the paradox of belonging simultaneously to an oppressed minority and an oppressed majority, and for good measure being left-handed in a right-handed world. As a self-supporting woman who has the responsibility for elderly relatives, the opportunity for education and employment consonant with my potentialities and training has been a matter of personal survival.

Moreover, in more than 30 years of intensive study of human rights and deep involvement in the civil rights movement I have observed the interrelationships between what is often referred to as racism and sexism (Jim Crow and Jane Crow), and have been unable to avoid the conclusion that discrimination because of one's sex is just as degrading, dehumanizing, immoral, unjust, indefensible, infuriating and capable of producing societal turmoil as discrimination because of one's race....

In matters of discrimination, although it is true that manifestations of racial prejudice have often been more brutal than the subtler manifestations of sex bias—for example, the use of ridicule of women as the psychic counterpart of violence against Negroes—it is also true that the rights of women and the rights of Negroes are only different phases of the fundamental and indivisible issue of human rights for all.

There are those who would have us believe that the struggle against racism is the No. 1 issue of human relations in the United States and must take priority over all other issues. I must respectfully dissent from this view. The struggle against sexism is equally urgent. More than half of all Negroes and other ethnic minorities are women. The costly lesson of our own history in the United States is that when the rights of one group are affirmed and those of another group are ignored, the consequences are tragic.

Whenever political expediency has dictated that the recognition of basic human rights be postponed, the resulting dissension and conflict has been aggravated. This lesson has been driven home to us time after time—in the Civil War, the women's suffrage movement, the violent upheavals of labor, and in the Negro revolt of the 1960's....

It seems clear that we are witnessing a worldwide revolution in human rights in which traditionally excluded or alienated groups—blacks, women, youth, various ethnic minorities and social minorities, the handicapped, and so forth—are all demanding the right to be accepted as persons and to share fully in making the decisions which shape their destinies.

Negroes and women are the two largest groups of minority status in the United States. The racial problem has been made visible and periodically more acute because of the peculiar history of black slavery and racial caste which produced a civil war and its bloody aftermath.

The acuteness of racism has forced us to engage in national self-examination and the growing militancy of our black minority has compelled us as a nation to reverse our former racist policies, at least in a formal legal sense. In neglecting to appreciate fully the indivisibility of human rights, however, we have often reacted with the squeaky-wheel-gets-the-grease approach and not given sufficient attention to the legitimate claims of other disadvantaged groups—poor whites, women, American Indians, Americans of Puerto Rican, Mexican, and Oriental origin, and the like. In so doing, we have often set in motion conditions which have created a backlash and which, if developed to an intense degree, would threaten to destroy the gains which Negroes have made over the past few decades, meager as these gains may have been for the masses of blacks.

The fact that women constitute more than 51 percent of the population, the very pervasiveness of sex discrimination which cuts across all racial, religious, ethnic, economic, and social groups, and the fact that women have cause to believe they are not taken seriously—all these combine to make the revitalized movement for women's liberation in the 1970's an instrument for potential widespread disruption if its legitimate claims are not honored.

Given the tendency of privileged groups to retain their power and privilege and to play one disadvantaged group off against another, and given the accelerating militancy of Women's Liberation, there is a grave danger of a head on collision of this movement with the movement for black liberation unless our decision makers recognize and implement the rights of all. [...]

Men have become enslaved by their dependency as well as their dominance. They pay a heavy price in shortened lives, military casualties, broken homes and the heartbreak of parents whose children are alienated from them. Many men find themselves unable to live up to the expectations of masculinity which men have defined for themselves, and many are now chagrined to find that women are no longer willing to accept the role of femininity which men have defined for women.

Just as blacks have found it necessary to opt for self-definition, women are seeking their own image of themselves nurtured from within rather than imposed from without. I am led to the hypothesis that we will be unable to eradicate racism in the United States unless and until we simultaneously remove all sex barriers which inhibit the development of individual talents. I am further convinced that the price of our survival as a nation is the sharing of our power and wealth—or rather the redistribution of this power and wealth—among black and white, rich and poor, men and women, old and young, red and brown and all the in-betweens.

This requires more than "objectivity." It demands a sensitivity, a recognition that individual human beings lie behind those depressing facts which have been assembled here. It demands that we women, who are the petitioners before Congress symbolized by this subcommittee, keep before us the goal of liberating our own humanity and that of our male counterparts. It demands from those who hold formal power—predominantly white males—something closely akin to conversion, the imagination and vision to realize that an androgynous society is vastly superior to a patriarchal society—which we now are—and that the liberation of women through legislation, through a restructuring of our political and social institutions, and through a change of our cultural conditioning may well hold the key to many of the complex social issues for which we do not now have answers....

I respectfully submit that in light of the widespread discrimination against women in many areas and in light of the need to protect all groups of minority status against actual or potential discrimination, as a rule of thumb all antidiscrimination measures should include sex along with race, color, religion, national origin, age, and other prohibited bases of discrimination....

42.

PAT MAINARDI
(b. 1942)

"The Politics of Housework"
(UNITED STATES, 1970)

While liberal women in the United States influenced by the civil rights struggle helped revive feminism in the 1960s, a younger generation of women steeped in New Left and antiwar politics forged a women's liberation movement. They considered women an oppressed group and sought a revolution in consciousness to free women from what Emma Goldman had referred to as the "internal tyrants." Radical feminists coined the phrase "the personal is political" to call attention to the exercise of power in the private arenas of sexuality, health, and interpersonal relationships. In consciousness-raising groups around the country, women shared their insights about oppressive practices that men in the New Left considered too trivial for political analysis. Pat Mainardi, a member of the New York Redstockings collective, captured the spirit of this process in her serious yet humorous treatment of housework. The essay circulated in the earliest women's liberation journals and reached a wider audience when Robin Morgan included it in her 1970 anthology Sisterhood Is Powerful. *Its insights continue to resonate, for in families throughout the world women still perform many more hours of housework than do men, even when both partners have full-time jobs.*

> Though women do not complain of the power of husbands, each complains of her own husband, or of the husbands of her friends. It is the same in all other cases of servitude; at least in the commencement of the emancipatory movement. The serfs did not at first complain of the power of the lords, but only of their tyranny.
>
> —JOHN STUART MILL, *On the Subjection of Women*

Liberated women—very different from women's liberation! The first signals all kinds of goodies, to warm the hearts (not to mention other parts) of the most radical men. The other signals—*housework*. The first brings sex without marriage, sex before marriage, cozy housekeeping arrangements ("You see, I'm living with this chick") and the self-content of knowing that you're not the kind of man who wants a doormat instead of a woman. That will come later. After all, who wants that old commodity anymore, the Standard American Housewife, all husband, home and kids. The New Commodity, the Liberated Woman, has sex a lot and has a Career, preferably something that can be fitted in with the household chores—like dancing, pottery, or painting.

On the other hand is women's liberation—and housework. What? You say this is all trivial? Wonderful! That's what I thought. It seemed perfectly reasonable. We both had careers, both had to work a couple of days a week to earn enough to live on, so why shouldn't we share the housework? So I suggested it to my mate and he agreed—most men are too hip to turn you down flat. "You're right," he said. "It's only fair."

Then an interesting thing happened. I can only explain it by stating that we women have been brainwashed more than even we can imagine. Probably too many years of seeing television women in ecstasy over their shiny waxed floors or breaking down over their dirty shirt collars. Men have no such conditioning. They recognize the essential fact of housework right from the very beginning. Which is that it stinks. Here's my list of dirty chores: buying groceries, carting them home and putting them away; cooking meals and washing dishes and pots; doing the laundry, digging out the place when things get out of control; washing floors. The list could go on but the sheer necessities are bad enough. All of us have to do these things, or get some one else to do them for us. The longer my husband contemplated these chores the more repulsed he became, and so proceeded the change from the normally sweet considerate Dr. Jekyll into the crafty Mr. Hyde who would stop at nothing to avoid the horrors of—*housework*. As he felt himself backed into a corner laden with dirty dishes, brooms, mops, and reeking garbage, his front teeth grew longer and pointier, his fingernails haggled and his eyes grew wild. Housework trivial? Not on your life! Just try to share the burden.

So ensued a dialogue that's been going on for several years. Here are some of the high points:

"I don't mind sharing the housework, but I don't do it very well. We should each do the things we're best at."

Meaning: Unfortunately I'm no good at things like washing dishes or cooking. What I do best is a little light carpentry, changing light bulbs, moving furniture (*how often do you move furniture?*).

Also Meaning: Historically the lower classes (black men and us) have had hundreds of years experience doing menial jobs. It would be a waste of manpower to train someone else to do them now.

Also Meaning: I don't like the dull stupid boring jobs, so you should do them.

"I don't mind sharing the work, but you'll have to show me how to do it."

Meaning: I ask a lot of questions and you'll have to show me everything everytime I do it because I don't remember so good. Also don't try to sit down and read while I'm doing my jobs because I'm going to annoy hell out of you until it's easier to do them yourself.

"We used to be so happy!" (Said whenever it was his turn to do something.)

Meaning: I used to be so happy.

Meaning: Life without housework is bliss. (*No quarrel here. Perfect agreement.*)

"We have different standards, and why should I have to work to your standards. That's unfair."

Meaning: If I begin to get bugged by the dirt and crap I will say "This place sure is a sty" or "How can anyone live like this?" and wait for your reaction. I know that all women have a sore called "Guilt over a messy house" or "Household work is ultimately my responsibility." I know that men have caused that sore—if anyone visits and the place *is* a sty, they're not going to leave and say, "He sure is a lousy housekeeper." You'll take the rap in any case. I can outwait you.

Also Meaning: I can provoke innumerable scenes over the housework issue. Eventually doing all the housework yourself will be less painful to you than trying to get me to do half. Or I'll suggest we get a maid. She will do my share of the work. You will do yours. It's women's work.

"I've got nothing against sharing the housework, but you can't make me do it on your schedule."

Meaning: Passive resistance. I'll do it when I damned well please, if at all. If my job is doing dishes, it's easier to do them once a week. If taking out laundry, once a month. If washing the floors, once a year. If you don't like it, do it yourself oftener, and then I won't do it at all.

"I *hate* it more than you. You don't mind it so much."

Meaning: Housework is garbage work. It's the worst crap I've ever done. It's degrading and humiliating for someone of *my* intelligence to do it. But for someone of *your* intelligence...

"Housework is too trivial to even talk about."

Meaning: It's even more trivial to do. Housework is beneath my status. My purpose in life is to deal with matters of significance. Yours is to deal with matters of insignificance. You should do the housework.

"This problem of housework is not a man-woman problem! In any relationship between two people one is going to have a stronger personality and dominate."

Meaning: That stronger personality had better be *me*.

"In animal societies, wolves, for example, the top animal is usually a male even where he is not chosen for brute strength but on the basis of cunning and intelligence. Isn't that interesting?"

Meaning: I have historical, psychological, anthropological, and biological justification for keeping you down. How can you ask the top wolf to be equal?

"Women's liberation isn't really a political movement."

Meaning: The Revolution is coming too close to home.

Also Meaning: I am only interested in how *I* am oppressed, not how I oppress others. Therefore the war, the draft, and the university are political. Women's liberation is not.

"Man's accomplishments have always depended on getting help from other people, mostly women. What great man would have accomplished what he did if he had to do his own housework?

Meaning: Oppression is built into the System and I, as the white American male receive the benefits of this System. I don't want to give them up.

POSTSCRIPT

Participatory democracy begins at home. If you are planning to implement your politics, there are certain things to remember.

1. He *is* feeling it more than you. He's losing some leisure and you're gaining it. The measure of your oppression is his resistance.
2. A great many American men are not accustomed to doing monotonous repetitive work which never ushers in any lasting let alone important achievement. This is why they would rather repair a cabinet than wash dishes. If human endeavors are like a pyramid with man's highest achievements at the top, then keeping oneself alive is at the bottom. Men have always had servants (us) to take care of this bottom strata of life while they have confined their efforts to the rarefied upper regions. It is thus ironic when they ask of women—where are your great painters, statesmen, etc? Mme. Matisse ran a millinery shop so he could paint. Mrs. Martin Luther King kept his house and raised his babies.
3. It is a traumatizing experience for someone who has always thought of himself as being against any oppression or exploitation of one human being by another to realize that in his daily life he has been accepting and implementing (and benefiting from) this exploitation; that his

rationalization is little different from that of the racist who says "Black people don't feel pain" (women don't mind doing the shitwork); and that the oldest form of oppression in history has been the oppression of 50 percent of the population by the other 50 percent.

4. Arm yourself with some knowledge of the psychology of oppressed peoples everywhere, and a few facts about the animal kingdom. I admit playing top wolf or who runs the gorillas is silly but as a last resort men bring it up all the time. Talk about bees. If you feel really hostile bring up the sex life of spiders. They have sex. She bites off his head.

The psychology of oppressed people is not silly. Jews, immigrants, black men, and all women have employed the same psychological mechanisms to survive: admiring the oppressor, glorifying the oppressor, wanting to be like the oppressor, wanting the oppressor to like them, mostly because the oppressor held all the power.

5. In a sense, all men everywhere are slightly schizoid—divorced from the reality of maintaining life. This makes it easier for them to play games with it. It is almost a cliché that women feel greater grief at sending a son off to war or losing him to that war because they bore him, suckled him, and raised him. The men who foment those wars did none of those things and have a more superficial estimate of the worth of human life. One hour a day is a low estimate of the amount of time one has to spend "keeping" oneself. By foisting this off on others, man gains seven hours a week—one working day more to play with his mind and not his human needs. Over the course of generations it is easy to see whence evolved the horrifying abstractions of modern life.

6. With the death of each form of oppression, life changes and new forms evolve. English aristocrats at the turn of the century were horrified at the idea of enfranchising working men—were sure that it signaled the death of civilization and a return to barbarism. Some working men were even deceived by this line. Similarly with the minimum wage, abolition of slavery, and female suffrage. Life changes but it goes on. Don't fall for any line about the death of everything if men take a turn at the dishes. They will imply that you are holding back the Revolution (their Revolution). But you are advancing it (your Revolution).

7. Keep checking up. Periodically consider who's actually *doing* the jobs. These things have a way of backsliding so that a year later once again the woman is doing everything. After a year make a list of jobs the man has rarely if ever done. You will find cleaning pots, toilets, refrigerators and ovens high on the list. Use time sheets if necessary. He will accuse you of being petty. He is above that sort of thing—(housework). Bear in mind what the worst jobs are, namely the ones that have to be done

every day or several times a day. Also the ones that are dirty—it's more pleasant to pick up books, newspapers, etc. than to wash dishes. Alternate the bad jobs. It's the daily grind that gets you down. Also make sure that you don't have the responsibility for the housework with occasional help from him. "I'll cook dinner for you tonight" implies it's really your job and isn't he a nice guy to do some of it for you.

8. Most men had a rich and rewarding bachelor life during which they did not starve or become encrusted with crud or buried under the litter. There is a taboo that says that women mustn't strain themselves in the presence of men: we haul around 50 pounds of groceries if we have to but aren't allowed to open a jar if there is someone around to do it for us. The reverse side of the coin is that men aren't supposed to be able to take care of themselves without a woman. Both are excuses for making women do the housework.

9. Beware of the double whammy. He won't do the little things he always did because you're now a "Liberated Woman," right? Of course he won't do anything else either...

I was just finishing this when my husband came in and asked what I was doing. Writing a paper on housework. Housework? He said, *Housework?* Oh my god how trivial can you get. A paper on housework.

43.

Boston Women's Health Book Collective

Our Bodies, Ourselves

(UNITED STATES, 1973)

Renewed attention to the politics of personal life inspired feminist analyses of the body, health, and sexuality. Earlier activists had also been concerned about women's health, criticizing tight-laced corsets in the nineteenth century and campaigning for birth control in the twentieth century. In the consciousness-raising groups of the 1960s, women increasingly shared their dissatisfaction with both medical treatment and cultural images of female bodies. A session on "women and their bodies" at a conference held in Boston in 1969 gave rise to an ongoing discussion by a group of women who later formed the Boston Women's Health Book Collective. From their research they created a course, circulated "Women and Their Bodies" (1970), and in 1973 published Our Bodies, Ourselves, *which became a worldwide publishing phenomenon. A bestseller in the United States in the 1970s, the book was first translated into Spanish and eventually into nineteen languages. The contents, which reflected the self-help ethos of the women's health movement, offered concrete information about topics such as menstruation, masturbation, sexual diseases, and natural childbirth. It also affirmed women's sexual desires, including lesbianism, and attempted to demystify medical expertise. The book helped spawn an international women's health movement of service and advocacy projects.*

From the very beginning of working together, first on the course that led to this book and then on the book itself, we have felt exhilarated and energized by our new knowledge. Finding out about our bodies and our bodies' needs, starting to take control over that area of our life, has released for us an energy that has overflowed into our work, our friendships, our relationships with men and women, for some of us our marriages and our parenthood. In trying to figure out why this has had such a life-changing effect on us, we have come up with several important ways in which this kind of body education has been liberating for us and may be a starting point for the liberation of many other women.

First, we learned what we learned equally from professional sources—textbooks, medical journals, doctors, nurses—and from our own experiences. The facts were important, and we did careful research to get the information we had not had in the past. As we brought the facts to one another we learned a good deal, but in sharing our personal experiences relating to those facts we learned still more. Once we had learned what the "experts" had to tell us, we found that we still had a lot to teach and to learn from one another. For instance, many of us had "learned" about the menstrual cycle in science or biology classes—we had perhaps even memorized the names of the menstrual hormones and what they did. But most of us did not remember much of what we had learned. This time when we read in a text that the onset of menstruation is a normal and universal occurrence in young girls from ages ten to eighteen, we started to talk about our first menstrual periods. We found that, for many of us, beginning to menstruate had not felt normal at all, but scary, embarrassing, mysterious. We realized that what we had been told about menstruation and what we had not been told, even the tone of voice it had been told in—all had had an effect on our feelings about being female. Similarly, the information from enlightened texts describing masturbation as a normal, common sexual activity did not really become our own until we began to pull up from inside ourselves and share what we had never before expressed—the confusion and shame we had been made to feel, and often still felt, about touching our bodies in a sexual way....

A second important result of this kind of learning has been that we are better prepared to evaluate the institutions that are supposed to meet our health needs—the hospitals, clinics, doctors, medical schools, nursing schools, public health departments, Medicaid bureaucracies, and so on. For some of us it was the first time we had looked critically, and with strength, at the existing institutions serving us. The experience of learning just how little control we had over our lives and bodies, the coming together out of isolation to learn from each other in order to define what we needed, and the experience of supporting one another in demanding the changes that grew out of our developing critique—all were crucial and formative political experiences for us. We have felt our potential power as a force for political and social change.

The learning we have done while working on *Our Bodies, Ourselves* has been such a good basis for growth in other areas of life for still another reason. For women throughout the centuries, ignorance about our bodies has had one major consequence—pregnancy. Until very recently pregnancies were all but inevitable, biology *was* our destiny—that is, because our bodies are designed to get pregnant and give birth and lactate, that is what all or most of us did. The courageous and dedicated work of people like Margaret Sanger started in the early twentieth century to spread and make available birth control methods that women could use, thereby freeing us from the traditional lifetime of pregnancies. But the societal expectation that a woman above all else will have babies does not die easily. When we first started talking to each other about this we found that that old expectation had nudged most of us into a fairly rigid role of wife-and-motherhood from the moment we were born female. Even in 1969 when we first started the work that led to this book, we found that many of us were still getting pregnant when we didn't want to. It was not until we researched carefully and learned more about our reproductive systems, about birth-control methods and abortion, about laws governing birth control and abortion, not until we put all this information together with what it meant to us to be female, did we begin to feel that we could truly set out to control whether and when we would have babies.

This knowledge has freed us to a certain extent from the constant, energy-draining anxiety about becoming pregnant. It has made our pregnancies better, because they no longer happen to us; we actively choose them and enthusiastically participate in them. It has made our parenthood better, because it is our choice rather than our destiny. This knowledge has freed us from playing the role of mother if it is not a role that fits us. It has given us a sense of a larger life space to work in, an invigorating and challenging sense of time and room to discover the energies and talents that are in us, to do the work we want to do. And one of the things we most want to do is to help make this freedom of choice, this life space, available to every woman. That is why people in the women's movement have been so active in fighting against the inhumane legal restrictions, the imperfections of available contraceptives, the poor sex education, the highly priced and poorly administered health care that keeps too many women from having this crucial control over their bodies.

There is a fourth reason why knowledge about our bodies has generated so much new energy. For us, body education is core education. Our bodies are the physical bases from which we move out into the world; ignorance, uncertainty—even, at worst, shame—about our physical selves create in us an alienation from ourselves that keeps us from being the whole people that we could be. Picture a woman trying to do work and to enter into equal and satisfying relationships with other people—when she feels physically weak because she has never tried to be strong; when she drains her energy trying to change her face, her figure, her hair, her smells, to match some ideal norm set by magazines, movies, and TV; when she feels confused and ashamed of the menstrual blood that every month appears from some dark place in her body; when her internal body processes are a mystery to her and surface only to cause her trouble (an unplanned pregnancy, or cervical cancer); when she does not understand nor enjoy sex and concentrates her sexual drives into aimless romantic fantasies, perverting and misusing a potential energy because she has been brought up to deny it. Learning to understand, accept, and be responsible for our physical selves, we are freed of some of these preoccupations and can start to use our untapped energies. Our image of ourselves is on a firmer base, we can be better friends and better lovers, better *people*, more self-confident, more autonomous, stronger, and more whole.

44.

MARIAROSA DALLA COSTA
(b. 1943)

"A General Strike"

(ITALY, 1974)

Feminists such as Sheila Rowbotham in England and Mariarosa Dalla Costa in Italy, influenced by Marxist theory but critical of its narrow focus on men's economic contributions, redefined "work" to incorporate female labor in the home, including reproduction and housework. In 1971 Dalla Costa helped found Lotta Femminista (Feminist Struggle) in Padua, Italy. Along with British socialist feminist Selma James she wrote The Power of Women and the Subversion of the Community *(1972), which called for working-class women to receive wages for housework. Radical and socialist feminists in Italy, England, and Canada organized to demand state support for women's work in the home, as well as equal pay for all wage labor. Dalla Costa gave the following speech at a 1974 celebration of International Women's Day in Mestre, Italy. In it she addressed a range of feminist concerns, from child care to abortion to the double day of wage-earning women who also perform household labor. Adopting the rhetoric of the male labor movement, she called for a general strike to win shorter working hours, adequate pay, and holidays for all women.*

Today the feminist movement in Italy is opening the campaign for Wages for Housework. As you have heard from the songs, as you have seen from the photograph exhibition, as you have read on the placards, the questions we are raising today are many: the barbarous conditions in which we have to face abortion, the sadism we are subjected to in obstetric and gynaecological clinics, our working conditions—in jobs outside the home our conditions are always worse than men's, and at home we work without wages—the fact that social services either don't exist or are so bad that we are afraid to let our children use them, and so on.

Now at this point some people might ask, what is the connection between the campaign we are opening today, the campaign for Wages for Housework, and all these things that we have raised today, that we have exposed and are fighting against? All these things that we have spoken about, that we have made songs about, that we have shown in our exhibition and in films?

We believe that the weakness of all women—that weakness that's behind our having been crossed out of history, that's behind the fact that when we leave the home we must face the most revolting, underpaid and insecure jobs—this weakness is based on the fact that all of us women, whatever we do, are wearied and exhausted at the very outset by 13 hours of housework that no-one has ever recognised, that no-one has ever paid for.

And this is the basic condition that forces women to be satisfied with nurseries like the "Pagliuca," "Celestini," "OMNI."* This weakness forces us to pay half a million lire [£300/$750] for an abortion and this, let's spell it out clearly, happens in every city and every country—and on top of that we risk death and imprisonment.

We all do housework; it is the only thing all women have in common, it is the only base on which we can gather our power, the power of millions of women.

---

*"Pagliuca" and "Celestini"—both notoriously brutal nurseries. "OMNI"—the State nurseries which are poorly equipped and badly run.

It is no accident that reformists of every stripe have always carefully avoided the idea of our organising on the basis of housework. They have always refused to recognise housework as work, precisely because it is the only work that we all have in common. It is one thing to confront two or three hundred women workers in a shoe factory, and quite another to confront millions of housewives. And since all women factory workers are housewives, it is still another matter to confront these two or three hundred factory workers united with millions of housewives.

But this is what we are putting on the agenda today in this square. This is the first moment of organisation. We have decided to organise ourselves around that work we all do, in order to have the power of millions of women.

For us, therefore, *the demand for Wages for Housework is a direct demand for power, because housework is what millions of women have in common.*

If we can organise ourselves in our millions on this demand—and already today there are quite a lot of us here in this square—we can get so much power that we need no longer be in a position of weakness when we go out of the home. We can bring about new working conditions in housework itself—if I have money of my own in my pocket I can even buy a dishwasher without feeling guilty and without having to beg my husband for it for months on end while he, who doesn't do the washing-up, considers a dishwasher unnecessary.

So if I have money of my own, paid into my own hands, I can change the conditions of housework itself. And moreover I will *be able to choose* when I want to go out to work. If I have 120,000 lire for housework I'll never again sell myself for 60,000 lire in a textile factory, or as someone's secretary, or as a cashier or usherette at the cinema. In the same way, if I already have a certain amount of money in my own hands, if I already have with me the power of millions of women, I will be able to dictate a completely new quality of services, nurseries, canteens and all those facilities that are indispensable in reducing working hours and in enabling us to have a social life.

We want to say something else. For a long time—particularly strongly in the last 10 years, but let's say always—male workers have come out to struggle against their hours of work and for more money, and have gathered in this square.

In the factories at Porto Marghera there have been many strikes, many struggles. We well remember the marches of male workers who started in Porto Marghera, crossed the Mestre bridge and arrived here in this square.

But let's make this clear. *No strike has ever been a general strike.* When half the working population is at home in the kitchens, while the others are on strike, *it's not a general strike.*

We've never seen a general strike. We've only seen men, generally men from the big factories, come out on the streets; while their wives, daughters, sisters, mothers, went on cooking in the kitchens.

Today in this square, with the opening of our mobilisation for Wages for Housework, we put on the agenda *our working hours, our holidays, our strikes and our money.*

When we win a level of power that enables us to reduce our 13 or more working hours a day to eight hours or even less than eight, when at the same time we can put on the agenda our holidays—because it's no secret to anyone that on Sundays and during vacation time women never have a holiday—then, perhaps, we'll be able to talk for the first time of a 'general' strike of the working class.

45.

Committee on the Status of Women in India

Towards Equality

(INDIA, 1974)

In India, feminists have pressed for education and equal rights for women since the era of British rule. When India gained independence in 1949, the constitution promised equality to all citizens. By 1970, however, many women, particularly in rural areas, had little access to education. Economic discrimination remained powerful, and the proportion of women in office had declined from the post-independence movement era. In 1971, the Ministry of Education and Social Welfare created a Committee on the Status of Women to study education and employment, as well as the problems of housewives. Based on surveys and interviews, the committee produced a report of over four hundred pages detailing obstacles to women's progress. The report called for programs to enhance women's earning power and insisted that only by addressing all social inequalities would women's status improve. In addition to inspiring government action, Towards Equality *helped establish academic research on women in India.*

While it is true that the status of women constitutes a problem in almost all societies, and has emerged today as a fundamental crisis in human development, we found that sex inequality cannot in reality be differentiated from the variety of social, economic and cultural inequalities in Indian society. The inequalities inherent in our traditional social structure, based on caste, community and class have a very significant influence on the status of women in different spheres. Socially accepted rights and expected roles of women, norms governing their behaviour and of others towards them vary among different groups and regions. They are closely affected by the stage and methods of development, and the position held by the group in the social hierarchy. All this makes broad generalisations regarding women's status unrealistic. It was, therefore, necessary to understand the reality of women's roles and status in the different strata of our society....

We believe:

1. that equality of women is necessary, not merely on the grounds of social justice, but as a basic condition for social, economic and political development of the nation;
2. that in order to release women from their dependent and unequal status, improvement of their employment opportunities and earning power has to be given the highest priority;
3. that society owes a special responsibility to women because of their child-bearing function. Safe bearing and rearing of children is an obligation that has to be shared by the mother, the father and society;
4. that the contribution made by an active housewife to the running and management of a family should be admitted as economically and socially productive and contributing to national savings and development;
5. that marriage and motherhood should not become a disability in women's fulfilling their full and proper role in the task of national

development. Therefore, it is important that society, including women themselves, must accept their responsibility in this field;

6. that disabilities and inequalities imposed on women have to be seen in the total context of a society, where large sections of the population—male and female, adults and children—suffer under the oppression of an exploitative system. It is not possible to remove these inequalities for women only. Any policy or movement for the emancipation and development of women has to form a part of a total movement for removal of inequalities and oppressive social institutions, if the benefits and privileges won by such action are to be shared by the entire women population and not be monopolised by a small minority.

7. that if our society is to move in the direction of the goals set by the Constitution, then special temporary measures will be necessary, to transform *de jure* into *de facto* equality....

It should be a woman's right to play a dual role. A woman should not be penalised for her important contribution as mother in the perpetuation of society. Childbearing is treated as purely a matter concerning women and hence the attitude that a woman must either give up her job or her right to bear children. A distinction between man's work and woman's work in respect of household jobs will have to be removed. If what are called woman's jobs come to be respected by society, men will cease to hesitate doing these jobs. This attitude needs to be built into the socialization process of children, both in the home and in the school.

It is necessary to make adequate provisions to give women opportunity to do both their jobs efficiently and satisfactorily. To this end, it is necessary to provide for creches, nurseries, and labour saving devices. Since all families cannot afford to buy gadgets it will be necessary to provide gadgets to do washing, vegetable chopping, chapati making and such other things which make household work a drudgery....

Prostitution is the worst form of exploitation of women and as an institution it speaks of man's tolerance of this exploitation on an organised level in society. Woman is viewed solely as a sex object and as an outlet for man's baser instincts. The condemnation of the woman and not the man is the continuance of the standards of dual morality which prevail in most countries with regard to men and women. Some societies have continued to regard prostitution as a necessary evil and have tolerated it as such.

Prostitution represents the exploitation of the poor by the rich and of women by men. If women have really to reach the level of equality with men, society should be in a position to ensure economic, social and psychological security for the traditionally exploited women folk. Prostitution is the worst form of women's exploitation and inequality.

What must be emphasised is the growing commercialization in the exploitation of women and girls. While the urbanization process and industrialisation with its accompanying evils, particularly socio-economic insecurity, poor living conditions, etc., are important forces for the increase of prostitution in recent years, this profession like any other, operates on a commercial basis according to the law of demand and supply. The growing incidence of prostitution in metropolitan cities and urban areas is an indication of the growing demand on the one hand and poverty on the other. Some sociologists have emphasised the role of economic factors over and above the traditional and customary factors, such as poverty, low wages, lack of gainful employment, partial or complete unemployment are contributory factors that constrain helpless women to embrace prostitution....

These women need to be rehabilitated and their emotional and psychological problems are to be tackled with understanding. The most significant aspect is preventive. This applies particularly to women and girls in moral danger. An important segment of this group are women who are victims of family discord. Counselling services could help them and prevent their taking recourse to this profession. Counselling centres should also have homes for such women....

The reviews of the disabilities and constraints on women, which stem from sociocultural institutions, indicates that the majority of women are still very far from enjoying the rights and opportunities guaranteed to them by the Constitution. Society has not yet succeeded in framing the required norms or institutions to enable women to fulfil the multiple roles that they are expected to play in India today. On the other hand, the increasing incidence of practices like dowry, indicate a further lowering of the status of women. They also indicate a process of regression from some of the norms developed during the Freedom Movement. We have been perturbed by the findings of the content analysis of periodicals in the regional languages, that concern for women and their problems, which received an impetus during the Freedom Movement, has suffered a decline in the last two decades. The social laws that sought to mitigate the problems of women in their family life have remained unknown to a large mass of women in this country, who are as ignorant of their legal rights today as they were before independence.

We realise the changes in social attitudes and institutions cannot be brought about very rapidly. It is, however, necessary to accelerate this process of change by deliberate and planned efforts. Responsibility for this acceleration has to be shared by the State and the community, particularly that section of the community which believes in the equality of women. We, therefore, urge that community organisations, particularly women's organisations, should mobilise public opinion and strengthen social efforts against oppressive institutions like polygamy, dowry, ostentatious expenditure on weddings and child marriage, and mount a campaign for the dissemination of information about the legal rights of women to increase their awareness. This is a joint responsibility, which has to be shared by community organisations, legislators, who have helped to frame these laws and the Government which is responsible for implementing them. . . .

Our investigation of the progress of women's education in India reveals that while there has been a tremendous increase in the number of girls receiving formal education in the period after Independence, the gap between the enrollment of boys and girls has continued to increase at all levels and the proportion of girls in the relevant age groups covered by the school system still remains for below the constitutional target of universal education upto the age at 14. Social attitudes to the education of girls range from acceptance of the need to one of the absolute in difference. The reasons for the variation in social attitude and the consequent slow progress of women's education are both social and economic, which are intensified by inadequate facilities and the ambivalent attitude regarding the purpose of educating girls. . . .

The challenge of the widening illiteracy gap will have to be borne in mind in determining priorities in educational development in the years to come. The claims of the formal educational system which can cater to the need of only a minority for a long time will have to be balanced against the claims of eradication of illiteracy. This stands out as the most important and imperative need to raise the status of women who are already adults and constitute the largest group. While the constitutional directive of universal education upto the age of 14 must receive the highest priority in the formal system.... an alternative system has to be designed to provide basic education to adult women, particularly in the 15–25 age group....

Though women's participation in the political process has increased, both in elections and in their readiness to express their views on issues directly concerning their day-to-day life, their ability to produce an impact on the political process has been negligible because of the inadequate attention paid to their political education and mobilisation by both political parties and women's organisations. Parties have tended to see women voters as appendages of the males. Among women, the leadership has become diffused and diverse—with sharp contradictions in their regard and concern for the inequalities that affect the status of women in every sphere—social, economic and political. The revolution in status of women for which constitutional equality was to be only the instrument still remains a very distant objective, while the position of some groups have changed for the better, the large masses of women continue to lack spokesmen in the representative bodies of the State. Though women do not constitute a minority numerically, they are acquiring the features of one by the inequality of class, status and political power. In this sense, the new rights have proved to be only concessional. Our recommendations aim to make women's political rights more functional as required by the needs of a democratic system.

In order to provide greater opportunities to women to actively participate in the decision-making process, it is imperative to recognise the true nature of the social inequalities and disabilities that hamper them. This can best be achieved by providing them with special opportunities for participation in the representative structure of local government. The present form of associating women in these bodies, through cooption or nomination, has become a kind of tokenism. The time has come to move out of this token provision to a more meaningful association of women in local administration, and to counteract the general apathy and indifference of the local bodies to women's development and change of status....

We recommend that political parties should adopt a definite policy regarding the percentage of women candidates to be sponsored by them for elections to Parliament and State Assemblies. While they may initially start with 15%, this should be gradually increased so that in time to come the representation of women in the legislative bodies has some relationship to their position in the total population of the country or the State.

46.

Susan Brownmiller
(b. 1935)

Against Our Will: Men, Women and Rape
(UNITED STATES, 1975)

*The women's liberation movement in Europe and North America insisted
that sexuality was a political, and not merely a personal, matter. In 1970,
Kate Millet's book* Sexual Politics *coined the phrase that encapsulated
this approach to understanding how sexual relations can perpetuate patriarchal control of women. Feminists had already begun to speak out
about prostitution, rape, and the harassment of women on the streets,
breaking silence by publicly naming women's sexual vulnerabilities. The
journalist Susan Brownmiller, who had been a civil rights activist in the
1960s, previously believed that rape was not a feminist issue but an individual crime. Involved in the women's liberation movement in New
York City, Brownmiller helped plan a conference on rape at which she
was shocked to learn how vulnerable she and other women felt in a climate of sexual intimidation. Her research for* Against Our Will *uncovered an extensive history of rape during wartime, pogroms, conquest,
slavery, and within families. The book, which confronted myths about
mad rapists, black rapists, and women's rape fantasies, argued that the
threat of rape supports male dominance by keeping women in fear and
thus dependent on men's protection. Brownmiller's reconceptualization of
rape as a political act, along with the popularity of her book, helped publicize the burgeoning antirape movement in the United States, which established rape crisis centers and self-defense classes, monitored rape
trials, and worked for legal reforms.*

Man's discovery that his genitalia could serve as a weapon to generate fear must rank as one of the most important discoveries of prehistoric times, along with the use of fire and the first crude stone axe. From prehistoric times to the present, I believe, rape has played a critical function. It is nothing more or less than a conscious process of intimidation by which *all men* keep *all women* in a state of fear....

The Greek warrior Achilles used a swarm of men descended from ants, the Myrmidons, to do his bidding as hired henchmen in battle. Loyal and unquestioning, the Myrmidons served their master well, functioning in anonymity as effective agents of terror. Police-blotter rapists in a very real sense perform a myrmidon function for all men in our society. Cloaked in myths that obscure their identity, they, too, function as anonymous agents of terror. Although they are the ones who do the dirty work, the actual *attentat*, to other men, their superiors in class and station, the lasting benefits of their simple-minded evil have always accrued.

A world without rapists would be a world in which women moved freely without fear of men. That some men rape provides a sufficient threat to keep all women in a constant state of intimidation, forever conscious of the knowledge that the biological tool must be held in awe for it may turn to weapon with sudden swiftness borne of harmful intent. Myrmidons to the cause of male dominance, police-blotter rapists have performed their duty well, so well in fact that the true meaning of their act has largely gone unnoticed. Rather than society's aberrants or "spoilers of purity," men who commit rape have served in effect as front-line masculine shock troops, terrorist guerrillas in the longest sustained battle the world has ever known....

Women are trained to be rape victims. To simply learn the word "rape" is to take instruction in the power relationship between males and females. To talk about rape, even with nervous laughter, is to acknowledge a woman's special victim status. We hear the whispers when we are children: *girls get raped.* Not boys. The message becomes clear. Rape has something to do with our sex. Rape is something awful that happens to females: it is the dark at the top of the stairs, the undefinable abyss that is just around the corner, and unless we watch our step it might become our destiny.

Rape seeps into our childhood consciousness by imperceptible degrees. Even before we learn to read we have become indoctrinated into a victim mentality. Fairy tales are full of a vague dread, a catastrophe that seems to befall only little girls. Sweet, feminine Little Red Riding Hood is off to visit her dear old grandmother in the woods. The wolf lurks in the shadows, contemplating a tender morsel. Red Riding Hood and her grandmother, we learn, are equally defenseless before the male wolf's strength and cunning. His big eyes, his big hands, his big teeth—"The better to see you, to catch you, to eat you, my dear." The wolf swallows both females with no sign of a struggle. But enter the huntsman—he will right this egregious wrong. The kindly huntsman's strength and cunning are superior to the wolf's. With the twist of a knife Red Riding Hood and her grandmother are rescued from inside the wolf's stomach. "Oh, it was so dark in there," Red Riding Hood whimpers. "I will never again wander off into the forest as long as I live…"

Red Riding Hood is a parable of rape. There are frightening male figures abroad in the woods—we call them wolves, among other names—and females are helpless before them. Better stick close to the path, better not be adventurous. If you are lucky, a *good, friendly* male may be able to save you from certain disaster. ("Funny, every man I meet wants to protect me," says Mae West. "I can't figure out what from.") In the fairy-tale code book, Jack may kill giants but Little Red Riding Hood must look to a kindly huntsman for protection. Those who doubt that the tale of Red Riding Hood contains this subliminal message should consider how well Peter fared when he met his wolf, or even better, the survival tactics of the Three Little (male) Pigs. Who's Afraid of the Big Bad Wolf? Not they.…

There is good reason for men to hold tenaciously to the notion that "All women want to be raped." Because rape is an act that men do in the name of their masculinity, it is in their interest to believe that women also want rape done, in the name of femininity. In the dichotomy that they have established, one does and one "is done to." This belief is more than arrogant insensitivity; it is a belief in the supreme rightness of male power.

Once the proposition that all women secretly wish to be ravished has been established, it is bolstered by the claim that "No woman can be raped against her will." A variation runs "You can't thread a moving needle," used with wicked wit by Balzac in one of his *Droll Stories*, and retold *ad nauseam*, I am informed, by law professors seeking to inject some classroom humor into their introductory lectures on criminal law. The concept seems to imply at first hearing that if the will of a woman is strong, or if she is sufficiently agile, she can escape unscathed. Four hundred rape-murders a year in this country, and the percentage of gang rapes, should offer strong testament to the cruel lie of this statement, but "No woman can be raped against her will" is not intended to encourage women to do battle against an aggressor—rather, it slyly implies that there is no such thing as forcible rape, and that it is the *will* of women to be ravished.

"She was asking for it" is the classic way a rapist shifts the burden of blame from himself to his victim. The popularity of the belief that a woman seduces or "cock-teases" a man into rape, or precipitates a rape by incautious behavior, is part of the smoke screen that men throw up to obscure their actions. The insecurity of women runs so deep that many, possibly most, rape victims agonize afterward in an effort to uncover what it was in their behavior, their manner, their dress that triggered this awful act against them.

The last little maxim that we must consider with a jaundiced eye, "If you're going to be raped, you might as well relax and enjoy it," deliberately makes light of the physical violation of rape, pooh-poohs the insult and discourages resistance. The humorous advice that a violent sexual encounter not of your choosing can be fun if you play along and suspend your own judgments and feelings is predicated on two propositions: (a) the inevitability of male triumph and (b) "All women want to be raped."

Do women want to be raped? Do we crave humiliation, degradation and violation of our bodily integrity? Do we psychologically need to be seized, taken, ravished and ravaged? Must a feminist deal with this preposterous question?

The sad answer is yes, it must be dealt with, because the popular culture that we inhabit, absorb, and even contribute to, has so decreed. Actually, as we examine it, the cultural messages often conflict. Sometimes the idea is floated that all women want to be raped and sometimes we hear that there is no such thing as rape at all, that the cry of rape is merely the cry of female vengeance in postcoital spite. Either way, the woman is at fault....

Once we accept as basic truth that rape is not a crime of irrational, impulsive, uncontrollable lust, but is a deliberate, hostile, violent act of degradation and possession on the part of a would-be conqueror, designed to intimidate and inspire fear, we must look toward those elements in our culture that promote and propagandize these attitudes, which offer men, and in particular, impressionable, adolescent males, who form the potential raping population, the ideology and psychologic encouragement to commit their acts of aggression *without awareness, for the most part, that they have committed a punishable crime*, let alone a moral wrong. The myth of the heroic rapist that permeates false notions of masculinity, from the successful seducer to the man who "takes what he wants when he wants it," is inculcated in young boys from the time they first become aware that being a male means access to certain mysterious rites and privileges, including the right to buy a woman's body. When young men learn that females may be bought for a price, and that acts of sex command set prices, then how should they not also conclude that that which may be bought may also be taken without the civility of a monetary exchange?...

A law that reflects the female reality and a social system that no longer shuts women out of its enforcement and does not promote a masculine ideology of rape will go a long way toward the elimination of crimes of sexual violence, but the last line of defense shall always be our female bodies and our female minds. In making rape a *speakable* crime, not a matter of shame, the women's movement has already fired the first retaliatory shots in a war as ancient as civilization. When, just a few years ago, we began to hold our speak-outs on rape, our conferences, borrowing a church meeting hall for an afternoon, renting a high-school auditorium and some classrooms for a weekend of workshops and discussion, the world out there, the world outside of radical feminism, thought it was all very funny.

"You're talking about rape? Incredible! A *political* crime against women? How is a sex crime political? You're actually having women give testimony about their own rapes and what happened to them afterwards, the police, the hospitals, the courts? Far out!" And then the nervous giggles that betray confusion, fear and shame disappeared and in their place was the dim recognition that in daring to speak the unspoken, women had uncovered yet another part of our oppression, perhaps the central key: historic physical repression, a conscious process of intimidation, guilt and fear.

Within two years the world out there had stopped laughing, and the movement had progressed beyond the organizational forms of speak-outs and conferences, our internal consciousness-raising, to community outreach programs that were imaginative, original and unprecedented: rape crisis centers with a telephone hot line staffed twenty-four hours a day to provide counseling, procedural information and sisterly solidarity to recent rape victims and even to those whose assault had taken place years ago but who never had the chance to talk it out with other women and release their suppressed rage; rape legislation study groups to work up model codes based on a fresh approach to the law and to work with legislators to get new laws adopted; anti-rape projects in conjunction with the emergency ward of a city hospital, in close association with policewomen staffing newly formed sex crime analysis squads and investigative units. With pamphlets, newsletters, bumper stickers, "Wanted" posters, combative slogans—"STOP RAPE"; "WAR—WOMEN AGAINST RAPE"; "SMASH SEXISM, DISARM RAPISTS!"— and with classes in self-defense, women turned around and seized the offensive....

Fighting back. On a multiplicity of levels, that is the activity we must engage in, together, if we—women—are to redress the imbalance and rid ourselves and men of the ideology of rape.

Rape can be eradicated, not merely controlled or avoided on an individual basis, but the approach must be long-range and cooperative, and must have the understanding and good will of many men as well as women.

My purpose in this book has been to give rape its history. Now we must deny it a future.

47.

HÉLÈNE CIXOUS
(b. 1937)

"The Laugh of the Medusa"
(FRANCE, 1975)

In the 1970s, the women's liberation movement in France inspired an out-pouring of feminist theoretical writing, continuing the exploration of gender initiated by Simone de Beauvoir. Academic and literary feminists championed competing theories of women's liberation, some emphasizing the social construction of womanhood and others the deep psychic structures that shaped female experience. The novelist, playwright, and literary scholar Hélène Cixous belonged to the latter group, known as Psych et Po, for Psychoanalysis and Politics. Born in Algeria of Sephardic Jewish background and educated in France, Cixous offered a theory of écriture féminine, or feminine writing. In response to the erasure of women from a male-defined, phallocentric culture, she urged women to write, to unleash from repression a female unconscious deeply connected to the sexual. Cixous invoked "a universal woman subject" with unique erotic potential. Other French feminists, including de Beauvoir, disagreed with Cixous's emphasis on an essential female body and her assumption of a single female nature that could be articulated through writing. The title of Cixous's essay imagines the mythical bloody head of Medusa, with hair of serpents, as a laughing rather than frightening figure.

I shall speak about women's writing: about *what it will do*. Woman must write her self: must write about women and bring women to writing, from which they have been driven away as violently as from their bodies—for the same reasons, by the same law, with the same fatal goal. Woman must put herself into the text—as into the world and into history—by her own movement.

The future must no longer be determined by the past. I do not deny that the effects of the past are still with us. But I refuse to strengthen them by repeating them, to confer upon them an irremovability the equivalent of destiny, to confuse the biological and the cultural. Anticipation is imperative.

Since these reflections are taking shape in an area just on the point of being discovered, they necessarily bear the mark of our time—a time during which the new breaks away from the old, and, more precisely, the (feminine) new from the old (*la nouvelle de l'ancien*). Thus, as there are no grounds for establishing a discourse, but rather an arid millennial ground to break, what I say has at least two sides and two aims: to break up, to destroy; and to foresee the unforeseeable, to project.

I write this as a woman, toward women. When I say "woman," I'm speaking of woman in her inevitable struggle against conventional man; and of a universal woman subject who must bring women to their senses and to their meaning in history. But first it must be said that in spite of the enormity of the repression that has kept them in the "dark"—that dark which people have been trying to make them accept as their attribute—there is, at this time, no general woman, no one typical woman. What they have *in common* I will say. But what strikes me is the infinite richness of their individual constitutions: you can't talk about *a* female sexuality, uniform, homogeneous, classifiable into codes—any more than you can talk about one unconscious resembling another. Women's imaginary is inexhaustible, like music, painting, writing: their stream of phantasms is incredible.

I have been amazed more than once by a description a woman gave me of a world all her own which she had been secretly haunting since early childhood. A world of searching, the elaboration of a knowledge, on the basis of a systematic experimentation with the bodily functions, a passionate and precise interrogation of her erotogeneity. This practice, extraordinarily rich and inventive, in particular as concerns masturbation, is prolonged or accompanied by a production of forms, a veritable aesthetic activity, each stage of rapture inscribing a resonant vision, a composition, something beautiful. Beauty will no longer be forbidden.

I wished that that woman would write and proclaim this unique empire so that other women, other unacknowledged sovereigns, might exclaim: I, too, overflow; my desires have invented new desires, my body knows unheard-of songs. Time and again I, too, have felt so full of luminous torrents that I could burst—burst with forms much more beautiful than those which are put up in frames and sold for a stinking fortune. And I, too, said nothing, showed nothing; I didn't open my mouth, I didn't repaint my half of the world. I was ashamed. I was afraid, and I swallowed my shame and my fear. I said to myself: You are mad! What's the meaning of these waves, these floods, these outbursts? Where is the ebullient, infinite woman who, immersed as she was in her naiveté, kept in the dark about herself, led into self-disdain by the great arm of parental-conjugal phallocentrism, hasn't been ashamed of her strength? Who, surprised and horrified by the fantastic tumult of her drives (for she was made to believe that a well-adjusted normal woman has a...divine composure), hasn't accused herself of being a monster? Who, feeling a funny desire stirring inside her (to sing, to write, to dare to speak, in short, to bring out something new), hasn't thought she was sick? Well, her shameful sickness is that she resists death, that she makes trouble.

And why don't you write? Write! Writing is for you, you are for you; your body is yours, take it. I know why you haven't written. (And why I didn't write before the age of twenty-seven.) Because writing is at once too high, too great for you, it's reserved for the great—that is, for "great men"; and it's "silly." Besides, you've written a little, but in secret. And it wasn't good, because it was in secret, and because you punished yourself for writing, because you didn't go all the way; or because you wrote, irresistibly, as when we would masturbate in secret, not to go further, but to attenuate the tension a bit, just enough to take the edge off. And then as soon as we come, we go and make ourselves feel guilty—so as to be forgiven; or to forget, to bury it until the next time.

Write, let no one hold you back, let nothing stop you: not man; not the imbecilic capitalist machinery, in which publishing houses are the crafty, obsequious relayers of imperatives handed down by an economy that works against us and off our backs; and not *yourself*. Smug-faced readers, managing editors, and big bosses don't like the true texts of women—female-sexed texts. That kind scares them.

I write woman: woman must write woman. And man, man. So only an oblique consideration will be found here of man; it's up to him to say where his masculinity and femininity are at: this will concern us once men have opened their eyes and seen themselves clearly.*

Now women return from afar, from always: from "without," from the heath where witches are kept alive; from below, from beyond "culture"; from their childhood which men have been trying desperately to make them forget, condemning it to "eternal rest." The little girls and their "ill-mannered" bodies immured, well-preserved, intact unto themselves, in the mirror. Frigidified. But are they ever seething underneath! What an effort it takes—there's no end to it—for the sex cops to bar their threatening return. Such a display of forces on both sides that the struggle has for centuries been immobilized in the trembling equilibrium of a deadlock.

Here they are, returning, arriving over and again, because the unconscious is impregnable. They have wandered around in circles, confined to the narrow room in which they've been given a deadly brainwashing. You can incarcerate them, slow them down, get away

---

*Men still have everything to say about their sexuality, and everything to write. For what they have said so far, for the most part, stems from the opposition activity/passivity, from the power relation between a fantasized obligatory virility meant to invade, to colonize, and the consequential phantasm of woman as a "dark continent" to penetrate and to "pacify." (We know what "pacify" means in terms of scotomizing the other and mis-recognizing the self.) Conquering her, they've made haste to depart from her borders, to get out of sight, out of body. The way man has of getting out of himself and into her whom he takes not for the other but for his own, deprives him, he knows, of his own bodily territory. One can understand how man, confusing himself with his penis and rushing in for the attack, might feel resentment and fear of being "taken" by the woman, of being lost in her, absorbed, or alone.

with the old Apartheid routine, but for a time only. As soon as they begin to speak, at the same time as they're taught their name, they can be taught that their territory is black: because you are Africa, you are black. Your continent is dark. Dark is dangerous. You can't see anything in the dark, you're afraid. Don't move, you might fall. Most of all, don't go into the forest. And so we have internalized this horror of the dark.

Men have committed the greatest crime against women. Insidiously, violently, they have led them to hate women, to be their own enemies, to mobilize their immense strength against themselves, to be the executants of their virile needs. They have made for women an antinarcissism! A narcissism which loves itself only to be loved for what women haven't got! They have constructed the infamous logic of antilove.

We the precocious, we the repressed of culture, our lovely mouths gagged with pollen, our wind knocked out of us, we the labyrinths, the ladders, the trampled spaces, the bevies—we are black and we are beautiful.

We're stormy, and that which is ours breaks loose from us without our fearing any debilitation. Our glances, our smiles, are spent; laughs exude from all our mouths; our blood flows and we extend ourselves without ever reaching an end; we never hold back our thoughts, our signs, our writing; and we're not afraid of lacking.

What happiness for us who are omitted, brushed aside at the scene of inheritances; we inspire ourselves and we expire without running out of breath, we are everywhere!

From now on, who, if we say so, can say no to us? We've come back from always.

It is time to liberate the New Woman from the Old by coming to know her—by loving her for getting by, for getting beyond the Old without delay, by going out ahead of what the New Woman will be, as an arrow quits the bow with a movement that gathers and separates the vibrations musically, in order to be more than her self....

She must write her self, because this is the invention of a *new insurgent* writing which, when the moment of her liberation has come, will allow her to carry out the indispensable ruptures and transformations in her history, first at two levels that cannot be separated.

a) Individually. By writing her self, woman will return to the body which has been more than confiscated from her, which has been turned into the uncanny stranger on display—the ailing or dead figure, which so often turns out to be the nasty companion, the cause and location of inhibitions. Censor the body and you censor breath and speech at the same time.

Write your self. Your body must be heard. Only then will the immense resources of the unconscious spring forth. Our naphtha will spread, throughout the world, without dollars—black or gold—nonassessed values that will change the rules of the old game.

To write. An act which will not only "realize" the decensored relation of woman to her sexuality, to her womanly being, giving her access to her native strength; it will give her back her goods, her pleasures, her organs, her immense bodily territories which have been kept under seal; it will tear her away from the superegoized structure in which she has always occupied the place reserved for the guilty (guilty of everything, guilty at every turn: for having desires, for not having any; for being frigid, for being "too hot"; for not being both at once; for being too motherly and not enough; for having children and for not having any; for nursing and for not nursing...)—tear her away by means of this research, this job of analysis and illumination, this emancipation of the marvelous text of her self that she must urgently learn to speak. A woman without a body, dumb, blind, can't possibly be a good fighter. She is reduced to being the servant of the militant male, his shadow. We must kill the false woman who is preventing the live one from breathing. Inscribe the breath of the whole woman.

b) An act that will also be marked by woman's *seizing* the occasion to *speak,* hence her shattering entry into history, which has always been based *on her suppression.* To write and thus to forge for herself the antilogos weapon. To become *at will* the taker and initiator, for her own right, in every symbolic system, in every political process.

It is time for women to start scoring their feats in written and oral language.

Every woman has known the torment of getting up to speak. Her heart racing, at times entirely lost for words, ground and language slipping away—that's how daring a feat, how great a transgression it is for a woman to speak—even just open her mouth—in public. A double distress, for even if she transgresses, her words fall almost always upon the deaf male ear, which hears in language only that which speaks in the masculine.

It is by writing, from and toward women, and by taking up the challenge of speech which has been governed by the phallus, that women will confirm women in a place other than that which is reserved in and by the symbolic, that is, in a place other than silence. Women should break out of the snare of silence. They shouldn't be conned into accepting a domain which is the margin or the harem....

It is impossible to *define* a feminine practice of writing, and this is an impossibility that will remain, for this practice can never be theorized, enclosed, coded—which doesn't mean that it doesn't exist. But it will always surpass the discourse that regulates the phallocentric system; it does and will take place in areas other than those subordinated to philosophico-theoretical domination. It will be conceived of only by subjects who are breakers of automatisms, by peripheral figures that no authority can ever subjugate....

Write! and your self-seeking text will know itself better than flesh and blood, rising, insurrectionary dough kneading itself, with sonorous, perfumed ingredients, a lively combination of flying colors, leaves, and rivers plunging into the sea we feed. "Ah, there's her sea," he will say as he holds out to me a basin full of water from the little phallic mother from whom he's inseparable. But look, our seas are what we make of them, full of fish or not, opaque or transparent, red or black, high or smooth, narrow or bankless; and we are ourselves sea, sand, coral, seaweed, beaches, tides, swimmers, children, waves.... More or less wavily sea, earth, sky—what matter would rebuff us? We know how to speak them all.

Heterogeneous, yes. For her joyous benefit she is erogenous; she is the erotogeneity of the heterogeneous: airborne swimmer, in flight, she does not cling to herself; she is dispersible, prodigious, stunning, desirous and capable of others, of the other woman that she will be, of the other woman she isn't, of him, of you....

48

COMBAHEE RIVER COLLECTIVE

"A Black Feminist Statement"
(UNITED STATES, 1977)

Like Sojourner Truth, Anna Julia Cooper, and Pauli Murray, the Combahee River Collective—a group of young African American women who began meeting in Boston in 1974—refused to separate the politics of race and of gender. In contrast to liberal black feminists, who had formed the National Black Feminist Organization in 1973, this radical collective embraced elements of socialist feminism, black nationalism, and lesbian feminism. They named their group after a river where Harriet Tubman had freed hundreds of slaves. The collective created a space apart from both white women and black men, forming study groups and cultural retreats where they addressed not only "antiracist and antisexist" politics but also "heterosexism and economic oppression under capitalism." The statement they issued in 1977 (written by collective members Barbara Smith, Beverly Smith, and Demita Frazier) became a classic text of American feminist theory. In an influential articulation of "identity politics," they argued that all forms of liberation flow from an understanding of one's own oppression and thus require separate organizing. At the same time, however, and in contrast to lesbian separatists who withdrew from mixed organizations, the members of the Combahee River Collective proclaimed solidarity with "progressive black men." Like other feminists of color, they criticized racism within the women's movement and created their own cultural and political institutions.

Above all else, our politics initially sprang from the shared belief that black women are inherently valuable, that our liberation is a necessity not as an adjunct to somebody else's but because of our need as human persons for autonomy. This may seem so obvious as to sound simplistic, but it is apparent that no other ostensibly progressive movement has ever considered our specific oppression a priority or worked seriously for the ending of that oppression. Merely naming the pejorative stereotypes attributed to black women (e.g., mammy, matriarch, Sapphire, whore, bulldagger), let alone cataloguing the cruel, often murderous, treatment we receive, indicates how little value has been placed upon our lives during four centuries of bondage in the Western hemisphere. We realize that the only people who care enough about us to work consistently for our liberation is us. Our politics evolve from a healthy love for ourselves, our sisters, and our community which allows us to continue our struggle and work.

This focusing upon our own oppression is embodied in the concept of identity politics. We believe that the most profound and potentially the most radical politics come directly out of our own identity, as opposed to working to end somebody else's oppression. In the case of black women this is a particularly repugnant, dangerous, threatening, and therefore revolutionary concept because it is obvious from looking at all the political movements that have preceded us that anyone is more worthy of liberation than ourselves. We reject pedestals, queenhood, and walking ten paces behind. To be recognized as human, levelly human, is enough.

We believe that sexual politics under patriarchy is as pervasive in black women's lives as are the politics of class and race. We also often find it difficult to separate race from class from sex oppression because in our lives they are most often experienced simultaneously. We know that there is such a thing as racial-sexual oppression which is neither solely racial nor solely sexual, e.g., the history of rape of black women by white men as a weapon of political repression.

Although we are feminists and lesbians, we feel solidarity with progressive black men and do not advocate the fractionalization that white women who are separatists demand. Our situation as black people necessitates that we have solidarity around the fact of race, which white women of course do not need to have with white men, unless it is their negative solidarity as racial oppressors. We struggle together with black men against racism, while we also struggle with black men about sexism.

We realize that the liberation of all oppressed peoples necessitates the destruction of the political-economic systems of capitalism and imperialism as well as patriarchy. We are socialists because we believe the work must be organized for the collective benefit of those who do the work and create the products and not for the profit of the bosses. Material resources must be equally distributed among those who create these resources. We are not convinced, however, that a socialist revolution that is not also a feminist and antiracist revolution will guarantee our liberation. We have arrived at the necessity for developing an understanding of class relationships that takes into account the specific class position of black women who are generally marginal in the labor force, while at this particular time some of us are temporarily viewed as doubly desirable tokens at white-collar and professional levels. We need to articulate the real class situation of persons who are not merely raceless, sexless workers, but for whom racial and sexual oppression are significant determinants in their working/economic lives. Although we are in essential agreement with Marx's theory as it applied to the very specific economic relationships he analyzed, we know that this analysis must be extended further in order for us to understand our specific economic situation as black women.

A political contribution which we feel we have already made is the expansion of the feminist principle that the personal is political. In our consciousness-raising sessions, for example, we have in many ways gone beyond white women's revelations because we are dealing with the implications of race and class as well as sex. Even our black women's style of talking/testifying in black language about what we have experienced has a resonance that is both cultural and political. We have spent a great deal of energy delving into the cultural and experiential nature of our oppression out of necessity because none of these matters have ever been looked at before. No one before has ever examined the multilayered texture of black women's lives.

crazy

The psychological toll of being a black woman and the difficulties this presents in reaching political consciousness and doing political work can never be underestimated. There is a very low value placed upon black women's psyches in this society, which is both racist and sexist. As an early group member once said, "We are all damaged people merely by virtue of being black women." We are dispossessed psychologically and on every other level, and yet we feel the necessity to struggle to change our condition and the condition of all black women. In "A Black Feminist's Search for Sisterhood," Michele Wallace arrives at this conclusion:

> We exist as women who are black who are feminists, each stranded for the moment, working independently because there is not yet an environment in this society remotely congenial to our struggle—because, being on the bottom, we would have to do what no one else has done: we would have to fight the world.

Wallace is not pessimistic but realistic in her assessment of black feminists' position, particularly in her allusion to the nearly classic isolation most of us face. We might use our position at the bottom, however, to make a clear leap into revolutionary action. If black women were free, it would mean that everyone else would have to be free since our freedom would necessitate the destruction of all the systems of oppression....

The reaction of black men to feminism has been notoriously negative. They are, of course, even more threatened than black women by the possibility that black feminists might organize around our own needs. They realize that they might not only lose valuable and hardworking allies in their struggles but that they might also be forced to change their habitually sexist ways of interacting with and oppressing black women. Accusations that black feminism divides the black struggle are powerful deterrents to the growth of an autonomous black women's movement.

Still, hundreds of women have been active at different times during the three-year existence of our group. And every black woman who came, came out of a strongly felt need for some level of possibility that did not previously exist in her life....

During our time together we have identified and worked on many issues of particular relevance to black women. The inclusiveness of our politics makes us concerned with any situation that impinges upon the lives of women, Third World, and working people. We are of course particularly committed to working on those struggles in which race, sex, and class are simultaneous factors in oppression. We might, for example, become involved in workplace organizing at a factory that employs Third World women or picket a hospital that is cutting back on already inadequate health care to a Third World community, or set up a rape crisis center in a black neighborhood. Organizing around welfare or daycare concerns might also be a focus. The work to be done and the countless issues that this work represents merely reflect the pervasiveness of our oppression.

Issues and projects that collective members have actually worked on are sterilization abuse, abortion rights, battered women, rape, and health care. We have also done many workshops and educationals on black feminism on college campuses, at women's conferences, and most recently for high school women.

One issue that is of major concern to us and that we have begun to publicly address is racism in the white women's movement. As black feminists we are made constantly and painfully aware of how little effort white women have made to understand and combat their racism, which requires among other things that they have a more than superficial comprehension of race, color, and black history and culture. Eliminating racism in the white women's movement is by definition work for white women to do, but we will continue to speak to and demand accountability on this issue.

In the practice of our politics we do not believe that the end always justifies the means. Many reactionary and destructive acts have been done in the name of achieving "correct" political goals. As feminists we do not want to mess over people in the name of politics. We believe in collective process and a nonhierarchical distribution of power within our own group and in our vision of a revolutionary society. We are committed to a continual examination of our politics as they develop through criticism and self-criticism as an essential aspect of our practice. As black feminists and lesbians we know that we have a very definite revolutionary task to perform and we are ready for the lifetime of work and struggle before us.

49

AUDRE LORDE

(1934–92)

"The Master's Tools Will Never Dismantle the Master's House"

(UNITED STATES, 1979)

In the 1970s, women of color and lesbians in the United States called on feminist scholars to recognize their own discriminatory practices and to analyze the intersections of racial, sexual, and gender hierarchies. At an academic feminist conference commemorating the thirtieth anniversary of the publication of de Beauvoir's The Second Sex, *the lesbian poet and literature professor Audre Lorde articulated the frustrations of women treated as tokens, the sole black or lesbian speaker invited to participate in a predominantly white movement. Her influential remarks impelled women's studies courses, programs, and conferences to expand their vision and embrace, rather than fear, differences among women. Lorde knew firsthand the dilemmas of bridging cultures. Raised in Harlem by Caribbean immigrant parents, she had been one of the few black women within the lesbian bar culture that flourished in post–World War II New York City. Her poetry increasingly dealt with multiple identities. "I who am bound by my mirror / as well as my bed / see causes in color / as well as sex," she wrote in "The Black Unicorn" (New York: Norton, 1978). Along with members of the Combahee River Collective, Lorde helped found Kitchen Table–Women of Color Press. Her autobiographical prose includes* The Cancer Journals *(1980) and* Zami: A New Spelling of My Name *(1982).*

I agreed to take part in a New York University Institute for the Humanities conference a year ago, with the understanding that I would be commenting upon papers dealing with the role of difference within the lives of american women: difference of race, sexuality, class, and age. For the absence of these considerations weakens any feminist discussion of the personal and the political.

It is a particular academic arrogance to assume any discussion of feminist theory in this time and in this place without examining our many differences, and without a significant input from poor women, black and third-world women, and lesbians. And yet, I stand here as a black lesbian feminist, having been invited to comment within the only panel at this conference where the input of black feminists and lesbians is represented. What this says about the vision of this conference is sad, in a country where racism, sexism and homophobia are inseparable. To read this progam is to assume that lesbian and black women have nothing to say of existentialism, the erotic, women's culture and silence, developing feminist theory, or heterosexuality and power. And what does it mean in personal and political terms when even the two black women who did present here were literally found at the last hour? What does it mean when the tools of a racist patriarchy are used to examine the fruits of that same patriarchy? It means that only the most narrow perimeters of change are possible and allowable.

The absence of any consideration of lesbian consciousness or the consciousness of third world women leaves a serious gap within this conference and within the papers presented here. For example, in a paper on material relationships between women, I was conscious of an either/or model of nurturing which totally dismissed my knowledge as a black lesbian. In this paper there was no examination of mutuality between women, no systems of shared support, no interdependence as exists between lesbians and women-identified women. Yet it is only in the patriarchal model of nurturance that women "who attempt to emancipate themselves pay perhaps too high a price for the results," as this paper states.

For women, the need and desire to nurture each other is not pathological but redemptive, and it is within that knowledge that our real power is rediscovered. It is this real connection, which is so feared by a patriarchal world. For it is only under a patriarchal structure that maternity is the only social power open to women.

Interdependency between women is the only way to the freedom which allows the "I" to "be," not in order to be used, but in order to be creative. This is a difference between the passive "be" and the active "being."

Advocating the mere tolerance of difference between women is the grossest reformism. It is a total denial of the creative function of difference in our lives. For difference must be not merely tolerated, but seen as a fund of necessary polarities between which our creativity can spark like a dialectic. Only then does the necessity for interdependency become unthreatening. Only within that interdependency of different strengths, acknowleged and equal, can the power to seek new ways to actively "be" in the world generate, as well as the courage and sustenance to act where there are no charters.

Within the interdependence of mutual (non-dominant) differences lies that security which enables us to descend into the chaos of knowledge and return with true visions of our future, along with the concomitant power to effect those changes which can bring that future into being. Difference is that raw and powerful connection from which our personal power is forged.

As women, we have been taught to either ignore our differences or to view them as causes for separation and suspicion rather than as forces for change. Without community, there is no liberation, only the most vulnerable and temporary armistice between an individual and her oppression. But community must not mean a shedding of our differences, nor the pathetic pretense that these differences do not exist.

Those of us who stand outside the circle of this society's definition of acceptable women; those of us who have been forged in the crucibles of difference; those of us who are poor, who are lesbians, who are black, who are older, know that *survival is not an academic skill*. It is learning how to stand alone, unpopular and sometimes reviled, and how to make common cause with those other identified as outside the structures, in order to define and seek a world in which we can all flourish. It is learning how to take our differences and make them strengths. *For the master's tools will never dismantle the master's house.* They may allow us temporarily to beat him at his own game, but they will never enable us to bring about genuine change. And this fact is only threatening to those women who still define the master's house as their only source of support.

Poor and third world women know there is a difference between the daily manifestations and dehumanizations of marital slavery and prostitution, because it is our daughters who line 42nd Street. The Black panelists' observation about the effects of relative powerlessness and the differences of relationship between black women and men from white women and men illustrate some of our unique problems as black feminists. If white american feminist theory need not deal with the differences between us, and the resulting difference in aspects of our oppressions, then what do you do with the fact that the women who clean your houses and tend your children while you attend conferences on feminist theory are, for the most part, poor and third world women? What is the theory behind racist feminism?

In a world of possibility for us all, our personal visions help lay the groundwork for political action. The failure of the academic feminists to recognize difference as a crucial strength is a failure to reach beyond the first patriarchal lesson. Divide and conquer, in our world, must become define and empower.

Why weren't other black women and third world women found to participate in this conference? Why were two phone calls to me considered a consultation? Am I the only possible source of names of black feminists? And although the black panelist's paper ends on a important and powerful connection of love between women, what about interracial co-operation between feminists who don't love each other?

In academic feminist circles, the answer to these questions is often "We did not know who to ask." But that is the same evasion of responsibility, the same cop-out, that keeps black women's art out of women's exhibitions, black women's work out of most feminist publications except for the occasional "Special Third World Women's Issue," and black women's texts off of your reading lists. But as Adrienne Rich pointed out in a recent talk, white feminists have educated themselves about such an enormous amount over the past ten years, how come you haven't also educated yourselves about black women and

Summary sentence

the differences between us—white and black—when it is key to our survival as a movement?

Women of today are still being called upon to stretch across the gap of male ignorance, and to educate men as to our existence and our needs. This is an old and primary tool of all oppressors to keep the oppressed occupied with the master's concerns. Now we hear that it is the task of black and third world women to educate white women, in the face of tremendous resistance, as to our existence, our differences, our relative roles in our joint survival. This is a diversion of energies and a tragic repetition of racist patriarchal thought.

Simone de Beauvoir once said:

"It is in the knowledge of the genuine conditions of our lives that we must draw our strength to live and our reasons for acting."

Racism and homophobia are real conditions of all our lives in this place and this time. *I urge each one of us here to reach down into that deep place of knowledge inside herself and touch that terror and loathing of any difference that lives there. See whose face it wears.* Then the personal as the political can begin to illuminate all our choices.

50.

UNITED NATIONS

Convention on the Elimination of All
Forms of Discrimination
Against Women

(1979)

Since its charter in 1945, the United Nations has attempted to implement equal rights for women through its constituent organizations, establishing a Commission on the Status of Women in 1947 and declaring 1975 as International Women's Year. During the U.N. "Decade for Women," three international conferences met: in Mexico City in 1975, Copenhagen in 1980, and Nairobi in 1985. At the Mexico City meeting, delegates drafted a Convention on the Elimination of All Forms of Discrimination Against Women (CEDAW), which the U.N. General Assembly passed in 1979. CEDAW reiterates earlier U.N. commitments to both women's rights and the importance of families; it also addresses the effects of poverty on women, the need to abolish apartheid and all forms of racism and colonialism, and the importance of national self-determination for "the attainment of full equality between men and women." Significantly, the document refers to the common responsibility of men and women for raising children. By 2006, 90 percent of the U.N. member countries (but not the United States) had ratified the treaty. Although CEDAW provides leverage for achieving women's rights, ratification by no means ensures compliance, for many signatory states continue to discriminate against women in law and practice. Nonetheless, the convention illustrates an ideal of gender justice that gained legitimacy in the late twentieth century.

PART I

Article 1

For the purposes of the present Convention, the term "discrimination against women" shall mean any distinction, exclusion or restriction made on the basis of sex which has the effect or purpose of impairing or nullifying the recognition, enjoyment or exercise by women, irrespective of their marital status, on a basis of equality of men and women, of human rights and fundamental freedoms in the political, economic, social, cultural, civil or any other field.

Article 2

States Parties condemn discrimination against women in all its forms, agree to pursue by all appropriate means and without delay a policy of eliminating discrimination against women and, to this end, undertake:

(a) To embody the principle of the equality of men and women in their national constitutions or other appropriate legislation if not yet incorporated therein and to ensure, through law and other appropriate means, the practical realization of this principle;

(b) To adopt appropriate legislative and other measures, including sanctions where appropriate, prohibiting all discrimination against women;

(c) To establish legal protection of the rights of women on an equal basis with men and to ensure through competent national tribunals and other public institutions the effective protection of women against any act of discrimination;

(d) To refrain from engaging in any act or practice of discrimination against women and to ensure that public authorities and institutions shall act in conformity with this obligation;

(e) To take all appropriate measures to eliminate discrimination against women by any person, organization or enterprise;

(f) To take all appropriate measures, including legislation, to modify or abolish existing laws, regulations, customs and practices which constitute discrimination against women;

(g) To repeal all national penal provisions which constitute discrimination against women.

Article 3

States Parties shall take in all fields, in particular in the political, social, economic and cultural fields, all appropriate measures, including legislation, to ensure the full development and advancement of women, for the purpose of guaranteeing them the exercise and enjoyment of human rights and fundamental freedoms on a basis of equality with men.

Article 4

1. Adoption by States Parties of temporary special measures aimed at accelerating de facto equality between men and women shall not be considered discrimination as defined in the present Convention, but shall in no way entail as a consequence the maintenance of unequal or separate standards; these measures shall be discontinued when the objectives of equality of opportunity and treatment have been achieved.
2. Adoption by States Parties of special measures, including those measures contained in the present Convention, aimed at protecting maternity shall not be considered discriminatory.

Article 5

States Parties shall take all appropriate measures:

(a) To modify the social and cultural patterns of conduct of men and women, with a view to achieving the elimination of prejudices and customary and all other practices which are based on the idea of the inferiority or the superiority of either of the sexes or on stereotyped roles for men and women;
(b) To ensure that family education includes a proper understanding of maternity as a social function and the recognition

of the common responsibility of men and women in the upbringing and development of their children, it being understood that the interest of the children is the primordial consideration in all cases.

Article 6

States Parties shall take all appropriate measures, including legislation, to suppress all forms of traffic in women and exploitation of prostitution of women.

PART II

Article 7

States Parties shall take all appropriate measures to eliminate discrimination against women in the political and public life of the country and, in particular, shall ensure to women, on equal terms with men, the right:

(a) To vote in all elections and public referenda and to be eligible for election to all publicly elected bodies;

(b) To participate in the formulation of government policy and the implementation thereof and to hold public office and perform all public functions at all levels of government;

(c) To participate in non-governmental organizations and associations concerned with the public and political life of the country.

Article 8

States Parties shall take all appropriate measures to ensure to women, on equal terms with men and without any discrimination, the opportunity to represent their Governments at the international level and to participate in the work of international organizations.

Article 9

1. States Parties shall grant women equal rights with men to acquire, change or retain their nationality. They shall ensure in particular that neither marriage to an alien nor change of nationality by the husband during marriage shall automatically change the nationality of the wife, render her stateless or force upon her the nationality of the husband.
2. States Parties shall grant women equal rights with men with respect to the nationality of their children.

PART III

Article 10

States Parties shall take all appropriate measures to eliminate discrimination against women in order to ensure to them equal rights with men in the field of education and in particular to ensure, on a basis of equality of men and women:

(a) The same conditions for career and vocational guidance, for access to studies and for the achievement of diplomas in educational establishments of all categories in rural as well as in urban areas; this equality shall be ensured in pre-school, general, technical, professional and higher technical education, as well as in all types of vocational training;

(b) Access to the same curricula, the same examinations, teaching staff with qualifications of the same standard and school premises and equipment of the same quality;

(c) The elimination of any stereotyped concept of the roles of men and women at all levels and in all forms of education by encouraging coeducation and other types of education which will help to achieve this aim and, in particular, by the revision of textbooks and school programmes and the adaptation of teaching methods;

(d) The same opportunities to benefit from scholarships and other study grants;

(e) The same opportunities for access to programmes of continuing education, including adult and functional literacy programmes, particulary those aimed at reducing, at the earliest possible time, any gap in education existing between men and women;

(f) The reduction of female student drop-out rates and the organization of programmes for girls and women who have left school prematurely;

(g) The same opportunities to participate actively in sports and physical education;

(h) Access to specific educational information to help to ensure the health and well-being of families, including information and advice on family planning.

Article 11

1. States Parties shall take all appropriate measures to eliminate discrimination against women in the field of employment in order to ensure, on a basis of equality of men and women, the same rights, in particular:

(a) The right to work as an inalienable right of all human beings;

(b) The right to the same employment opportunities, including the application of the same criteria for selection in matters of employment;

(c) The right to free choice of profession and employment, the right to promotion, job security and all benefits and conditions of service and the right to receive vocational training and retraining, including apprenticeships, advanced vocational training and recurrent training;

(d) The right to equal remuneration, including benefits, and to equal treatment in respect of work of equal value, as well as equality of treatment in the evaluation of the quality of work;

(e) The right to social security, particularly in cases of retirement, unemployment, sickness, invalidity and old age and other incapacity to work, as well as the right to paid leave;

(f) The right to protection of health and to safety in working conditions, including the safeguarding of the function of reproduction.

2. In order to prevent discrimination against women on the grounds of marriage or maternity and to ensure their effective right to work, States Parties shall take appropriate measures:

(a) To prohibit, subject to the imposition of sanctions, dismissal on the grounds of pregnancy or of maternity leave and discrimination in dismissals on the basis of marital status;

(b) To introduce maternity leave with pay or with comparable social benefits without loss of former employment, seniority or social allowances;

(c) To encourage the provision of the necessary supporting social services to enable parents to combine family obligations with work responsibilities and participation in public life, in particular through promoting the establishment and development of a network of child-care facilities;

(d) To provide special protection to women during pregnancy in types of work proved to be harmful to them.

3. Protective legislation relating to matters covered in this article shall be reviewed periodically in the light of scientific and technological knowledge and shall be revised, repealed or extended as necessary.

Article 12

1. States Parties shall take all appropriate measures to eliminate discrimination against women in the field of health care in order to ensure, on a basis of equality of men and women, access to health care services, including those related to family planning.

2. Notwithstanding the provisions of paragraph I of this article, States Parties shall ensure to women appropriate services in connection with pregnancy, confinement and the post-natal period, granting free services where necessary, as well as adequate nutrition during pregnancy and lactation.

Article 13

States Parties shall take all appropriate measures to eliminate discrimination against women in other areas of economic and social life in order to ensure, on a basis of equality of men and women, the same rights, in particular:

(a) The right to family benefits;
(b) The right to bank loans, mortgages and other forms of financial credit;
(c) The right to participate in recreational activities, sports and all aspects of cultural life.

Article 14

1. States Parties shall take into account the particular problems faced by rural women and the significant roles which rural women play in the economic survival of their families, including their work in the non-monetized sectors of the economy, and shall take all appropriate measures to ensure the application of the provisions of the present Convention to women in rural areas.

2. States Parties shall take all appropriate measures to eliminate discrimination against women in rural areas in order to ensure, on a basis of equality of men and women, that they participate in and benefit from rural development and, in particular, shall ensure to such women the right:

(a) To participate in the elaboration and implementation of development planning at all levels;
(b) To have access to adequate health care facilities, including information, counselling and services in family planning;
(c) To benefit directly from social security programmes;
(d) To obtain all types of training and education, formal and non-formal, including that relating to functional literacy, as well as, inter alia, the benefit of all community and extension services, in order to increase their technical proficiency;

    (e) To organize self-help groups and co-operatives in order to obtain equal access to economic opportunities through employment or self employment;

    (f) To participate in all community activities;

    (g) To have access to agricultural credit and loans, marketing facilities, appropriate technology and equal treatment in land and agrarian reform as well as in land resettlement schemes;

    (h) To enjoy adequate living conditions, particularly in relation to housing, sanitation, electricity and water supply, transport and communications.

PART IV

Article 15

1. States Parties shall accord to women equality with men before the law.
2. States Parties shall accord to women, in civil matters, a legal capacity identical to that of men and the same opportunities to exercise that capacity. In particular, they shall give women equal rights to conclude contracts and to administer property and shall treat them equally in all stages of procedure in courts and tribunals.
3. States Parties agree that all contracts and all other private instruments of any kind with a legal effect which is directed at restricting the legal capacity of women shall be deemed null and void.
4. States Parties shall accord to men and women the same rights with regard to the law relating to the movement of persons and the freedom to choose their residence and domicile.

Article 16

1. States Parties shall take all appropriate measures to eliminate discrimination against women in all matters relating to marriage and family relations and in particular shall ensure, on a basis of equality of men and women:

(a) The same right to enter into marriage;

(b) The same right freely to choose a spouse and to enter into marriage only with their free and full consent;

(c) The same rights and responsibilities during marriage and at its dissolution;

(d) The same rights and responsibilities as parents, irrespective of their marital status, in matters relating to their children; in all cases the interests of the children shall be paramount;

(e) The same rights to decide freely and responsibly on the number and spacing of their children and to have access to the information, education and means to enable them to exercise these rights;

(f) The same rights and responsibilities with regard to guardianship, wardship, trusteeship and adoption of children, or similar institutions where these concepts exist in national legislation; in all cases the interests of the children shall be paramount;

(g) The same personal rights as husband and wife, including the right to choose a family name, a profession and an occupation;

(h) The same rights for both spouses in respect of the ownership, acquisition, management, administration, enjoyment and disposition of property, whether free of charge or for a valuable consideration.

2. The betrothal and the marriage of a child shall have no legal effect, and all necessary action, including legislation, shall be taken to specify a minimum age for marriage and to make the registration of marriages in an official registry compulsory.

51.

DOMITILA BARRIOS DE LA CHUNGARA
(b. 1937)

"The Woman's Problem"

(BOLIVIA, 1980)

At the international conference on women held in Mexico City in 1975 to launch the United Nations Decade of Women (1975–85), an indigenous woman born in the Bolivian Andes confronted American feminists, including Betty Friedan, to insist that the conference address the concerns of her class. Domitila Barrios de la Chungara had been invited by the U.N. to report on her efforts to organize the wives of miners in Bolivia. After a childhood of poverty and abuse, and with a grade-school education, she had married a miner and had seven children. In 1963 Barrios de la Chungara joined the Housewives Committee of Siglo XX, a group of miners' wives founded two years earlier that supported imprisoned male union members and monitored local food prices. Despite initial opposition from her husband and from the miners' union, she became increasingly active as a community organizer, staging local protests over inadequate medical care and running for office. In her speaking and writing she urged other women to share their complaints and to educate themselves politically. As the following excerpt from a pamphlet based on her talks to peasant women illustrates, Barrios de la Chungara rejected middle-class feminist aspirations for equality with men, even as she sharply criticized patriarchy. Her views reflect those of other grassroots activists who insist on women's rights within the context of labor and revolutionary movements. The publication of her book, Let Me Speak *(translated into English in 1978), brought into wider public view the plight of Bolivian workers and their families.*

First we shall talk about the woman's problem in general. Woman, not only in Bolivia, but all over the world, is being subjugated, relegated to a fourth place in society. She is subjugated in such a way that she is not allowed to participate—as we can see in everyday life—even at the level of trade union organization.

We are looked down upon right from birth. Let us begin by looking at what happens to the woman in the home. When a boy is born, *companeras*, what does the father do? He goes off and celebrates because a man has been born. There has to be celebration because the child is male. Isn't this true? But what do they say when it's a girl? "Ah this good-for-nothing, what use is she, let her die!" And even the women sometimes say: "What a shame it's a little girl, what use is she? It would be better if she died." They have taught us to look down on ourselves, isn't this true?

Where would the world be without women? It wouldn't get very far. But we are used to looking down on ourselves and undermining our own abilities. There are women who criticize us for being in trade unions or political parties. They say: "Those idle women have nothing to do. Why do they interfere?" Thus, even women criticize us because, since birth, we have been brought up in this way, with this mentality, not only in Bolivia but in the whole world. Throughout history, however, women have shown themselves just as capable of taking part in cultural, political and union activities as men. They have also shown that they can fight on battle-fields, fight beside the men. We have many examples of this in our country, the women who fought alone in La Coronilla, other women who fought alongside the men in the War of Independence. Men and women have also fought together in other countries, such as Nicaragua.

What I want to tell you, *companeras*, is that we women were born with all our rights. In Bolivia there is a law that guarantees women's participation in everything. In 1948, all the countries of the world came together in the United Nations. There, laws were created about human rights, and amongst these was one that gave women the right to participate in everything, as human beings. Thus, we women have the right to participate in clubs, in unions, in political parties, We have the same rights to education as a man does, and the right to receive equal wages with men. We are all covered by these laws. Even Bolivia has said "We agree that Bolivian women should participate in everything," and the government has signed this document. But, since 1948 up to the present day, what government has really bothered about educating, training and encouraging women to participate? None. If they have created laws for women, it has only been so that they can use them to serve a certain political party, a certain social class. Later the women are forgotten. A woman is like a piece of cloth, used to clean a dirty table and then hidden away in a corner until next time. This is how they use us, and it is we ourselves who are to blame. We allow ourselves to be used and manipulated. We criticize ourselves. How many times have we been called lazy and idle when we participated in unions? They also say that we join the union looking for an affair with one of the leaders and the leaders themselves sometimes think that we go to the meetings to flirt with them. What we must do is decide exactly what we are looking for, because women all over the world are fighting for their liberation in different ways and for different reasons.

At the International Women's Conference in Mexico in 1975, I could see two types of liberation. One type involves those who think women will only be free when they equal men in all their vices. This is called feminism. It means that women must fight against men for the right to smoke and drink as they do. For example, they said in this conference: "If the man goes out to enjoy himself tonight, tomorrow I must go out and do the same."

But *companeras*, do we really want to smoke cigarettes? Do we really want to go out drinking and living it up like our husbands? I don't think so. If the man has ten mistresses, does this mean I have to do the same? What would we be doing? We would be degrading people, nothing more. But we should not fight against our *companeros* or imitate their vices, but we should try to imitate our husbands' good points.

This fight is typical of the wealthy, women who have everything and only want to imitate men's bad habits. But for us, from our class position, what type of liberation do we want? The liberation that rich women and American women want? Or the other type, which consists of women being respected as human beings, who can solve problems and participate in everything—culture, art, literature, politics, trade-unionism—a liberation that means our opinion is respected at home and outside the home! Because sometimes even as mothers are we not allowed to give our opinion or correct our children, because the father comes along and beats us and takes away our authority. In the end, the children lose all respect for us, and when their father dies they tell us to shut up and treat us like idiots. Isn't that true? And why does all this happen? Because it has been proved in practice, women are more thoughtful, more firm in their positions, more honest. When a woman reaches a position of leadership, she doesn't sell out like a man because she has fewer vices, and is more conscious in her struggle. That is why our exploiters don't want us women to get involved in anything.

Many comrades say that women should organize themselves in unions, but sometimes, what happens is that they are very enthusiastic at first, then later they get demoralized. There are times when our husbands are conscious, helping in the struggle. Then, when the repression comes, what does the woman do? She starts saying to her husband, "Well, now you must choose between me and your children, or the union and your party." Or she says "You're not going to the union, or I will leave." This is why they sometimes blame us women, saying that instead of being a help and encouraging them to go on with the fight, we are a hindrance. Some women have actually denounced their own husbands.

It is good if we women are interested in why our husbands organize themselves. We must encourage them and work together with them. Because, what also happens is that when women begin to emerge, the men become jealous, and think their wives are going to take over. By working together, this problem could be solved.

I was saying that there were international agreements saying that women can participate, but that in practice this does not happen. For example, in Bolivia, broad guarantees have been given out to many of those women's organizations who serve whichever government happens to be in power at the time. There's CONIF (National Confederation of Feminine Institutions), the Rotary Club, the Lions ladies, the civic action groups and I don't know what else. Last year they remembered that thousands of children get no breakfast, so they gave them all cups of chocolate, and with this they thought that they had wiped away the misery those children had suffered for all the year. These organizations are supported by the government. They know no repression, these women get all types of support. But what happens when the wives of workers begin to organize in a conscious way? They are repressed. It follows us just as it follows the men. They want to shut us up, they want to scare us, and sometimes we are scared and we say, "Well, I'm not going to get involved any longer." And who benefits when we do this? The capitalists who exploit us.

We know from our own experience that women are not used to being activists. We never dared to be; since we were little we were told that the man's place was in the street, and the woman's was in the home, that the woman must look after the kids, and cook and sew while the man could go into the street, get involved in politics and go to the cinema or to meetings. Isn't that right? They even use religion to keep women down because religion says that "the head of the family is the man." So, even if the man is unjust, we must obey him in everything because he is the boss. He made him in His own image and likeness; then He made a woman. But did He make her from man's head, so that she could be above him? Or perhaps from the soles of his feet, so that he could walk all over her? No. It says that to make woman, God took one of man's ribs, this means that she is his companion. She is neither superior, nor inferior, to be walked over by man. Man and woman should go together and be trained in the same way.

Happily, there is an awakening all over the place—not just in Bolivia—of women who want to start to participate and to be trained. In our country there are already groups of women who are well oriented and who are doing something.

52

Association of African Women for Research and Development

"A Statement on Genital Mutilation"

(SENEGAL, 1980)

At the United Nations–sponsored conferences on women, delegates from the developing regions echoed the words of Shareefeh Hamid Ali when they warned of the dangers of Western ethnocentric attitudes, which often overlooked the structural causes of gender inequality. African women pointed to the limits of European and North American feminist critiques of the genital cutting of girls, a coming-of-age ritual long practiced in parts of Africa and the Middle East. In 1980, the Association of African Women for Research and Development (AAWORD) issued a forceful statement against both the practice of genital mutilation and any simplistic or sensationalized approach to the problem. Founded in Senegal in 1977, AAWORD soon expanded throughout Africa. Although millions of young women continue to experience genital cutting, African women's groups have successfully implemented a broad strategy to undermine the practice through female literacy, family law reform, and women's health education, as well as through substituting new rituals to replace the custom of genital cutting.

In the last few years, Western public opinion has been shocked to find out that in the middle of the 20th Century thousands of women and children have been "savagely mutilated" because of "barbarous customs from another age." The good conscience of Western society has once again been shaken. Something must be done to help these people, to show public disapproval of such acts.

There have been press conferences, documentary films, headlines in the newspapers, information days, open letters, action groups—all this to mobilize public opinion and put pressure on governments of the countries where genital mutliation is still practised.

This new crusade of the West has been led out of the moral and cultural prejudices of Judaeo-Christian Western society: aggressiveness, ignorance or even contempt, paternalism and activism are the elements which have infuriated and then shocked many people of good will. In trying to reach their own public, the new crusaders have fallen back on sensationalism, and have become insensitive to the dignity of the very women they want to "save." They are totally unconscious of the latent racism which such a campaign evokes in countries where ethnocentric prejudice is so deep-rooted. And in their conviction that this is a "just cause," they have forgotten that these women from a different race and a different culture are also *human beings*, and that solidarity can only exist alongside self-affirmation and mutual respect.

This campaign has aroused three kinds of reaction in Africa:
1) the highly conservative, which stresses the right of cultural difference and the defence of traditional values and practices whose supposed aim is to protect and elevate women; this view denies Westerners the right to interfere in problems related to culture;
2) which, while condemning genital mutilation for health reasons, considers it premature to open the issue to public debate;
3) which concentrates on the aggressive nature of the campaign and considers that the fanaticism of the new crusaders only serves to draw attention away from the fundamental problems of the economic

exploitation and oppression of developing countries, which contribute to the continuation of such practices.

Although all these reactions rightly criticize the campaign against genital mutilation as imperialist and paternalist, they remain passive and defensive. As is the case with many other issues, we refuse here to confront our cultural heritage and to criticize it constructively. We seem to prefer to draw a veil of modesty over certain traditional practices, whatever the consequences may be. However, it is time that Africans realized they must take a position on all problems which concern their society, and to take steps to end any practice which debases human beings.

AAWORD, whose aim is to carry out research which leads to the liberation of African people and women in particular, *firmly condemns* genital mutilation and all other practices—traditional or modern—which oppress women and justify exploiting them economically or socially, as a serious violation of the fundamental rights of women.

AAWORD intends to undertake research on the consequences of genital mutilation for the physical and mental health of women. The results of these studies could be used as the basis of an information and educational campaign, and could help to bring about legislation on all aspects of this problem.

However, as far as AAWORD is concerned, the fight against genital mutilation, although necessary, should not take on such proportions that the wood cannot be seen for the trees. Young girls and women who are mutilated in Africa are usually among those who cannot even satisfy their basic needs and who have to struggle daily for survival. This is due to the exploitation of developing countries, manifested especially through the impoverishment of the poorest social classes. In the context of the present world economic crisis, tradition, with all of its constraints, becomes more than ever a form of security for the peoples of the Third World, and especially for the "wretched of the earth," For these people, the modern world, which is primarily Western and bourgeois, can only represent aggression at all levels—political, economic, social and cultural. It is unable to propose viable alternatives for them.

Moreover, to fight against genital mutilation without placing it in the context of ignorance, obscurantism, exploitation, poverty, etc., without questioning the structures and social relations which perpetuate this situation, is like "refusing to see the sun in the middle of the day," This, however, is precisely the approach taken by many Westerners, and is highly suspect, especially since Westerners necessarily profit from the exploitation of the peoples and women of Africa, whether directly or indirectly.

Feminists from developed countries—at least those who are sincerely concerned about this situation rather than those who use it only for their personal prestige—should understand this other aspect of the problem. They must accept that it is a problem for *African women*, and that no change is possible without the conscious participation of African women. They must avoid ill-timed interference, maternalism, ethnocentrism and misuse of power. These are attitudes which can only widen the gap between the Western feminist movement and that of the Third World.

African women must stop being reserved and shake themselves out of their political lethargy. They must make themselves heard on all national and international problems, defining their priorities and their special role in the context of social and national demands.

On the question of such traditional practices as genital mutilation, African women must no longer equivocate or react only to Western inteference. They must speak out in favour of the total eradication of all these practices, and they must lead information and education campaigns to this end within their own countries and on a continental level.

The Lusaka Regional Conference on the Integration of Women in Development (3–7 December 1979) ought to provide an occasion to denounce these practices and to recommend to the governments of the region to take steps to suppress them in the context of a global strategy for improving the situation of women.

At the World Mid-Decade Conference on Women at Copenhagen (July 1980), the African delegations should not let themselves be diverted by those who want to confuse "the wood with the trees." The women's question is a political problem; the African delegations have a duty to place it firmly within the context of the demand for a new international order.

53

ANONYMOUS

"How It All Began: I Have Had an Abortion"

(GERMANY, 1981)

Despite criminal sanctions, abortion has been widely practiced by women seeking to limit childbearing. Most nineteenth-century feminists preferred voluntary motherhood, while the early birth control movement championed contraception as an alternative to abortion. In Germany, however, some liberal feminists called for the decriminalization of abortion as early as 1904. Not until the 1960s did an abortion reform movement in Europe and North America publicize the high death rates from illegal abortions and the complaints of physicians who felt unnecessarily restricted by the laws. The women's liberation movement soon broke the long historical silence about the extent of abortion and campaigned for its decriminalization. In April 1971, the Mouvement de Libération des Femmes published a manifesto in the French press, signed by 343 women who revealed publicly that they had had abortions. Simone de Beauvoir's name was at the top of the list. German women debated whether to protest the anti-abortion law in their country through a similar campaign. Within a few months they had published a confession signed by hundreds of women who demanded legal change. Over the next decades, Germany and most Western nations, including predominantly Catholic countries, lifted their bans and witnessed immediate declines in mortality from abortion. In the United States and elsewhere, however, the issue remained contentious, pitting "pro-life" against "pro-choice" activists.

Historically, privileged people have never freely given up their rights. That's why we demand: Women must become a power factor in the battle to be waged! Women must organize, because they must recognize their most basic problems and learn to represent their interests. Applause from the majority. Boos from some. It was late afternoon already when these now-historic utterances resounded over the mike. Sentences with which—fifty years after the death of the first German Women's Movement—the second German Women's Movement was born. Location: the Youth Hostel in Frankfurt on the banks of the Main River. Midwives: about 450 women from forty groups from the entire Federal Republic gathered here for the first Federal Women's Congress.

There were stormy months preceding these statements. And had someone prophesied to these 450 women a year previously that they would be participating in the rebirth of feminism—most among them would have shaken their heads in disbelief. For at that time the concept of feminism was a pejorative term—especially among the ranks of politicized women. After the first protest in the wake of the 1968 Protest Movement, the beginning of the 1970s seemed to have a deadly calm in terms of women.

In search of a photogenic Women's Lib at home, the magazine *Brigitte* complained coquettishly as late as Spring of 1971: "German women don't burn bras and wedding dresses, don't storm any beauty contests and anti-emancipation editorial boards, do not advocate getting rid of marriage and do not compose manifestos for eradicating men. There are no witches, daughters of Lilith, like in the United States not even Dolle Minnas with a sense of humor like in Holland, there are no aggressive magazines. No anger."

Well, there was anger. More than *Brigitte* and *Kompagnon* liked. It was quickly directed towards the abortion law and the dictates of femininity. The catalyst was the anti-abortion law (Article 218). The background for it was the increasing infamy and schizophrenia of women's new role. At that time, the much-propagated double burden was beginning to peak: Hold down a job on the side and at the same time be the perfect housewife, good mother, smooth lover—that was the new ideal that we were to attain. Only the spark was missing from the powder keg—but who was going to ignite it?

In April of 1971, 343 French women declared openly: "We have had an abortion and we demand the right to free abortions for every woman." The action was initiated by the Paris Women's Movement, the MLF. The Left newspaper *Le Nouvel Observateur* had published their appeal. It was by chance that the movement spread so rapidly to neighboring Germany. Alice Schwarzer, at that time correspondent in Paris and herself active in the MLF, transported the idea to her German sisters. Determined to keep the feminist impetus of the action, she looked for comparable women's groups and, on the other hand, for an avenue for publication. *Stern*, which had recognized the dramatic aspect of the action, agreed. Thus we had the ticklish, but ultimately successful short mésalliance between the Hamburg men's magazine and the women's project. The women had their forum and the *Stern* its scandal. If *Stern* had actually known whom it was helping, it would surely have kept its hands off the whole thing. The next step was to find women who would participate. Since it soon became clear that there was no women's group like the Parisian one, which could carry the project centrally, Alice pounded on a lot of doors—including those of SPD, DKP and trade union women, but all refused. Argument: "Such a project would only harm us—it doesn't sound serious." Or, "It would only shock the grass roots." However, from the total of four women's groups remaining, three were prepared to go along with it: (1) the "Frauenaktion 70" in Frankfurt—it had arisen out of the Humanistic Union, consisted of largely middle class working women, and had already taken to the streets with the slogan "My belly belongs to me." (2) The Socialist Women's Federation in Berlin, and (3) The "Red Women" of Munich. Piqued, the student-dominated Women's Council of Frankfurt rejected the project, finding it unpolitical and reformist. On that Friday in May, on which Alice submitted the plan to the "Red Women," the group split spontaneously. One part kept to its schoolings; the others jumped at the chance: "We were delighted to be able to do something for once."

Feverish activities began. The three women's groups gathered about one-half of the 374 signatures in less than a month, and the rest snowballed in. One woman told another, friends, colleagues, neighbors decided together. The courage of these women was enormous. No one can imagine today what it meant to admit to an abortion at all, not to mention a public confession. Thanks to this campaign, the topic of abortion has, to be sure not yet been solved, but has largely lost its taboo. At that time it was simply a monstrosity, which you didn't admit even to your best friend. Contrary to later propaganda, most of the 374 women were anything but of the priveleged class. Among the first 374 only nine were actresses. The rest were secretaries, housewives (a *lot* of housewives), students, workers, white-collar women. The oldest was seventy-seven, the youngest twenty-one. The campaign was daring on all levels: daring in its collaboration with *Stern* and in the personal risk for each woman. But precisely this risk, the resoluteness of the women not to follow the rules which weren't theirs, and the demonstration of their solidarity constituted the action's immense effect. On July 6, 1971, the open confession of the 374 broke the plot of silence. Millions of copies of *Stern* were at the newsstands, with names and faces of well-known and unknown women who declared in common: "We've had an abortion. We don't demand alms from lawmakers and reform in portions! We demand the cancellation of Article 218 and no substitute laws!"

But really revolutionary was the demand to abolish 218 via the demand attached to it that the woman determine her own destiny! These first weeks and months after June 6 were exciting and radicalizing for all who took part. Ute Geissler: "When I signed the document I was very afraid. And then, when this police raid took place a few months later, it became clear that we wouldn't allow ourselves to be intimidated any more." The police actions "by night and fog," like those in Munich where a raid took place, no longer weakened the campaign, but rather strengthened it, brought a wave of sympathy to it, and—a further wave of women seeking help. Thus the women of Project 218 were initially alone—with the thousands of women who needed counselling and abortions. The only way out was to break the law in their own country or travel abroad. The first contacts with foreign countries were made. On November 1971, women took to the street in almost all Western countries for the right to abortion and self-determination of women. In Paris alone, over 4,000 demonstrated.

54.

MONIQUE WITTIG
(1935–2003)

"One Is Not Born a Woman"
(FRANCE, 1981)

In contrast to writers such as Hélène Cixous, who celebrated sexual dif-
ference, the French novelist, socialist, and feminist theorist Monique Wit-
tig argued that "woman" is a political rather than natural category.
Invoking Simone de Beauvoir's critique of biology as destiny, "One Is Not
Born a Woman" emphasizes the material conditions that give meaning to
women's reproductive and sexual choices and rejects the "myth" of the
natural category of "woman." Here and in her other work Wittig partic-
ularly explored lesbianism as a means of exposing the limitations of het-
erosexuality for all women. Her experimental novel Les guérillières
(1969) imagined a futuristic world in which lesbian warriors affirmed
female sexuality and rejected patriarchy. Wittig's goal, however, was not
to replace patriarchy with matriarchy but rather to undermine distinc-
tions between male and female, and between heterosexual and homosex-
ual, by recognizing their social construction. One of the founders of the
Mouvement de Libération des Femmes in France in 1970 and a co-
founder, with de Beauvoir, of the journal Questions feministes
(1977–80), Wittig immigrated in 1976 to the United States, where she
taught literature and women's studies.

A materialist feminist approach to women's oppression destroys the idea that women are a "natural group": "a racial group of a special kind, a group perceived *as natural*, a group of men considered as materially specific in their bodies." What the analysis accomplishes on the level of ideas, practice makes actual at the level of facts: by its very existence, lesbian society destroys the artificial (social) fact constituting women as a "natural group." A lesbian society pragmatically reveals that the division from men of which women have been the object is a political one and shows how we have been ideologically rebuilt into a "natural group." In the case of women, ideology goes far since our bodies as well as our minds are the product of this manipulation. We have been compelled in our bodies and in our minds to correspond, feature by feature, with the *idea* of nature that has been established for us. Distorted to such an extent that our deformed body is what they call "natural," what is supposed to exist as such before oppression. Distorted to such an extent that in the end oppression seems to be a consequence of this "nature" within ourselves (a nature which is only an *idea*). What a materialist analysis does by reasoning, a lesbian society accomplishes practically: not only is there no natural group "women" (we lesbians are a living proof of it), but as individuals as well we question "woman," which for us, as for Simone de Beauvoir thirty years ago, is only a myth. She said: "One is not born, but becomes a woman. No biological, psychological, or economic fate determines the figure that the human female presents in society: it is civilization as a whole that produces this creature, intermediate between male and eunuch, which is described as feminine."

However, most of the feminists and lesbian-feminists in America and elsewhere still believe that the basis of women's oppression *is biological as well as* historical. Some of them even claim to find their sources in Simone de Beauvoir. The belief in mother right and in a "prehistory" when women created civilization (because of a biological predisposition) while the coarse and brutal men hunted (because of a biological predisposition), is symmetrical with the biologizing interpretation of history produced up to now by the class of men. It is still the same method of finding in women and men a biological explanation of their division, outside of social facts. For me this could never constitute a lesbian approach to women's oppression, since it assumes that the basis of society or the beginning of society lies in heterosexuality. Matriarchy is no less heterosexual than patriarchy: it is only the sex of the oppressor that changes. Furthermore, not only is this conception still imprisoned in the categories of sex (woman and man), but it holds onto the idea that the capacity to give birth (biology) is what defines a woman. Although practical facts and ways of living contradict this theory in lesbian society, there are lesbians who affirm that "women and men are different species or races (the words are used interchangeably): men are biologically inferior to women; male violence is a biological inevitability . . ." By doing this, by admitting that there is a "natural" division between women and men, we naturalize history, we assume that men and women have always existed and will always exist. Not only do we naturalize history, but also consequently we naturalize the social phenomena which express our oppression, making change impossible. For example, instead of seeing giving birth as a forced production, we see it as a "natural," "biological" process, forgetting that in our societies births are planned (demography), forgetting that we ourselves are programmed to produce children, while this is the only social activity "short of war" that presents such a great danger of death. Thus, as long as we will be "unable to abandon by will or impulse a lifelong and centuries-old commitment to childbearing as *the* female creative act," gaining control of the production of children will mean much more than the mere control of the material means of this production: women will have to abstract themselves from the definition "woman" which is imposed upon them.

A materialist feminist approach shows that what we take for the cause or origin of oppression is in fact only the *mark* imposed by the oppressor: the "myth of woman," plus its material effects and manifestations in the appropriated consciousness and bodies of women. Thus, this mark does not preexist oppression: Colette Guillaumin has shown that before the socioeconomic reality of black slavery, the concept of race did not exist, at least not in its modern meaning, since it was applied to the lineage of families. However, now, race, exactly like sex, is taken as an "immediate given," a "sensible given," "physical features," belonging to a natural order. But what we believe to be a physical and direct perception is only a sophisticated and mythic construction, an "imaginary formation," which reinterprets physical features (in themselves as neutral as any others but marked by the social system) through the network of relationships in which they are perceived. (They are seen *black*, therefore they *are* black; they are seen as *women*, therefore, they *are* women. But before being *seen* that way, they first had to be *made* that way.) A lesbian consciousness should always remember and acknowledge how "unnatural," compelling, totally oppressive, and destructive being "woman" was for us in the old days before the women's liberation movement. It was a political constraint and those who resisted it were accused of not being "real" women. But then we were proud of it, since in the accusation there was already something like a shadow of victory: the avowal by the oppressor that "woman" is not something that goes without saying, since to be one, one has to be a "real" one. We were at the same time accused of wanting to be men. Today this double accusation has been taken up again with enthusiasm in the context of the women's liberation movement by some feminists and also, alas, by some lesbians whose political goal seems somehow to be becoming more and more "feminine." To refuse to be a woman, however, does not mean that one has to become a man. Besides, if we take as an example the perfect "butch," the classic example which provokes the most horror, whom Proust would have called a woman/man, how is her alienation different from that of someone who wants to become a woman? Tweedledum and Tweedledee. At least for a woman, wanting to become a man proves that she escapes her initial programming. But even if she would like to, with all her strength, she cannot become a man. For becoming a man would demand from a woman not only the external appearance of a man but his consciousness as well, that is, the consciousness of one who disposes by right of at least two "natural" slaves during his life span. This is impossible and one feature of lesbian oppression consists precisely of making women out of reach for us, since women belong to men. Thus a lesbian *has to* be something else, a not-woman, a not-man, a product of society, not a product of nature, for there is no nature in society.

The refusal to become (or to remain) heterosexual always meant to refuse to become a man or a woman, consciously or not. For a lesbian this goes further than the refusal of the *role* "woman." It is the refusal of the economic, ideological, and political power of a man. This, we lesbians, and nonlesbians as well, knew before the beginning of the lesbian and feminist movement. However, as Andrea Dworkin emphasizes, many lesbians recently "have increasingly tried to transform the very ideology that has enslaved us into a dynamic, religious, psychologically compelling celebration of female biological potential." Thus, some avenues of the feminist and lesbian movement lead us back to the myth of woman which was created by men especially for us, and with it we sink back into a natural group. Thirty years ago we stood up to fight for a sexless society. Now we find ourselves entrapped in the familiar deadlock of "woman is wonderful." Thirty years ago Simone de Beauvoir underlined particularly the false consciousness which consists of selecting among the features of the myth (that women are different from men) those which look good and using them as a definition for women. What the concept of "woman is wonderful" accomplishes is that it retains for defining women the best features (best according to whom?) which oppression has granted us, and it does not radically question the categories "man" and "woman," which are political categories and not natural givens. It puts us in a position of fighting within the class "women" not as the other classes do, for the disappearance of our class, but for the defense of "woman" and its reenforcement. It leads us to develop with complacency "new" theories about our specificity: thus, we call our passivity "nonviolence," when the main and emergent point for us is to fight our passivity (our fear, rather, a justified one). The ambiguity of the term "feminist" sums up the whole situation. What does "feminist" mean? Feminist is formed with the word "femme," "woman," and means: someone who fights for women. For many of us it means someone who fights for women as a class and for the disappearance of this class. For many others it means someone who fights for woman and her defense—for the myth, then, and its reenforcement. But why was the word "feminist" chosen if it retains the least ambiguity? We chose to call ourselves "feminists" ten years ago, not in order to support or reenforce the myth of woman nor to identify ourselves with the oppressor's definition of us, but rather to affirm that our movement had a history and to emphasize the political link with the old feminist movement....

Marxism has refused the attribute of being a subject to the members of oppressed classes. In doing this, Marxism, because of the ideological and political power this "revolutionary science" immediately exercised upon the workers' movement and all other political groups, has prevented all categories of oppressed peoples from constituting themselves historically as subjects (subjects of their struggle, for example). This means that the "masses" did not fight for themselves but for *the* party or its organizations. And when an economic transformation took place (end of private property, constitution of the socialist state), no revolutionary change took place within the new society, because the people themselves did not change.

For women, Marxism had two results. It prevented them from being aware that they are a class and therefore from constituting themselves as a class for a very long time, by leaving the relation "women/men" outside of the social order, by turning it into a natural relation, doubtlessly for Marxists the only one along with the relation of mothers to children to be seen this way, and by hiding the class conflict between men and women behind a natural division of labor (*The German Ideology*).... In addition, Marxist theory does not allow women any more than other classes of oppressed people to constitute themselves as historical subjects, because Marxism does not take into account the fact that a class also consists of individuals one by one. Class consciousness is not enough. We must try to understand philosophically (politically) these concepts of "subject" and "class consciousness" and how they work in relation to our history. When we discover that women are the objects of oppression and appropriation, at the very moment that we become able to perceive this, we become subjects in the sense of cognitive subjects, through an operation of abstraction. Consciousness of oppression is not only a reaction to (fight against) oppression. It is also the whole conceptual reevaluation of the social world, its whole reorganization with new concepts, from the point of view of oppression. It is what I would call the science of oppression created by the oppressed. This operation of understanding reality has to be undertaken by every one of us: call it a subjective, cognitive practice. The movement back and forth between the levels of reality (the conceptual reality and the material reality of oppression, which are both social realities) is accomplished through language.

It is we who historically must undertake the task of defining the individual subject in materialist terms. This certainly seems to be an impossibility since materialism and subjectivity have always been mutually exclusive. Nevertheless, and rather than despairing of ever understanding, we must recognize the *need* to reach subjectivity in the abandonment by many of us to the myth "woman" (the myth of woman being only a snare that holds us up). This real necessity for everyone to exist as an individual, as well as a member of a class, is perhaps the first condition for the accomplishment of a revolution, without which there can be no real fight or transformation. But the opposite is also true; without class and class consciousness there are no real subjects, only alienated individuals. For women to answer the question of the individual subject in materialist terms is first to show, as the lesbians and feminists did, that supposedly "subjective," "individual," "private" problems are in fact social problems, class problems; that sexuality is not for women an individual and subjective expression, but a social institution of violence. But once we have shown that all so-called personal problems are in fact class problems, we will still be left with the question of the subject of each singular woman—not the myth, but each one of us. At this point, let us say that a new personal and subjective definition for all humankind can only be found beyond the categories of sex (woman and man) and that the advent of individual subjects demands first destroying the categories of sex, ending the use of them, and rejecting all sciences which still use these categories as their fundamentals (practically all social sciences).

To destroy "woman" does not mean that we aim, short of physical destruction, to destroy lesbianism simultaneously with the categories of sex, because lesbianism provides for the moment the only social form in which we can live freely. Lesbian is the only concept I know of which is beyond the categories of sex (woman and man), because the designated subject (lesbian) is *not* a woman, either economically, or politically, or ideologically. For what makes a woman is a specific social relation to a man, a relation that we have previously called servitude, a relation which implies personal and physical obligation as well as economic obligation ("forced residence," domestic corvée, conjugal duties, unlimited production of children, etc.), a relation which lesbians escape by refusing to become or to stay heterosexual. We are escapees from our class in the same way as the American runaway slaves were when escaping slavery and becoming free. For us this is an absolute necessity; our survival demands that we contribute all our strength to the destruction of the class of women within which men appropriate women. This can be accomplished only by the destruction of heterosexuality as a social system which is based on the oppression of women by men and which produces the doctrine of the difference between the sexes to justify this oppression.

55.

ADRIENNE RICH
(b. 1929)

"Notes Toward a Politics of Location"
(UNITED STATES, 1984)

*During the 1970s, the award-winning poet Adrienne Rich contributed to
the development of radical feminist theory in the United States. Her book*
Of Woman Born *portrayed the social and political institution of motherhood, while the poems in her collection* The Dream of a Common
Language *explored both women's culture and love between women. Like
other American feminists, however, in the 1980s Rich began to question
the universality of womanhood. Given the racial, class, and national tensions that emerged within the United States and at the U.N. Decade for
Women conferences, white, western feminists began to place their experiences within the contexts of international conflicts and cross-cultural differences. In this essay, Rich acknowledged her own "politics of location" as
a North American, white, Jewish lesbian, and she criticized "the faceless,
raceless classless category of all women as a creation of white, western,
self-centered women." In revising Virginia Woolf's rejection of nationalism, Rich explained how one's country deeply influenced one's view of the
world and of womanhood.*

I am to speak these words in Europe, but I have been searching for them in the United States of America. A few years ago I would have spoken of the common oppression of women, the gathering movement of women around the globe, the hidden history of women's resistance and bonding, the failure of all previous politics to recognize the universal shadow of patriarchy, the belief that women now, in a time of rising consciousness and global emergency, may join across all national and cultural boundaries to create a society free of domination, in which "sexuality, politics,... work,... intimacy... thinking itself will be transformed."*

I would have spoken these words as a feminist who "happened" to be a white United States citizen, conscious of my government's proven capacity for violence and arrogance of power, but as self-separated from that government, quoting without second thought Virginia Woolf's statement in *Three Guineas* that "as a woman I have no country. As a woman I want no country. As a woman my country is the whole world."

This is not what I come here to say in 1984. I come here with notes but without absolute conclusions. This is not a sign of loss of faith or hope. These notes are the marks of a struggle, to keep moving, a struggle for accountability.

Beginning to write, then getting up. Stopped by the movements of a huge early bumblebee which has somehow gotten inside this house and is reeling, bumping, stunning itself against windowpanes and sills. I open the front door and speak to it, trying to attract it outside. It is looking for what it needs, just as I am, and, like me, it has gotten trapped in a place where it cannot fulfill its own life. I could open the jar of honey on the kitchen counter, and perhaps it would take honey from that jar; but its life process, its work, its mode of being cannot be fulfilled inside this house.

And I, too, have been bumping my way against glassy panes, falling

*Adrienne Rich, *Of Woman Born: Motherhood as Experience and Institution* (New York: W. W. Norton, 1976), p. 286.

half-stunned, gathering myself up and crawling, then again taking off, searching.

I don't hear the bumblebee any more, and I leave the front door. I sit down and pick up a secondhand, faintly annotated student copy of Marx's *The German Ideology*, which "happens" to be lying on the table.

I will speak these words in Europe, but I am having to search for them in the United States of North America. When I was ten or eleven, early in World War II, a girlfriend and I used to write each other letters which we addressed like this:

Adrienne Rich
14 Edgevale Road
Baltimore, Maryland
The United States of America
The Continent of North America
The Western Hemisphere
The Earth
The Solar System
The Universe

You could see your own house as a tiny fleck on an ever-widening landscape, or as the center of it all from which the circles expanded into the infinite unknown.

It is that question of feeling at the center that gnaws at me now. At the center of what?

As a woman I have a country; as a woman I cannot divest myself of that country merely by condemning its government or by saying three times "As a woman my country is the whole world." Tribal loyalties aside, and even if nation-states are now just pretexts used by multinational conglomerates to serve their interests, I need to understand how a place on the map is also a place in history within which as a woman, a Jew, a lesbian, a feminist I am created and trying to create.

Begin, though, not with a continent or a country or a house, but with the geography closest in—the body. Here at least I know I exist, that living human individual whom the young Marx called "the first premise of all human history."* But it was not as a Marxist that I

*Karl Marx and Frederick Engels, *The German Ideology*, ed. C. J. Arthur (New York: International Publishers, 1970), p. 42.

turned to this place, back from philosophy and literature and science and theology in which I had looked for myself in vain. It was as a radical feminist.

The politics of pregnability and motherhood. The politics of orgasm. The politics of rape and incest, of abortion, birth control, forcible sterilization. Of prostitution and marital sex. Of what had been named sexual liberation. Of prescriptive heterosexuality. Of lesbian existence.

And Marxist feminists were often pioneers in this work. But for many women I knew, the need to begin with the female body—our own—was understood not as applying a Marxist principle *to* women, but as locating the grounds from which to speak with authority *as* women. Not to transcend this body, but to reclaim it. To reconnect our thinking and speaking with the body of this particular living human individual, a woman. Begin, we said, with the material, with matter, mma, madre, mutter, moeder, modder, etc., etc.

Begin with the material. Pick up again the long struggle against lofty and privileged abstraction. Perhaps this is the core of revolutionary process, whether it calls itself Marxist or Third World or feminist or all three. Long before the nineteenth century, the empirical witch of the European Middle Ages, trusting her senses, practicing her tried remedies against the anti-material, anti-sensuous, anti-empirical dogmas of the Church. Dying for that, by the millions. "A female-led peasant rebellion"?—in any event, a rebellion against the idolatry of pure ideas, the belief that ideas have a life of their own and float along above the heads of ordinary people—women, the poor, the uninitiated.*

Abstractions severed from the doings of living people, fed back to people as slogans.

Theory—the seeing of patterns, showing the forest as well as the trees—theory can be a dew that rises from the earth and collects in the rain cloud and returns to earth over and over. But if it doesn't smell of the earth, it isn't good for the earth.

I wrote a sentence just now and x'd it out. In it I said that women have always understood the struggle against free-floating abstraction even

*Barbara Ehrenreich and Deirdre English, *Witches, Midwives and Nurses: A History of Women Healers* (Old Westbury, N.Y.: Feminist Press, 1973).

when they were intimidated by abstract ideas. I don't want to write that kind of sentence now, the sentence that begins "Women have always...." We started by rejecting the sentences that began "Women have always had an instinct for mothering" or "Women have always and everywhere been in subjugation to men." If we have learned anything in these years of late twentieth-century feminism, it's that that "always" blots out what we really need to know: When, where, and under what conditions has the statement been true?

The absolute necessity to raise these questions in the world: where, when, and under what conditions have women acted and been acted on, as women? Wherever people are struggling against subjection, the specific subjection of women, through our location in a female body, from now on has to be addressed. The necessity to go on speaking of it, refusing to let the discussion go on as before, speaking where silence has been advised and enforced, not just about our subjection, but about our active presence and practice as women. We believed (I go on believing) that the liberation of women is a wedge driven into all other radical thought, can open out the structures of resistance, unbind the imagination, connect what's been dangerously disconnected. Let us pay attention now, we said, to women: let men and women make a conscious act of attention when women speak; let us insist on kinds of process which allow more women to speak; let us get back to earth—not as paradigm for "women," but as place of location.

Perhaps we need a moratorium on saying "the body." For it's also possible to abstract "the" body. When I write "the body," I see nothing in particular. To write "my body" plunges me into lived experience, particularity: I see scars, disfigurements, discolorations, damages, losses, as well as what pleases me. Bones well nourished from the placenta; the teeth of a middle-class person seen by the dentist twice a year from childhood. White skin, marked and scarred by three pregnancies, an elected sterilization, progressive arthritis, four joint operations, calcium deposits, no rapes, no abortions, long hours at a typewriter—my own, not in a typing pool—and so forth. To say "the body" lifts me away from what has given me a primary perspective. To say "my body" reduces the temptation to grandiose assertions.

This body. White, female; or female, white. The first obvious, lifelong facts. But I was born in the white section of a hospital which separated Black and white women in labor and Black and white babies in the nursery, just as it separated Black and white bodies in its morgue. I was defined as white before I was defined as female.

The politics of location. Even to begin with my body I have to say that from the outset that body had more than one identity. When I was carried out of the hospital into the world, I was viewed and treated as female, but also viewed and treated as white—by both Black and white people. I was located by color and sex as surely as a Black child was located by color and sex—though the implications of white identity were mystified by the presumption that white people are the center of the universe.

To locate myself in my body means more than understanding what it has meant to me to have a vulva and clitoris and uterus and breasts. It means recognizing this white skin, the places it has taken me, the places it has not let me go.

The body I was born into was not only female and white, but Jewish—enough for geographic location to have played, in those years, a determining part. I was a *Mischling*, four years old when the Third Reich began. Had it been not Baltimore, but Prague or Lódz or Amsterdam, the ten-year-old letter writer might have had no address. Had I survived Prague, Amsterdam, or Lódz and the railway stations for which they were deportation points, I would be some body else. My center, perhaps, the Middle East or Latin America, my language itself another language. Or I might be in no body at all.

But I am a North American Jew, born and raised three thousand miles from the war in Europe.

Trying as women to see from the center. "A politics," I wrote once, "of asking women's questions."* We are not "the woman question" asked by somebody else; we are the women who ask the questions.

Trying to see so much, aware of so much to be seen, brought into the light, changed. Breaking down again and again the false male uni-

*Adrienne Rich, *On Lies, Secrets, and Silence: Selected Prose 1966–1978* (New York: W. W. Norton, 1979), p. 17.

versal. Piling piece by piece of concrete experience side by side, comparing, beginning to discern patterns. Anger, frustration with Marxist or Leftist dismissals of these questions, this struggle. Easy now to call this disillusionment facile, but the anger was deep, the frustration real, both in personal relationships and political organizations. I wrote in 1975: *Much of what is narrowly termed "politics" seems to rest on a longing for certainty even at the cost of honesty, for an analysis which, once given, need not be reexamined. Such is the deadendedness—for women—of Marxism in our time.* *

And it has felt like a dead end wherever politics has been externalized, cut off from the ongoing lives of women or of men, rarefied into an elite jargon, an enclave, defined by little sects who feed off each others' errors.

But even as we shrugged away Marx along with the academic Marxists and the sectarian Left, some of us, calling ourselves radical feminists, never meant anything less by women's liberation than the creation of a society without domination; we never meant less than the making new of all relationships. The problem was that we did not know whom we meant when we said "we."

The power men everywhere wield over women, power which has become a model for every other form of exploitation and illegitimate control. I wrote these words in 1978 at the end of an essay called "Compulsory Heterosexuality and Lesbian Existence." Patriarchy as the "model" for other forms of domination—this idea was not original with me. It has been put forward insistently by white Western feminists, and in 1972 I had quoted from Lévi-Strauss: *I would go so far as to say that even before slavery or class domination existed, men built an approach to women that would serve one day to introduce differences among us all.*†

Living for fifty-some years, having watched even minor bits of history unfold, I am less quick than I once was to search for single "causes" or origins in dealings among human beings. But suppose that we could trace back and establish that patriarchy has been everywhere

Ibid., p. 193.
[A.R., 1986: For a vigorous indictment of dead-ended Marxism and a call to "revolution in permanence," see Raya Dunayevskaya, *Women's Liberation and the Dialectics of Revolution* (Atlantic Highlands, N.J.: Humanities Press, 1985).]
†Rich, *On Lies, Secrets, and Silence*, p. 84.

the model. To what choices of action does that lead us in the present? Patriarchy exists nowhere in a pure state; we are the latest to set foot in a tangle of oppressions grown up and around each other for centuries. This isn't the old children's game where you choose one strand of color in the web and follow it back to find your prize, ignoring the others as mere distractions. The prize is life itself, and most women in the world must fight for their lives on many fronts at once.

We ... often find it difficult to separate race from class from sex oppression because in our lives they are most often experienced simultaneously. We know that there is such a thing as racial-sexual oppression which is neither solely racial nor solely sexual. ... We need to articulate the real class situation of persons who are not merely raceless, sexless workers but for whom racial and sexual oppression are significant determinants in their working/economic lives.

This is from the 1977 Combahee River Collective statement, a major document of the U.S. women's movement, which gives a clear and uncompromising Black-feminist naming to the experience of simultaneity of oppressions.*

Even in the struggle against free-floating abstraction, we have abstracted. Marxists and radical feminists have both done this. Why not admit it, get it said, so we can get on to the work to be done, back down to earth again? The faceless, sexless, raceless proletariat. The faceless, raceless, classless category of "all women." Both creations of white Western self-centeredness.

To come to terms with the circumscribing nature of (our) whiteness.† Marginalized though we have been as women, as white and Western makers of theory, we also marginalize others because our lived experience is thoughtlessly white, because even our "women's cultures" are rooted

---

*Barbara Smith, ed., *Home Girls: A Black Feminist Anthology* (New York: Kitchen Table/Women of Color Press, 1983), pp. 272–83. See also Audre Lorde, *Sister Outsider: Essays and Speeches* (Trumansburg, N.Y.: Crossing Press, 1984). See Hilda Bernstein, *For Their Triumphs and for Their Tears: Women in Apartheid South Africa* (London: International Defence and Aid Fund, 1978), for a description of simultaneity of African women's oppressions under apartheid. For a biographical and personal account, see Ellen Kuzwayo, *Call Me Woman* (San Francisco: Spinsters/Aunt Lute, 1985).
†Gloria I. Joseph, "The Incompatible Ménage à Trois: Marxism, Feminism and Racism," in *Women and Revolution*, ed. Lydia Sargent (Boston: South End Press, 1981).

in some Western tradition. Recognizing our location, having to name the ground we're coming from, the conditions we have taken for granted—there is a confusion between our claims to the white and Western eye and the woman-seeing eye,* fear of losing the centrality of the one even as we claim the other.

How does the white Western feminist define theory? Is it something made only by white women and only by women acknowledged as writers? How does the white Western feminist define "an idea"? How do we actively work to build a white Western feminist consciousness that is not simply centered on itself, that resists white circumscribing?

It was in the writings but also the actions and speeches and sermons of Black United States citizens that I began to experience the meaning of my whiteness as a point of location for which I needed to take responsibility. It was in reading poems by contemporary Cuban women that I began to experience the meaning of North America as a location which had also shaped my ways of seeing and my ideas of who and what was important, a location for which I was also responsible. I traveled then to Nicaragua, where, in a tiny impoverished country, in a four-year-old society dedicated to eradicating poverty, under the hills of the Nicaragua-Honduras border, I could physically feel the weight of the United States of North America, its military forces, its vast appropriations of money, its mass media, at my back; I could feel what it means, dissident or not, to be part of that raised boot of power, the cold shadow we cast everywhere to the south.

I come from a country stuck fast for forty years in the deep-freeze of history. Any United States citizen alive today has been saturated with Cold War rhetoric, the horrors of communism, the betrayals of socialism, the warning that any collective restructuring of society spells the end of personal freedom. And, yes, there have been horrors and betrayals deserving open opposition. But we are not invited to consider the butcheries of Stalinism, the terrors of the Russian counterrevolution alongside the butcheries of white supremacism and Manifest Destiny. We are not urged to help create a more human society here in response

*See Marilyn Frye, *The Politics of Reality* (Trumansburg, N.Y.: Crossing Press, 1983), p. 171.

to the ones we are taught to hate and dread. Discourse itself is frozen at this level. Tonight as I turned a switch searching for "the news," that shinily animated silicone mask was on television again, telling the citizens of my country we are menaced by communism from El Salvador, that communism—Soviet variety, obviously—is on the move in Central America, that freedom is imperiled, that the suffering peasants of Latin America must be stopped, just as Hitler had to be stopped.

The discourse has never really changed; it is wearingly abstract. (Lillian Smith, white anti-racist writer and activist, spoke of the "deadly sameness" of abstraction.)* It allows no differences among places, times, cultures, conditions, movements. Words that should possess a depth and breadth of allusions—words like *socialism, communism, democracy, collectivism*—are stripped of their historical roots, the many faces of the struggles for social justice and independence reduced to an ambition to dominate the world.

Is there a connection between this state of mind—the Cold War mentality, the attribution of all our problems to an external enemy—and a form of feminism so focused on male evil and female victimization that it, too, allows for no differences among women, men, places, times, cultures, conditions, classes, movements? Living in the climate of an enormous either/or, we absorb some of it unless we actively take heed.

In the United States large numbers of people have been cut off from their own process and movement. We have been hearing for forty years that we are the guardians of freedom, while "behind the Iron Curtain" all is duplicity and manipulation, if not sheer terror. Yet the legacy of fear lingering after the witch hunts of the fifties hangs on like the aftersmell of a burning. The sense of obliquity, mystery, paranoia surrounding the American Communist party after the Khrushchev Report of 1956: the party lost 30,000 members within weeks, and few who remained were talking about it. To be a Jew, a homosexual, any kind of marginal person was to be liable for suspicion of being "Communist." A blanketing snow had begun to drift over the radical history of the United States.

And, though parts of the North American feminist movement actually sprang from the Black movements of the sixties and the student

*Lillian Smith, "Autobiography as a Dialogue between King and Corpse," in *The Winner Names the Age*, ed. Michelle Cliff (New York: W. W. Norton, 1978), p. 189.

left, feminists have suffered not only from the burying and distortion of women's experience, but from the overall burying and distortion of the great movements for social change.*

The first American woman astronaut is interviewed by the liberal-feminist editor of a mass-circulation women's magazine. She is a splendid creature, healthy, young, thick dark head of hair, scientific degrees from an elite university, an athletic self-confidence. She is also white. She speaks of the future of space, the potential uses of space colonies by private industry, especially for producing materials which can be advantageously processed under conditions of weightlessness. Pharmaceuticals, for example. By extension one thinks of chemicals. Neither of these two spirited women speak of the alliances between the military and the "private" sector of the North American economy. Nor do they speak of Depo-Provera, Valium, Librium, napalm, dioxin. *When big companies decide that it's now to their advantage to put a lot of their money into production of materials in space ... we'll really get the funding that we need*, says the astronaut. No mention of who "we" are and what "we" need funding for; no questions about the poisoning and impoverishment of women here on earth or of the earth itself. Women, too, may leave the earth behind.†

The astronaut is young, feels her own power, works hard for her exhilaration. She has swung out over the earth and come back, one more time passed all the tests. It's not that I expect her to come back to earth as Cassandra. But this experience of hers has nothing as yet to do with the liberation of women. A female proletariat—uneducated, ill nourished, unorganized, and largely from the Third World—will create the profits which will stimulate the "big companies" to invest in space.

On a split screen in my brain I see two versions of her story: the backward gaze through streaming weightlessness to the familiar globe, pale blue and green and white, the strict and sober presence of it, the true intuition of relativity battering the heart; and the swiftly calculated move to a farther suburb, the male technocrats and the women

*See Elly Bulkin, "Hard Ground: Jewish Identity, Racism, and Anti-Semitism," in E. Bulkin, M.B. Pratt, and B. Smith, *Yours in Struggle: Three Feminist Perspectives on Anti-Semitism and Racism* (Brooklyn, N.Y.: Long Haul, 1984; distributed by Firebrand Books, 141 The Commons, Ithaca, NY 14850).
†*Ms.* (January 1984): 86.

they have picked and tested, leaving the familiar globe behind: the toxic rivers, the cancerous wells, the strangled valleys, the closed-down urban hospitals, the shattered schools, the atomic desert blooming, the lilac suckers run wild, the blue grape hyacinths spreading, the ailanthus and kudzu doing their final desperate part—the beauty that won't travel, that can't be stolen away.

A movement for change lives in feelings, actions, and words. Whatever circumscribes or mutilates our feelings makes it more difficult to act, keeps our actions reactive, repetitive: abstract thinking, narrow tribal loyalties, every kind of self-righteousness, the arrogance of believing ourselves at the center. It's hard to look back on the limits of my understanding a year, five years ago—how did I look without seeing, hear without listening? It can be difficult to be generous to earlier selves, and keeping faith with the continuity of our journeys is especially hard in the United States, where identities and loyalties have been shed and replaced without a tremor, all in the name of becoming "American." Yet how, except through ourselves, do we discover what moves other people to change? Our old fears and denials—what helps us let go of them? What makes us decide we have to re-educate ourselves, even those of us with "good" educations? A politicized life ought to sharpen both the senses and the memory.

The difficulty of saying I—a phrase from the East German novelist Christa Wolf.* But once having said it, as we realize the necessity to go further, isn't there a difficulty of saying "we"? *You cannot speak for me. I cannot speak for us.* Two thoughts: there is no liberation that only knows how to say "I"; there is no collective movement that speaks for each of us all the way through.

And so even ordinary pronouns become a political problem.†

- 64 cruise missiles in Greenham Common and Molesworth.
- 112 at Comiso.
- 96 Pershing II missiles in West Germany.
- 96 for Belgium and the Netherlands.

*Christa Wolf, *The Quest for Christa T*, trans. Christopher Middleton (New York: Farrar, Straus & Giroux, 1970), p. 174.
†See Bernice Reagon, "Turning the Century," in Smith, pp. 356–68; Bulkin, pp. 103, 190–93.

That is the projection for the next few years.*

- Thousands of women, in Europe and the United States, saying *no* to this and to the militarization of the world.

An approach which traces militarism back to patriarchy and patriarchy back to the fundamental quality of maleness can be demoralizing and even paralyzing.... Perhaps it is possible to be less fixed on the discovery of "original causes." It might be more useful to ask, How do these values and behaviors get repeated generation after generation?†

The valorization of manliness and masculinity. The armed forces as the extreme embodiment of the patriarchal family. The archaic idea of women as a "home front" even as the missiles are deployed in the backyards of Wyoming and Mutlangen. The growing urgency that an anti-nuclear, anti-militarist movement must be a feminist movement, must be a socialist movement, must be an anti-racist, anti-imperialist movement. That it's not enough to fear for the people we know, our own kind, ourselves. Nor is it empowering to give ourselves up to abstract terrors of pure annihilation. The anti-nuclear, anti-military movement cannot sweep away the missiles as a movement to save white civilization in the West.

The movement for change is a changing movement, changing itself, demasculinizing itself, de-Westernizing itself, becoming a critical mass that is saying in so many different voices, languages, gestures, actions: *It must change; we ourselves can change it.*

We who are not the same. We who are many and do not want to be the same.

Trying to watch myself in the process of writing this, I keep coming back to something Sheila Rowbotham, the British socialist feminist, wrote in *Beyond the Fragments:*

A movement helps you to overcome some of the oppressive distancing of theory and this has been a ... continuing creative endeavour of women's liberation. But some

---

*Information as of May 1984, thanks to the War Resisters League.
†Cynthia Enloe, *Does Khaki Become You? The Militarisation of Women's Lives* (London: Pluto Press, 1983), ch. 8.

> *paths are not mapped and our footholds vanish....I see what I'm writing as part of a wider claiming which is beginning. I am part of the difficulty myself. The difficulty is not out there.**

My difficulties, too, are not out there—except in the social conditions that make all this necessary. I do not any longer *believe*—my feelings do not allow me to believe—that the white eye sees from the center. Yet I often find myself thinking as if I still believed that were true. Or, rather, my thinking stands still. I feel in a state of arrest, as if my brain and heart were refusing to speak to each other. My brain, a woman's brain, has ex-ulted in breaking the taboo against women thinking, has taken off on the wind, saying, *I am the woman who asks the questions.* My heart has been learning in a much more humble and laborious way, learning that feel-ings are useless without facts, that all privilege is ignorant at the core.

The United States has never been a white country, though it has long served what white men defined as their interests. The Mediterranean was never white. England, northern Europe, if ever absolutely white, are so no longer. In a Leftist bookstore in Manchester, England, a Third World poster: *WE ARE HERE BECAUSE YOU WERE THERE.* In Europe there have always been the Jews, the original ghetto dwellers, identified as a racial type, suffering under pass laws and special entry taxes, enforced relocations, massacres: the scapegoats, the aliens, never seen as truly European but as part of that darker world that must be controlled, eventually exterminated. Today the cities of Europe have new scapegoats as well: the diaspora from the old colo-nial empires. Is anti-Semitism the model for racism, or racism for anti-Semitism? Once more, where does the question lead us? Don't we have to start here, where we are, forty years after the Holocaust, in the churn of Middle Eastern violence, in the midst of decisive ferment in South Africa—not in some debate over origins and prece-dents, but in the recognition of simultaneous oppressions?

I've been thinking a lot about the obsession with origins. It seems a way of stopping time in its tracks. The sacred Neolithic triangles, the

---

*Sheila Rowbotham, Lynne Segal, and Hilary Wainwright, *Beyond the Fragments: Feminism and the Making of Socialism* (Boston: Alyson, 1981), pp. 55–56.

Minoan vases with staring eyes and breasts, the female figurines of Anatolia—weren't they concrete evidence of a kind, like Sappho's fragments, for earlier woman-affirming cultures, cultures that enjoyed centuries of peace? But haven't they also served as arresting images, which kept us attached and immobilized? Human activity didn't stop in Crete or Çatal Hüyük. We can't build a society free from domination by fixing our sights backward on some long-ago tribe or city.

The continuing spiritual power of an image lives in the interplay between what it reminds us of—what it *brings to mind*—and our own continuing actions in the present. When the labrys becomes a badge for a cult of Minoan goddesses, when the wearer of the labrys has ceased to ask herself what she is doing on this earth, where her love of women is taking her, the labrys, too, becomes abstraction—lifted away from the heat and friction of human activity. The Jewish star on my neck must serve me both for reminder and as a goad to continuing and changing responsibility.

When I learn that in 1913, mass women's marches were held in South Africa which caused the rescinding of entry permit laws; that in 1956, 20,000 women assembled in Pretoria to protest pass laws for women, that resistance to these laws was carried out in remote country villages and punished by shootings, beatings, and burnings; that in 1959, 2,000 women demonstrated in Durban against laws which provided beerhalls for African men and criminalized women's traditional home brewing; that at one and the same time, African women have played a major role alongside men in resisting apartheid, I have to ask myself why it took me so long to learn these chapters of women's history, why the leadership and strategies of African women have been so unrecognized as theory in action by white Western feminist thought. (And in a book by two men, entitled *South African Politics* and published in 1982, there is one entry under "Women" [franchise] and no reference anywhere to women's political leadership and mass actions.)*

---

* *Women under Apartheid* (London: International Defence and Aid Fund for Southern Africa in cooperation with the United Nations Centre Against Apartheid, 1981), pp. 87–99; Leonard Thompson and Andrew Prior, *South African Politics* (New Haven, Conn.: Yale University Press, 1982). An article in *Sechaba* (published by the African National Congress) refers to "the rich tradition of organization and mobilization by women" in the Black South African struggle ([October 1984]: p. 9).

When I read that a major strand in the conflicts of the past decade in Lebanon has been political organizing by women of women, across class and tribal and religious lines, women working and teaching together within refugee camps and armed communities, and of the violent undermining of their efforts through the civil war and the Israeli invasion, I am forced to think.* Iman Khalife, the young teacher who tried to organize a silent peace march on the Christian-Moslem border of Beirut—a protest which was quelled by the threat of a massacre of the participants—Iman Khalife and women like her do not come out of nowhere. But we Western feminists, living under other kinds of conditions, are not encouraged to know this background.

And I turn to Etel Adnan's brief, extraordinary novel *Sitt Marie Rose*, about a middle-class Christian Lebanese woman tortured for joining the Palestinian Resistance, and read:

> She was also subject to another great delusion believing that women are protected from repression, and that the leaders considered political fights to be strictly between males. In fact, with women's greater access to certain powers, they began to watch them more closely, and perhaps with even greater hostility. Every feminine act, even charitable and seemingly unpolitical ones, were regarded as a rebellion in this world where women had always played servile roles. Marie Rose inspired scorn and hate long before the fateful day of her arrest.†

Across the curve of the earth, there are women getting up before dawn, in the blackness before the point of light, in the twilight before sunrise; there are women rising earlier than men and children to break the ice, to start the stove, to put up the pap, the coffee, the rice, to iron the pants, to braid the hair, to pull the day's water up from the well, to boil water for tea, to wash the children for school, to pull the vegetables and start the walk to market, to run to catch the bus for the work that is paid. I don't know when most women sleep. In big cities at dawn women are traveling home after cleaning offices all night, or

---

*Helen Wheatley, "Palestinian Women in Lebanon: Targets of Repression," *TWANAS*, *Third World Student Newspaper*, University of California, Santa Cruz (March 1984).
†Etel Adnan, *Sitt Marie Rose*, trans. Georgina Kleege (Sausalito, Calif.: Post Apollo Press, 1982), p. 101.

waxing the halls of hospitals, or sitting up with the old and sick and frightened at the hour when death is supposed to do its work.

In Peru: "Women invest hours in cleaning tiny stones and chaff out of beans, wheat and rice; they shell peas and clean fish and grind spices in small mortars. They buy bones or tripe at the market and cook cheap, nutritious soups. They repair clothes until they will not sustain another patch. They...search...out the cheapest school uniforms, payable in the greatest number of installments. They trade old magazines for plastic washbasins and buy second-hand toys and shoes. They walk long distances to find a spool of thread at a slightly lower price."*

This is the working day that has never changed, the unpaid female labor which means the survival of the poor.

In minimal light I see her, over and over, her inner clock pushing her out of bed with her heavy and maybe painful limbs, her breath breathing life into her stove, her house, her family, taking the last cold swatch of night on her body, meeting the sudden leap of the rising sun.

In my white North American world they have tried to tell me that this woman—politicized by intersecting forces—doesn't think and reflect on her life. That her ideas are not real ideas like those of Karl Marx and Simone de Beauvoir. That her calculations, her spiritual philosophy, her gifts for law and ethics, her daily emergency political decisions are merely instinctual or conditioned reactions. That only certain kinds of people can make theory; that the white-educated mind is capable of formulating everything; that white middle-class feminism can know for "all women"; that only when a white mind formulates is the formulation to be taken seriously.

In the United States, white-centered theory has not yet adequately engaged with the texts—written, printed, and widely available—which have been for a decade or more formulating the political theory of Black American feminism: the Combahee River Collective statement, the essays and speeches of Gloria I. Joseph, Audre Lorde, Bernice Reagon, Michele Russell, Barbara Smith, June Jordan, to name a few of the most obvious. White feminists have read and taught from the anthology *This Bridge Called My Back: Writings by Radical*

*Blanca Figueroa and Jeanine Anderson, "Women in Peru," *International Reports: Women and Society* (1981). See also Ximena Bunster and Elsa M. Chaney, *Sellers and Servants: Working Women in Lima, Peru* (New York: Praeger, 1985), and Madhu Kishwar and Ruth Vanita, *In Search of Answers: Indian Women's Voices from "Manushi"* (London: Zed, 1984), pp. 56–57.

Women of Color, yet often have stopped at perceiving it simply as an angry attack on the white women's movement. So white feelings remain at the center. And, yes, I need to move outward from the base and center of my feelings, but with a corrective sense that my feelings are not *the* center of feminism.*

And if we read Audre Lorde or Gloria Joseph or Barbara Smith, do we understand that the intellectual roots of this feminist theory are not white liberalism or white Euro-American feminism, but the analyses of Afro-American experience articulated by Sojourner Truth, W.E.B. Du Bois, Ida B. Wells-Barnett, C.L.R. James, Malcolm X, Lorraine Hansberry, Fannie Lou Hamer, among others? That Black feminism cannot be marginalized and circumscribed as simply a response to white feminist racism or an augmentation of white feminism; that it is an organic development of the Black movements and philosophies of the past, their practice and their printed writings? (And that, increasingly, Black American feminism is actively in dialogue with other movements of women of color within and beyond the United States?)

To shrink from or dismiss that challenge can only isolate white feminism from the other great movements for self-determination and justice within and against which women define ourselves.

Once again: Who is *we?*

This is the end of these notes, but it is not an ending.

*Gloria Anzaldúa and Cherríe Moraga, eds., *This Bridge Called My Back: Writings by Radical Women of Color* (Watertown, Mass.: Persephone, 1981; distributed by Kitchen Table/Women of Color Press, Albany, New York).

56.

GLORIA ANZALDÚA
(1942–2004)

"La Conciencia de la Mestiza: Toward a New Consciousness"

(UNITED STATES, 1987)

Women of color in the United States increasingly wrote about the challenges that race, sexuality, and ethnicity posed for their identities as feminists. In 1981, Kitchen Table–Women of Color Press published an influential anthology, This Bridge Called My Back: Writings by Radical Women of Color, *edited by Chicana feminists Cherríe Moraga and Gloria Anzaldúa. In essays and poems, women from Mexican American, Native American, and Asian American backgrounds confronted racism in the women's movement as well as exclusions from their communities of origin because of their sexuality and politics. Women from Spanish-speaking backgrounds in particular probed the ways that language represented both a link to family and community and a potential barrier to understanding across ethnicities. In her own collection of essays,* Borderlands/La Frontera: The New Mestiza *(1987), Anzaldúa posited a borderlands identity, akin to the geographical U.S.-Mexican border. It encompassed psychological, sexual, and spiritual distinctions, reinforced in her writing by interspersing Spanish and English. At a time when academic feminists invoked postmodern theory to question fixed identities, writers like Anzaldúa and Moraga modeled a mestiza consciousness, born at the intersections of racial, gender, and sexual difference.*

Por la mujer de mi raza
hablará el espíritu.[1]

Jose Vascocelos, Mexican philosopher, envisaged *una raza mestiza, una mezcla de razas afines, una raza de color—la primera raza síntesis del globo.* He called it a cosmic race, *la raza cósmica,* a fifth race embracing the four major races of the world.[2] Opposite to the theory of the pure Aryan, and to the policy of racial purity that white America practices, his theory is one of inclusivity. At the confluence of two or more genetic streams, with chromosomes constantly "crossing over," this mixture of races, rather than resulting in an inferior being, provides hybrid progeny, a mutable, more malleable species with a rich gene pool. From this racial, ideological, cultural and biological cross-pollinization, an "alien" consciousness is presently in the making—a new *mestiza* consciousness, *una conciencia de mujer.* It is a consciousness of the Borderlands.

UNA LUCHA DE FRONTERAS /
A STRUGGLE OF BORDERS

Because I, a *mestiza,*
continually walk out of one culture
and into another,
because I am in all cultures at the same time,
alma entre dos mundos, tres, cuatro,
me zumba la cabeza con lo contradictorio.
Estoy norteada por todas las voces que me hablan
simultáneamente.

The ambivalence from the clash of voices results in mental and emotional states of perplexity. Internal strife results in insecurity and indecisiveness. The mestiza's dual or multiple personality is plagued by psychic restlessness....

In a constant state of mental nepantilism, an Aztec word meaning torn between ways, *la mestiza* is a product of the transfer of the cultural and spiritual values of one group to another. Being tricultural, monolingual, bilingual, or multilingual, speaking a patois, and in a state of

[1] This is my own "take off" on Jose Vasconcelos' idea. Jose Vasconcelos, *La Raza Cósmica: Missión de la Raza Ibero-Americana* (Mexico: Aguilar S.A. de Ediciones, 1961).
[2] Vasconcelos.

perpetual transition, the *mestiza* faces the dilemma of the mixed breed: which collectivity does the daughter of a darkskinned mother listen to?

El choque de un alma atrapado entre el mundo del espíritu y el mundo de la técnica a veces la deja entullada. Cradled in one culture, sandwiched between two cultures, straddling all three cultures and their value systems, *la mestiza* undergoes a struggle of flesh, a struggle of borders, an inner war. Like all people, we perceive the version of reality that our culture communicates. Like others having or living in more than one culture, we get multiple, often opposing messages. The coming together of two self-consistent but habitually incompatible frames of reference[3] causes *un choque*, a cultural collision.

Within us and within *la cultura chicana*, commonly held beliefs of the white culture attack commonly held beliefs of the Mexican culture, and both attack commonly held beliefs of the indigenous culture. Subconsciously, we see an attack on ourselves and our beliefs as a threat and we attempt to block with a counterstance.

But it is not enough to stand on the opposite river bank, shouting questions, challenging patriarchal, white conventions. A counterstance locks one into a duel of oppressor and oppressed; locked in mortal combat, like the cop and the criminal, both are reduced to a common denominator of violence. The counterstance refutes the dominant culture's views and beliefs, and, for this, it is proudly defiant. All reaction is limited by, and dependent on, what it is reacting against. Because the counterstance stems from a problem with authority—outer as well as inner—it's a step towards liberation from cultural domination. But it is not a way of life. At some point, on our way to a new consciousness, we will have to leave the opposite bank, the split between the two mortal combatants somehow healed so that we are on both shores at once and, at once, see through serpent and eagle eyes. Or perhaps we will decide to disengage from the dominant culture, write it off altogether as a lost cause, and cross the border into a wholly new and separate territory. Or we might go another route. The possibilities are numerous once we decide to act and not react.

[3]Arthur Koestler termed this "bisociation." Albert Rothenberg, *The Creative Process in Art, Science, and Other Fields* (Chicago, IL: University of Chicago Press, 1979), 12.

A TOLERANCE FOR AMBIGUITY

These numerous possibilities leave *la mestiza* floundering in uncharted seas. In perceiving conflicting information and points of view, she is subjected to a swamping of her psychological borders. She has discovered that she can't hold concepts or ideas in rigid boundaries. The borders and walls that are supposed to keep the undesirable ideas out are entrenched habits and patterns of behavior; these habits and patterns are the enemy within. Rigidity means death. Only by remaining flexible is she able to stretch the psyche horizontally and vertically. *La mestiza* constantly has to shift out of habitual formations; from convergent thinking, analytical reasoning that tends to use rationality to move toward a single goal (a Western mode), to divergent thinking,[4] characterized by movement away from set patterns and goals and toward a more whole perspective, one that includes rather than excludes.

The new *mestiza* copes by developing a tolerance for contradictions, a tolerance for ambiguity. She learns to be an Indian in Mexican culture, to be Mexican from an Anglo point of view. She learns to juggle cultures. She has a plural personality, she operates in a pluralistic mode—nothing is thrust out, the good the bad and the ugly, nothing rejected, nothing abandoned. Not only does she sustain contradictions, she turns the ambivalence into something else.

She can be jarred out of ambivalence by an intense, and often painful, emotional event which inverts or resolves the ambivalence. I'm not sure exactly how. The work takes place underground—subconsciously. It is work that the soul performs. That focal point or fulcrum, that juncture where the mestiza stands, is where phenomena tend to collide. It is where the possibility of uniting all that is separate occurs. This assembly is not one where severed or separated pieces merely come together. Nor is it a balancing of opposing powers. In attempting to work out a synthesis, the self has added a third element which is greater than the sum of its severed parts. That third element is a new consciousness—a mestiza consciousness—and though it is a source of intense pain, its energy comes from continual creative motion that keeps breaking down the unitary aspect of each new paradigm.

En unas pocas centurias, the future will belong to the mestiza. Because

[4]In part, I derive my definitions for "convergent" and "divergent" thinking from Rothenberg, 12–13.

the future depends on the breaking down of paradigms, it depends on the straddling of two or more cultures. By creating a new mythos—that is, a change in the way we perceive reality, the way we see ourselves, and the ways we behave—*la mestiza* creates a new consciousness.

The work of *mestiza* consciousness is to break down the subject-object duality that keeps her a prisoner and to show in the flesh and through the images in her work how duality is transcended. The answer to the problem between the white race and the colored, between males and females, lies in healing the split that originates in the very foundation of our lives, our culture, our languages, our thoughts. A massive uprooting of dualistic thinking in the individual and collective consciousness is the beginning of a long struggle, but one that could, in our best hopes, bring us to the end of rape, of violence, of war.

LA ENCRUCIJADA / THE CROSSROADS

A chicken is being sacrificed
at a crossroads, a simple mound of earth
a mud shrine for *Eshu*,
Yoruba god of indeterminacy,
who blesses her choice of path.
She begins her journey.

Su cuerpo es una bocacalle. La mestiza has gone from being the sacrificial goat to becoming the officiating priestess at the crossroads.

As a *mestiza* I have no country, my homeland cast me out; yet all countries are mine because I am every woman's sister or potential lover. (As a lesbian I have no face, my own people disclaim me; but I am all races because there is the queer of me in all races.) I am cultureless because, as a feminist, I challenge the collective cultural/religious male-derived beliefs of Indo-Hispanics and Anglos; yet I am cultured because I am participating in the creation of yet another culture, a new story to explain the world and our participation in it, a new value system with images and symbols that connect us to each other and to the planet. *Soy un amasamiento*, I am an act of kneading, of uniting and joining that not only has produced both a creature of darkness and a creature of light, but also a creature that questions the definitions of light and dark and gives them new meanings.

We are the people who leap in the dark, we are the people on the knees of the gods. In our very flesh, (r)evolution works out the clash of cultures. It makes us crazy constantly, but if the center holds, we've made some kind of evolutionary step forward. *Nuestra alma el trabajo*, the opus, the great alchemical work; spiritual *mestizaje*, a "morphogenesis,"[5] an inevitable unfolding. We have become the quickening serpent movement.

Indigenous like corn, the *mestiza* is a product of crossbreeding, designed for preservation under a variety of conditions. Like an ear of corn—a female seed-bearing organ—the *mestiza* is tenacious, tightly wrapped in the husks of her culture. Like kernels she clings to the cob; with thick stalks and strong brace roots, she holds tight to the earth— she will survive the crossroads.

Lavando y remojando el maíz en agua de cal, despojando el pellejo. Moliendo, mixteando, amasando, haciendo tortillas de masa.[6] She steeps the corn in lime, it swells, softens. With stone roller on *metate*, she grinds the corn, then grinds again. She kneads and moulds the dough, pats the round balls into *tortillas*.

> We are the porous rock in the stone *metate*
>   squatting on the ground.
> We are the rolling pin, *el maíz y agua,*
>   *la masa harina. Somos el amasijo.*
>   *Somos lo molido en el metate.*
> We are the *comal* sizzling hot,
>   the hot *tortilla*, the hungry mouth.
> We are the coarse rock.
> We are the grinding motion,
>   the mixed potion, *somos el molcajete.*
> We are the pestle, the *comino, ajo, pimienta,*
>   We are the *chile colorado,*
>   the green shoot that cracks the rock.
>   We will abide....

[5] To borrow chemist Ilya Prigogine's theory of "dissipative structures," Prigogine discovered that substances interact not in predictable ways as it was taught in science, but in different and fluctuating ways to produce new and more complex structures, a kind of birth he called "morphogenesis," which created unpredictable innovations. Harold Gilliam, "Searching for a New World View," *This World* (January, 1981), 23.

[6] *Tortillas de masa harina:* corn tortillas with two types, the smooth uniform ones made in a tortilla press and usually bought at a tortilla factory or supermarket, and *gorditas*, made by mixing *masa* with lard or shortening or butter (my mother sometimes puts bits of bacon or *chicharrones*).

57.

GUERRILLA GIRLS

"When Sexism and Racism
Are No Longer Fashionable"
and
"Do Women Have To Be Naked
To Get into the Met. Museum?"

(UNITED STATES, 1989)

Second Wave feminism unleashed a wealth of artistic creativity across the genres of fiction, poetry, theater, painting, and sculpture. Writers and artists explored the diversity of female experience and questioned assumptions about gender, race, and sexuality. Even as the literary establishment in the United States began to recognize the talents of feminist writers, women artists continued to face serious obstacles to exhibiting their work. In 1970, a group called Women Artists in Revolution, or WAR, formed to protest the fact that only five percent of the artists represented at New York's Whitney Museum were female. Since 1985 the political activists and performance artists known as the Guerrilla Girls have continually confronted the art world. Members of this anonymous group dress in gorilla suits and masks, taking the names of women artists such as Käthe Kollwitz and Frida Kahlo. They employ both humor and cutting criticism to expose "sexism and racism in the art world and the culture at large." In addition to dozens of posters and exhibits, the Guerrilla Girls have published several books about stereotypes of women in art history and popular culture. They continue to target museums for their racial and gender exclusivity and to address feminist issues such as reproductive and lesbian rights.

58

KATHLEEN HANNA/BIKINI KILL

"Riot Grrrl Manifesto"
(UNITED STATES, 1992)

In the 1990s, despite American media descriptions of a "postfeminist" culture that took for granted the gains of earlier social movements, a new generation of activists confronted persistent obstacles to women's equality. The problems of girls, ranging from low self-esteem to eating disorders to sexual abuse, stimulated a range of "girl power" campaigns to counteract societal pressures. Within the punk rock musical subculture, young women who felt marginalized by men reclaimed the term "girl," proclaiming their strength in a variety of "riot grrrl" fanzines. With graphic language and hard-driving music, female punk bands such as Bikini Kill screamed with rage against male abuse, celebrated an independent female sexuality, and called for a grrrl-style revolution. The following declaration written by Kathleen Hanna of Bikini Kill illustrates the political spirit of this movement, which questioned male dominance in music and throughout society. Her critique of capitalism and rejection of internalized sexism echoes the anarchist feminism of Emma Goldman, while the band's music added a queer sexual sensibility that embraced lesbian as well as heterosexual pleasure.

BECAUSE us girls crave records and books and fanzines that speak to US that WE feel included in and can understand in our own ways.

BECAUSE we wanna make it easier for girls to see/hear each other's work so that we can share strategies and criticize-applaud each other.

BECAUSE we must take over the means of production in order to create our own meanings.

BECAUSE viewing our work as being connected to our girlfriends-politics-real-lives is essential if we are gonna figure out how we are doing impacts, reflects, perpetuates, or DISRUPTS the status quo.

BECAUSE we recognize fantasies of Instant Macho Gun Revolution as impractical lies meant to keep us simply dreaming instead of becoming our dreams AND THUS seek to create revolution in our own lives every single day by envisioning and creating alternatives to the bullshit christian capitalist way of doing things.

BECAUSE we want and need to encourage and be encouraged in the face of all our own insecurities, in the face of beergutboyrock that tells us we can't play our instruments, in the face of "authorities" who say our bands/zines/etc are the worst in the US and

BECAUSE we don't wanna assimilate to someone else's (boy) standards of what is or isn't cool.

BECAUSE we are unwilling to falter under claims that we are reactionary "reverse sexists" AND NOT THE TRUEPUNKROCK-SOULCRUSADERS THAT WE KNOW we really are.

BECAUSE we know that life is much more than physical survival and are patently aware that the punk rock "you can do anything" idea is crucial to the coming angry grrrl rock revolution which seeks to save the psychic and cultural lives of girls and women everywhere, according to their own terms, not ours.

BECAUSE we are interested in creating non-hierarchical ways of being AND making music, friends, and scenes based on communication + understanding, instead of competition + good/bad categorizations.

BECAUSE doing/reading/seeing/hearing cool things that validate and challenge us can help us gain the strength and sense of community that we need in order to figure out how bullshit like racism, able-bodieism, ageism, speciesism, classism, thinism, sexism, anti-semitism and heterosexism figures in our own lives.

BECAUSE we see fostering and supporting girl scenes and girl artists of all kinds as integral to this process.

BECAUSE we hate capitalism in all its forms and see our main goal as sharing information and staying alive, instead of making profits or being cool according to traditional standards.

BECAUSE we are angry at a society that tells us Girl = Dumb, Girl = Bad, Girl = Weak.

BECAUSE we are unwilling to let our real and valid anger be diffused and/or turned against us via the internalization of sexism as witnessed in girl/girl jealousy and self defeating girltype behaviors.

BECAUSE I believe with my wholeheartmindbody that girls constitute a revolutionary soul force that can, and will change the world for real.

59

REBECCA WALKER

"Becoming the Third Wave"
(UNITED STATES, 1992)

When the African American lawyer Anita Hill testified to the U.S. Senate Judiciary Committee in 1992 that Supreme Court nominee Clarence Thomas had sexually harassed her, the interrogation of Hill by the male legislators and their disbelief of her charges catalyzed feminist activism around the country. In addition to inspiring women to run for office, the Hill-Thomas testimonies unleashed personal stories of sexual harassment in the workplace and on the streets. Dismayed by the treatment of Hill, then college student Rebecca Walker, the daughter of the acclaimed African American feminist writer Alice Walker, called for young women to create a Third Wave of feminism. Rebecca Walker rejected the idea of "postfeminism" and worked to engage young women in politics. After launching a voter registration campaign to counter youth apathy, Walker and others created the Third Wave Foundation to help finance young women's political projects. In 1995 Walker published an anthology, To Be Real: Telling the Truth and Changing the Face of Feminism, *which helped popularize Third Wave feminism in the United States.*

I am not one of the people who sat transfixed before the television, watching the Senate hearings. I had classes to go to, papers to write, and frankly, the whole thing was too painful. A black man grilled by a panel of white men about his sexual deviance. A black woman claiming harassment and being discredited by other women.... I could not bring myself to watch that sensationalized assault of the human spirit.

To me, the hearings were not about determining whether or not Clarence Thomas did in fact harass Anita Hill. They were about checking and redefining the extent of women's credibility and power. Can a woman's experience undermine a man's career? Can a woman's voice, a woman's sense of self-worth and injustice, challenge a structure predicated upon the subjugation of our gender? Anita Hill's testimony threatened to do that and more. If Thomas had not been confirmed, every man in the United States would be at risk. For how many senators never told a sexist joke? How many men have not used their protected male privilege to thwart in some way the influence or ideas of a woman colleague, friend, or relative?

For those whose sense of power is so obviously connected to the health and vigor of the penis, it would have been a metaphoric castration. Of course this is too great a threat.

While some may laud the whole spectacle for the consciousness it raised around sexual harassment, its very real outcome is more informative. He was promoted. She was repudiated. Men were assured of the inviolability of their penis/power. Women were admonished to keep their experiences to themselves.

The backlash against U.S. women is real. As the misconception of equality between the sexes becomes more ubiquitous, so does the attempt to restrict the boundaries of women's personal and political power. Thomas' confirmation, the ultimate rally of support for the male paradigm of harassment, sends a clear message to women: "Shut up! Even if you speak, we will not listen."

I will not be silenced.

I acknowledge the fact that we live under siege. I intend to fight back. I have uncovered and unleashed more repressed anger than I thought possible. For the umpteenth time in my 22 years, I have been radicalized, politicized, shaken awake. I have come to voice again, and this time my voice is not conciliatory.

The night after Thomas' confirmation I ask the man I am intimate with what he thinks of the whole mess. His concern is primarily with Thomas' propensity to demolish civil rights and opportunities for people of color. I launch into a tirade. "When will progressive black men prioritize my rights and well-being? When will they stop talking so damn much about 'the race' as if it revolved exclusively around them?" He tells me I wear my emotions on my sleeve. I scream "I need to know, are you with me or are you going to help them try to destroy me?"

A week later I am on a train to New York. A beautiful mother and daughter, both wearing green outfits, sit across the aisle from me. The little girl has tightly plaited braids. Her brown skin is glowing and smooth, her eyes bright as she chatters happily while looking out the window. Two men get on the train and sit directly behind me, shaking my seat as they thud into place. I bury myself in *The Sound and the Fury*. Loudly they begin to talk about women. "Man, I fucked that bitch all night and then I never called her again." "Man, there's lots of girlies over there, you know that ho, live over there by Tyrone? Well, I snatched that shit up."

The mother moves closer to her now quiet daughter. Looking at her small back I can see that she is listening to the men. I am thinking of how I can transform the situation, of all the people in the car whose silence makes us complicit.

Another large man gets on the train. After exchanging loud greetings with the two men, he sits next to me. He tells them he is going to Philadelphia to visit his wife and child. I am suckered into thinking that he is different. Then, "Man, there's a ton of females in Philly, just waitin' for you to give 'em some." I turn my head and allow the fire in my eyes to burn into him. He takes up two seats and has hands with huge swollen knuckles. I imagine the gold rings on his fingers slamming into my face. He senses something, "What's your name, sweetheart?" The other men lean forward over the seat.

A torrent explodes: "I ain't your sweetheart, I ain't your bitch, I ain't your baby. How dare you have the nerve to sit up here and talk about women that way, and then try to speak to me." The woman/mother chimes in to the beat with claps of sisterhood. The men are momentarily stunned. Then the comeback: "Aw, bitch, don't play that woman shit over here 'cause that's bullshit." He slaps the back of one hand against the palm of the other. I refuse to back down. Words fly.

My instinct kicks in, telling me to get out. "Since I see you all are not going to move, I will." I move to the first car. I am so angry that thoughts of murder, of physically retaliating against them, of separatism, engulf me. I am almost out of body, just shy of being pure force. I am sick of the way women are negated, violated, devalued, ignored. I am livid, unrelenting in my anger at those who invade my space, who wish to take away my rights, who refuse to hear my voice. As the days pass, I push myself to figure out what it means to be a part of the Third Wave of feminism. I begin to realize that I owe it to myself, to my little sister on the train, to all of the daughters yet to be born, to push beyond my rage and articulate an agenda. After battling with ideas of separatism and militancy, I connect with my own feelings of powerlessness. I realize that I must undergo a transformation if I am truly committed to women's empowerment. My involvement must reach beyond my own voice in discussion, beyond voting, beyond reading feminist theory. My anger and awareness must translate into tangible action.

I am ready to decide, as my mother decided before me, to devote much of my energy to the history, health, and healing of women. Each of my choices will have to hold to my feminist standard of justice.

To be a feminist is to integrate an ideology of equality and female empowerment into the very fiber of my life. It is to search for personal clarity in the midst of systemic destruction, to join in sisterhood with women when often we are divided, to understand power structures with the intention of challenging them.

While this may sound simple, it is exactly the kind of stand that many of my peers are unwilling to take. So I write this as a plea to all women, especially the women of my generation: Let Thomas' confirmation serve to remind you, as it did me, that the fight is far from over. Let this dismissal of a woman's experience move you to anger. Turn that outrage into political power. Do not vote for them unless they work for us. Do not have sex with them, do not break bread with them, do not nurture them if they don't prioritize our freedom to control our bodies and our lives.

I am not a postfeminism feminist. I am the Third Wave.

60.

UNITED NATIONS, FOURTH WORLD CONFERENCE ON WOMEN

Speeches
(1995)

Ten years after the Decade for Women, the United Nations authorized a fourth international conference in Beijing, China, to assess progress and set agendas for future policies to ensure women's equality. The Declaration and Platform of Action adopted by official delegates to the conference insisted that women's rights were human rights, a theme articulated as well by more than twenty thousand activists who attended the Non-Governmental Organization (NGO) forum held simultaneously outside Beijing. The following four presentations illustrate common themes of the conference: that promoting equality for women contributes to the health and well-being of all family members and that achieving full women's rights is impossible without addressing poverty, violence, and the environment. In her opening address, Gertrude Mongella of Tanzania, the secretary general of the conference, emphasized this holistic approach, closing with a plea to end armed conflicts. Native American environmentalist Winona LaDuke drew connections between the oppression of women and the exploitation of natural resources. Palesa Beverley Ditsie, a lesbian activist from South Africa, implored the conference to include sexual orientation in its list of human rights to be protected, but a majority of the delegates refused to do so. As Norwegian Prime Minister Gro Haarlem Brundtland acknowledged when she referred to abortion in her closing address, the topics of sexual and reproductive rights for women remained most vulnerable to conservative opposition.

GERTRUDE MONGELLA

(TANZANIA)

Opening Address, Plenary Session

At long last, we are here in Beijing participating in the Fourth World Conference on Women—a conference which is phenomenal in several aspects. It has generated much interest and debate globally, among men and women, old and young, from country to country. It has brought together the largest gathering of persons ever to attend any United Nations Conference on any subject. All the indications point to a social revolution in the making!...

This Platform is a global tapestry woven by women, men and youth with strands from all nations, races and religions alike. Its needlecraft has been carefully, objectively and caringly embroidered through the various consultations, conferences and meetings which had been organized at the national, regional and international levels. The Platform is a document for the world; but for women, it is their document since it embodies the aspirations, hopes and actions which will guide us all into the twenty-first century. In fact, the Platform is for everyone. There can be no spectators, no side-liners, no abstainers for this is a crucial social agenda which affects all humanity.

It is for this reason that I wish to appeal to each woman participating in this conference and in the NGO Forum not only to serve as representatives of their governments and NGOs but also to become committed crusaders in the struggle in which we have been engaged for many, many years. As I noted at the opening of the NGOs Forum 1995, "millions have placed their trust in us. We must not fail them."

I would like to highlight a few salient features that became obvious during the process toward Bejing:

First, there is the need to look at women's issues in a holistic manner and to address them as part of overall societal and developmental concerns. It will not be possible to attain sustainable development without cementing the partnership of women and men in all aspects of life. Women have all along struggled with their men-folk for the abolition of slavery, the liberation of countries from colonialism, the dismantling of apartheid, and the struggle for peace. It is now the turn of men to join women in their struggle for equality.

Second, because of the crosscutting nature of women's issues, it is imperative that each issue is given due weight and consideration.

Third, there is the need to recognize the inter-generational link which is unique to women, as well as the cumulative effect since unresolved problems tend to deteriorate in subsequent phases.

Finally, since [the United Nations First World Conference on Women in] Mexico (1975), some twenty years ago, women have learned that achieving equality depends on themselves. Necessary actions will not be taken for them based on some theoretical principle of equality. Women have researched and they have been the subject of research. The statistics are much too gloomy in several key sectors such as poverty, education and illiteracy, health, violence against women, governance and politics, and human rights. With the statistics and facts now well documented, there is no denying that women fare badly relative to men. Only last month, the 1995 edition of *The World's Women: 1990–1995 Trends and Statistics* showed irrefutably the changes that had occurred and the remaining obstacles.

Ladies and gentlemen, we are at the crucial last decade of the twentieth century and the solidarity that binds us in our common experiences, irrespective of race, color, and religion should become the instrument to propel us all into the twenty-first century armed with vision, imagination and actions which can make the difference in our own lives and to those of our children and our grandchildren. We have been saying all along that women and men must work together if we are to bring this world safely and successfully into the coming century—so too, must we ensure the participation of the youth. They are our hope and future and society can only be the beneficiary.

Our agenda must address eradication of illiteracy, ill-health, poverty, unemployment, violence and promotion of decision making and empowerment. It must focus on actions that will eliminate discrimination, marginalization, and social exclusion.

The basis for change is here; what is lacking is the commitment which will ensure actions which could bring about change. When the facts and statistics are disaggregated, the undeniable fact is that action is required to change the status quo. Action is the only way forward. There is no substitute.

Excellencies, the Fourth World Conference on Women must elicit commitments to action coupled with commitment of resources, nationally and internationally. This is the mission of Beijing. Each government must now set priorities, specify the resources it will contribute and declare what steps it will take to hold itself accountable to the world's women. This conference must preserve achievements and agreements reached in earlier Conferences and move beyond the rhetoric to work toward genuine change.

I must conclude now with an issue that is close to my heart and the hearts of many women by posing the following questions.

–How long will women toil to contribute to the purchase of arms?
–How long will women continue to give life just to see it taken away by the use of arms?
–And how long will the world continue to ignore women's tears during armed conflicts?

This platform will not see light as long as the issue of peace is not properly addressed.

I thank you for your attention.

WINONA LaDUKE
(UNITED STATES)

"The Indigenous Women's Network: Our Future, Our Responsibility"

... The Earth is our Mother. From her we get our life ... and our ability to live. It is our responsibility to care for our Mother, and in caring for our Mother, we care for ourselves. Women, all females, are the manifestation of Mother Earth in human form. We are her daughters and in my cultural instructions: Minobimaatisiiwin. We are to care for her. I am taught to live in respect for Mother Earth. In Indigenous societies, we are told that Natural Law is the highest law, higher than the law made by nations, states, municipalities and the World Bank. That one would do well to live in accordance with Natural Law. With those of our Mother. And in respect for our Mother Earth of our relations—indinawaymuguni took.

One hundred years ago, one of our Great Leaders—Chief Seattle— stated, "What befalls the Earth, befalls the People of the Earth." And that is the reality of today, and the situation of the status of women, and the status of Indigenous women and Indigenous peoples....

The origins of this problem lie with the predator-prey relationship industrial society has developed with the Earth, and subsequently, the people of the Earth. This same relationship exists *vis-à-vis* women. We, collectively, find that we are often in the role of the prey, to a predator society, whether for sexual discrimination, exploitation, sterilization, absence of control over our bodies, or being the subjects of repressive laws and legislation in which we have no voice. This occurs not only on an individual level, but, equally, and more significantly, on a societal level. It is also critical to point out at this time that most matrilineal societies, societies in which governance and decision-making are largely controlled by women, have been obliterated from the face of the Earth by colonialism, and subsequently industrialism. The only matrilineal societies which exist in the world today are those of Indigenous nations. We are the remaining matrilineal societies. Yet we also face obliteration.

On a worldwide scale and in North America, Indigenous societies historically, and today, remain in a predator-prey relationship with industrial society, and prior to that colonialism and imperialism. We are the peoples with the land—land and natural resources required for someone else's development program and the amassing of wealth. The wealth of the United States, that nation which today determines much of world policy, easily expropriated from our lands. Similarly the wealth of Indigenous peoples of South Africa, Central, South American countries, and Asia was taken for the industrial development of Europe, and later for settler states which came to occupy those lands. That relationship between development and underdevelopment adversely affected the status of our Indigenous societies, and the status of Indigenous women.

The rapid increase in dioxin, organichlorides, and PCBs (polychlorinated byphenyls) chemicals in the world, as a result of industrialization, has a devastating impact on Indigenous peoples, Indigenous women, and other women. Each year, the world's paper industry discharges from 600 to 3,200 grams of dioxin equivalents into water, sludge and paper products according to United States Environmental Protection agency statistics. This quantity is equal to the amount which would cause 58,000 to 294,000 cases of cancer every year, based on the Environmental Protection Agency's estimate of dioxin's carcinogenicity. According to a number of recent studies, this has significantly increased the risk of breast cancer in women. Similarly, heavy metals and PCBs contamination of Inuit women of the Hudson Bay region of the Arctic indicates that they have the highest levels of breast milk contamination in the world. In a 1988 study, Inuit women were found to have contamination levels up to 28 times higher than the average of women in Quebec, and ten times higher than that considered "safe" by the government....

Consequently, it is clear to us that the problems also found in the south, like the export of chemicals and bio-accumulation of toxins, are also very much our problems, and the problems clearly manifested in our women. These are problems which emanate from industrial societies' mis-treatment and disrespect for our Mother Earth, and subsequently are reflected in the devastation of the collective health and well-being of women.

In summary, I have presented these arguments for a purpose. To illustrate that these are very common issues for women, not only for Indigenous women, but for all women. What befalls our Mother Earth, befalls her daughter—the women who are the Mothers of our nations. Simply stated, if we can no longer nurse our children, if we can no longer bear children, and if our bodies, themselves are wracked with poisons, we will have accomplished little in the way of determining our destiny, or improving our conditions. And, these problems, reflected in our health and well being, are also inherently resulting in a decline of the status of women, and are the result of a long set of historical processes. Processes, which we as women, will need to challenge if we will ultimately be in charge of our own destinies, our own self-determination, and the future of our Earth our Mother....

If we are to seek and struggle for common ground of all women, it is essential to struggle on this issue. It is not that the women of the dominant society in so-called first world countries should have equal pay and equal status, if that pay and status continues to be based on a consumption model which is not only unsustainable, but causes constant violation of the human rights of women and nations elsewhere in the world. It is essential to collectively struggle to recover our status as Daughters of the Earth. In that is our strength and the security; not in the predator, but in the security of our Mother, for our future generations. In that we can ensure our security as the Mothers of our Nations.

PALESA BEVERLEY DITSIE
(SOUTH AFRICA)

Statement of the International Gay and Lesbian Human Rights Commission

It is a great honor to have the opportunity to address this distinguished body on behalf of the International Gay and Lesbian Human Rights Commission, the International Lesbian Information Service, the International Lesbian and Gay Association, and over fifty other organizations. My name is Palesa Beverley Ditsie and I am from Soweto, South Africa, where I have lived all my life and experienced both tremendous joy and pain within my community. I come from a country that has recently had an opportunity to start afresh, an opportunity to strive for a true democracy where the people govern and where emphasis is placed on the human rights of all people. The Constitution of South Africa prohibits discrimination on the basis of race, gender, ethnic or social origin, colour, sexual orientation, age, disability, religion, conscience, belief, culture, or language. In his opening parliamentary speech in Cape Town on the 9th of April 1994, His Excellency Nelson Rolihlahla Mandela, State President of South Africa, received resounding applause when he declared that never again would anyone be discriminated against on the basis of sexual orientation.

The Universal Declaration of Human Rights recognizes the "inherent dignity and ... the equal and inalienable rights of all members of the human family," and guarantees the protection of the fundamental rights and freedoms of all people "without distinction of any kind, such as race, color, sex, language ... or other status" (art. 2). Yet every day, in countries around the world, lesbians suffer violence, harassment and discrimination because of their sexual orientation. Their basic human rights—such as the right to life, to bodily integrity, to freedom of association and expression—are violated. Women who love women are fired from their jobs; forced into marriages; beaten and murdered in their homes and on the streets; and have their children taken away by hostile courts. Some commit suicide due to the isolation and stigma that they experience within their families, religious institutions and their broader community. These and other abuses are documented in a recently released report by the International Gay and Lesbian Human Rights Commission on sexual orientation and women's human rights, as well as in reports by Amnesty International. Yet the majority of these abuses have been difficult to document because although lesbians exist everywhere in the world (including Africa), we have been marginalized and silenced and remain invisible in most of the world. In 1994, the United Nations Human Rights Committee declared that discrimination based on sexual orientation violates the right to non-discrimination and the right to privacy guaranteed in the International Covenant of Civil and Political Rights. Several countries have passed legislation prohibiting discrimination based on sexual orientation. If the World Conference on Women is to address the concerns of all women, it must similarly recognize that discrimination based on sexual orientation is a violation of basic human rights. Paragraphs 48 and 226 of the Platform for Action recognize that women face particular barriers in their lives because of many factors, including sexual orientation. However, the term "sexual orientation" is currently in brackets. If these words are omitted from the relevant paragraphs, the Platform for Action will stand as one more symbol of the discrimination that lesbians face, and of the lack of recognition of our very existence.

No woman can determine the direction of her own life without the ability to determine her sexuality. Sexuality is an integral, deeply ingrained part of every human being's life and should not be subject to debate or coercion. Anyone who is truly committed to women's human rights must recognize that every woman has the right to determine her sexuality free of discrimination and oppression.

I urge you to make this a conference for all women, regardless of their sexual orientation, and to recognize in the Platform for Action that lesbian rights are women's rights and that women's rights are universal, inalienable, and indivisible human rights. I urge you to remove the brackets from sexual orientation. Thank you.

GRO HAARLEM BRUNDTLAND
(NORWAY)

Closing Address

We came here to answer the call of billions of women who have lived—and of billions of women who will live. We now need a tidal change—Women will no longer accept the role as second-rate citizens.

Our generation must answer that call. Undoubtedly, we have moved forward. But the measure of our success cannot be fully assessed today. It will depend on the will of us all to fulfill what we have promised.

The views expressed here—and the news which escaped from here—will irrevocably shape world opinion. The story of Beijing cannot be untold.

What will be remembered? Zealous security? The palms of policemen? Visas not granted? Yes, but such practices cannot, and will not, long endure. Let us today count our strategic victories, not the tactical defeats. What we have achieved is to unbracket the lives of girls and women.

Now we must move on. All history of liberation struggles tells us that life, freedom, equality and opportunity have never been given. They have always been taken.

We cannot maintain the illusion, that someone else is going to do the job and establish equality with men. Women, and men working with us, men who understand, we all must fight for that freedom.

Today we know that women's contribution[s] to the economy are decisive for growth and social development. We know that countries will continue to live in poverty if women remain under the heel of oppression. We know the costs of a continuing genderized apartheid.

Today, there isn't a single country in the world—not one—where men and women enjoy equal opportunities. So we must go back from Beijing,

- go back to the shantytowns of Third World megacities,
- go back to the croplands at the desert's edge in Africa,
- to the indigenous communities of Latin American rain forests,
- go home to change values and attitudes.

But not only there.
* no, we must go the boardrooms,
* to the suburbia of Europe and North America,
* to all of our local communities,
* our governments,
and to the United Nations' headquarters.

This is where change is required. Both in the North and in the South. What must be done to fulfill the hopes and aspirations of generations living and yet unborn?

Not only must women become free and equal to make choices about their own lives. Not only must women have the right, the formal and protected right, to take part in the shaping of society.

No, far more, women must make use of that right. Women power is a formidable force. Women's values have a lot to give. We need women at all levels of management and government—local as well as national government. We all agree that women must have education, not only experience—but we still are far from a world that makes use of it.

To take one example from the political field: There are cabinets and parliaments in the world with few or even no women. This situation cannot and will not last. And if the transition towards more real political representation is sluggish, affirmative action will work.

It did, in Scandinavia. When I first became prime minister 15 years ago, it was a cultural shock to many Norwegians. Today, four-year-olds ask their mommies: "but can a man be prime minister?"

We are adopting a comprehensive Platform for Action. All of its elements are important in this agenda for change. Let me focus on some of its most compelling thrusts:

We agree that women's education is essential. This year's Human Development Report makes it emphatically clear: The economic returns on investing in women's education are fully comparable to those for men. But the social returns from educating women far exceed those of educating men. Schooling of girls is one of the unlocking keys to development.

There has been a difficult debate on how Beijing should define the human rights of women. As if there could be one set of human rights for men and another, more restricted one, for women.

I even have heard the following allegation from a country not to be named: "The West, to be frank, is attempting to impose its cultural pattern as an international model."

Wrong; most countries are today strongly defending their own cultures. And there is more respect and mutual understanding of the value of other cultures and religions than ever before.

But the point is a different one: There are limits to the practices that countries can expect the international community to accept, or condone, even when such practices have deep cultural roots. This is where human rights enter the picture.

Violence against women, also domestic violence, can be said to be part of a "cultural pattern," in most countries including my own. We receive too many appalling reports of plain wife beating.

And clearly, freedom from violence and coercion must apply also in the sexual sphere of life. This conference has rightly made clear what the existing human rights must mean in practice.

The state becomes an accomplice if violence against women is seen as a separate cultural category of behavior extraneous to the realm of justice and law enforcement.

There are stains on the world map of girl-child maltreatment. Genital mutilation of girls is just that. It does not become sacrosanct or elevated beyond the realm of politics, just because that practice can be said to be part of a "cultural pattern."

We are familiar with the terrible discrimination against girls, even before birth. What has obscurely been described as "pre-natal sex selection," and the fatal neglect of infant girls, are tragic testimonies.

There are often ancient root causes of such practices. But they are committed by people who live today. Why are there astonishingly more boys than girls in certain countries? The question may be unpleasant for governments, who do not encourage these crimes. But we will all be found guilty if we close our eyes.

Why are girl children given less and poorer food than their brothers? Why do they receive less health care and less education? Why are they subjected to the horrible tradition of sexual exploitation?

Ingrained, centuries-old attitudes are not easily changed, but these which I have mentioned must be. The task requires vigorous action on the part of governments, religious groups and private, nongovernmental organizations.

Greater equality in the family is to the good for men, women and children. The allegation that this Conference is against motherhood and family is plainly absurd.

Today, we recognize that poverty has a gender bias. Increasingly, poverty discriminates between men and women.

The myth that men are the economic providers and women, mainly, are mothers and care-givers in the family has now been thoroughly refuted.

This family pattern has never been the norm, except in a narrow middle-class segment.

Women have always worked, in all societies—and at all times. As a rule they have worked harder than men, and—as a rule,—without pay and acknowledgment. Their contribution has been essential for national economies as well as to their families, where women have been the breadwinners, often quite superior to men.

As defined by statistics, societies have often kept women at arm's length. Women who work 10–12 hours a day in subsistence agriculture may be registered as "housewives" in the national censuses.

But overlooking women's contribution to the economy has had more severe damaging effects. Often women cannot even obtain a modest loan to become more independent and productive. In many countries, women own nothing, they inherit nothing and are unable to offer security. On top of that laws often work against them.

No, women will not become more empowered merely because we want them to be, but through change of legislation, increased information and by redirecting resources.

Ministers of finance and planning may rue their former practice faced with what Beijing says about the economic role of women. Unleashing women from the chains of poverty is not only a question of justice. It is a question of sound economic growth and improved welfare for everyone. It is high time that we genderize development plans and government budgets.

The 20/20 concept is a promising path forward. It requires mutual commitment, the solidarity of the international community and the responsibility of each national government to provide basic social services. It is not possible to meet the aspirations of our people, nor to fulfill our commitments without allocating at least 20 percent of national budgets to basic social services. And those 20 percent need to be genderized.

We learned a lesson at the Population Conference in Cairo last year. Improving the status of women and sound family planning is the key to lower fertility rates. The risky pattern of "too many, too soon, too late and too close" is also strongly detrimental to the survival of infants and children. There is no morality in condemning women to a life of perpetual childbearing and fatigue. Where appeals for justice for women have not been listened to, perhaps the necessity of a sounder economy and sounder population trends may.

Fortunately, we managed to erect a dike against the stormy waves threatening the Cairo consensus. But here in Beijing we managed more than just a defence of past achievements. When I said at the Cairo conference that, at the very least, we should decriminalize women who had seen no other solution than to go through an abortion, it caused an uproar. And I fail to understand, why also here in Beijing—why those who most vocally speak for what many of us favour, a caring society where all women can safely have their children, why they have held so strongly that these most dramatically difficult decisions should be cause for public prosecution.

We should focus on human suffering, not on recrimination against the weakest and most vulnerable.

Every second a baby boy and baby girl are born into this world of diversity and inequality. They all deserve love and care, a future and opportunities. There is nothing so thoroughly, so unconditionally trusting as the look in the eyes of a newborn girl or boy child. From that privilege, we must depart, and make ourselves worthy of the look in those eyes.

61.

SYLVIANE AGACINSKI
(b. 1945)

Parity of the Sexes
(FRANCE, 1998)

In the 1990s, several French feminists proposed a policy termed parité—
*akin to electoral quotas established in other nations for racial or ethnic
minorities—to rectify the underrepresentation of women in political office. The French feminists argued that because women make up half of the
population, half of the candidates for office should ideally be female. In
1993, a letter supporting* parité, *signed by equal numbers of men and
women, appeared in the popular French newspaper* Le Monde. *Some
feminists disliked* parité's *emphasis on sex, rather than the neutral category of citizenship, as a qualification for office. Feminist philosopher Sylviane Agacinski insisted that* parité *did not adopt a theory of natural
sexual difference but instead tried to make sense of the culturally produced political difference that excluded women from office. In 2001, under socialist prime minister Lionel Jospin (Agacinski's husband), France
instituted* parité *by reducing state funding for political parties if they
failed to field equal numbers of female and male candidates. As a result,
at the next election women's share of seats on city councils doubled, to almost half. By the early twenty-first century, more than a dozen
countries—including Argentina, Germany, India, Israel, Sweden, Tanzania, and Venezuela—required at least minimal representation of
women in local or national legislatures.*

The idea of parity was put forward for the first time by one of the most audacious French feminists, Hubertine Auclert, the very same woman who in 1880, in a letter to the prefect, refused to pay her taxes as long as she could not vote: "I leave to the men who enjoy the power to govern the privilege of paying the taxes they vote for and distribute as they please.... I have no rights, thus I have no burden. I do not vote, I do not pay." The argument's strength struck public opinion but was not enough to move the parliament nor, moreover, women in general who were more preoccupied with the attainment of civil rights. A few years later in 1884, Hubertine Auclert again demanded that the supposedly "universal" suffrage be extended to women and at the same time suggested that the assemblies be composed of "as many women as men."

In a single move, this demand situated itself on an entirely new plane. It was not simply a question of putting an end to the masculine monopoly on democratic and republican power and abolishing the exclusion of women from the state by giving them the right to vote or be elected. It was a question of a completely unheard-of idea: that of men and women sharing political power. For Hubertine, it went without saying that the political equality she was calling for must mean the recognition of women *as such* as the other part of the sovereign people. Men and women should thus constitute, *together and equally*, the body of the electorate as well as that of the elected.

This utopic vision, then, of power sharing between the sexes is the one reappearing today. Not, it seems, under an inevitably arithmetic form, but as a demand for a balance of men and women among the leading authorities. This vision is what, in 1996, inspired the Charter of Rome and the Manifesto of the Ten. It is this vision, again, that informs public opinion when there is unanimous outrage at the very small number of women in the National Assembly and the Senate— about 5 percent in 1996!—and when it is declared desirable for women and men to participate equally in decision making. Numerous polls attest to this trend in public opinion. Even more: the gap between the principle of equality posited by the law and the reality of political fact, showing the law to be almost exclusively masculine, is everywhere denounced.

But it would be wrong, in this case, to oppose the equality of rights to the reality of facts. Equality only implies, as we have remarked, that rights are *the same* for women and for men (the right to vote and to be eligible to hold office). The equality of men and women *before the law* has never meant that there should be as many women as men electors or elected—that is, a quantitative equality *between* men and women. Obviously, there are *approximately* as many women electors as men—and even a few more—as a result of the approximately equal distribution of the population between men and women. On the other hand, as it is beginning to dawn on us, there are almost no women elected in France. Is it a question, as we often hear said, of a "scandalous" functioning of our institutions, indeed, a "failure of democracy"? Hardly. The classical concept of democracy, even after the right to vote was extended to women, never included the need for a definite proportion of women among those elected. Neither the idea of equal rights nor the idea of democracy refers to an ideal of actual *mixity* in elected authority—still less to an equal or equitable *sharing* of power. Only the idea of *parity* contains this demand for sharing. It is in this that parity is original and perfectly new, both from the point of view of principles and democratic life itself....

Parity really constitutes a political interpretation of sexual difference. This difference ceases to be the pretext for segregation and becomes the justification for *sharing*. Parity posits that the interest in things public and the responsibilities attached devolve to men and women equally. This *sharing* constitutes a realization of sexual difference that does not hierarchize, according to traditional schema, nor neutralize, according to a universalist conception. If it is possible to escape the hierarchical programming of difference, it really would be by inventing original solutions not by denying a priori that this difference takes on political meaning.

However, if many invoke an ideal of actual mixity for political proceedings (even the fiercest adversaries of the institution of parity, indeed of quotas), few ask themselves on what principle this idea of mixity should be founded. No one dares contest this ideal, as if it were self-evident, but they recoil in the face of the questions it raises, because these questions inevitably lead back to the status of sexual difference about which French universalism wants to know nothing.

Even those who wish that political power were *more* shared between men and women are often loath to accept implementing the *means* to arrive at this end, because it seems so shocking to institute mixity through regulations, institutional measures, or—horror of horrors—constitutional changes. Some remain so inconsistent, calling loudly and strongly for "more women" in the Assembly while refusing to take gender difference into account in the civic arena. But if the civic space shouldn't recognize gender, there's no reason to raise the question of the number of men or women in institutions. In reality, those who are so frightened by the means are hardly convinced of the legitimacy of the ends themselves.

This is why, before addressing these new stakes in the relations between the sexes represented today by parity, I returned at length in the preceding pages to the nature, validity, and universality of sexual difference.

If being a woman truly constitutes *one of two essential ways of being a human being*—and only if we agree on this point—then we must admit that a people, no matter what people, also exists according to this double mode. We cannot agree that man (in the generic sense) only exists as divided and deny a nation this double way of being. I agree with Blandine Kriegel's analysis, which bases the legitimacy of sexual equality, according to the model of parity, more on the doctrine of the rights of man than on that of citizenship. It is the equal humanity of men and women that is at stake, more pertinent here than any category of citizenship.

In this sense I would say that the universal mixity of humanity must also find its expression in the definition of the people and must be included in the concept of democracy and the principles of political life.

If we admit this point—which is everything—the debates on the constitutional or legal obstacles become as irrelevant as the constitutionalists' objections to extending voting rights to women once were. Either the cause seems just and the legal consequences must follow, or it doesn't and the fundamental issue must be debated.

Moreover, it is the sovereign people themselves who must judge the soundness of this position and the justice of this cause. According to the Constitution, the people can express themselves by way of Congress or through referendum. Democracy, and this is its strength, has within its means the ability to transform itself: parity, as a *new idea* of democracy, must thus become the object of a decision that is, itself, democratic....

It is now clear that the equitable *representation* of women in the assemblies does not mean that the women elected must be the mouthpieces of women: this vision of things would be a return to a segmenting by categories. As subtle as the difference between these two ways of conceiving of representation may seem—as reflection or figure—we must maintain them and not confuse the democratic demand for a good "representation" of the social body with what Francine Demichel calls, in rejecting it, "a photography of social diversity."

Parity thus means that the actual mixity of the assemblies must *figure* the human mixity of the nation. The equitable *representation of men and women*—because neither sex should be considered unilaterally— if it is not the faithful *reflection* of the diverse components of the population considered in its empirical reality at a given time, should thus be a *relevant figure* of what the people are, universally, that is, a people made up of men and women. Through their *presence* in the Assembly, men and women "embody" the nation for the period of their mandate.

62.

JONAH GOKOVA
(b. 1956)

"Challenging Men to Reject
Gender Stereotypes"
(ZIMBABWE, 1998)

Since the 1970s, male allies within the feminist antirape movement have attempted to undermine violence against women. Some of their projects socialize boys to refuse to participate in the objectification or stereotyping of women, while others teach men incarcerated for rape and battery about the consequences of their actions and the importance of respecting women. In Zimbabwe, Padare/Enkundleni, which means "a gathering place," formed in 1993 to provide a Men's Forum on Gender. The organization has expanded to include more than a dozen branches in Zimbabwe, where it holds workshops to address the links between sexual health, violence against women, and the spread of HIV/AIDS. Padare creates support groups to help men who have been raised to believe they have a right to possess women to change their vision of masculinity. Founder and chair Jonah Gokova, a 2001 recipient of the Africa Prize for Leadership for his efforts to stop the spread of HIV/AIDS, is active in the Global Network of Men, organized in 2000 through the YMCA and the World Council of Churches. He also works for African debt relief, arguing that African nations could better use their resources to control HIV/AIDS.

Living in a patriarchal society, I ask myself questions. Why do I as a man have so many privileges? If men are equal in standing to women, they also profit—for example, through shared responsibility and more freedom to express themselves. That is why circumstances keeping women back must be eliminated.

The term "gender" is not synonymous for "women" but is often used in that way. The view that gender issues only concern women has served as an excuse to avoid addressing the gender stereotypes that have imprisoned men and women. Moreover, men have taken little, if any, interest in responding to the challenges women have been raising over the years. Nevertheless, gender issues demand men's participation since men need to change to realize overall change.

Men have allowed themselves to dominate or ignore reproductive rights, parenting, and active participation in family-planning matters instead of sharing those responsibilities. Many women are largely denied the freedom to decide whether they can have children or not. Ending domestic violence must become men's responsibility. They should further see themselves as partners in addressing the problem of other men's lack of interest and concern about educating one another about their role in HIV/AIDS awareness education.

The implication of all this is that men need to change their attitude towards sex. They should begin to see it as an opportunity to communicate mutually with women rather than as a chance to dominate and conquer. Men must consciously take the decision to think and behave differently.

Generally, men enjoy privileges associated with gender roles assigned to them at the expense of women. Why then do they find special privileges necessary when they claim to be stronger, braver and more creative and intelligent than women? One soon realizes that men have been living a myth that needs to be challenged. Padare/Enkundleni/Men's Forum on Gender (Padare), an antisexist organization for men in Zimbabwe, encourages men to respond to gender inequality in our society. Its message is clear: men must welcome women's invitation to help create a gender-sensitive society. To enjoy being truly human and to build a just society, men must recognize women as equal partners.

> My wife and I decided not to raise our daughters according to the prevailing norms. We want to show them life as it should be. That means that they see daddy cooking, changing nappies and making the bed. They see me washing dishes and my wife going to work every day. Do you know what I really liked? A few days ago my 5-year-old daughter asked: 'Daddy, why do you both wear pants but not dresses?' My daughter is beginning to look around her. It was an important question for her and I was happy she asked it....

Men have not realized how much they pay in insisting on separate gender roles. Patriarchy forces men, whether they are aware of it or not, to be collaborators in a system that oppresses women. Men deny themselves the experience of being human, particularly insofar as their relationship with women is concerned. They miss important lessons of life derived from challenging relationships in which women play an equal role.

Living the myth of male superiority has sometimes resulted in men suffering from stress, even early death, because of pressure to project an image that is not naturally theirs and that is not sustainable. For example, men cannot openly express themselves. They are not supposed to cry or admit weaknesses in the presence of women.

The separation of gender roles also restricts male creativeness. In Zimbabwe and most countries in Southern Africa, for example, men are not supposed to work in the kitchen as this is considered women's domain. Expression of love is also limited in the sense that they cannot make their girlfriends, wives, sisters or mothers a nice meal for fear of being misunderstood as compromising their "manhood."

One other assumption also needs to be challenged. So often when we talk about gender inequality we think of heterosexual people. The concept of gender should also apply equally to gay men and lesbian women. While their sexual orientation is a departure from heterosexual definitions, some of them remain imprisoned in stereotyped gender roles in their relationships. This has resulted in violence and abuse in gay communities....

What men need to do is to come together and talk, talk, talk about the way they have been raised. What assumptions about women and men have we picked up that have made us oppressive and unhelpful in creating meaningful relationships between men and women? Where do we need to change?

Men who are involved in this process need to be more visible in society. Padare encourages men to recognize and reject destructive assumptions and perceptions that result in gender inequality. Out of this process, a new definition of manhood is emerging. Men are understanding that the gender struggle is not about lifting women to the position of men. After all, men have been elevated to a super-human position through patriarchy and the tensions that result from such a life of pretense are quite high, unhealthy and unsustainable for men and society in the long term.

Men need to cooperate with women who have been working on gender issues, sometimes in isolation and sometimes dealing with hostile men threatened by the prospect of change. For example, many times men in Zimbabwe have stood in the way of women's access to information that is likely to increase their knowledge and status. Cooperation will allow men to help rather than block that access.

Our vision for the creation of a society established on gender justice requires the involvement of every man and woman. We recognize, however, that men have a particular responsibility in this effort. Men need to be challenged continually to seek change. This means openly and publicly rejecting the current image of manhood. Developing a new man whose existence does not depend on any form of violence and abuse of women is possible!

63

Jennifer Baumgardner
(b. 1970)

and

Amy Richards
(b. 1970)

Manifesta: Young Women, Feminism, and the Future
(UNITED STATES, 2000)

Young activists who came of age a generation after the Second Wave of feminism in the United States reshaped the women's movement in their own image. In the 1990s, a flurry of writing by self-defined Third Wavers built on past struggles within American women's movements to insist that racial justice and queer and lesbian rights were central to feminism. These writers both condemned sexual violence and rejected sexual victimization, insisting on a sex-positive view. Third Wave feminist magazines, with titles such as Bitch *and* Bust, *attempted to reject misogynistic terms and to reclaim female imagery. In their book* Manifesta, *journalists Jennifer Baumgardner and Amy Richards surveyed Third Wave feminism and obstacles to it, along with offering guidelines for political participation by young women. Richards help found the Third Wave Foundation and worked to register young voters in the 1990s. Both authors served as editors at* Ms. *magazine and have continued to foster feminist activism.*

THIRD WAVE MANIFESTA:
A THIRTEEN-POINT AGENDA

1. To out unacknowledged feminists, specifically those who are younger, so that Generation X can become a visible movement and, further, a voting block of eighteen- to forty-year-olds.

2. To safeguard a woman's right to bear or not to bear a child, regardless of circumstances, including women who are younger than eighteen or impoverished. To preserve this right throughout her life and support the choice to be childless.

3. To make explicit that the fight for reproductive rights must include birth control; the right for poor women and lesbians to have children; partner adoption for gay couples; subsidized fertility treatments for all women who choose them; and freedom from sterilization abuse. Furthermore, to support the idea that sex can be—and usually is—for pleasure, not procreation.

4. To bring down the double standard in sex and sexual health, and foster male responsibility and assertiveness in the following areas: achieving freedom from STDs; more fairly dividing the burden of family planning as well as responsibilities such as child care; and eliminating violence against women.

5. To tap into and raise awareness of our revolutionary history, and the fact that almost all movements began as youth movements. To have access to our intellectual feminist legacy and women's history; for the classics of radical feminism, womanism, *mujeristas*, women's liberation, and all our roots to remain in print; and to have women's history taught to men as well as women as a part of all curricula.

6. To support and increase the visibility and power of lesbians and bisexual women in the feminist movement, in high schools, colleges, and the workplace. To recognize that queer women have always been at the forefront of the feminist movement, and that there is nothing to be gained—and much to be lost—by downplaying their history, whether inadvertently or actively.

7. To practice "autokeonony" ("self in community"): to see activism not as a choice between self and community but as a link between them that creates balance.

8. To have equal access to health care, regardless of income, which includes coverage equivalent to men's and keeping in mind that women use the system more often than men do because of our reproductive capacity.

9. For women who so desire to participate in all reaches of the military, including combat, and to enjoy all the benefits (loans, health care, pensions)

offered to its members for as long as we continue to have an active military. The largest expenditure of our national budget goes toward maintaining this welfare system, and feminists have a duty to make sure women have access to every echelon.

10. To liberate adolescents from slut-bashing, listless educators, sexual harassment, and bullying at school, as well as violence in all walks of life, and the silence that hangs over adolescents' heads, often keeping them isolated, lonely, and indifferent to the world.

11. To make the workplace responsive to an individual's wants, needs, and talents. This includes valuing (monetarily) stay-at-home parents, aiding employees who want to spend more time with family and continue to work, equalizing pay for jobs of comparable worth, enacting a minimum wage that would bring a full-time worker with two children over the poverty line, and providing employee benefits for freelance and part-time workers.

12. To acknowledge that, although feminists may have disparate values, we share the same goal of equality, and of supporting one another in our efforts to gain the power to make our own choices.

13. To pass the Equal Rights Amendment so that we can have a constitutional foundation of righteousness and equality upon which future women's rights conventions will stand.

64

REVOLUTIONARY ASSOCIATION OF THE WOMEN OF AFGHANISTAN

"Statement on the Occasion of International Women's Day"

(AFGHANISTAN, 2004)

Democratic and industrial revolutions laid the groundwork for feminist politics, and the absence of these historical conditions pose the greatest challenges to women's rights. Afghanistan during the 1990s represented an extreme case, in which the ruling Taliban imposed a strict patriarchal state. Women could not appear in public without a male relative or work for wages, and widows who had no male relatives to provide for them had to beg for support. Part of an underground movement kindling women's rights, the Revolutionary Association of the Women of Afghanistan (RAWA), founded in Kabul in 1977, had resisted Soviet occupation and, after the Taliban gained power in 1992, opposed Islamic fundamentalism. From exile in Pakistan, RAWA provided schools and health care for women refugees from Afghanistan. After the defeat of the Taliban, RAWA both provided social services within the country and publicized internationally the continuing violence and limited economic and educational opportunities for girls and women. As their 2004 International Women's Day statement illustrates, the group remained vigilant about the threat to democracy and women's rights posed by fundamentalist influences on regional politics.

Women's emancipation is achievable only by themselves!

During the medieval and tyrannical rule of Taliban, the major international and Western media began and ended with a focus on women's oppression. It seemed as though this country would not have had a problem if all that torture and gradual death were not enforced on women and the Taliban had showed a little mercy! And when the U.S. came out to punish her hirelings, the first and last word was about the abuse of women by Taliban—even the flyers that were thrown by U.S. military aircraft on cities contained photos that portrayed Taliban barbarism against women.

Of course after the U.S. attack and installation of the interim government, raising women's banner steadily continued: the Women's Ministry and various other commissions were created and a few women became so-called "authorities." And now that two years have passed since these events, who is to deny the fact that the condition of 99% of women in Afghanistan has not seen fundamental changes? There are no longer Taliban who lash women because their hair or feet came out of the Burqa. But how can women go out unveiled and have normal life without the fear of warlords who like hunting dogs annoy, insult and rape them?

Out of extreme suffocation and terror in Herat, grabbed in the filthy grip of the terrorist "amir" Ismail Khan, hundreds of girls and women have committed suicide by self-immolation in less than a year to free themselves from a painful life under the dagger of a corrupted and freedom-killing regime. The burnt bodies of these innocent victims keep the faces of Ismail Khan and his accomplices in "Northern Alliance" black with shame.

Despite the above dreadful realities, if talking about Afghanistan is confined only to abuse of women then in fact it is throwing dust into the eyes of the world. Regardless of the multitude of oppressions against women, men are also not free. If the Taliban are not in charge, their Jehadi brethren, the "Northern Alliance," embrace the power in the country. Hence if all these atrocities and disasters, i.e. the presence of fundamentalist warlords, are not rooted out from Afghanistan, no serious issues including freedom and prosperity of women and men can be solved even if more ministries and commissions are created for women.

The freedom of a nation is to be achieved by itself—similarly the real emancipation of women can be realized only by themselves. If that freedom is bestowed by others, it may be seized and violated any time....

We now have a constitution that has nothing to guarantee the trial of warlord criminals, allows the misuse of religion, and has not abolished the various crimes against women in the name of religion and tradition. The Constitution is just a piece of paper that gives legitimacy to the tyrannical rule of warlords.

It is quite natural that the voter registration, particularly of women, for the upcoming election may have the lowest possible figure. What value does an election have for the hopeless people who have no bread and no work and are being tormented by criminal fundamentalists? The presence of every woman and man in the future assemblies is meaningful only when they represent the people, and, like Malalai Joya, spit at the fundamentalists in their cage with courage and honor. Otherwise they should be called a cat's-paw of religious fascists and their accomplices. They would compromise and hunger for power, not to be forgiven by the people.

The experience of Iran has made it clear that democratic forces cannot achieve their goals within the framework of a brutal religious regime or relying on a so-called "moderate" regime. People and democratic forces in Iran paid a heavy price for their participation in the bloody game of an Islamic regime. Supporters of democratic forces in Afghanistan should have learned enough from Iran's example and should never make cease-fires or deal with this or that faction of fundamentalists. The only benchmark to measure the loyalty to freedom in a country is the degree of boldness, determination and honesty of a person or group in the struggle against religious fascism.

It is up to our conscious women that organize tens and hundreds of thousands of freedom-loving women and create a great anti-fundamentalism movement for democracy across this terrorism and fundamentalism blighted country. While organizing such a massive movement, we can play an effective role for women's emancipation on the basis of freedom of the country. Now we should no longer talk about a "silent majority," but an uprising, a decisive and aggressive majority, and translate our solidarity to the struggle of all freedom-loving women in the remote places of the world from words into practice.

While celebrating International Women's Day with all justice-seeking women of the world, Revolutionary Association of the Women of Afghanistan (RAWA) sends warmest regards to all the freedom-loving women imprisoned in the torturous prison of Iran and Turkey. We wish that the women of Afghanistan celebrate this day in Afghanistan free of the fetters of fundamentalism and on the road to democracy and prosperity.

Sources for Documents

Christine de Pizan. *The Book of the City of Ladies.* Earl Jeffrey Richards, trans. New York: Persea Books, 1982 (pp. 3–5, 62–64, 142, 164–65, 256–57).

François Poullain de la Barre. *On the Equality of the Two Sexes.* In *Three Cartesian Feminist Treatises,* Vivien Bosley, trans. Chicago: University of Chicago Press, 2002 (pp. 82–83, 90–91, 106–107).

Sor Juana Inés de la Cruz. "The Reply to Sor Philothea." In *A Sor Juana Anthology:* Alan S. Trueblood, trans. Cambridge, Mass.: Harvard University Press, 1988 (pp. 226–27, 229–30, 232–33, 235–36).

A Lover of Her Sex [Mary Astell]. *A Serious Proposal to the Ladies, For the Advancement of their true and greatest interest.* London: R. Wilkin, 1694, and Anonymous [Mary Astell]. *A Serious Proposal to the Ladies: Part II: Wherein a Method is offer'd for the Improvement of their Minds.* London: Richard Wilkin, 1697, repr. in *A Serious Proposal to the Ladies: Parts I and II.* Patricia Springborg, ed. Peterborough, Ont.: Broadview Press, 2002 (pp. 73, 74, 76–77, 80, 81, 231–32, 233–34).

Mary Wollstonecraft. *A Vindication of the Rights of Woman with Strictures on Political and Moral Subjects.* New ed., with an introduction by Mrs. Henry Fawcett. New York: Humboldt Publishing Co., [1891?] (pp. 23–25, 26–27, 148, 149, 150, 152–57, 184, 192–93, 196–200).

Li Ju-chen. *Flowers in the Mirror.* Lin Tai-yi, trans., ed. Berkeley: University of California Press, 1965 (pp. 107–14).

Sarah M. Grimké. "On the Condition of Women in the United States." In *Letters on the Equality of the Sexes and Other Essays*. Elizabeth Ann Bartlett, ed. New Haven: Yale University Press, 1988 (pp. 56–61).

Flora Tristan. "The Emancipation of Working Class Women." Gisele Pincetl, trans. *Harvest Quarterly* 7 (Fall 1977): 10–14.

Elizabeth Cady Stanton, "Declaration of Sentiments." In *History of Woman Suffrage: Vol. 1 1848–1861*. Elizabeth Cady Stanton, Susan B. Anthony, and Matilda Joslyn Gage, eds. New York: Fowler & Wells, 1881 (pp. 70–73).

Sojourner Truth Speech, *Anti-Slavery Bugle* (Salem, Ohio), June 21, 1851, repr. in C. Peter Ripley, ed. *The Black Abolitionist Papers,* Volume 4: The United States, 1847–1858. Chapel Hill: University of North Carolina Press, 1991 (pp. 81–83); "Address of Sojourner Truth to the 1st Anniversary Meeting of the American Equal Rights Association, May 1867, New York." In *Proceedings of the First Anniversary of the American Equal Rights Association: Held at the Church of the Puritans, New York, May 9 and 10, 1867*. New York: Robert J. Johnston, 1867 (pp. 20–21).

Harriet Taylor Mill. "The Enfranchisement of Women." *Westminster Review*, 1851, repr. in Jo Ellen Jacobs, ed., *The Complete Works of Harriet Taylor Mill*. Bloomington: Indiana University Press, 1998 (pp. 51–73).

John Stuart Mill. *The Subjection of Women*. New York: D. Appleton and Company, 1869 (pp. 22–34, 55–59, 87–89, 91–93, 148–49, 153, 187, 188).

Susan B. Anthony. "Social Purity." In Ida Husted Harper, *The Life and Work of Susan B. Anthony: Including Public Addresses, Her Own Letters and Many from Her Contemporaries During Fifty Years*. Vol 2. Indianapolis: Bowen-Merrill Company, 1898 (pp. 1004–12).

Henrik Ibsen. *The Doll's House: A Play*. Henrietta Frances Lord, trans. New York: D. Appleton & Co., 1889 (pp. 135–42, 145–48).

Kishida Toshiko. "Daughters in Boxes." *Liberty Times*. November 20, 1883 (pp. 2–3), November 21, 1883 (p. 2), Rebecca Copeland and Aiko Okamoto MacPhail, trans. In *The Modern Murasaki: Women Writers of Meiji Japan*. Eds. Rebecca Copeland and Melek Ortabasi. New York: Columbia University Press, 2006.

Friedrich Engels. *The Origin of the Family, Private Property, and the State*. New York: International Publishers, 1942 (pp. 43, 46–50, 54–55, 57–58, 65–66, 72).

Francisca Senhorinha da Motta Diniz. "Equality of Rights." In June E. Hahner, *Emancipating the Female Sex: The Struggle for Women's Rights in Brazil, 1850–1940*. Durham: Duke University Press, 1990 (pp. 213–15).

Anna Julia Cooper. *A Voice from the South*. Xenia, Ohio: The Aldine Printing House, 1892 (pp. 31–33, 56–61, 108–11, 120–21).

Elizabeth Cady Stanton. "The Solitude of Self." Reprinted in *The American Magazine* 1–11, no. 8 (1889–Nov. 1896): 93–95. Originally published in *The Woman's Journal* Vol. 23:4 (January 23, 1892) pp. 25, 32.

Charlotte Perkins Gilman. *"The Yellow Wallpaper." New England Magazine*. January 1892 (pp. 647–56). Reprinted in *The Charlotte Perkins Gilman Reader*, ed. Ann J. Lane. New York: Pantheon, 1980 (pp. 3–19).

Qasim Amin. "The Liberation of Women." In Samiha Sidhom Peterson, trans. *The Liberation of Women and The New Woman: Two Documents in the History of Egyptian Feminism*. Cairo: The American University in Cairo Press, 2000 (pp. 3, 6–9, 35–36, 40–43, 56, 60–61).

Rokeya Sakhawat Hossain. "Sultana's Dream." Calcutta: S. K. Lahiri & Co., 1908. Originally published in *The Indian Ladies Magazine*, Madras, India, 1905.

Qiu Jin. "Stones of the Jingwei Bird." In Amy D. Dooling and Kristina M. Torgeson, eds. and trans. *Writing Women in Modern China: An Anthology of Women's Literature from the Early Twentieth Century*. New York: Columbia University Press, 1998 (pp. 43–45).

Emma Goldman. "The Tragedy of Woman's Emancipation." In *Mother Earth* 1 (March 1906): 9–18. See also Candace Falk, ed. *Emma Goldman: A Documentary History of the American Years. Vol. Two: Making Speech Free, 1902–1909*. Berkeley: University of California Press, 2005 (pp. 178–81, 182, 183–84, 185).

Alexandra Kollontai. "The Social Basis of the Woman Question." In *Selected Writings of Alexandra Kollontai*. Alex Holt, trans. Westport, Conn.: Lawrence Hill and Company, 1977 (pp. 58–60, 63, 64, 65, 66–67, 72, 73).

Three Poems:

Sara Estela Ramírez. "Rise Up! To Woman." *La Cronica* (Laredo, Texas) August 9, 1910: 3. Inés Hernandez, trans., in "Sara Estela Ramírez: Sembradora." *Legacy: A Journal of Nineteenth-Century American Women Writers* 6 no. 1 (Spring 1989): 13–26.

Yosano Akiko. "The Day the Mountains Move." In Laurel Rasplica Rodd, "Yosano Akiko and the Taisho Debate Over the 'New Woman.'" In *Recreating Japanese Women, 1600–1945*. Gail Lee Bernstein, ed. Berkeley: University of California Press, 1991 (p. 180).

James Oppenheim. "Bread and Roses." *American Magazine* 73 (2): 214.

Luisa Capetillo. *A Nation of Women: An Early Feminist Speaks Out: Mi opinión sobre las libertades, derechos y deberes de la mujer.* Félix V. Matos Rodríguez, ed. Alan West-Durán, trans. Houston: Arte Público Press, 2004 (pp. 19–23, 28).

Emmeline Pankhurst speech. In *Suffrage Speeches from the Dock: Made at the Conspiracy Trial, Old Bailey, May 15th–22nd, 1912.* London: Woman's Press [1912?], (pp. 26–28, 30, 33–35, 37–39, 43–44).

Women's International League for Peace and Freedom. Resolutions at the Zurich Convention. http://www.wilpf.int.ch/statements/1919.htm (accessed August 26, 2006).

W.E.B. Du Bois. "The Damnation of Women." In *Darkwater: Voices from Within the Veil.* New York: Harcourt, Brace and Howe, 1920 (pp. 164–65, 179–84, 185–86).

Margaret Sanger. *Woman and the New Race.* New York: Truth Publishing Company, 1920 (pp. 1–5, 7–8, 177–81, 183).

Shareefeh Hamid Ali. "East and West in Cooperation," 1935. Box 1, folder 8, International Alliance of Women Papers. Sophia Smith Collection, Smith College, Northampton, Mass.

Virginia Woolf. *Three Guineas.* San Diego: Harcourt Brace & Company, 1966 (pp. 3, 4–5, 12–14, 16, 22, 30, 33–34, 35, 37, 39, 40, 58–59, 66, 85, 103–6, 108–9, 144).

Alva Myrdal. *Nation and Family: The Swedish Experiment in Democratic Family and Population Policy.* London: Kegan Paul, Trench, Trubner & Co., Ltd., 1945 (pp. 398, 399, 400–1, 402–3, 403, 414, 417, 424–25, 425–26).

Ding Ling. "Thoughts on March 8." Gregor Benton, trans. In *I Myself Am a Woman: Selected Writings of Ding Ling,* Tani E. Barlow and Gary J. Bjorge, eds. Boston: Beacon Press, 1989 (pp. 317–21).

Huda Shaarawi. Speeches at Arab Feminist Conference. Ali Badran and Margot Badran, trans. In *Opening the Gates: An Anthology of Arab Feminist Writing,* 2nd ed., Margot Badran and Miriam Cooke, eds. Bloomington: Indiana University Press, 2004 (pp. 338–40).

Funmilayo Ransome-Kuti. "For Women: She Speaks for Nigeria/We Had Equality Till Britain Came." *Daily Worker* (London), August 18, 1947 (p. 4).

Simone de Beauvoir. *The Second Sex.* H. M. Parshley, trans., ed. New York: Alfred A. Knopf, 1978 (pp. xiii–xxiv, xxvi–xxix)

Federation of South African Women. Women's Charter and Aims. In Cherryl Walker, *Women and Resistance in South Africa.* London: Onyx Press, 1982 (pp. 279–82).

Betty Friedan, *The Feminine Mystique*. New York: W. W. Norton & Company, 1963 (pp. 15–25, 29–32, 338, 342, 344, 370, 377–78).

Pauli Murray, Testimony before U.S. House Committee on Education and Labor, *Discrimination Against Women*, 91st Congress, 2d Session. Washington, D.C.: U.S. Government Printing Office, 1970.

Pat Mainardi. "The Politics of Housework." In *Sisterhood Is Powerful: An Anthology of Writings from the Women's Liberation Movement*. Robin Morgan, ed. New York: Vintage Books, 1970 (pp. 501–9).

The Boston Women's Health Book Collective. *Our Bodies, Ourselves: A Book by and for Women*. New York: Simon and Schuster, 1973 (pp. 2, 3).

Mariarosa Dalla Costa. "A General Strike." In *All Work and No Pay: Women, Housework, and the Wages Due*. Wendy Edmond and Suzie Fleming, eds. Frome, England: Power of Women Collective and the Falling Wall Press, 1975 (pp. 125–27).

Committee on the Status of Women in India. *Towards Equality: Report of the Committee on the Status of Women in India*. New Delhi: Government of India Ministry of Education & Social Welfare, Department of Social Welfare, December 1974 (pp. 3, 8, 91, 94, 96, 101, 368, 372).

Susan Brownmiller. *Against Our Will: Men, Women and Rape*. New York: Simon and Schuster, 1975 (pp. 14–15, 209, 309–10, 312–13, 391, 396–97, 404).

Hélène Cixous. "The Laugh of the Medusa." Keith Cohen and Paula Cohen, trans. *Signs: Journal of Women in Culture and Society* 1, no. 4 (1976): 875–78, 880–81, 883, 889–90.

Combahee River Collective. "A Black Feminist Statement." In *Capitalist Patriarchy and the Case for Socialist Feminism*. Zillah R. Eisenstein, ed. New York and London: Monthly Review Press, 1979 (pp. 364–67, 367–68, 369, 371–72).

Audre Lorde. "The Master's Tools Will Never Dismantle the Master's House." In *Sister Outsider*. Freedom, Calif.: Crossing Press, 1984 (pp. 110–13).

United Nations. Convention on the Elimination of All Forms of Discrimination Against Women, December 18, 1979. http://www.un.org/womenwatch/daw/cedaw/text/econvention.htm (accessed August 26, 2006).

Domitila Barrios de la Chungara. "Women and Organization." In *Third World—Second Sex: Women's Struggles and National Liberation Third World Women Speak Out*. Miranda Davies, ed. London: Zed Books, 1983, (pp. 40–43).

AAWORD. "A Statement on Genital Mutilation." In *Third World—Second Sex: Women's Struggles and National Liberation Third World Women Speak Out.* Miranda Davies, ed. London: Zed Books, 1983 (pp. 217–20).

Anon. "How It All Began: I Have Had an Abortion." Translated by Naomi Stephan. In *German Feminism: Readings in Politics and Literature.* Edith Hoshino Altbach, et al., eds. Albany: State University of Albany Press, 1984 (pp. 102–4).

Monique Wittig. "One Is Not Born a Woman." *Feminist Issues* 1, no. 2 (Winter 1981): 47–50, 52–53.

Adrienne Rich. "Notes Toward a Politics of Location." In *Blood, Bread, and Poetry: Selected Prose 1979–1985.* New York: W. W. Norton & Company, 1986 (pp. 210–31).

Gloria Anzaldúa. "La Conciencia de la Mestiza: Toward a New Consciousness." In *Borderlands/La Frontera: The New Mestiza.* San Francisco: Aunt Lute Books, 1987 (pp. 77–82).

Guerrilla Girls. "When Sexism and Racism Are No Longer Fashionable," and "Do Women Have To Be Naked To Get into the Met. Museum?" 1989. Available at http://www.guerrillagirls.com/posters/sexism2.shtml and http://www.guerrillagirls.com/posters/getnaked.shtml (accessed August 26, 2006).

Kathleen Hanna. "Riot Grrrl Manifesto." *Bikini Kill* (Olympia, Wash.) [1992], no. 2.

Rebecca Walker, "Becoming the Third Wave." *Ms.,* January–February 1992, 39–41.

United Nations. Fourth World Conference on Women 1995 Speeches: Gertrude Mongella. Opening Address Plenary Session, September 4, 1995. http://www.un.org/esa/gopher-data/conf/fwcw/conf/una/950904201423.txt (accessed August 26, 2006).

Winona LaDuke. "The Indigenous Women's Network: Our Future, Our Responsibility." http://www.ratical.org/co-globalize/WinonaLaDuke/Beijing95.html (accessed August 26, 2006).

Palesa Beverley Ditsie. International Gay and Lesbian Human Rights Commission Statement, September 13, 1995. http://www.hartford-hwp.com/archives/28/014.html (accessed August 26, 2006).

Gro Haarlem Brundtland. Closing Address, September 15, 1995. http://www.un.org/esa/gopherdata/conf/fwcw/conf/gov/950915135459.txt (accessed August 26, 2006).

Sylviane Agacinski. *Parity of the Sexes*. Lisa Walsh, trans. New York: Columbia University Press, 2001 (pp. 153–55, 156–58, 168).

Jonah K. Gokova. "Challenging Men to Reject Gender Stereotypes." *Sexual Health Exchange* 2 (1998), (pp. 1–3).

Jennifer Baumgardner and Amy Richards. *Manifesta: Young Women, Feminism, and the Future*. New York: Farrar, Straus and Giroux, 2000 (pp. 278–80).

Revolutionary Association of the Women of Afghanistan. "Statement on the Occasion of International Women's Day, 2004: Women's Emancipation Is Achievable Only by Themselves!" Available at http://www.rawa.org/mar8-04e.htm (accessed August 26, 2006).

SELECTED BIBLIOGRAPHY

In addition to the works in which documents appeared, the following scholarly studies provided historical context:

Anderson, Bonnie S., and Zinsser, Judith P. *A History of Their Own: Women in Europe from Prehistory to the Present.* 2 vols. New York: Harper and Row, 1988.

Anderson, Bonnie S. *Joyous Greetings: The First International Women's Movement, 1830–1860.* New York: Oxford University Press, 2000.

Breines, Winifred. *The Trouble Between Us: An Uneasy History of White and Black Women in the Feminist Movement.* New York: Oxford University Press, 2006.

Freedman, Estelle B. *No Turning Back: The History of Feminism and the Future of Women.* New York: Ballantine Books, 2002.

Hahner, June E. *Emancipating the Female Sex: The Struggle for Women's Rights in Brazil, 1850–1940.* Durham, N.C. Duke University Press, 1990.

Herman, Sondra R. "Dialogue: Children, Feminism, and Power: Alva Myrdal and Swedish Reform, 1929–1956." *Journal of Women's History* 4, no. 2 (1992): 98.

Horowitz, Daniel. *Betty Friedan and the Making of The Feminine Mystique: The American Left, The Cold War, and Modern Feminism.* Amherst: University of Massachusetts Press, 1998.

Jardine, Alice. "Interview with Simone de Beauvoir." *Signs* 5, 2 (Winter, 1979), 224–36.

Johnson-Odim, Cheryl, and Nina Emma, Mba. *For Women and Nation: Funmilayo Ransome-Kuti of Nigeria.* Urbana: University of Illinois Press, 1997.

Lane, Ann J., ed. "Introduction." In *The Charlotte Perkins Gilman Reader: The Yellow Wallpaper, and Other Fiction.* New York: Pantheon Books, 1980.

Lerner, Gerda. *The Creation of Feminist Consciousness: From the Middle Ages to 1870.* New York: Oxford University Press, 1993.

Lerner, Gerda. *The Feminist Thought of Sarah Grimké.* New York: Oxford University Press, 1998.

Mohanty, Chandra Talpade. *Feminism without Borders: Decolonizing Theory, Practicing Solidarity.* Durham, N.C.: Duke University Press, 2003.

Offen, Karen. *European Feminisms, 1700–1950: A Political History,* Stanford, Calif.: Stanford University Press, 2000.

Painter, Nell Irwin. *Sojourner Truth: A Life, a Symbol.* New York: W. W. Norton, 1996.

Perry, Ruth. *The Celebrated Mary Astell: An Early English Feminist.* Chicago: University of Chicago Press, 1986.

Ray, Bharati. *Early Feminists of Colonial India: Sarala Devi Chaudhurani and Rokeya Sakhawat Hossain.* New Delhi: Oxford University Press, 2002.

Ropp, Paul S. "The Seeds of Change: Reflections on the Condition of Women in the Early and Mid Ch'ing." *Signs* 2, no. 1 (Autumn, 1976): 5–23.

Rupp, Leila. *Worlds of Women: The Making of An International Women's Movement.* Princeton, N.J.: Princeton University Press, 1997.

Scott, Joan. *Only Paradoxes to Offer: French Feminists and the Rights of Man.* Cambridge, Mass.: Harvard University Press, 1996.

Scott, Nina M. " 'If You Are Not Pleased to Favor Me, Put Me Out of Your Mind…': Gender and Authority in Sor Juana Inés de la Cruz and the Translation of the Letter to the Reverend Father Maestro Antonio Nunez of the Society of Jesus." *Women's Studies International Forum* 11, no. 5(1988): 429–38.

Shaarawi, Huda. *Harem Years: The Memoirs of an Egyptian Feminist (1879–1924).* Trans., ed. Margot Badran. London: Virago, 1986.

———. "Egyptian Women's Movement." In Elizabeth Warnock Fernea and Baasima Qattan Bezirgan, eds, *Middle Eastern Women Speak.* Austin: University of Texas Press, 1977.

Sklar, Kathryn Kish. *Women's Rights Emerges within the Anti-slavery Movement, 1830–1870: A Brief History with Documents*. Boston: Bedford/St. Martin's, 2000.

Templeton, Joan. *Ibsen's Women*. New York: Cambridge University Press, 1997.

Welch, Marcelle Maistre. "Introductions." In *Three Cartesian Feminist Treatises*. Trans. Vivien Bosley. Chicago: University of Chicago Press, 2002.

ACKNOWLEDGMENTS

Compiling *The Essential Feminist Reader* has renewed my appreciation both for the authors of these feminist works and for the community of scholars who have uncovered, translated, and analyzed this history. I could not have completed this collection without the expert assistance of Brenda Frink. Her skills as a historical detective greatly eased the search for documents and permissions, and her thoughtful comments improved the introduction and headnotes. I dedicate this book to John D'Emilio, not only for the wise counsel he offered as I edited, wrote, and revised but especially for his lifelong feminist friendship. My partner Susan Krieger offered both critical insight and personal encouragement throughout this project, and I thank her deeply. Leila Rupp gave generously from her extensive knowledge of feminist history when she suggested documents and responded to my historical overviews. I am grateful to Purnima Mankekar and Caroline Winterer for their helpful responses to the introduction and to Julia Cheiffetz at Random House for her comments and for inviting me to edit this collection.

Although not all of the texts they suggested are included here, I thank the many colleagues who responded to my inquiries about locating and contextualizing essential feminist writing, particularly Dalit Baum, Sandra Barnes, Jennifer Baumgardner, Joel Beinin, Marilyn Booth, Renate Bridenthal, Berenice Carroll, Akku Chowdhury, Rebecca Copeland, Paula Findlen, Shelley Fisher Fishkin, Abosede George, Huma Ghosh, Bryna Goodman, Susan Hartmann, Sally Hastings, Gail Hershatter, Selina Hossain, Teruko

Inoue, Saori Kamano, Hal Kahn, Diana Khor, Robin Khundkar, Purnima Mankekar, Paula Moya, Amy Richards, Esther Rothblum, Vicki Ruiz, Caroline Springer, Takako Takeda, Chizuko Ueno, Kären Wigen, Claire Williams, Yvonne Yarbro-Bejarano, Kari Zimmerman, and the members of the UCLA Workshop on Teaching U.S. Women's History.

PERMISSION ACKNOWLEDGMENTS

Grateful acknowledgment is made to the following for permission to reprint previously published material:

ARTE PÚLICO PRESS: "Mi Opinión" by Luisa Capetillo from *A Nation of Women*, edited by Felix V. Matos Rodriguez, translated by Alan West-Durán (Houston, TX: Arte Público Press, 2004). Reprinted by permission of Arte Público Press.

AUC PRESS: Excerpt from *The Liberation of Women and the New Woman: Two Documents in the History of Egyptian Feminism* by Qasim Amin, translated by Samiha Sidhom Peterson (Cairo: The American University in Cairo Press, 2000). Reprinted by permission of AUC Press.

AUNT LUTE BOOKS: Excerpt from "La conciencia de la mestiza/Towards a New Consciousness" by Gloria Anzaldúa from *Borderlands/La Frontera: The New Mestiza*, copyright © 1987, 1999 by Gloria Anzaldúa. Reprinted by permission of Aunt Lute Books.

THE BANGLA ACADEMY: "Sultana's Dream" by Rokeya Hossain, originally published in *Indian Ladies Magazine*, 1905. Reprinted by permission of The Bangla Academy.

BEACON PRESS: "Thoughts on March 8" from *I Myself Am a Woman: Selected Writings of Ding Ling* edited by Tani E. Barlow and Gary J. Bjorge, copyright © 2003 by Beacon Press. Reprinted by permission of Beacon Press, Boston.

JONAH K. GOKOVA: "Challenging Men to Reject Gender Stereotypes" by Jonah K. Gokova. Reprinted by permission of Jonah K. Gokova.

GUERRILLA GIRLS, INC.: "When Sexism and Racism Are No Longer Fashionable" and "Do Women Have To Be Naked To Get into the Met. Museum?" Courtesy www.guerillagirls.com.

HARCOURT, INC.: Excerpts from *The Three Guineas* by Virginia Woolf, copyright © 1938 by Harcourt, Inc. and copyright renewed 1966 by Leonard Woolf. Reprinted by permission of Harcourt, Inc.

HARVARD UNIVERSITY PRESS: Excerpts from pp. 226–236 from *A Sor Juana Anthology*, translated by Alan S. Trueblood (Cambridge, MA: Harvard University Press, 1988), copyright © 1988 by the Presidents and Fellows of Harvard College. Reprinted by permission of Harvard University Press.

INTERNATIONAL PUBLISHERS CO.: Excerpt from *The Origins of the Family, Private Property, and the State* by Frederick Engels. Reprinted by permission of International Publishers Co.

KEGAN PAUL LTD.: Excerpts from *Nation and Family* by Alva Myrdal. Reprinted by permission of Kegan Paul Ltd., London.

ALFRED A. KNOPF, A DIVISION OF RANDOM HOUSE, INC.: Excerpts from *The Second Sex* by Simone de Beauvoir, translated by H. M. Parshley, copyright © 1952 and renewed 1980 by Alfred A. Knopf, Inc. Reprinted by permission of Alfred A. Knopf, a division of Random House, Inc.

PATRICIA MAINARDI: "The Politics of Housework" by Pat Mainardi, copyright © 1970 by Pat Mainardi. Reprinted by permission of the author.

MONTHLY REVIEW FOUNDATION: Excerpt from "The Combahee River Collective: A Black Feminist Statement" from *Capitalist Patriarchy and the Case for Socialist Feminism* edited by Zillah R. Eisenstein, copyright © 1978 by Monthly Review Press. Reprinted by permission of Monthly Review Foundation.

THE CHARLOTTE SHEEDY LITERARY AGENCY, INC.: "The Master's Tools Will Never Dismantle the Master's House" from *Sister Outsider: Essays and Speeches* by Audre Lorde (Berkeley, CA: The Crossing Press, 1984), copyright © 1984 by Audre Lorde. Reprinted by permission The Charlotte Sheedy Literary Agency, Inc.

W.W. NORTON & COMPANY, INC.: Excerpts from *The Feminine Mystique* by Betty Friedan, copyright © 1983, 1974, 1973, 1963 by Betty Friedan; "Notes Towards a Politics of Location" from *Arts of the Possible: Essays and Conversations* by Adrienne Rich, copyright © 2001 by Adrienne Rich. Reprinted by permission of W. W. Norton & Company, Inc.

PEOPLE'S PRINTING SOCIETY/MORNING STAR: "We Had Equality Till Britain Came" by Funmilayo Ransome-Kuti in *The Daily Worker* (1947). Reprinted by permission of the People's Printing Society/Morning Star.

PERSEA BOOKS, INC.: Excerpt from *The Book of the City of Ladies* by Christine de Pizan, translated by Earl Jeffrey Richards, copyright © 1982, 1998 by Persea Books, Inc. Reprinted by permission of Persea Books, Inc. (New York).

GISELE PINCETL: Excerpts from "The Emancipation of Working Class Women" by Flora Tristan, translated by Gisele Pincetl. Reprinted by permission of Gisele Pincetl.

PETER OWEN LTD.: Excerpts from *Flowers in the Mirror* by Li Ju-Chen. Reprinted by permission of Peter Owen Ltd., London.

SIMON AND SCHUSTER, INC.: Abridged excerpt from pp. 2–3 of the Preface by Wilma Vilunya Diskin and Wendy Coppedge Sanford from *Our Bodies, Ourselves: A Book By and For Women* by The Boston Women's Health Book Collective, copyright © 1971, 1973 by The Boston Women's Health Book Collective, Inc.; excerpts from *Against Our Will* by Susan Brownmiller, copyright © 1975 by Susan Brownmiller. Reprinted by permission of Simon and Schuster Adult Publishing Group, a division of Simon and Schuster, Inc.

STATE UNIVERSITY OF NEW YORK: "How It All Began: I Have Had an Abortion" (Anon.) translated by Naomi Stephan, in *German Feminism: Readings in Politics and Literature* edited by Edith H. Altbach, Jeannette Clausen, Dagmar Schultz, and Naomi Stephan, copyright © State University of New York Press, 1984. All rights reserved. Reprinted by permission of the State University of New York Press.

TRANSACTION PUBLISHERS: "One is Not Born a Woman" by Monique Wittig, originally published in *Feminist Issues* volume 1, issue 2 (1981), copyright © 1981. Reprinted by permission of Transaction Publishers.

UNIVERSITY OF CHICAGO PRESS: Excerpts from *Three Cartesian Feminist Treatises* by François Poullain de la Barre, introductions and annotations by Marcelle Maistre Welch, translation by Vivien Bosley, copyright © 2002 by University of Chicago. Reprinted by permission of the University of Chicago Press.

UNIVERSITY OF CHICAGO PRESS, HÉLÈNE CIXOUS AND KEITH COHEN: Excerpt from "The Laugh of the Medusa" by Hélène Cixous, translated by Keith Cohen and Paula Cohen in SIGNS 1:4 (1976) pp. 875–881,

881–882, 883, 889–890, 893. Reprinted by permission of the University of Chicago Press, Hélène Cixous, and Keith Cohen.

UNIVERSITY OF NEBRASKA PRESS: "Rise Up!" by Sara Estela Ramírez from *Legacy: A Journal of Nineteenth-Century Women Writers*, v. 6, no. 1 (Spring, 1989), copyright © 1989 by *Legacy, A Journal, Inc.* Reprinted by permission of the University of Nebraska Press.

WILLIAM MORRIS AGENCY, LLC: "Becoming the Third Wave" by Rebecca Walker, originally published in *Ms.* Magazine, 1992, copyright © 1992 by Rebecca Walker. Reprinted by permission of the William Morris Agency, LLC on behalf of the author.

YALE UNIVERSITY PRESS: Excerpt from *Sarah Grimké: Letters on the Equality of the Sexes and Other Essays* by Sarah Grimké, edited and with an introduction by Elizabeth Ann Bartlett, copyright © 1988 by Yale University. Reprinted by permission of Yale University Press.

ZED BOOKS LTD.: "The Women's Problem" by Domitila Barrios de la Chungara and "A Statement on Genital Mutilation" by the Association of African Women for Research and Development from *Third World Second Sex: Women's Struggles and National Liberation: Third World Women Speak Out* by Miranda Davies, editor (Zed Books, 1983). Reprinted by permission of Zed Books Ltd.

INDEX

About the Editor

ESTELLE B. FREEDMAN, the Edgar E. Robinson Professor in U.S. History at Stanford University, is cofounder of the Program in Feminist Studies at Stanford. She is the recipient of numerous honors, including the Rhodes Prize for Excellence in Undergraduate Teaching at Stanford and the Nancy Lyman Roelker Mentorship Award for graduate mentorship from the American Historical Association. Freedman is the author of several books, including *No Turning Back: The History of Feminism and the Future of Women*. Freedman lives in San Francisco.